T0204281

The Spiritual Gift of Madness

"*The Spiritual Gift of Madness* is a work of extraordinary intellectual courage. Not since the death of psychiatrist R. D. Laing in 1989 has anyone written about mad people with such insight and respect. Like Laing, Farber will be accused of romanticizing 'schizophrenia.' But his interviews with six mental patients speak for themselves. In 1970 Laing, a countercultural icon, publicly repudiated his trademark brand of spiritual-political activism, expressed most profoundly in his 1967 campus bestseller *The Politics of Experience.* In a manner of speaking, *The Spiritual Gift of Madness* may be regarded as the sequel to *The Politics of Experience*—the book that Laing himself did not dare to write."

RAY RUSS, PH.D.,
EDITOR OF *THE JOURNAL OF MIND AND BEHAVIOR*

"Seth Farber has dedicated his decades of professional life to not merely destigmatizing 'mental illness' but to giving us an all-inclusive, spiritual perspective on the evolution of consciousness that will, hopefully, end the iatrogenic suffering caused to so many in 'the doctor's efforts to heal.' The existence of this book is, in itself, uplifting; its many cogent insights will surely inspire similarly dedicated readers to further this great humanitarian work."

"Seth Farber makes a powerful case for the Mad Pride movement based on a challenge to the normative humanism of modernity. He draws on a number of thinkers, prominently the redemptive-messianic vision of Sri Aurobindo, who saw the human as a 'transitional being' and earth as the habitation for a divine life. This is a valuable addition to the expanding library of handbooks for charting a new passage to the future through what Michel Foucault has called 'an insurrection of subjugated knowledges.'"

"Seth Farber is one of the most provocative and original thinkers in America. Like his mentor, R. D. Laing, Farber believes schizophrenics are prophets. They called Laing mad, as they will Farber. This is often the fate of those who are crazy for God or fools for Christ in a secular culture. Farber brings us to the threshold of the only questions that really matter: the demarcation lines between imagination and objective reality and between 'madness' and 'sanity.' *The Spiritual Gift of Madness* is an important book that could revolutionize the way progressive religious people regard what is called mental health."

The Spiritual Gift of Madness

The Failure of Psychiatry and the Rise of the Mad Pride Movement

SETH FARBER, Ph.D.

Inner Traditions
Rochester, Vermont • Toronto, Canada

Inner Traditions
One Park Street
Rochester, Vermont 05767
www.InnerTraditions.com

Library of Congress Cataloging-in-Publication Data

Farber, Seth, 1951–
  The spiritual gift of madness : the failure of psychiatry and the rise of the mad
pride movement / Seth Farber.
      p. cm.
  Summary: "A bold call for the 'insane' to reclaim their rightful role as prophets
of spriutal and cultural transformation"— Provided by publisher.
  Includes bibliographical references and index.
  ISBN 978-1-59477-448-5 (pbk.) — ISBN 978-1-59477-703-5 (e-book)
  1. Antipsychiatry. 2. Psychiatry—Social aspects. 3. Psychiatric errors.
4. Psychotherapy patients. 5. Ex-mental patients. 6. Prophets—Calling of. I. Title.
  RC437.5.F354 2012
  616.89—dc23

                                                                          2012003984

Printed and bound in the United States by Thomson-Shore

10 9 8 7 6 5 4 3 2 1

Text design by Virginia Scott Bowman
Text layout by Priscilla Baker
This book was typeset in Garamond Premier Pro with Dali and Avenir used as
display typefaces

"David's Story" from *Madness, Heresy, and the Rumor Angels* by Seth Farber,
copyright © 1998 by Seth Farber, reprinted by permission of Open Court
Publishing Company, a division of Carus Publishing Company, Chicago, Illinois.

To send correspondence to the author of this book, mail a first-class letter to the
author c/o Inner Traditions • Bear & Company, One Park Street, Rochester, VT
05767, and we will forward the communication.

To my parents, Don and Ann Farber, in gratitude.
And to Sri Aurobindo, whose vision of the divine life on Earth
gave me the courage to endure the night of humanity
and to herald the new dawn.

The culture as a whole and most of its members are insane. The culture is driven by a death urge, an urge to destroy life.

DERRICK JENSEN, *ENDGAME: THE PROBLEM OF CIVILIZATION*

The wolf shall dwell with the lamb and the leopard shall lie with the kid, and a calf with a lion's cub and a fatling together, and a small child shall lead them. . . . They will not harm or destroy on all my holy mountain, for the earth shall be full of the knowledge of God as the waters cover the sea.

ISAIAH 11:6–9

The Messianic outlook is rooted in the prophetic temper. It maintains that all people are made in God's image, it is passionately concerned with social justice, and it is actually or incipiently democratic in character, expecting God's will to be implemented in historical time in ways that disclose the truth and that will rally all of humanity to its senses.

DANIEL BURSTON, *THE CRUCIBLE OF EXPERIENCE*

As Jung prophesied, an epochal shift is taking place in the contemporary psyche, reconciliation between the two great polarities, a union of opposites: a hieros gamos (sacred marriage) between the long dominant but now alienated masculine and the long suppressed but now ascending feminine. . . . We seem to be witnessing, suffering the birth of a new reality, a new form of human existence, a "child" that would be the fruit of this great archetypal marriage, and that would bear within itself all its antecedents in a new form.

RICHARD TARNAS, *THE PASSION OF THE WESTERN MIND*

Contents

Part One
The Failure of the Psychiatric System and the Biomedical Myth

Part Five
Awakenings in History and Social Activism

Foreword

Kate Millett

I have great respect for Seth Farber; his knowledge of history—not only American but world history—is extraordinary. It's as if he has been reading all his life and remembering everything, from Socrates to Plato to the modern Indian seer Sri Aurobindo, then putting it all aside toward his one purpose: the understanding of the human psyche. What motivates a human being—what fears, what depths of loneliness, what hopes and joys, what visions? He has read widely and deeply with that one question in mind. Dr. Farber is an uncommon man: he has had lots of time to think, to speculate also on America, with its diversity of religions, enthusiasms, and immigrant cultures.

Dr. Farber has read R. D. Laing and David Cooper (the inventor of the term *antipsychiatry*), Freud in his entirely, but also Ferenczi. There are social factors to consider: "You lost your job, now you are homeless. How does that make you feel?" The psycho-person's one tireless question turned on its head, over and over: "How does that make you feel?"

"Actually it makes me feel pretty awful, Doctor, pretty wrong, pretty failed, already. How would it make you feel, Doctor Pill Pusher? Oh, I forgot: You do have a job. Listening to me, making me feel bad, reviled, discombobulated—crazy."

The diagnosis is everything; as Farber puts it, it's a sentence that the condemned person spends the rest of a lifetime living with. It can mean divorce from your family, your own people, many if not all of your friends, and even your neighbors when they find out. You are diseased, evil. Everyone is afraid of you. If you have a problem it's your own fault, for staying up late at night, for going out alone; whatever you did, you did it wrong. You are living a "shameful" life, for spending "too much money," for calling home—even at the right time of day (not too late, not too early), even if you are happy. Still it is the wrong call, the wrong tone to take.

"Are you taking your meds?" Always, that question from everyone: from your siblings, from your own friends—who drink enough themselves, even drink more than you do. Your friends brag over lunch and say they are taking classes in everything. You find the classes silly, juvenile (young men have taken over the college, which used to be a really good school for women); for them it's on the right subway line.

"Are you taking your meds?"

What's happening in the world today? I burn for my own mismanaged country. But then, I'm Irish. I've always known America was a good idea, which never does work out. It gives you baseball, General MacArthur—who let Japan keep its emperor, the one thing they had left. Japan had never been conquered—until it was conquered utterly by American bombs at Hiroshima and Nagasaki and now by its own nuclear power plants. Never mind—the Japanese will figure it out without any help from us.

We have our own problems: At Yucca Mountain nuclear waste repository, 100 million gallons of radioactive waste sit on top of several earthquake faults; finally the Department of Energy decided last year that we'd better look for another place to store it. But where? Meanwhile American greedy bastards, just like Japanese CEOs, are planning to build more nuclear power plants!

Compared to the cynicism of the United States of America, Dr. Farber is romantic hope, trailing clouds of glory behind him, still optimistic. He wrote me recently:

> I think I should tell you that despite the optimism of my book, in my day-to-day life I often find myself becoming despondent: The world strikes me as so shockingly awful these days that I often think it's too late—that every effort to change the world is futile. I say this

not as a qualification of any statement I make in my book, but just to admit that I'm not absolutely confident that we can avoid the deluge. I don't doubt that my criticisms of society are valid. And I am grateful for the opportunity to criticize not only the psychiatric system, but those "realists" who advocate making adjustments, and chic French philosophers who denigrate "grand narratives" and "grandiose" visions. It seemed providential that I even found a publisher.

I read an article recently by David Ray Griffin, the Christian theologian (famous now as a 9/11 skeptic). After discussing global warming and polluting technologies, he concluded, "The projections based upon purely ecological matters are bad enough; when this growing scarcity of land, food, and other resources is combined with increasing ethnic and cultural animosities, the proliferation of nuclear weapons, and arms sales generally, any realistic picture of the future based on present trends is completely terrifying. We live in a world that is essentially good, created by divine power. But it is a world that is, even more fully than was the world in New Testament times, presently in the grip of demonic power."

He wrote that in 1993—certainly today it's worse. In fact every month it gets worse. When thousands of people are killed in Japan and millions are subjected to the prospect of radiation sickness, and even the more liberal wing of the American establishment (e.g., *The New York Times*) urges that we take precautions *before* building *more* nuclear power plants, one feels powerless in the face of evil. I believe in the immortality of the soul, in reincarnation—so I expect to be around. But when will the suffering be o'er? Round and round, life after life.

Back in the seventeenth century Jews would take leave of each other with the salutation, "Next year in Jerusalem." This meant universal salvation, as in Isaiah (before political Zionism eclipsed the pristine universalist vision). Ah, to have that kind of imminent expectation again—like it was in the '60s—instead now it's only the echo of the bard singing in the town square, "How many times must a man look up before he can see the sky? And how many ears must one man have before he can hear people cry? How many deaths will it take till he knows that too many people have died? The answer, my friend, is blowin' in the wind." How many deaths? How many years? Lifetimes? Millennia? How long? "The answer is blowin in the wind." What kind of apocalyptic, man-caused horrors lie ahead? Can we prevent hell on Earth? (It's already hell for many. It could get worse.)

I admit, I don't know. I believe in the vision of an Aurobindo, of a Christ—the divine life on Earth—free from even the shadow of death. But when? I have seen so many wise souls who have been ruined by the mental health system. At least my book will liberate some of these gentle, creative souls from psychiatry. In the back of my mind I first conceived the notion twenty-five years ago that the "schizophrenics" have a key role to play in the drama of salvation. I imagine that somehow they will take off their Clark Kent/Lois Lane disguises, shocking the sleepwalkers—Laing's name for normal people—around them. The shock would be so great that the sleepwalkers will awaken from their collective death-trance for just long enough for the mad to cast a new magic spell, allowing all of them to feel for a brief while the bliss of an eternal love that is pure enough to defeat the demonic—long enough to glimpse the vision of a new dawn. And then, they too, awakened, will choose life over death—for all of us.

That is only a daydream. But it is one of the few things that gives me hope.

I have great respect for Dr. Seth Farber because his knowledge of history is so rich and he draws on it to answer certain questions: What makes the human mind tick? What stimulus, what forces? This is something unusual in an American and still more unusual in a psychologist. The function of American psychology seems so often to deny its own historical past and to function as if there were no history at all—no terrible past of machinery to still the hands of children who masturbated, to put away wives who disobeyed, people who were too poor and burdensome to be supported by their relatives, people abandoned because they were inconvenient to their masters, or husbands, or gentrified relations, or ambitious bosses. A history that simply "put the unfortunates away," consigned them to a nut house and went back home relieved of the burden of the unwanted, the unwell. This history put away the wife who wouldn't do her conjugal "duty," wouldn't change the beds, till the fields, or "act normal" and who had aspirations above her station, longed for dance, theater, to paint, or something "crazy" like that—impractical, "far out" as we used to say.

I am reminded of one of my experiences helping someone who was considered mad: a boy from the American South who jumped off the Brooklyn Bridge and lived. My husband and I would visit him at Bellevue because he was the brother to a Southerner who was our friend in art. This wonderful young man was not given a prize for surviving, only a trip to the local asylum as a reward. We finally got him out and sent him home.

Being an artist was simply too hard a thing to be: too uncertain, impractical, and unremunerative. We were young then, carefree, had lots of time to visit strangers who were friends too; we were practically hobos ourselves. Another friend was rich but an embarrassment to her relations because she "wrote verses," had some "second sight," and could recite William Butler Yeats's poems all afternoon—to the astonishment of the psychiatrists at Bellevue. She was in and out of the hospital and became merely—sadly—a permanent patient. She was only a vulnerable woman when I met her, pliable, dependent on her relatives, relying only on another young woman who lived at my farm in the beginning.

My husband, the Japanese sculptor Fumio Yoshimura, was sympathetic to them both, just as he was to my other lesbian friends—one of whom was an architectural theorist, as was his own friend, Arakawa—and to Madeline Gins, who switched from painting to architecture. Arakawa had been at Waseda, where I had taught English literature under Prince Ijima, the Shakespearian scholar. We gathered together in New York—old friends, trusted friends, but open to a whole bunch of new friends too: blacks, Koreans, eccentrics of all kinds, fellow artists from all over the country. It was New York, the melting pot of American art and writing. We were still young, unpretentious, and unafraid; we were "crazy artists." The world was different then.

All this time Dr. Farber was a youngster looking for answers. After he went to grad school in the early 1980s he became a family therapist and a follower of Laing and Szasz—the two leading "antipsychiatrists" in the world—even though they did not like the term, nor each other. Like a great many people, I owe my very survival to Dr. Thomas Szasz.

The summer I spent working as an aide at St. Peter's asylum in southern Minnesota, near St. Paul, Seth Farber was a child and I had not yet heard of Szasz. We have a joke among us: "There is the happy life in St. Paul and the hellish life at St. Peter's." I lost twenty pounds the first fortnight. What a job: counting silverware after every meal, eating the same food as the patients but unable to keep it down. I remember trying to persuade the cruel nurse not to put a straitjacket on the woman who was having a "fit"—a "lifer" who simply needed some sympathy, some kindness. She was not prepared to defecate on command—having been awakened at 4:30 in the morning, ordered to wash, fitted into an undershirt (a dress if there was one), shoes, and stockings, if there were any.

The rest of these abandoned women had to go naked all day—the most humiliating form of punishment—reduced to a "twin forked thing" as King Lear put it on his heath. They had committed no crime: they were just poor and old. The floor stank; the stench was terrible. The place had been built during the Civil War. The wood of those heavy plank floors had seen every suffering known to humanity: blood, shit, and urine. That was the night shift on the Geriatric Ward.

Meanwhile, I read the entire library; they had a good one—all of Freud, of course, but also his opposite number: Ferenczi and Menninger. They also had all the newest and "best" treatments, including electroshock and insulin shock therapies. Of course, as a Millett, I couldn't believe a word of it. These unfortunates were simply being warehoused—at the will of their "masters" if they were women, and the men at the command of their bosses, rich relatives, or the adversaries of their will in probate court, stewards of their land and inheritors of their money. Even if their inheritance was only forty dollars, their brothers would put them away for it.

Once "perceived" as mad, there is no end of the scandal. The English rolled it into the Cheshire Cat and Alice and the Red Queen. There are a lot of laughs in madness, but it is a waste of time and money. A great industry is built on it today—Big Pharma.

Madness has even embroiled soldiers, victims of "post-traumatic stress disorder." How many thousands suffer this in America after Iraq and Afghanistan? "Shell shock," they used to call it. Drunk all the time, we call it now. So there are painkillers, amphetamines, "antipsychotics," legalized doping. Hemingway so dreaded another lockup in the Mayo Clinic that he just shot himself. Lots of people have simply offed themselves rather than suffer the loony-bin again. To a writer, the loneliness of our profession—when cursed with the further burden of "Did you take your lithium today?" on the other end of a phone line—becomes simply too much to bear.

Diagnosis is all, and Dr. Farber will tell you, the diagnosis is enough to kill you. You are "perceived" as insane, which is almost the same as being insane. You are also broke and deprived of your liberty, which is everything. From now on, someone else will make your decisions for you, pay your bills—or neglect to pay them. You will lose your job, your house, your passport, your prospects. You become a nothing: whether someone whose chances are all gone, who never had any, or who had some but never got to do what he or she wanted.

The sexes are very different here. Patriarchy, of course, must be observed, especially in the art world, where being a painter is regarded as somewhat effeminate for a man. So the male must compensate—at the woman's expense. One is obliged to drip paint onto the canvas, drive too fast, swear like a trooper, dismiss all women as puppets, use them, abuse them, sometimes even kill them. Or force yourself on them, let them conceive your child, then leave them unceremoniously.

When I came home after my summer of horrors, I found my younger sister had polio mellitus and the house I came back to was quarantined. Mother said, "Go back there and tell them you are now a volunteer."

"Why? Can't I write it up for the *St. Paul Pioneer Press and Dispatch*? It's shocking how the poor are abandoned this way."

"No one will believe you, you are only eighteen. Go back there now. You've earned enough so you no longer deserve a salary; I can take you off my income tax. See if you can do any good there."

I went back.

Fortunately I knew Rosie, a head nurse, who also had an interest in psychology. She was young and adventurous and could drive a car and keep me out of trouble. We quarreled with the men's side, who believed in brutality and practiced it daily on their victims. She was wary of the "sensitive souls" who wanted to listen to classical music with me but were really discredited doctors who regularly raped patients with the willing collusion of the male guards.

Rosie was sympathetic to my idea of musical therapy and tennis lessons for the patients. So the ward would nod off to Stravinsky and Albinoni and Hayden and exercise to Purcell's "When Come Ye Sons of Art," and the gang came alive to "The Firebird." Then when we had done two weeks of this stuff, I got permission to take the patients out of the hospital and onto the grounds, which were, of course, beautiful. We chased tennis balls. I chased more balls than I ever had before. A few of us actually hit some balls! Everyone had a good day.

On wet days, we would smoke cigarettes, rolled by my expert machine, on the great porches. (Buying cigarettes and Baby Ruth candy bars for abandoned women had become too costly.) They were contented. We even got permission for a handful to "go home," which meant usually to the same home from which they had escaped, so they usually came back.

My younger sister survived her polio. Mother said I had to go back to college and finish my course in abnormal psychology, which had started me on this adventure. My parents got divorced. Mother started to sell life insurance. I had to become her squire, driving her car and teaching her to drive it too. I had to go into retail, selling stockings every afternoon, then taking the streetcar down to town with mother's college friends, Dr. and Mrs. Thorson, to see the dentist about my braces.

The job gave me a little latitude to buy books, drink malted milk, and take the streetcar home, passing Aunt Dorothy's house on Virginia Avenue. She eventually sent me to Oxford, where I discovered real scholarship. It is such a pity that American scholarship has slipped the point of paying the mortgage and no one ever seems to read books that are not meant for children.

As a feminist, I must point out that the Mad movement has degenerated into patriotic/patriarchal belief in pill-pusher psychiatry, forgotten even to honor and read its male doctors like Peter Breggin and its civilian forces like Leonard Frank and Michel Foucault. It sadly neglects its female authorities like Dr. Phyllis Chesler—not to mention Susan Brownmiller, Sylvia Plath, Jessica Mitford, Eve Figes, Sally Zinman, Judi Chamberlin, Ellen Frankfort, Mary Daly, Elizabeth Davis, Barbara Ehrenreich, Judy Graham, Janet Frame, and Frances Farmer. One could read all about "institutional psychiatry" in one short story by Anton Chekov called *Ward 6*. Or one could dip into Holocaust studies a bit: the mental patients were the first to be exterminated in Germany. The struggle continues—all over the world now.

Of course, being Irish, I have a sense of humor, a special point of view. You have to laugh at the insanity of the world: consider the alternative.

KATE MILLETT, PH.D., prominent feminist and author, was born in St. Paul, Minnesota, in 1934. She graduated from the University of Minnesota magna cum laude and Phi Beta Kappa and in 1956 attended St. Hilda's College at Oxford University. She obtained her Ph.D., with distinction, from Columbia University in 1970. Active in feminist politics in the late 1960s and the 1970s, in 1966 she became chairwoman of the education committee of the newly formed National Organization for Women (NOW). In 1970, her book *Sexual Politics* was published. An amplification of her Ph.D. thesis, it was and continues to be a bestseller and remains a classic statement of radical feminist theory. In 1990 Simon and Schuster published *The Loony-Bin Trip,* the autobiographical story of her struggles with manic depression and her brave decision to go off her prescription drug, lithium. Other works include *The Prostitution Papers: A Candid Dialogue,* published in 1973 and again in 1976; *Flying* (1974); *Sita* (1977); *Going to Iran* (1981); *The Politics of Cruelty: An Essay on the Literature of Political Imprisonment* (1994); and *A.D.* (1995). She lives in Poughkeepsie, New York, where she oversees the Women's Art Colony Farm, a community of female artists and writers.

Preface

This is a book about the Mad Pride movement. I had various goals in mind in writing and editing this book; these goals are all complementary. First, I wanted to publicize the new Mad Pride movement—to make both the public at large and those who have been psychiatrically labeled as "mentally ill" and/or "psychotic" aware of its existence, what it has done, and what it is doing. I want readers to be aware that it provides an alternative to the "mental health" system. Second, and most important, I wanted to help "mental patients" or "psychiatric survivors" (to use the current term) free themselves from the psychiatric net in which they may have become entangled.

To do this I present the stories of several persons—considered "seriously mentally ill" by Psychiatry—who proved the system wrong: they overcame their problems and now live extraordinary lives, far exceeding the low expectations about what they could achieve conveyed to them by psychiatrists. They are role models: reading their stories may instill in patients the conviction that they too can break away from psychiatry, can transcend the identity of the chronic "mental patient" and lead creative lives—often as "creatively maladjusted" persons (to borrow a phrase from Martin Luther King Jr.) devoted to changing the world.

Third, I wanted to present and update the argument I have been making for twenty years against the mental health system. In accord with this I included a discussion of the theories of psychiatrists and social critics R. D. Laing and John Weir Perry. It is an unfortunate fact that despite Laing's status as a countercultural icon and intellectual celebrity in the 1960s and 1970s, his work has been neglected by the psychiatric survivors' movement—formerly the "mental patients' liberation movement"—and he is virtually unknown by Mad Pride.

Finally, I wanted to provide a rationale for the existence of the Mad Pride movement—as distinct from (albeit not in conflict with) the psychiatric survivors' movement. While I was working on this book, new developments took place in the Mad Pride movement; I thus became aware of conflicting tendencies within it. I explain what I believe are the sources of these tensions and argue that in order for Mad Pride to fulfill its potential, it must make a choice; it must abjure the secular postmodern pluralist zeitgeist and affirm instead a fully spiritual messianic vision of madness and social change. This would be a courageous move in an age when even the term *messianic* is equated with anachronistic superstitious religious views (e.g., premillennialism)—or with psychopathology, that is, "psychosis"!

On the other hand, for neomessianic forces (e.g., New Age) to associate themselves with the mad would be for them to risk being discredited by virtue of association with the most stigmatized group in society—"schizophrenics." However, the conditions for this coalescence are more propitious than in the past. Due to the arguments of mavericks like Laing, Perry, and Ken Kesey, and as a result of the psychedelics and cultural revolution in the 1960s, "psychosis" has assumed a more romantic status among influential subcultures, particularly bohemian writers and artists. Thus the association of madness and messianism appears in a more favorable light than in the past—from both sides.

In order to make the argument that mad persons have a distinctive contribution to make to the salvation of the planet, I attempt in the final section of this book to rehabilitate the reputation of the messianic or "utopian" vision. I do this by reexamining the two most messianic periods of cultural revitalization in American history—the Second Awakening of the early nineteenth century and the 1960s' period of countercultural ferment and New Left activism. The examination of these two disparate periods of profound cultural revitalization demonstrate the socially progressive (to use a modern term) nature and spiritual depth of messianism. I briefly discuss the cultural change theories of John Perry, William McLoughlin, and H. Richard Niebuhr, which support my argument for a messianic-redemptive model of madness and social change. I also briefly discuss the social perspective of (in my view) the most important and neglected seer of the modern age, the neo-Hindu philosopher and yogi Sri Aurobindo (1872–1950).

Fortunately, while writing this book I discovered the writings of Paul Levy, who—as a mad person (a former mental patient who had spiritual visions) and a spiritual educator strongly influenced by the writings of Carl Jung—also takes, as I do, an unabashedly messianic view of human potential. Following Jung, Levy writes of the "Christification" of humanity: all of us are called on to act as "messiahs." I cite Levy on a number of occasions (besides the interview) as his views are further confirmation of my own.

With the increasingly murderous and brutal policies of corporate capitalism fueled by spiritual emptiness and greed and the assault on the Earth, we now face the prospect of permanent war and the threat of the ecological destruction of the conditions necessary for life on Earth. Or rather some of us face it; most look the other way. The American ruling political elite has abdicated its democratic responsibilities and is now enacting policies in the service of the corporate Leviathan that, unless reversed, may lead within this century to the extinction of the human species. The communal mind is in a state of acute distress and confusion.

The emergence of Mad Pride and the foundation of The Icarus Project (TIP) was an auspicious development; it was initially an "evolutionary bid" to change the consciousness of humanity. At this point, it is uncertain if Mad Pride will decide to forsake its more messianic aspirations and accommodate itself to the postmodern ethos.

I hope that the argument I make in this book and particularly in the concluding chapter will prompt a serious reexamination—by Mad Pride and by all persons interested in social change—of the much maligned redemptive-messianic vision, which I believe is the only solution to the current spiritual crisis of humanity.

Acknowledgments

I am indebted to my editors at Inner Traditions: Jon Graham, Jennifer Marx—whose astute and thoughtful reading of the book made it considerably less obscure—and Anne Dillon. I want to thank the following people for their support as friends or help with the book, or both: Hardina Dahl, Dr. Stuart Sovatsky, Peter Lehmann, Professor Daniel Burston, Claude M., Dr. John Breeding, Dr. David Cohen, Dr. Ray Russ, Ingrid Vien, Dr. Richard Gosden, Dr. Linda Morrison, my sister Pat and her husband Sal, Pasquale Galante, Elizabeth Smith, Antonia Dunbar, Harold Channer, Bill Kaufman, Steve Apodaca, Judith Greenberg, Tom Oakley, Danielle Deschamps, Carol Goss, Luisa Castaganara, Ruth Campbell, Laura Levine, Julian O'Neill, Ady Linda, George Fish, J. Pavia, Steve Pearlman, Serine Forino, Chris Launois, Melissa Lande, Lauren Tenney, Mitch Cohen, Joe Dubovy, Van Howell, Jeff Levy, Francesca Spiegel, Dr. Mychael Gleason, and others to whom I am no less indebted but are too numerous to mention.

There were several very articulate people I interviewed whom I could not include in the book either because they had not had the requisite experience (e.g., Zool had not had a degrading experience in a psychiatric ward and had far more knowledge about the brutal foreign policies of our government than he did about the mental health system) or because I had too much material to include in one book. Dianne Dragon eloquently recounted a powerful story about her very extraordinary experiences in the military (in training)—they were emotionally overwhelming—but since many are exposed to the same stresses it's surprising more soldiers are not driven crazy by them. The implications of her story would have required a discussion of many more pages.

Introduction

Discovering the Higher Sanity within Madness

"Mad Pride"* is the new twenty-first-century rallying cry of three generations of radical ex-mental patients who refuse to genuflect before the altar of Psychiatry. The Mad Pride movement is a recent outgrowth of the larger mental patients' liberation movement—now called the psychiatric survivors' movement—that originated in the early 1970s and is composed today of thousands of "schizophrenics," "bipolars," "schizotypals," "borderline personality disorders," and whatever new categories of the "severely mentally ill" are invented and christened by the psychiatric establishment. The mad constitute an increasing percentage of the population in the United States. According to the National Institute of Mental Health, over eight million Americans have bipolar disorder or schizophrenia, the two most common forms of "psychosis."

The Mad Pride movement is not merely a movement for mental patients' rights. It is a movement about the right to be different. Where will it lead? Will it become a broad-based revolt against the psychiatric-pharmaceutical complex, against the corporate capitalist system and its destruction of the Earth, against the bureaucratic state, which has become a tool of psychiatry and of other corporate interests, against the pervasiveness of the surveillance and social control of "deviants" in the

---

*I am using the term *Mad Pride* to refer to the Mad Pride movement or the theories of Mad Pride formulated by participants.

1

modern world, against the legitimacy granted to the Psychiatric "scientific" authorities who sanctify adjustment to the current criminally insane social order as "mental health"?

Clearly the leading activists in Mad Pride would like to see such a movement. But what is the basis of its alternative vision? In the name of *what* will it protest? Will it spread its wings and become a movement based on an affirmation of the holiness of the Earth, of the preciousness of all sentient life, of the freedom of the spirit, of the fraternity of humanity, of the sanctity of the imagination? Will it affirm a messianic (i.e., utopian) vision of redemption? Or will Mad Pride lose its way in the miasma of postmodern cultural pluralism and domesticated identity politics?

This book is a contribution to telling the emerging story of the birth of the Mad Pride movement. I tried to convey a sense of what this movement is about through interviewing and describing the heroic triumphs of six mad persons, each of whom can pass as normal today, all but one of whom do not take any psychiatric "medication," and all of whom far exceeded the low expectations of them conveyed to them by Psychiatry. Four are leaders in the Mad Pride movement and the other two (one a medical researcher and the other a spiritual teacher) speak powerfully and eloquently about how madness was for them an initiation into a higher, more conscious mode of being.

Paul Levy (see the interview with him in chapter 16) eloquently described the initiation process in general terms—but in a manner that clearly reflected his own life journey. "The ordeals, trials, and tribulations that inevitably come our way as part of life and put us 'through the fire' are initiations, designed by a higher, divine intelligence, uniquely crafted for and by our soul to burn away our false, egoic personality traits so as to liberate our latent, higher psycho-spiritual potentials."[1]

In the past year Mad Pride has become the object of increasing publicity and journalistic interest. Clearly it is a force that is just beginning to grow. As written eloquently in a recent *Newsweek* article,

Mad Pride [is] a budding grassroots movement, where people who have been defined as mentally ill reframe their conditions and celebrate unusual (some call them "spectacular") ways of processing information and emotion. Icarus members cast themselves as a dam in the cascade of new diagnoses like bipolar and ADHD. The group [The Icarus Project—which will be discussed in depth in part 3], which now has a membership of 8,000 people across the United States, argues that mental-health conditions can be made into "something beautiful." They mean that one can transform what are often considered simply horrible diseases into an ecstatic, creative, productive, or broadly "spiritual" condition. As Will Hall puts it, he hopes Icarus will "push the emergence of mental diversity."[2]

Insanity and Madness

I have introduced in this book a semantic distinction between the words *insane* and *mad*. I use the former in an evaluative (pejorative) sense. I define *insanity* as a state of spiritual derangement and *sanity* as a condition in which one is in accord with process of spiritual growth, whereas I use *madness* to refer nonpejoratively to "altered states of consciousness" (ASC) that are nonrational. (The term "altered state of consciousness" was first used to describe persons under the influence of LSD or other hallucinogens.) A mad person has had or has ASCs. *Madness,* as I use the term, is not evaluative or normative—it can be *either* good or bad or neither—but I argue that in many, if not most cases, such altered states, however painful, are "good," meaning that they are potentially valuable experiences. (I do not necessarily claim this about states induced by LSD or other chemicals.)

Someone who is mad has often had a "breakdown," but a breakdown can lead to a breakthrough (see chapter 5). Madness is potentially regenerative. To interpret it as "insanity" or "mental illness" is to misunderstand its meaning and possibilities. By my definitions one could thus be both mad and sane. I believe this same distinction between madness and insanity is *implied* in R. D. Laing's work, particularly in *The Politics of Experience*.

The term *insane as I use it* always includes a "value judgment," it denotes a negative condition; it's never seen as positive or neutral (like brown eyes). In this way it is like the term *evil*. According to the convention I am following in this book and elsewhere, when I state that someone is insane, I do not mean that the person is insane by psychiatric ("psychotic") or legal criteria. She may or may not be.

When I use the term *insane,* for example, I could be using it to refer to the well-known murderer Charles Manson (who is "psychotic" by psychiatric criteria) or to the former U.S. Secretary of Defense Donald Rumsfeld (who is "normal"), who is responsible for initiation of the widespread torture of prisoners of war—because I regard both of them as insane.

The persons I call "insane" are most likely to be very well-adjusted, normal people. Often they appear stable and are emotionally content since they have the ability, as David Oaks states, to deny "inconvenient truths." On the other hand, in society the term *insane* is almost always used to refer to those deemed "psychotic" by psychiatry. Somewhat less often it is used by social critics in the way I am using it, to refer to a person (or society) who is spiritually deranged. Critics infer that a person is insane or spiritually deranged from the fact that they committed acts that are both evil and unintelligible or absurd. An evil act is not necessarily insane. It has to include an element of absurdity or what I call objective unintelligibility. That is, an insane act is both evil and "objectively" unintelligible or absurd.

I frequently use the term *insane* to apply to society. If certain practices are routine in a society then I believe they are a product of that society. To pick an example I use frequently, the United States is a society in which our political and business leaders either deny or ignore ecological threats and promote practices that unless stopped could lead, according to our best climate scientists, to the annihilation of life on Earth. At best it will lead to the death of millions of people and nonhuman animals.

Our ecologically destructive policies are not accidental. They occur systematically. Thus I say they are a feature of our society. But to destroy the conditions for human survival is insane. Thus I am led to conclude, "American society or the American social system is insane." It is evil, but not *merely* evil. It defies explanation. It is intrinsically, "objectively" unintelligible. It is deranged, absurd, insane.

Many people have adjusted to our insane society because they do not have the spiritual maturity and courage to fight against it. Or because they—understandably—feel hopeless. The antonym of *insane* is not *sanity,* which is a neutral term, but *wisdom,* which is a higher sanity that transcends the condition of the average person. Wisdom is *highly* intelligible, it possesses a plenitude of meaningfulness. Our great prophets are always men or women of wisdom—of a higher sanity—who are invariably critics of our insane society.

From Mental Patients' Liberation to Mad Pride

Mad Pride was officially launched in England in 1999 with the foundation of the organization Mad Pride, which soon spread to the United States. The movement found institutional embodiment with the formation of The Icarus Project. It subsists alongside of the psychiatric survivors' movement. How does the Mad Pride movement differ from the psychiatric survivors' movement? The major difference stems from the fact that the primary goal of the latter is opposing human rights violations (whether legal or illegal) that are endemic in the mental health system, including involuntary psychiatric drugging, electroshock, and inpatient and outpatient commitment laws. It seeks to change, to reform the "mental health system." *Thus its philosophical emphasis has been on the fundamental similarity between "ex-mental patients"* (psychiatric survivors) *and "normal" people,* and the rights of the former to equal treatment under the law. Mad Pride's goals, as will be shown, are empowering the mad and, more broadly speaking, effecting profound changes in society. *Its philosophical emphasis is on the distinctiveness of the mad, the ways in which they are different from normal people*; at the same time it acknowledges the interconnectedness and the existential equality of all persons.

The philosophical foundation of the psychiatric survivors' movement was established by psychiatrist Thomas Szasz, who argued that mental illness was a myth and that those labeled "mentally ill" were suffering—as all persons do at times—from "problems in living." Szasz asserted that the so-called mentally ill were similar to normal people in all important respects: above all, they are moral agents, just as normal people are, and are thus entitled to the same constitutional and legal rights—particularly liberty—and conversely should be held to the same standards of legal responsibility. (Szasz opposed the insanity defense.) These goals do not conflict with those of Mad Pride, although Szasz himself has rejected the existence of madness and thus of Mad Pride.

The mental patients' liberation movement paralleled the emergence in the public arena in the 1960s and 1970s of a variety of outspoken nonconformist mental health professionals, including the three most prominent dissident psychiatrists in the country: Thomas Szasz, the late R. D. Laing (he died in 1989, unexpectedly at age sixty-one), and Peter Breggin. Despite the dissidents' diversity of views, they were and are united in their rejection of the dominant medical model of psychology and its root metaphor, mental illness. They all rejected the central premise of the medical model—that the categorization of behaviors and experiences as "mental illness" by psychiatrists is based on objective medical (scientific) criteria.

To the contrary, the dissidents claimed that the diagnosis of mental illnesses was based on psychiatrists' subjective values and biases, usually reflecting the biases of the culture. (The most salient example in support of this claim was the American Psychiatric Association's decision to recategorize homosexuality from a mental illness to a normative sexual orientation in the 1970s.)[3] The dissidents also agreed that diagnosing clients as "mentally ill" is the sine qua non of a process that leads to their transformation from persons and citizens—and moral agents—to patients. Once defined as mental patients, persons are deemed incompetent and deprived of their constitutional rights, above all, of their right to liberty—including their liberty to refuse specific medical "treatments," such as the forcible administration sanctioned by the courts, the state, of psychiatric drugs or (less commonly) of electroshock. Szasz's writings repeatedly attacked the violation of the principle of the separation of church and state; the psychiatric religion counts on the power of the state to force citizens to submit to its dictates.

But in one respect the approach of R. D. Laing was singular and profound. Unlike most of the critics of the psychiatric system, Laing focused on some of the ways in which "schizophrenics" (and other "psychotics") *were* genuinely *different from*—not inferior to—normal people. Laing's most important book, *The Politics of Experience* (published in 1967), prefigured the ideas of the Mad Pride movement that first arose three decades later. His radicalism consisted of his belief that far from being mentally defective, the mad were *superior* in certain important respects to normal people: many schizophrenics, Laing said—he meant "most"—were more sensitive and more spiritually aware than "normal" persons, who tended to be oblivious to the "inner world" of their psyches.[4] Although in its early stages the mental patients' liberation movement had embraced some Laingian themes, as its battle to attain equal rights for mental patients increasingly became its main focus, it turned its back on Laing's spiritual model of madness. (Laing also distanced himself for his own reasons from the ex-patients' movement.)

It is the contention of this book that the recent emergence of Mad Pride represents a new, more mature, and "higher" stage of the development of the psychiatric survivors'/ex-patients' movement. Mad Pride is based on an emphasis on the Laingian theme (although Laing is rarely mentioned or even read) of the distinctiveness of the mad. In this regard it parallels the trajectory of the movements of other minorities, which at first sought to establish their members' similarities to the majority and to end the discrimination to which they had been subjected and later went on to affirm the distinctiveness of their group and discover in its differences from the norm, the source of new values.

The founders of Mad Pride both in England and in America often drew an analogy between Gay Pride or Black Pride and Mad Pride. They stated or implied that there is something distinctive and positive about being mad—about having experienced altered states of consciousness, so-called "psychotic episodes." The Icarus Project collective wrote, "We are a website community, a support network of local and campus Groups . . . created by and for people living with *dangerous gifts* that are commonly diagnosed and labeled as 'mental illnesses.' We believe we have mad gifts to be cultivated and taken care of, rather than diseases or disorders to be suppressed or eliminated. By joining together as individuals and as a community, the intertwined threads of madness, creativity, and collaboration can inspire hope and transformation in an oppressive and damaged world." The term *dangerous gifts*—coined by Sascha DuBrul, the cofounder of The Icarus Project who associated these gifts with the wings of wax in the myth of Icarus—became a shibboleth for the perspective of The Icarus Project (see chapter 8).

Szasz had been the first to demonstrate that diagnoses were based on social and psychiatric biases, but Szasz was not specific in regard to the nature of these biases. Laing was, and Mad Pride is today—sometimes.

Mad Pride activists often argue that since our society is individualistic, competitive, materialistic, and rationalistic, the conformist bias of mental health professionals manifests itself in an inability to appreciate the communal, the cooperative, the nonrational, and the spiritual or religious dimensions of existence. Thus the mental health experts tend to interpret altered states of consciousness—which one might term "varieties of religious experiences" (borrowing William James's phrase)—as psychopathological syndromes such as "schizophrenia" or "bipolar disorder."

Repudiation of the Psychiatric Narrative

The interviews contained herein are with Mad Pride activists or sympathizers of the movement who are or had been mad. (I use the term *mad* to refer to anyone who experienced altered states of consciousness or "psychotic episodes"—as labeled by psychiatric "authorities"—who still regard these experiences as constitutive of their identity.) They are the protagonists and heroes or heroines of this book. All but one (Caty Simon, see chapter 7) believed that there was something valuable in their "psychotic episodes," which gave them access to transcendent, mystical, and/or supernatural dimensions of life. Each one of them is a witness for Mad Pride and against the mental health system. For each subject there was a moment (or a period) of decision: Would she accept and affirm the psychiatric view of her altered states of consciousness as psychopathology and of herself as "chronically mentally ill"? Would she accept her "incorporation into the psychiatric narrative," or would she develop a "resistant identity and an alternative narrative"?[5]

Each protagonist repudiated the mentally ill identity and affirmed "a positive identity of the self."[6] Her new identity after her mad experience and her disentanglement from the mental health system was based (Caty Simon excepted) on the reinterpretation of her "psychotic episodes" as revelatory or initiatory experiences. All the protagonists went on to lead active and creative lives (all but one without psychiatric drugs), thus refuting the psychiatric contention that they suffer from chronic mental illnesses. But they did not become well-adjusted, rather they became creatively *mal*adjusted. Five of the six interviewees (six out of seven if we include the psychiatrist) are involved in an ongoing effort to change society, and their views are in accord with my theory that the mad constitute a vanguard in the effort to bring change to an insane world.

Revealingly, all of the protagonists affirmed several or (infrequently) all of the following contentions that I believe are at the root of the Mad Pride movement. One, there is a distinctive mad sensibility different from that of "normal" persons. Two, this sensibility is an asset, not a defect—and thus provides a basis for "Mad Pride." Three, madness—the "psychotic episode"—has value, it has the potential to shed light on the human situation, to promote spiritual growth; it is not a mental illness or a symptom of a brain defect. (The idea that madness has value goes back, of course, to Socrates and Plato.*) Four, since the mad experience has value, society ought to provide supportive sanctuaries where people can undergo this experience without the adverse consequences of standard psychiatric treatment. Five, society as it exists today is insane; in the words of Laing, it is existentially or "ontologically *off course*." (Every person I interviewed agreed on this point!) Six, the purpose of the mental health system is social control—helping or forcing people to adjust to society as is, to the status quo. Finally, if society is insane, adjustment to society is not a sign of mental health, of spiritual well-being.

Many of these contentions provide the basis for an agenda different from—though not in conflict with—that of (other) radical organizations such as Mind Freedom, which still identifies itself not as Mad Pride but as an advocacy organization for the psychiatric survivors' movement. (Mind Freedom also has a Mad Pride division, which sponsors Mad Pride events.) Mind Freedom founder David Oaks calls for "a nonviolent revolution in the mental health system" (see chapter 3). (Mind Freedom also operates a clearing house, a referral service, and a self-empowerment website.) However, if the purpose of the mental health system as it exists is to help persons adjust to society, then how could there be a revolution in the mental health system without changing society? It is inconceivable that one could have a progressive or humanitarian mental health system in an insane society—a society programmed for self-destruction. And if society were to radically change, what need would there be to have a mental health system at all?

Oaks seems to be aware of this conundrum but since the mandate

---

*Socrates allegedly said, "God-sent madness is far superior to any self-restraint of human origin."

of Mind Freedom as a nongovernmental organization (NGO) is to act—as it does, often very effectively—as a pressure group to oppose human rights violations within the mental health system, Oaks tends to dwell on (at least in his public talks) revolutionizing the mental health system rather than revolutionizing society (although, it should be noted that Oaks has also promoted the idea of creative maladjustment, as discussed below). Also, Oaks must realize that since the adversary of Mind Freedom is the multibillion-dollar psychiatric-pharmaceutical complex—and the government that supports it—a successful "revolution" in the mental health system is more unlikely today than it was when he first became active. (When Oaks first became an activist in the late 1970s, psychiatry was a shaky force, which had not yet decided to sacrifice its independence by wedding its fortune to the pharmaceutical companies.)[7]

In contrast to the survivors' movement, which focuses on changing the mental health system, the implicit if not explicit goal of the Mad Pride movement is a transformation of society as a whole. (Let me emphasize again that most persons in the survivors' movement support Mad Pride.) Yet there is a catch-22: it is impossible for society to change radically as long as mad people are suppressed because mad people constitute a large proportion of society's visionaries and prophets, and visionaries and prophets are the catalysts of social change. Thus, the mental health system is critical to maintaining the status quo.

Many, if not most, of the great prophets in the past (Isaiah, St. Paul, George Fox) had experienced madness in a prototypical form. They experienced a breakdown followed by a breakthrough, spiritual death followed by rebirth. (This is termed the "metanoia" theory of madness.) These prophets lived in eras before psychiatry had established itself as the dominant social control agency in a society based on total surveillance (as Michel Foucault has argued in his many books) and the weeding out of those who deviate from the norm. The budding prophets of today are captured, "cured," and transformed into chronic mental patients by the psychiatric system before they have the opportunity to complete the death and rebirth process, to flower into prophets.

Mad Pride is *beginning* to reverse this process by creating collective self-help alternatives outside the system by providing the mad with myriad forms of social support, from the development of alternative communities like that based in Freedom Center (see chapter 6) to ad hoc groups on college campuses based on the Icarus model, to Internet forums as well as publicizing alternative "maps" of madness. Unlike Mind Freedom, the Mad Pride movement does *not* define its goal as the transformation of the mental health system; rather it seeks to constitute an alternative to this system. (Many of the mad still rely partially on the psychiatric system for services.) By providing these alternatives, Mad Pride is helping many mad people to complete the death and rebirth process and to accept being creatively maladjusted to an insane society.

For many mad people, adjustment to the status quo may not be feasible—as illustrated by the subjects in this book. Laing has written, "We all live under the constant threat of our own annihilation. We seem to seek death and destruction as much as life and happiness. . . . Only by the most outrageous violation of ourselves have we achieved our capacity to live in relative adjustment to a civilization apparently driven to its own destruction."[8] It may well be that many of the mad (like other unusual persons) lack the capacity to live in relative adjustment to such an insane society and that paradoxically the only way they can achieve a state of emotional stability is to become creatively *mal*adjusted—to become the prophets, activists, and spiritual leaders who will endeavor to bring the world closer to the visions they have had, to attempt to help humanity make the transition to a higher stage of consciousness, far beyond the status quo. As Martin Luther King Jr. put it long before there was a mental patients' liberation movement, "So let us be maladjusted, as maladjusted as the prophet Amos, who in the midst of the injustices of his day could cry out in words that echo across the centuries, 'Let justice run down like water and righteousness like a mighty stream.' Let us be as maladjusted as Abraham Lincoln, who had the vision to see that this nation could not exist half slave and half free. Let us be maladjusted as Jesus of Nazareth, who could look into the eyes of the men and women of his generation and cry out, 'Love your enemies.'"[9]

The Sociobiological Function of Madness: The Spiritual Evolution Narrative

The fact that the mad are "maladjusted" to society does not mean they are maladjusted to nature, to the underlying basis of the cosmos.

As Laing presciently wrote, "Our society may itself have become biologically dysfunctional, and some forms of schizophrenic alienation from the alienation of our society may have a sociobiological function that we have not recognized."[10] This stunning insight of Laing's has not been fully appreciated by psychiatric survivors. It is beginning to come to consciousness in Mad Pride, although few Mad Pride activists are familiar with the Laingian paradigm.

Let me put Laing's assertion about the sociobiological function of madness into the kind of narrative context that makes it more fully intelligible—and was only hinted at by Laing. The context—the premise of my own theory of Mad Pride (which is consistent with Laing's statements)—is this: the entire species, the entire Earth is involved in an evolutionary crisis that must be resolved if we are to survive. This assertion implies, of course, that "there is a purpose striving in creation."[11]

This idea is the basis of the vision of the eminent Indian philosopher and yogi Sri Aurobindo. Though we are presently mired in Ignorance, human beings sooner or later must ascend to a more enlightened state, we must realize the divine life, the eternal life, on Earth.* This will involve a profound change of society, of humanity, and of the cosmos itself: society will be based on a realization of the unity of humanity, not on, as at present, the division of humanity and the struggle for survival of the fittest (in reality, the most ruthless). The current "laws of nature" themselves will be transcended by "newer ones" more conducive to human happiness.[12] As Sri Aurobindo wrote, "The ascent of man into heaven is not the key, but rather his ascent here into the spirit and the descent also of the spirit into his normal humanity and the transformation of this earthly nature." This, and not "some post-mortem salvation," Aurobindo tells us, is "the new birth" for which humanity waits as "the crowning movement" of its "long, obscure and painful history."[13] The dream of heaven on Earth—the recovery of paradise that has haunted the collective imagination for millennia[14]—will be realized.

The human being must transform herself so that she can be the instrument of this planetary transformation. "Man is at highest a half-

---

*Of course, in the current age of ecological catastrophes the failure to resolve this crisis could lead to the destruction of the biosphere—and of humanity.

god who has risen out of the animal nature, and is splendidly abnormal in it, but the thing which man has started off to be, the whole God," wrote Aurobindo, "is something so much greater than what he is, that it seems to him as abnormal to himself as he is to the animal. This means a great and arduous labor of growth before him, but also a splendid crown of his race and his victory."[15] This new being would indeed be abnormal by the standards of society, of the mental health system. The process by which she would evolve spiritually might take unexpected turns, it might—and clearly often does—lead through madness. It might indeed *be* madness by our currents standards.

If we take into account this kind of evolutionary "utopian" vision, what then might we imagine Laing had in mind (consciously or unconsciously) by his reference to the "sociobiological function" of madness? Its function is to resolve the evolutionary crisis we are in, thus enabling the process of evolution to move to a higher level of spiritual evolution, a level beyond what humanity has yet attained in history as we know it. How exactly madness would effect this *collective* transformation was a question Laing did not address.

Dissident psychiatrist John Weir Perry had a theory. He believed that visionaries, prophets, and mad persons are able to descend into the deepest level of the unconscious and access new myths that guide societies in making transitions in times of crisis. Those who are leaders may "deliver the new myth" that is going to be accepted for the next phase of that culture's evolution. He explained the dynamic in *The Heart of History*, "The poetic and prophetic souls possessing the great vision of the new way would become the mouthpieces of the psyche in its dynamic upheaval of renewal. Their effect upon the culture would be to stir a momentous rush of enthusiasm into new concerns."[16]

Richard Gosden, in his discussion of Perry's work, writes that people in modern societies "who manifest schizophrenic symptoms are struggling to fulfill the same function" as visionaries in times of crises—to transmit new "myth-forms" that they have glimpsed in their moments of madness to society at large so that people can act to foster and adapt to social change. As will be discussed in chapter 5 Perry did not quite go as far as Gosden implies: he believed that schizophrenics are visionaries, but not prophets; only the latter seek to influence society at large. More specifically, Gosden has a prescient formulation: he writes that in modern society those who are "diagnosed with schizophrenia" are making "an evolutionary bid" for the transformation of consciousness.[17]

Paul Levy (interviewed in chapter 16), a mad person (that is, a former mental patient) and spiritual teacher, makes this bid quite explicit. As he wrote in a recent book (all emphases are mine), "Jung pointed out the *world-creating* significance of the consciousness manifested in man.' Because of its ability to help to create the universe, Jung called the consciousness manifesting in humanity 'a divine instrument.' We are being invited to consciously realize ourselves as apertures through which the divine imagination is able to materialize itself into, as, and through our universe. In an evolutionary leap in consciousness, we realize that instead of fighting with each other, we can *co-operate* with each other and literally and lucidly change the dream we are having. What a novel idea."[18] I will clarify: Levy claims that "reality" is but a collective dream that can be changed—by first changing our consciousness.

This bid to collectively change consciousness—to change the dream we are having—has rarely been made *explicitly* by the mad in the past, as it is by Levy and Whitney (interviewed in chapter 14). It is *implicit* in the visions and the accompanying communications of the mad. *Perry wrote that "almost universally" within "acute psychosis" lies a messianic vision of a new world order based on "equality and harmony, tolerance and love."*[19] This is invariably coupled with visions (often terrifying) of apocalyptic conflict; the visionary experience constellates the opposites in the psyche: paradise and hell. And hell on Earth is the likely consequence of our failure to address the developing ecological catastrophe. Perry found in the "messianic ideation" of his psychotic clients, in their "vision of oneness" a *prefiguration* of the new society that was "waiting to come about in the collective society of our time"[20]—the next phase, if we choose it, of our spiritual evolution.

Laing's views on this topic were similar, though not as fully developed as Perry's. In *The Politics of Experience* Laing presciently wrote, "If the human race survives, future men will look back on our enlightened epoch as a veritable Age of Darkness. The laugh's on us. They will see that what we call 'schizophrenia' was one of the forms in which, often through quite ordinary people, the light began to break in the cracks in our all-too-closed minds."[21] On the one hand, Laing refers to "the schizophrenic alienation from the alienation of our society";[22] on the other hand, he refers frequently in *The Politics of Experience* to the illumination experienced in madness (see chapter 4).

They are two sides of the same coin; together they constitute the traits that make the mad so different. It is as if a new mode of consciousness is seeking to manifest itself through the mad. Because the world needs to be changed, because we need to dream a new dream, because we need to break the trance of consensus reality *if the human species is to survive*, it makes sense to posit, as Laing did, that madness as an altered state of consciousness—teleologically considered—may have a "sociobiological function." I contend that this sociobiological function is often experienced by the mad as a *"calling"* to act as catalysts of spiritual evolution, of a messianic transformation. It is the basis of Mad Pride.

One can find support for these metaphysical ideas in a more secular source—the writings of the utopian socialist and neo-Marxist theoretician Ernst Bloch. From a Blochian perspective it is not surprising that messianic fantasies are expressed by the mad: Bloch found them throughout the interfacing realms of religion, literature, and personal fantasy. Unlike most Marxists, Bloch had a high estimate of religion; he believed that religious messianism in general expresses "the eternal human yearning for utopia on Earth." For Bloch religion is "the unconscious of utopia."[23] Utopia is "the preconscious of what is to come"; it is "the birthplace of the New."[24] The reformer should look for traces of utopia everywhere: it is the "anticipatory illuminations" of these utopian traces (undertaken by the philosopher or activist) that will enable them to become a reality; these illuminations are the link between hope and reality, dream and future.[25]

Of course, living in the age when the unfashionable mad—the "mentally ill"—were silenced, confined, and lobotomized, it would not have occurred to Bloch to look for utopian traces in the "hallucinations" of "schizophrenics." But today, as we have seen, the psychiatrists with the most sympathy for the mad are keenly aware of the profound messianic visions that haunt them. Mad Pride could provide a forum where these messianic traces (disparaged as symptoms of deep pathology by the benighted psychiatrist) could be revealed and illuminated—thus forging the link between hope and reality.

The first ex-mental patient I met and befriended (when I was a college student in the 1970s) used to whisper to me, "I am the mother of the new messianic age." Ed Whitney (see chapter 14) was absolutely convinced in the 1990s that the long-awaited day of peace and happiness for all was being inaugurated by the new messiah, the Lubavitcher rebbe. (Whitney was not a member of the Lubavitcher's group). Could it not be said of madness, as Bloch said of Christianity fifty years ago, that madness is now the new unconscious of utopia, the preconscious of the messianic age? In Christian terms one would say that the traces of utopia are signs that the kingdom of God is seeking to break into the world—in this case through the psyches of the mad. It is the calling of the Mad Pride movement to cooperate with this process, to facilitate it, to be the midwife—or at least one of the midwives—of the new age.

Mad Pride in Transition

I am speaking in a higher octave, in more messianic-utopian terms than most activists in the Mad Pride movement. (Although most of them have experienced the messianic visions of which I wrote, they have not consistently affirmed the relevance of these visions for the Mad Pride movement as explained throughout this book.) Sascha DuBrul spoke in terms very similar to my own soon after he formed The Icarus Project—before he reversed himself in 2008. So does Jacks Ashley McNamara, the cofounder of The Icarus Project. So does Paul Levy in the interview—although Levy does not speak as a representative of Mad Pride.

The mission statement of The Icarus Project has an unmistakably messianic tone. It reads like something written by Laing circa 1967 but that was then—in 2004. Despite the more somber pitch of the tone of Mad Pride today, the fact is that many mad people still report (as will be discussed in the next section, What Is to Be Done? Adopting a High Messianic Perspective), as Perry had observed, that they have been in contact with God and have been given a messianic mission to fulfill. I contend that the mad *do* have a redemptive-messianic mission to fulfill (we all do, in a sense)—to act as the midwives of the new order that exists within the womb of the old society, to use one of Karl Marx's phrases.

Let me be clear that I do not mean messianism in any funda-mentalist sense of the term. In the first part of the twentieth century Martin Buber wrote, "Messianism is Judaism's most profoundly original idea."[26] One could say that along with "the prophetic," the messianic was Judaism's gift to humanity. Buber explains messianism meant the coming of a "world of unity" in which sin would be forever destroyed.[27] Buber advocated an "active messianism" that did not wait passively for *the* Messiah, but "sought to prepare the world to be God's kingdom."[28] Buber wrote that according to the Jewish prophets, including Jesus, the future kingdom of God meant "the true community," "the perfection of men's life together." "The Kingdom of God is the community to come in which all those who hunger and thirst for righteousness will be satis-fied."[29] The modern Kabbalah scholar Moshe Idel shows how Buber's "distribution of the messianic function" among many persons, although more pronounced among "modern Jewish philosophies,"*[30] is prefigured in fifteenth-century Hasidism.[31]

The Mad Pride movement can help mad people fulfill their mission by encouraging them to affirm their madness, to resist the pressure to adjust to society—and above all, to take seriously the "delusional" idea that they have a messianic mission. My hope is to encourage the Mad Pride move-ment to be explicitly messianic or utopian. (Different people have strong preferences for one or the other term, although I think Bloch showed they pointed to the same phenomenon.) This may require of course that the mad subject their messianic visions to discussion and interpretation—and that they not repudiate messianism altogether out of fear of "ego infla-tion" (as Jung termed it), as discussed by Levy and DuBrul.

DuBrul, citing the influence of Eastern spirituality, repudiated in 2008 the Dionysian-messianic vision he had developed over the previous years; he feared it encouraged egotism. Levy, on the other hand, himself a Buddhist and a Jungian, considered "ego inflation" (as Jung called it) to be a nascent phase of spiritual awakening that initially helps one to break out of the "trance of consensus-reality" and then "falls away" as it becomes integrated into a broader perspective.

---

*According to Idel, "In modern Jewish philosophies . . . the assumption of multiple Messiahs has been advanced in order to fulfill the multiple messianic functions."

For the most part the psychiatric survivors' movement (see chapter 3), as opposed to Mad Pride (e.g., The Icarus Project), has embraced a secularist ideology in its effort to unite former mental patients and others who identify with the term *survivors of psychiatry* around the least common denominator—to emphasize their commonality with each other and with "normal" people—and thus to mobilize as many persons as possible to oppose the oppressiveness of the psychiatric system. In accord with this, it has treated the visions of the mad as private issues with no relevance to society or to the survivors' movement itself.

It is largely because of the failure of the psychiatric survivors' movement to treat madness as a socially significant phenomenon that the Mad Pride movement emerged in the first place. It arose spontaneously around ten years ago (started by a new generation), thirty years after the first mental patients' liberation organization was formed, as if in *compensation* finally for the one-sided *secularism* of the psychiatric survivors' movement—its public silence about mad people's most prominent trait (their spirituality)—which mirrored the *secularism* of society. The spontaneous character of Mad Pride was evidenced by the fact that Sascha DuBrul and Ashley McNamara, the founders of The Icarus Project—which became the largest Mad Pride organization in the United States—had not themselves even read the diverse intellectual theorists who had an influence on the mental patients' liberation movement from the time of its emergence in the 1970s. They had not even read Laing—whose ideas were strikingly similar to DuBrul's and McNamara's in their most radical phase. Neither DuBrul's nor McNamara's positive valuation of madness was a result of any kind of discernible intellectual influence, except for their readings on shamanism.

McNamara, a highly gifted writer, was expressing in essays she wrote between 2002 and 2006 (and posted on The Icarus Project's website) themes similar to Laing's writings on madness as spiritual revelation. However, when I communicated with her in 2007 she told me she knew nothing about Laing. In 2002 DuBrul had written a dramatic account about his breakdown, published in a large alternative magazine (see chapter 9). As DuBrul's piece was a conflicted apology for psychiatry, there was no reason to expect that within two years he would become an exponent and champion of Mad Pride. However, DuBrul is an artist and a mad person and, as such, an intuitive who is unusually sensitive to the needs of the time, which in this instance required compensating for the secularism of the psychiatric survivors' movement.

Levy has lucidly explicated this process of "compensation" as first described by Carl Jung. Levy writes,

> When our universe is viewed as a whole system composed of multiple dimensions . . . when something is out of balance in the system, whether it be on the level of the individual, family, community, nation or planet, the greater underlying field self-regulates and invariably manifests so as to compensate the one-sidedness in the system. . . . When there is an unconscious imbalance or disturbance in the field, a co-responding and reflexive compensatory process becomes activated . . . invariably resulting in an archetypal, healing figure incarnating in human form—whether we call this figure artist, shaman, healer, seer, or poet. The intuitive human beings who become channels for this process are tuned into and sensitive to the underlying unified field in a way that helps the field to unify. To quote Jung, "Whenever conscious life becomes one-sided or adopts a false attitude, these images 'instinctively' rise to the surface in dreams and in the vision of artists and seers to restore the psychic balance, whether of the individual or of the epoch."[32]

Mad Pride, in the form of The Icarus Project—at least at the time of its birth—*was an instance of this*: its founders were the intuitive human beings who were the channels for this process.

The hallmark of Mad Pride, the affirmation of the distinctiveness of the mad—first emphasized by DuBrul, with his idea of madness as composed of "dangerous gifts"—was a major step toward fostering the autonomy of the mad, toward discovering and affirming an identity for the Mad Pride movement in which the mad person's differences from the normal man or woman were highlighted rather than marginalized, suppressed, or treated as incidental. DuBrul's strength as a leader was his ability to impart to mad persons a sense of their uniqueness and to convey to them his conviction that they had the opportunity to make a distinctive contribution to saving the world.

The Icarus Project collective* wrote:

> There are so many of us out here who feel the world with thin skin and heavy hearts, who get called crazy because we are too full of fire and pain, who know that other worlds exist, and who are not comfortable with this version of reality. . . . We've been busting up out of sidewalks and blooming all kinds of misfit flowers for as long as people have been walking on this earth. . . . [Y]ou could think of us like dandelion roots that gather minerals from hidden layers of the soil that other plants don't reach. If we're lucky we share them with everyone on the surface. . . . A lot of us have visions about how things could be different, why they need to be different, and it's painful to keep them silent. Sometimes we get called sick and sometimes we get called sacred, but no matter how you label us we are a vital part of making this planet whole. [33]

For the first few years of The Icarus Project this was a leitmotif of DuBrul and McNamara: the mad "have visions about how things could be different, why they need to be different, and it's painful to keep them silent." Furthermore, the mad were "a vital part of making the planet whole." Whereas the psychiatric survivors' movement focused on fighting to revolutionize the mental health system, The Icarus Project set its sights on the world, as expressed in their mission statement, "We believe we have mad gifts to be cultivated and taken care of. . . . By joining together as individuals and as a community, the intertwined threads of madness and creativity can inspire hope and transformation in an oppressive and damaged *world*. . . ."[34] The name Icarus was chosen to indicate that these gifts could be dangerous if not treated with care.

Unfortunately by the time I interviewed him for this book in September 2009 (see chapter 9) DuBrul had undergone a major transformation and

---

*In 2007 when I first met DuBrul, The Icarus Project Collective (which DuBrul described as "the staff") consisted of two other people besides him and McNamara, the two cofounders. These two others were Will Hall and Madigan Shive. Hall, who is now in his forties, had been an activist in the antipsychiatric movement for over ten years and was the host of a radio show, *Madness Radio*. Madigan Shive, known as Bonfire Madigan, is a successful and talented cello player, singer, and songwriter who has a busy touring schedule.

had repudiated many of his previous ideas and retreated to a more conservative stance; this was a year after he had an unexpected breakdown. Although he still anticipated rejoining the movement in the future, he no longer thought mad people would play a "vanguard" role in transforming society. He still believed that the world was in a process of spiritual transformation, as evidenced (he said) by the people inspired by Eckhart Tolle, but he felt that the Mad Pride movement should be very modest about the contribution it can make to the process. "We have a role to play but . . . I don't have the audacity to think that we're that important," he said.

As of 2011, DuBrul has become active in Mad Pride again—though not with The Icarus Project. The question arises: What next? It seems The Icarus Project will continue to emphasize their spiritual differences from normal people. Will they evolve to the point—which DuBrul had ephemerally reached—where they come to define their identity in terms of a "calling" to act as catalysts of utopian/messianic transformation and spiritual evolution? This was clearly where DuBrul had seemed to be moving with his "dangerous gifts" idea, before he changed his mind in 2009. Furthermore he had written in 2008 that the mad are "the only ones that are crazy enough to think they can change the world and have the outlandish visions and drive to be able to do it" (see chapter 9).

McNamara espoused beliefs similar to DuBrul. She wrote that a few weeks of mania could give one access to a sense of understanding that it could take "years of meditation" to achieve, access to visions of "the wholeness" of the universe and "the interconnected nature of love, access to a sense of time and space that allows one to discern what is and what is not important."[35] Like several of the subjects interviewed she was aware that one often has these revelations "before you are ready to hold them in your head."[36] Yet she suspects that madness may be a key to "opening doors" in a society that is "rapidly constructing walls around possibility at every bend."[37] She writes in a more poetic and allusive manner than DuBrul, but she seemed to agree in the most general sense with the point stated—that the visions of the mad are key to the spiritual transformation of the planet. She wrote, "We need to imagine a globe without limits. . . . We are like seeds and we create words like millennia and madness that grow a world around us. . . . We need to imagine a place for visions like that, we need to imagine an atlas where the experiences we label 'psychosis' and 'mania' don't get written off the map. Or quarantined to hospitals and penitentiaries."[38] Like DuBrul she also became less radical—or at least less outspoken—after she had an unexpected breakdown in 2007, a year before DuBrul's so-called psychotic episode.

Some of the activists in Mad Pride tend to distrust the very idea of leadership. Madigan Shive wrote me in 2009 to warn me against making a hero of DuBrul. At that time she had read a brief summary of my book but not my profile of DuBrul, which might have surprised her since I frequently expressed disagreement with DuBrul's views. She warned me that "individual narratives" reflect and foster the individualistic ethos of capitalism, and she asserted that "collective liberation narratives" are the basis of Mad Pride. But I do not agree with this premise. I believe that individual narratives inspire and empower other individuals—of which the "masses" are composed—to break from psychiatry and join Mad Pride; individuals can be role models for other individuals.

I know that one person's life can be changed by reading or hearing the story of another person who "beat the odds." It is our nature to be influenced by "role models"; this is not pernicious. There is a dialectic between the individual and the mass. The denigration of individual narratives often derives from a collectivist ideology, which I consider repressive (but a discussion of this is beyond the scope of this book). Suffice it to state that creative and responsible individual leaders and new "collective" or organizational formations are both necessary if Mad Pride as a collective entity, a movement, is to grow and become (as stated in their mission statement) a transformative force "in an oppressive and damaged *world*. . . ."

New leaders—or whatever they want to call themselves—will inevitably emerge who will provide a theoretical orientation for Mad Pride, just as David Oaks (and Judi Chamberlin before him) provided a theoretical orientation (derived primarily from Thomas Szasz and Peter Breggin) for the psychiatric survivors' movement.[39] I wrote this book partly with the hope of influencing the development of this orientation and prompting a belated consideration of the 1960s Laingian paradigm that, as noted, had only an ephemeral effect on the mental patients' liberation movement. Of course Laing had become famous before the worldview of postmodern pluralism had eclipsed the Romantic messianic perspective that was popular in the countercultural 1960s.

As philosopher Richard Tarnas aptly wrote, "The underlying intellectual ethos [of our age] is one of disassembling established structures, deflating pretensions, exploding beliefs, unmaking appearances—a hermeneutics of suspicion in the spirit of Marx, Nietzsche and Freud."[40] Radical deconstruction is salutary but, I submit, only if it is complemented by the commitment to an overall vision of redemption, a vision of the unification of spirit and nature, of conscious and unconscious, male and female, sanity and madness, body and soul, the sacred and the profane—as envisioned, for example, by the Western Romantic philosophical tradition or by Sri Aurobindo or Christianity at its best. But such a vision or narrative is viewed from the postmodern perspective (which is dominant now even on the intellectual left, which was once a natural home for the "utopian" redemptive perspective in secular form) as "intellectual authoritarianism"—or religious superstition.

The hallmark of postmodernism is the valorization of *difference* and diversity and a rejection of "the tyranny of wholes" in favor of pluralism or relativism. Tarnas brilliantly captures the spirit of the postmodernist vantage point: "Grand theories and universal overviews cannot be sustained without producing empirical falsification and intellectual authoritarianism. To assert general truths is to impose a spurious dogma on the chaos of phenomena. Respect for contingency and discontinuity limits knowledge to the local and specific. Any alleged comprehensive, coherent outlook is at best no more than a temporary useful fiction masking chaos, at worst an oppressive fiction masking relationships of power, domination and subordination."[41] The virtual obliteration of any kind of unifying Romantic narrative—and of the redemptive-messianic vision in general—is a product of the postmodern era.

Since the mad are a marginal group, sensitive understandably to the threat of domination due to their experiences at the hands of Psychiatry, and inclined to celebrate diversity, the postmodern perspective (as defined above by Tarnas) has its appeal to Mad Pride activists. This appeal is strengthened by the apparent anachronism of Romantic or other messianic-redemptive narratives in a postmodern age when ironic detachment (as opposed to passionate involvement) is celebrated as one of the premium virtues and Romantic-utopian yearnings or messianic hopes are viewed as naive, or worse—dangerous.[42] But I believe its appeal to the mad is superficial—based on an evasion of confronting the metaphysical significance of madness. My own question is this: Will Mad Pride leaders have the courage, the "audacity," to go beyond postmodern pluralism, to go beyond identity politics and affirm—perhaps based on a sense of loyalty to revelations that came to them in moments of madness[*43]—a unifying messianic-redemptive vision?

With DuBrul temporarily in retirement from Mad Pride in 2010, Will Hall had often found himself in the spotlight as a leading spokesperson for The Icarus Project or the Mad Pride movement in general. Hall is a skillful and highly motivated organizer and a smart, intellectually inquisitive activist, but judging from his writings and his interviews as the moderator of *Madness Radio,* my sense is that he does not believe his role as a spokesperson for Mad Pride is to provide intellectual leadership for Mad Pride activists. Nor does he view the Mad Pride movement in neo-Laingian terms as the catalyst of a spiritual-social-ecological transformation or revolution.

He seems more inclined to raise intelligent questions than to provide answers—which he does very well as the moderator of *Madness Radio.* In fact, like many Mad Pride activists, he probably believes that presenting one narrative (however inspiring) or one perspective (however empowering) as *the* truth is old-fashioned or "authoritarian." I suspect he is temperamentally inclined to adopt a postmodern pluralistic approach that invites activists to entertain a variety of different perspectives on reality while at the same time retaining a critical view of the establishment.* In 2011 DuBrul wrote his latest views on Mad

---

*Kate Millett wrote, "But what if there were something on the other side of crazy, what if across that line there was a certain understanding, a special knowledge? Don't you remember so many times during it, telling yourself, swearing, that you would never forget what you saw and learned, precious enough to justify what you suffered? And didn't I then repudiate every vision—didn't I even disparage the knowledge I had last time, trample it underfoot in my haste to rejoin the sane and the sane-makers, the shrinks and the family?"

*For further reading, Bradley Lewis' book *Moving beyond Prozac, DSM, and the New Psychiatry: The Birth of Post-Psychiatry* is probably the most trenchant and brilliant critique of Psychiatry and scientistic (not scientific) propaganda written since the original

Pride—he does not agree with the perspective he expressed in the Icarus mission statement (see chapter 11). So the future today is uncertain.

What Is to Be Done? Adopting a High Messianic Perspective

Mad Pride, as noted, emerged spontaneously; its leaders did not evolve out of the psychiatric survivors' movement. From my perspective what is needed now is a more conscious, historically informed, and theoretically aware leadership to guide the Mad Pride movement, to mount a sustained, intellectually informed attack on the dominant materialist paradigm of modern society—the paradigm that defines madness as pathology and messianism as pathology or anachronistic. As noted below, one of the main weaknesses of DuBrul as a leader (a role he does not necessarily want) is that he had not (at the time of our last interview) familiarized himself with the variety of intellectual influences on the broader movement—of thousands of mental patients and a small group of dissident psychiatrists and other professionals—of which he was an heir. The mad need leaders (however temporary) who will encourage them—as DuBrul had begun to do as a "leader" of The Icarus Project—to make use of their dangerous gifts and creativity to undermine the hegemony of consensus reality and propagate a messianic-redemptive (utopian) vision of possibility, of "reality." They must encourage them to reach for the moon—a perspective DuBrul shied away from after 2008 (see chapter 9).

Since the moment of its inception Mad Pride has been empowering mad people to affirm their madness. *I am arguing in this book for the importance of taking this process one step further: I want to see the Mad Pride movement become a catalyst for an epochal spiritual transformation of humanity.* I believe the mad need a vast vision and an imposing sense of their own power in order to motivate them to overcome the

---

works of Szasz and Laing. Despite his epistemological radicalism—or perhaps because of it—his secular and pragmatistic premises seem to blind him to the idea that the very existence of Psychiatry is a *symptom* of a society that is ontologically thwarted as well as undemocratic. His agenda for the future of a reformed Psychiatry reveals the imaginative constrictiveness and conservatism of the postmodern vision—as compared to Romantic or messianic-redemptive visions.

obstacles that have been placed in their path by Psychiatry, to give them the courage to believe there can be a resolution to the problems of the world that impinge so acutely on their psyches. For their own sense of well-being, the mad need to be inspired by a confirmation of their own private messianic visions. Without appealing to a larger sense of mission based on a messianic-redemptive vision, the Mad Pride movement will eventually lose its élan and become just another self-help movement based on identity politics.

Looking at one of The Icarus Project forums ("Alternate Dimensions or Psychotic Delusions") I was struck by an online "conversation" in which several mad persons discussed having a sense of mission. "Serine" (each person used a working name) writes on The Icarus Project Forum on February 7, 2007:

> Hi, I am a 31 yr [sic] old single mom, and I have BP ["bipolar disorder"] with psychosis. When I go into mania, I have conversation with God and He has told me how He plans to bring together the plan for the ages. Or how he is going to bring about global awareness. And of course it is something that I have to do. Now every time I go into mania, I am consumed by it, when I come out I am 'normal' but still believe it. I mean what better thing is there to believe than God has chosen you to do an earthly mission for Him. Anybody else out there in the same boat? What do they call it . . . Grandious [sic] delusions?

One person responds, "I had a bit of a messiah complex once. I wasn't talking to god or anything, but I did feel 'chosen.'" Another forum member, "Hen," responds "Often times when I am so sick of my life there is something in me that thinks that God picked me to do something special. I have always felt that way and I think I am getting closer and closer to the path to something."

"Shaman 2012" advises Serine, "I believe I'm on a mission. I believe others know they are on a mission. But we cannot dwell in these thoughts, they can drive us mad." (Pun intended?) "Ianus" responds to Serine, "I frequently have a feeling of being, somehow divinely chosen. Main difference for me, is I kinda believe all people are in a way divinely chosen. The rational way I put this is everyone has their ability to effect [*sic*] the world around them in either positive or negative ways. Is there the possibility that there is some external force active and driving the universe to a nebulous end goal? Yes, but there is no way to scientifically prove such a theory." "Bisco" writes, "I've definitely felt I'm on a mission to save the world. Sometimes, I just get this feeling that by being here I am somehow helping to save the world, like I did my work, and now the world can go on." Forum member "Turbokat" writes philosophically, "I think the problem is that most people *don't* think they have a mission to save the world, they think they have a carte blanche to destroy it in little ways every day, and anyone who thinks they have a mission to save it is certifiable and to be pitied. But, God speaks through many religions of something like a mission to at least follow instructions and make the world a better place. One way around it is to simply not believe in God."[44]

Psychiatrists believe these sentiments and profound philosophical reflections are delusional, egocentric ("ideas of reference"), and "grandiose." From the shrunken reductionist Freudian or biopsychiatric view, messianic feelings constitute a psychotic and narcissistic compensation ("grandiose") for the low self-esteem of an ego that is ostensibly underdeveloped and "damaged" due to inadequate child rearing or, alternatively, an inexplicable product of a chemically imbalanced or defective brain. This disparaging and spiritually myopic view of the messianic feelings and often deeply spiritual and profound insights of the mad is adopted by virtually all mental health professionals today—even most of the transpersonal psychologists, following the lead of the erstwhile New Age spokesman and philosopher Ken Wilber.

But what is striking to me in the comments of the mad are the absence of arrogance (of "narcissism" as the shrinks call it)—in fact, the humility—with which these feelings are shared on The Icarus Project forum and the profound philosophical insights expressed by these mad people. Ianus's interpretation is astute: he (or she) believes "all people are in a way divinely chosen" and suggests perceptively that this feeling may arise because one is in accord with a "force" that is driving the universe to a goal. Turbokat thinks the problem is that *most* people do *not* think they have a mission to save the world! These comments demonstrate that those among the mad who have not yet reached a plateau of self-confidence and maturity (attaining such a state is a task greatly hindered by Psychiatry) need leaders who *have* reached such a stage of maturity (as have the "leaders" in the Mad Pride movement) and are willing to assure the mad that what they are able to do *is* of utmost importance—of messianic significance. They need leaders who will encourage their messianic feelings that they can bring "transformation" to an "oppressive and damaged world"—to quote again from the original mission statement of The Icarus Project. They need to be provided by Mad Pride with opportunities to make a contribution.

This kind of messianic perspective was affirmed by two of my interviewees, Ed Whitney and Paul Levy. Whitney believed at certain points that he was the messiah, as did Levy. However—just like the persons on The Icarus Project forum—neither was egocentric or arrogant about his claim. Both were all too eager to yield to others or to get others to share with them the burden and privilege of being the Messiah or a messiah. Levy's democratic approach was exemplary (and similar to Whitney's). He says, "When I was having my spiritual awakening . . . I was having the realization of being the messiah too, but I was realizing we all are the messiah. I actually made out these business cards that just said 'the messiah,' and I was giving them out to people, and I was saying 'Look, here's my card, and if you want some you can have some too, you can give them out to people'" (see Levy's interview in chapter 14). Society needs as many people as possible who believe that we can change the world: *we need as many messiahs as possible*—not egocentric but humble messiahs. It is quite possible to be humble and feel a sense of a calling to serve God. And who else but the mad—as DuBrul said—are "crazy enough to think they can change the world and have the outlandish visions and drive to be able to do it"?

Levy, a spiritual teacher today, still believes in a messianic transformation.

If people tell me I am a "dreamer" when I profess these idealistic and seemingly naïve beliefs, I will simply say, to quote the late John Lennon, "I am not the only one." There are ever-expanding numbers of us—millions? billions?—around the planet who in various ways are being drafted by the Self to be channels for a deeper process of awakening, enabling a vast range of entirely new and previously unimagined possibilities to become available to us. The universe is dreaming itself awake through us. When enough of us simply recognize . . . that the universe is waking itself up through us, we can "come together," I "imagine," and help each other to deepen and stabilize our mutually shared awakening, what I call "dreaming ourselves awake."[45]

Levy has explained this process from an esoteric-Christian perspective as developed by Carl Jung. This parallels the evolutionary explanation I gave above by Sri Aurobindo, but it also specifically explains why the term *messiah* may be meaningful to many mad people in the West. Levy writes:

We are being invited to stop limiting who we imagine ourselves to be, to allow our life to become imbued with a deeper sense of meaning. . . . *God, is incarnating not just through one man, as it did through Christ over 2000 years ago, but is incarnating through all of humanity.* Jung talked about, ". . . a broadening process of incarnation. Christ was the first attempt by God to incarnate and transform itself. Now humanity as a whole will be the subject of the divine incarnation process." What is happening in our world right now is the Second Coming of Christ, what Jung calls the "Christification of many."[46]

As Levy made clear, this means that many people must not only conform to the image of God, they must themselves assume—collectively—the messianic functions of Jesus, of Christ. The mad are among the first to feel God seeking to incarnate through all humanity. In other words, this process may be beginning today with the Christification of the mad, which includes, above all, assuming a "messianic" role—as a group, as Mad Pride.

Cultural transformation occurs when the "crack in the cosmic egg" splits apart and messianic possibilities become visible to the eye of the collective imagination. This is what happened in the 1960s. The crack began to widen again when The Icarus Project was formed and when

The Icarus Project Collective became catalysts for an autonomous Mad Pride movement—when DuBrul and McNamara were trusting their mad inspirations and writing that madness was the missing key to resolving the crisis of the modern world, the crisis of civilization.

DuBrul wrote that "because of the success of this incredible mad community of ours" he had found the courage to make spiritual explorations that he had shied away from in the past. DuBrul was clear in 2008: the mad have a leading role (as a *vanguard,* to use the term derived from Lenin) to play in the process of spiritual transformation. The Christification of the mad (he did not use those terms) was taking place, and The Icarus Project and DuBrul were catalysts. What the future holds is anybody's guess. When DuBrul had a couple of his breakdowns he thought he was the messiah. As he formulated it on his blog in spring 2008 the messianic function was distributed (Moshe Idel's phrase) among many of the mad (for further discussion of this point, look under the subheading Mad Pride: The Revolt Against the Monoculture). By 2009, DuBrul had eschewed these messianic ideas.

Of course, I am aware that everything I am saying is insane from the viewpoint of the established order (which, from my point of view, illustrates its insanity). The established order arrogates to itself, to its Scientists of the Mind—as psychiatrists, as psychiatric drug alchemists, as modern society's secular priesthood—the right and the power to define what is reality, what is sanity, what is normality, and to conceal its normative concepts and values in allegedly value-neutral medical language. But as an intellectual heretic and am not influenced by the psychiatric conception of reality. From my perspective—shared by everyone I interviewed—*normality is the state of insanity, of spiritual derangement that society must transcend.* As psychiatric heretic Laing wrote, "The condition of alienation, of being asleep, of being unconscious, of being *out of one's mind,* is the condition of the normal man. Society highly values its normal man. It educates children to lose themselves and to become absurd, and thus to be normal."[47] In Laing's mind normality is insanity, whereas madness may be a path to "hypersanity."[48]

Now is the time for transformation; the "hour of God" cannot be postponed. As the world founders on the verge of the abyss—as ecological disasters and wars become more prevalent—it seems apparent to me that we are approaching a momentous time, a *kairos*. "A kairos is a moment in history marked by the entry of the Kingdom of God into human affairs,"[49] so writes historian Robert Abzug in 1994, inspired by Paul Tillich's use of the term. The Second Awakening was such a kairos—or rather it was believed to be such by the reformers of the day, (e.g., the abolitionists) (see part 5), many of whom were certain as Christians that when slavery was abolished the kingdom of God would be inaugurated on Earth, ushering in a period of harmony, unity, and eternal life—as described by Isaiah and St. Paul (again, see my discussion in part 5).

The historian David Brion Davis has described a kairos as a period of reform in which an "eschatological leap" becomes possible, one that overcomes "demonic powers and then transcends the limits of previous political, racial and economic history."[50] Davis's definition enriches the one above since it refers also to a victory over demonic powers and mentions the worldly changes that have to be effected as the precondition for God's salvific action and ingression into the world. The Christians of this era were Reform activists, not fatalistic like the Christian right.

A kairos entails a crisis of the paradigms, a disenchantment with the old idols, and it presumes the messianic vision has entered into the consciousness of the masses. It is pitted against demonic powers that represent the old order. McLoughlin substitutes the term "cultural revitalization" for *kairos*—the two are synonymous. Cultural revitalizations constitute "the awakening of a people caught in an outmoded, dysfunctional world view to the necessity of converting their mindset, their behavior, and their institutions to more relevant or more functionally useful ways of understanding and coping with the changes in the world they live in."[51]

The outmoded order in the current situation consists of the corporate capitalist mentality and institutions. What the young anticorporate radicals call the 1 percent are the beneficiaries of the present order, but the order is sustained by the allegiance and habits of the masses of Americans who are completely oblivious—unaware if not indifferent—to the harm inflicted on other beings, including humans, and are deluded by cultural myths. The environmentalist Derrick Jensen writes:

Deluded by myths of progress and suffering from the psychosis of technomania complicated by addiction to depleting oil reserves, industrial society leaves a crescendo of atrocities in its wake. A very partial list would include the Bhopal chemical disaster, numerous oil spills, the illegal depleted uranium-spewing occupations of Iraq, Afghanistan, mountaintop removal, the nuclear meltdown of Fukushima, the permanent removal of 95 percent of the large fish from the oceans (not to mention full-on systemic collapse of those oceans), indigenous communities replacement by oil wells, the mining of coltan for cell phones and Playstations along the Democratic Republic of the Congo/Rwanda border—resulting in tribal warfare and the near-extinction of the Eastern Lowland gorilla. . . . As though 200 species going extinct each day were not enough, climate change, a direct result of burning fossil fuels, has proved not only to be as unpredictable as it is real, but as destructive as it is unpredictable.[52]

Even Occupy Wall Street, the most significant populist movement since the 1960s, seems unaware of the gravity of the danger humanity faces. Millions of people around the world have correctly identified the corporate vultures who are destroying society, ravaging the Earth. However there is not yet a sense of life or death urgency, not yet an awareness that the decisive battle is approaching: if the corporations win this battle humanity will be destroyed, all life on Earth may be destroyed. In 2007 James Hansen, the NASA climate scientist, wrote, "Our home planet is now dangerously near a tipping point. . . the planet has been warm enough to keep ice sheets off North America and Europe, but cool enough for ice sheets on Greenland and Antarctica to be stable." Global warming created by human use of fossil fuels has "brought us to the precipice of a great tipping point. If we go over the edge, it will be a transition to a different planet. . . . [T]he trip will exterminate a large fraction of the species on the planet." Hansen called this a "planetary emergency" and said "we must move onto a new energy direction within a decade to avoid setting in motion unstoppable climate change with irreversible effects."

Hansen is not alone: as David Orr, professor of environmental studies at Oberlin College pointed out, not only does humanity face the risk of being completely destroyed, by some accounts by the end of the century, but "we have been alerted, warned and warned again by ecologists, geologists, systems analysts, physicists, Pulitzer Prize winners, Nobel laureates, ... but so far without much effect."[53] Obama, who campaigned on saving the environment, has shown complete disregard for it once in power. The corporate capitalist economic system is completely dysfunctional.

Just as the psychiatrists I discuss in this book will sell people poison to make money, so will our corporations and the politicians they own destroy life on the planet and the dreams of their own children if it will boost next year's profit margins or get them reelected. They care neither about humanity nor the lives of their children, although they assume with enough money they can buy invulnerability for their families.

Two years ago British Petroleum accidentally dumped 180 million gallons of oil in the Gulf of Mexico, creating a nightmare for marine life and the people in the region. Many Americans watched TV with horror, transfixed by the images of birds too drenched in oil to fly. However, the deep-water oil drilling continues in America, and BP has resumed drilling in the Gulf; even without an accident, carbon emissions that cause global warming increase. The candidate who campaigned against deep-water oil drilling became the president with friends in the industry. Obama, unlike the Republicans, acknowledges the existence and seriousness of climate change. Does that make him more or less guilty?

Many of the mad—the people labeled "schizophrenic," "schizoaffective," and "bipolar"—seem to know all about this. They have seen it in their visions. They have felt it. Since the culture values apathy, ignorance, and "self-imposed denial in the face of all this sadistic exploitation and violence," these traits are considered normal signs of mental health. To lie awake at night worrying about birds drenched in oil is obviously abnormal—"mentally ill." John Weir Perry said of the visions of the mad, "I've been told, by people looking back on the experience, that one thing that stands out most of all, beyond the feeling of isolation, is the perception that everything that comes up is divided into opposites: Good and Bad, God and the Devil, Us and Them, or whatever. . . . It takes the form of experiencing the world as caught in the grip of opposing forces, whether they be political, spiritual, cultural, ideological, or even racial. In recent years I've noticed it's 'those who might destroy the planet' versus 'those who are ecologically minded.'"[54]

The mad have seen correctly; their visions mirror the deeper reality. Perry noticed this about his patients in 1982, before most people were talking about ecology. Perry points out that their visions unfold sequentially and that after the phase of conflict, the mad typically have seen a "messianic vision." Haunted by the horrors of the world, they still dream of redemption, of a return to Eden. As Perry wrote in the late 1990s, "This vision of oneness is expressed in the messianic ideation, along with the recognition that the world is going to be marked by a style of living emphasizing equality and tolerance, harmony and love."[55]

In the depths of their unconscious the mad have experienced the demons of war and greed and held fast to their vision of paradise. It is for this reason that I believe that from their ranks—once they get off toxic psychiatric drugs and realize that they are clairvoyant, not sick—will come many of the prophets who will help to make the messianic vision a force within history—to create the conditions for a kairos (see discussion in chapters 15 and 17).

As I will argue in later chapters, the Mad Pride movement—if it recovers the vision and sense of mission that provided the basis of its original inspiration—could well provide the spark that will set fire to the messianic tinder that has smoldered for centuries in the depths of the collective imagination of humanity. If this occurs, it will be said in hindsight that the new spiritual awakening was a success. It will be said that it so altered the commonsense conception of what is important, what is real, and what is possible that humanity was saved from self-annihilation—that we found the trust and courage to conquer the ruling demons of our age and to finally make the eschatological leap into a higher phase of our spiritual and historical evolution, and thus to continue on our divine journey.

Part One

The Failure of the Psychiatric System and the Biomedical Myth

1

Interview with Peter Stastny, M. D.

The Psychiatric-Pharmaceutical Complex and Its Critics

There are literally only a few psychiatrists in the United States who are critical of psychiatry. The two most well-known are octogenarian Thomas Szasz* (see chapter 4) and Peter Breggin.† Dr. Breggin was probably the first authority to document the harmful effects—particularly the brain-damaging and "brain-disabling" effects‡—of psychiatric drugs. He began to become popular after an appearance on Oprah Winfrey in the late 1980s. He was also the first psychiatrist to warn of the creation of a psychiatric-pharmaceutical industrial complex (he called it, less clearly,

---

*Szasz's first path-breaking book is *The Myth of Mental Illness*. His best book in my opinion is *The Manufacture of Madness: A Comparative Study of the Inquisition and the Mental Health Movement*. A more recent look at psychiatric practice is his *Coercion as Cure: A Critical History of Psychiatry*.

†Breggin's *Toxic Psychiatry* is his most comprehensive book and his best critique of the psychiatric system. It is accessible to the layperson.

‡*Psychiatric Drugs: Hazards to the Brain* is one of Breggin's early books that marshals copious studies to document his thesis that psychiatric drugs (particularly the

the "psycho-pharmaceutical complex") which began to develop in a barely perceptible way in the late 1970s when the American Psychiatric Association made a decision to accept drug company money.[1]

Dr. Breggin still believes that the alternative to psychiatric treatment (drugging) is psychotherapy. As a trained therapist myself, I have had the opportunity to learn and apply some of the alternative therapies that became popular in the 1970s and 1980s, including various kinds of family therapy as well as hypnotherapy. I do not doubt the efficacy of therapy, although unlike Dr. Breggin I am critical of the dependence on individual therapy (or I was in the 1980s before psychiatric drugs replaced everything else). However, the innovative therapies are rarely available today to persons in the public sector, where the emphasis lies always on psychiatric "medication," which, once commenced, is presumed to continue until the patient's death.

Therapy is merely an adjunct often not offered or not covered by Medicaid. Thus the most innovative therapies are only accessible to those able to afford to hire a therapist in the private sector. Despite my success with clients, in the late 1980s I was forced to resign from two clinics successively for encouraging clients to wean themselves off of psychiatric drugs. When I wrote my first book in the early 1990s[2] I believed that the mental patients' liberation movement could successfully apply pressure to the mental health system to force it to offer "alternative" treatments in the public sector. Today I believe that the only feasible alternative to Psychiatry in America is self-help associations created and run by patients themselves—and not funded by the drug companies. Since the death in 2004 of psychiatrist Loren Mosher (see chapter 2), Dr. Peter Stastny has been the leading psychiatric spokesperson for the patient self-help movement. He was a founding

---

"antipsychotics") have brain-damaging and "brain-disabling" effects and were known to have these effects by the psychiatrists who first discovered or used them. This early book was written in a more straightforward way as it was not aimed at a popular audience. Nevertheless, it powerfully makes its point: the "therapeutic effect" of the drugs—they made the patients less refractory and easier to manage—was caused by the brain damage. The idea that they correct a chemical imbalance was invented later and is not supported by the evidence. In 1997 Breggin updated his original thesis by examining the new treatments, as discussed in his *Brain-Disabling Treatments in Psychiatry: Drugs, Electroshock, and the Role of the FDA*.

member in 2005 of the International Network Toward Alternatives and Recovery (INTAR). The book he coedited with Peter Lehmann,* *Alternatives beyond Psychiatry,*[3] is an indispensable resource for all activists in the Mad Pride movement.

Peter Stastny was born in Vienna, Austria, where he graduated from medical school in 1976. He moved to New York in 1978, where today he is a practicing psychiatrist and author and/or editor of several books critical of mainstream psychiatry. He is an associate professor of Psychiatry at the Albert Einstein School of Medicine. As mentioned, the views in this interview are his own and are not necessarily representative of INTAR.

Description of INTAR

The International Network Toward Alternatives and Recovery is an international summit of world-renowned survivor leaders, psychiatrists, psychologists, family members, and other mental health professionals who meet annually to counter the belief that people with diagnoses such as schizophrenia or bipolar disorder can never completely recover.

INTAR believes that the dignity and autonomy of the person in crisis are of the utmost importance, that full recovery from distressing/altered mental states is possible, and that these two convictions should shape the social response. For these reasons, we find established psychiatry and public mental health systems in which many of us work, seek (or have been forced to seek) treatment (for ourselves or our loved ones) and do research, to be deficient. Instead, we seek, and some of us provide, alternative settings where people in crisis can find the care, connectedness, respect, and interventions they need and elect to use.

Our backgrounds range widely, from peer/user organizing to biomedicine and psychoanalytic training to Eastern meditative disciplines to family advocacy to academic research. But we are, each of us, committed to building safe spaces and positive relationships, wherein the ordeal presented by extreme states of mind can be met with preventive tools and seasoned presence. This includes people who have been through it before and know how to offer the steadfast support needed. As an international network, we undertake to document the

---

*Lehmann is a leader of the patients' rights movement in Germany.

effectiveness of such alternatives, to refine and expand their use, and to make them more accessible to people who need them.[4]

Farber: One of the things that's distinctive about INTAR was the belief that full recovery from extreme mental states, including so-called schizophrenia, is possible. This is heresy right now in the mental health field.

Dr. Stastny: It might be a little less heretical now—everybody *talks* about recovery nowadays, but I'm not sure what they all mean by it. I don't personally like to talk too much about recovery, because the term has been bandied about so much that it's becoming pretty much meaningless as far as I'm concerned.

Farber: Do you object on philosophical terms?

Dr. Stastny: No. I think the mental health industry has corrupted the term and is now using it to say everything is really going well; we all believe in recovery. I think it's a problematic term. In terms of the name INTAR I think the emphasis is really on alternative and recovery. Recovery is in there because (a), it makes a good acronym and (b), it's necessary to talk about. Primarily, we're interested in just a different way for people to get help.

Farber: Someone could object on Szaszian grounds, but that's not what you meant right? Szasz would say there's no mental illness so there's nothing to recover from.

Dr. Stastny: On Szaszian grounds, we could call it discovery or rediscovery rather than recovery, but I mean we're telling people the system is bad and it's hurting people and they're saying, "But what are we gonna do?" You have to have something to offer. Sure there are people like Dr. Szasz who say, "Oh well, just don't be crazy," or "Don't go to a shrink." But that's not good enough as far as I'm concerned.

Farber: The people in the mental health system who use the term *recovery*—do they imply that you can recover but only if you stay on so-called meds?

Dr. Stastny: Yes, I mean I haven't heard too many people talking about getting off medication at all. Whatever I'm saying shouldn't be taken as representing INTAR.

Farber: When was INTAR founded?

Dr. Stastny: Exactly five years ago. My main emphasis was people shouldn't be put on psychiatric drugs to begin with, because getting off of drugs is a much more complicated proposition than not getting on them in the first place.

Farber: I've seen so many people—they call me—whose lives have been ruined. A couple of women I'm thinking of in particular: they were put on meds when they were young and attractive, and now they weigh 300 pounds—and all these years they never had a love life, not since they were young. Now they're in their forties and are humiliated by the ways their bodies look. The drugs not only make them fat but oddly misshapen. So they just resigned themselves to being alone—and essentially having no life except going to day treatment or groups run by the psychiatric system.

Dr. Stastny: I worked with a woman who was hospitalized once, it was her first time, she was put on a bunch of drugs, and she came out not really recognizable to herself. This was only a short period of time, she was on drugs for maybe three or four months. She had gained a huge amount of weight, and she was completely destroyed. If people come off of drugs early they have a better chance of making it.

Farber: Yes, I'd like to get that message across to readers. Get off the drugs early—but gradually of course. The people I know who have been on the drugs for over ten years, even if they want to get off, it seems they can't.

Dr. Stastny: It's hard, very hard, but some people make it though. Peter Lehmann has collected a bunch of reports by people who have successfully come off drugs, but it also depends which drugs. Some drugs are easier to come off than others.

Farber: The antipsychotics are the most difficult, aren't they?

Dr. Stastny: Yes, but the SSRIs, or the selective serotonin reuptake inhibitors like Prozac, Effexor, the drugs used for depression are also very difficult to come off.

Farber: There was a report in *The New York Times Magazine* a year or so ago (2006–2007) about the guy who had a difficult time getting off of an SSRI. Did you see that?

Dr. Stastny: I saw a thing by a doctor that all of a sudden he's finding in his practice he has ten to twenty people who started out on SSRIs when they were adolescents and they're still on them fifteen years later. He doesn't know what to do with them because there's no research at all that talks about how to get them off. Psychiatrists are told that patients should just keep taking it for the rest of their lives. There's no protocol within the field on how to get off once someone has been on that stuff for a bunch of years.

Farber: Did you happen to know the story of Gianna Kali, who got off of drugs after fifteen years?

Dr. Stastny: I happen to know her story, yes.

Farber: She posted on her blog she was able to get off of them without going psychotic or being emotionally overwhelmed but she has no energy. She has a hard time doing things; of course she's only been completely off for a few months. It makes it harder to get off now, doesn't it? They put patients on a cocktail of drugs rather than one or two. When a young person has a breakdown and hears voices or whatever, in America they're told they have a disease and they'll need to be on the drugs for the rest of their life. Isn't that almost always the case?

Dr. Stastny: I don't think they're always explicitly told they have to be on the drugs for the rest of their life, but if they have a breakdown like that, they're probably told they should just stay on them until further notice: But no further notice ever comes. So that's why some people just take themselves off it.

Farber: What you are saying is unusual if not unique for a psychiatrist—that people don't need to be on these drugs.

Dr. Stastny: What I'm saying is that people who find themselves in trouble emotionally—or because people tell them they are in trouble—they have to have different options. It's not just the drugs that are damaging; it's the hospitals and the clinics that prescribe the drugs. I find the hospitals equally if not more problematic. It's a package deal that happens when people flip out or become very despondent or wonder if they should continue to live. All these things put people at risk for this package they're being offered, especially in this country, which means: emergency room, admission to a hospital—half the time involuntarily and the other half the time you're being tricked or you don't know what else to do or your family puts pressure on you. When patients agree to stay in the hospital they don't even know what they're agreeing to, they don't know what to expect. They have no idea that once they've entered the hospital, it's not a one-time thing. There are a lot of times people are quickly turned into mental patients; it happens very fast. I can speak about one person who unfortunately died. Mimi Kravitz, who recently gave an interview, eloquently described how quickly it happens that you're turned from a college student to a mental patient with a few gestures on the part of the doctor you know. You're told that you're sick: you have to wear pajamas all day, you have one bar of soap, you get a diagnosis, and there you are among the other mental patients. Presto! You are a mental patient. That happens so fast that it seems to me the medication alone is not as problematic as the package, including the often-terrifying responses of the doctors in the emergency rooms—not to mention the fact that no attention gets paid to what people actually are suffering and experiencing, why they ended up there in the first place.

Farber: Oh yes. Good point. The original problem is left unresolved; it doesn't even exist for psychiatrists who see everything as aberrant biochemistry. I was trained as a family therapist with Salvador Minuchin and then with Jay Haley.* That whole family therapy field has also been co-opted; they don't do real family therapy anymore. The

---

*Both Minuchin and Haley wrote numerous books, but the best introductions to their approaches are, from Minuchin, *Families and Family Therapy,* and from Haley, *Leaving Home.* Lynn Hoffman's book *Foundations of Family Therapy* is the best text for an overview of the family therapy field in the 1980s.

original methods of course were based on the idea that if one person is acting crazy, the entire family is dysfunctional; so there is really nothing wrong *inside* the person who becomes the "identified patient." Now family therapy in the clinics has been turned into the so-called psycho-educational model where the family sits together and talks with the therapist about how they're going to make or help Johnny—the identified patient—to accept his illness, his identity as a patient, and take his meds. It's the opposite of the original family therapy model, but it's now been adopted by almost all so-called family therapists. So, the family problems do not get addressed because the therapist joins in scapegoating the so-called patient. Johnny is locked forever into the sick role, and the drug companies and the psychiatrists—the pimps for the drug companies—are happy.

I believe this family therapy movement could have brought about a "revolution in mental health"—just like David Oaks advocates, and it appeared to be heading that way in the mid-1980s. The marginalization or co-optation of family therapy demonstrated that the agenda for the development of the "helping professions" was set by the pharmaceutical corporations and had nothing to with the needs of clients. Family therapists bear responsibility for distorting the ideas of innovators like Minuchin and Haley in order to be compatible with the dominant biopsychiatric theory that problems in living were the result of aberrant biochemistry, not family problems.

Dr. Stastny: Right. That has happened ever since the families in groups like NAMI*[5] have lobbied to be taken "off the hook." It's a lame excuse by the family movement to say, "Oh we've been accused of causing mental illness and therefore now we're just turning things around—and putting the blame on the illness." That's what they've done, and they oppose any kind of systemic therapy. For example, there is this movement in Finland that's called open dialogue, and it's a very

---

*National Alliance on Mental Illness. For most of its existence it was called National Alliance for the Mentally Ill. NAMI is composed primarily of parents of children or adult-children who have been labeled "mentally ill." A strong supporter of the biopsychiatric model and the use of psychiatric drugs, it serves as a lobby for the pharmaceutical companies from whom it receives large contributions.

different approach to families and to people. You go in to meet with a family, basically you become one team, and there's no separate team of therapists—you don't go back and discuss what's going on behind the family's back—it's an open dialogue and everything gets discussed openly. They've actually done research on that and found that has really great results. Most people who are seen by the therapists (and these are so-called psychotics) don't end up in the hospital, and a great number of people don't end up on medication.

Farber: Now one of the things that's so detrimental about the hospitalization is the powerful impact of being treated like a patient—people end up believing they're chronically mentally ill.

Dr. Stastny: Yes. A lot of people believe that, and they believe the diagnosis. Nowadays, people will tell you that they're quote-unquote schizophrenic-bipolar. People walk around and I meet them and I say, "Well, what have you been told?" They say, "Well, I'm schizophrenic-bipolar." It's like one word, *bipolar-schizophrenic:* people just buy that, and that explains why they take four different medications.

Farber: This completely undermines their sense of self-esteem, what Laing used to call the rituals of invalidation, of degradation, that take place in the hospital.

Dr. Stastny: To be honest, occasionally hospitals do work for people to some extent. I worked with a guy who had taken himself off psychiatric drugs and was experiencing weird stuff all the time. He had nowhere else to go. He was hearing voices so he thought that meant he had schizophrenia—the term itself should really be abolished because it's a delusion that the term *schizophrenia* denotes some kind of a common thing. To give people those psychiatric terms is very counterproductive. Psychiatry has not spent any effort in coming up with terminology that could actually be helpful to people. The voice-hearing movement[6] has been very interesting in this regard. In England, in Holland, in Europe, they've opened up the possibility that voice-hearing happens to many people, people who are otherwise "normal." It turns out it's not restricted to any diagnosis or any illness. It can be associated with being high on drugs, it can be associated with Wilson's disease (which is a disorder of copper metabolism), or it can be associated with nothing other than being very religious. So the Hearing Voices Network has been very helpful because it's offered people a lot more room to say, "I had something unusual happen to me, and I have my own explanation for it. Other people might have different explanations for it, so don't cubbyhole me." This movement has revolutionized in Europe what it means to be a voice-hearer.

Farber: So it's a form of Mad Pride? Instead of being ashamed people are proud.

Dr. Stastny: Exactly. It lets people breathe and live and be themselves without submitting to this medical identity.

Farber: Reading about England, many of them actually don't feel they're inferior anymore.

Dr. Stastny: Not at all, these people used to be very superior—in the time of the prophets everybody heard voices. That was the qualification to become a prophet.

Farber: It cannot happen in the United States. It's too much of a threat to the drug companies, and the psychiatrists won't allow it. They'd all lose millions of dollars. People would stop taking drugs and stop going to psychiatrists. I was reading in some article that the hearing-voices movement has had a major impact in England. They have self-help groups all over, and it's a substitute for psychiatrists and even therapists. I haven't met anyone in America who's been involved. I interviewed two people (see chapters 6 and 7) from the Freedom Center, and they were completely "cured" from so-called bipolar symptoms or so-called schizophrenia—and of all anxiety and depression—by a support group of other patients, most of whom do not take psych drugs. But Freedom Center is a one-of-a-kind thing in America.

Dr. Stastny: It's very interesting: in America, the Hearing Voices Network has not really taken off. Pat Deegan, a psychologist and ex-patient, is one person who has been promoting it. But it certainly has not taken off like it has in Europe. I was going to try to find out why. I don't really have the answer, but one answer is that I think the fear of the stigma of being labeled psychotic in America is more severe than in lots of other places. I tried to start a group of voice-hearers in the Bronx, and people don't want to come out and identify themselves like that. The genius thing that happened in Europe—and that never happened here—is that Marius Romme, this Dutch psychiatrist, went on TV in Holland with one of his patients, and they said, "Look, we don't know what we're doing here, we have no clue how to help this person, but let's hear from our audience about their experiences with voices and how they're dealing with it." To their surprise, lots of people contacted them, and they found that there are lots of people dealing with voices who have never even talked to a psychiatrist. That made a huge difference, and that kind of a thing has never been done in this country.

Farber: And it also couldn't be done on TV here because of the power of the pharmaceutical companies, no?

Dr. Stastny: Well, I don't know, do we even have this kind of call-in show in America? Maybe on radio but not TV so much. I think that was interesting how that happened on this Dutch TV show: immediately they had a movement, and people were willing to stay connected, and then it started groups all over. In this country some people tried it on the Internet, but it didn't happen.

Farber: People are told the only answer is the so-called antipsychotic drugs, which really ruin their life. They can't have any romantic or sexual life when they're on these antipsychotic drugs; they basically sit in their room, and the only interactions they have are in psychiatric groups with patients and doctors.

Dr. Stastny: Well, I wouldn't be so general about it. I think there are people who manage to make it, to do something and are able to have sex and relationships too, but it's a minority of people.

Farber: A minority, yes. But when I find someone on antipsychotics who seems to have some kind of real social life—and not just in psychiatric facilities—it turns out they are on lower dosages. This minority you speak of—haven't they lowered the dosage of the psychiatric drugs they're taking?

Dr. Stastny: Yes, that's absolutely true. When I first got into psychiatry in the late seventies or early eighties, it was a time when the dosages of drugs were drastically reduced. People had realized that giving someone seventy or eighty or one hundred milligrams of Haldol basically lobotomizes them; this was before the new antipsychotics in the early 1990s. So, they had all these people that were half-dead zombies, and the perspective of psychiatrists at that time was very simple: "We gotta get people on low dosages." Lo and behold people started to wake up, because instead of giving sixty or seventy milligrams of Haldol, people were taking three or five or six milligrams, and it made a huge difference to the quality of their life.

That has been reversed today, ever since the new atypical antipsychotics have replaced the older drugs. Now the dosages and combinations of drugs have increased to a point of madness, especially in hospitals. I work with people who come out of hospitals, and it usually takes me a year or half a year to get people off of these incredible combinations and dosages. This is what I call the third phase in the so-called drug revolution, which is, "Let's throw everything and the kitchen sink at people and let them fend for themselves without any therapy or support." The 1980s were a better time, because people were really on low dosages, and they were able to do a lot more.

The first phase was during the first forty years after they started using antipsychotics, and they used megadoses until the 1980s because all of a sudden people were talking about how Haldol causes terrible nerve diseases like tardive dyskinesia. Now it's back to the way it was. The same psychiatrists who talk about recovery from psychosis and self-help, they drug people to the gills.

Farber: There have been a number of articles in the *New York Times;* there was one that had the statistics from Minnesota (where the law requires them to keep statistics), and over one-third of the psychiatrists in 2005 (probably more today) were getting consultation fees from the drug companies, and the ones that got the consultation fees—even though they claimed they were objective—prescribed many more drugs, even to kids.*[7]

---

*On average, Minnesota psychiatrists—who received at least $5,000 from drug companies who manufactured atypical anti-psychotic drugs from 2000 to 2005—appear to have written three times as many atypical prescriptions for children as psychiatrists who recieved less or no money.

Dr. Stastny: Robert Whitaker [the author of *Mad in America*] would agree; he's going to come out with another book soon.

Farber: So what you are saying is that the so-called revolution with atypical drugs that was supposed to be a move forward—because they claim these drugs are less harmful than the older antipsychotics—was actually a move backward because the psychiatrists are putting people on higher dosages of these drugs?

Dr. Stastny: Absolutely. They're putting people on higher dosages, and they're putting people on multiple drugs [instead of one or two]. What seems to have happened in the past twenty or twenty-five years is that the pharmaceutical industry has completely gone out of control. This is what's happening in terms of health care reform also. These people have realized they can make huge amounts of money by pushing the drugs. The new drugs were incredibly lucrative for the drug companies: they recommended high dosages, and also they realized they can make more money by not competing with the other companies.

Farber: What do you mean by not competing?

Dr. Stastny: I'll give you an example. I once had a drug rep say to me, "Don't change anyone's drug regime, just add our drug." "Just add," they kept saying, "just add this and that." And this "just add" is exactly what's going on all the time nowadays, and it's horrifying. Take Risperdal: when it first came out people were usually on eight to twelve milligrams; the fact is one fourth of that amount is equally effective and has way fewer side effects. Now they're lowering Risperdal, but it's taken fifteen years to reverse that trend. I'm very frustrated with the way things are going. It's not about reforming the system anymore: to me the place to start is really with all those people that enter the system freshly. There are so many thousands every single day that enter the system. For example, a student in college may be going through some existential crisis and starting to feel suicidal, and that person could end up in the hospital, which could be a terrible experience. Occasionally it could be helpful to treat someone in a residence if you have a really nice place and you can talk and chill out and relax—and not be put on medication. Those places don't exist in America today; insurance won't pay for them. If you're in a hospital and you don't get put on medication, the insurance is going to say, "You are not sick and should not be in the hospital." It's a package deal, and that's what I'd like to change. I'd like to see people being treated differently from the get-go: that would be less expensive for the public because the person would not become a lifelong patient, as you show in this book.

Farber: Of course, in the seventies there were a few alternative residences for psychotics, and they were funded by the government. Nowadays they can't get any funding if they're not going to push psychiatric drugs.

Dr. Stastny: No, they cannot. Some of the more progressive psychiatrists are trying to introduce a waiting period of three days between the time a person gets admitted and when they get started on drugs. Even that is not acceptable—not even three days! I would propose at least three weeks without drugs as a normal waiting period.

Farber: Mosher [Loren Mosher, the psychiatrist who cofounded the Soteria Project] used to use small amounts of Valium when people were in a state of psychotic panic or couldn't sleep—on a temporary basis. He would not use antipsychotics.

Dr. Stastny: I'm a big believer that the benzodiazepines are the least noxious of the drugs. I once years ago came up with the hierarchy of the least toxic alternatives.

Farber: The psychiatric establishment acts like Valium is heroin nowadays.

Dr. Stastny: Klonopin is pretty widespread; it's less habit-forming than Valium, although both are far better than the antipsychotics. I personally think it's not a bad drug; some people use it like others use red wine. If you drink too much wine over a period of time, it's probably going to harm your liver or your brain, but Klonopin—it seems—is not really toxic to the system.

Farber: You know Henry Stack Sullivan used to use wine or some kind of alcohol to relax schizophrenics when they came into his hospital in Chestnut Lodge.

Dr. Stastny: Some people believe certain dosages of marijuana are helpful to certain people.

Farber: There is evidence for that with physical problems. What was your hierarchy?

Dr. Stastny: Neuroleptics, of course, are the most toxic. Some of the antiseizure drugs like Depakote and lithium are up there too, but probably the second-most toxic should be the SSRIs. Following them are the anticonvulsants, and at the bottom—the least toxic—are the benzodiazepines. Yes, I would say that they're the least toxic. Psychiatrists are so scared of causing people to become addicted to benzodiazepines, but then patients get dependent on neuroleptics and antidepressants instead.

Farber: One of the reasons people stay on the drugs is that hospitalization is such a traumatizing experience that they become terrified of having to go back. They're afraid if they don't keep taking these drugs they're going to end up back in the hospital again. Let me ask another question: to me, you seem to differ from psychiatrist Peter Breggin. Dr. Breggin seems to put all drugs in the same category, or at least his position is to never use any psychiatric drugs except to get off gradually.

Dr. Stastny: Yes, I do differ. Again certain benzodiazepines have been very helpful to people. I have met people who have been having a terrible time coming off Klonopin; addiction does happen; I think it's a minority though. I think it is really important that patients understand how the drug works for them. The whole business of maintenance medication is extremely problematic. I don't know how I feel about certain mood stabilizers; I know Depakote is a pretty terrible drug, and it's usually prescribed at way too high a dosage. I know a woman who goes through these states where she becomes really dysfunctional, she can't speak, she is almost catatonic, she just can't do anything, and she feels very down at the same time. It seems like for her taking a little Depakote even for a short period of time makes a difference. That's an odd thing, and we would never know that if she hadn't experimented with it. We figured it out together that even taking a little bit for a short period of time makes a difference. So, the unconventional uses of medications are more interesting to me than the sort of, "Why don't you keep taking this combination for the rest of your life?"

Farber: What do you advise someone to do who is stuck in Iowa—or even New York City—who does not want to be put on drugs? If they are in Massachusetts they can go to the Freedom Center, but anywhere else it's almost impossible to find a psychiatrist who is not a drug pusher. So what could you advise persons reading this who are constantly being told they're chronically mentally ill? How can they find help?

Dr. Stastny: With people who've been in the system for a long time, it's a more difficult problem than the people entering the system, because for those who are already on drugs there is a big risk that the brain has been irreversibly altered. If you want to improve your chances of succeeding in getting off the drugs, you have to have support, you have to read the literature—whether it's the *Coming Off Drugs* guide or something like it—and also have a different way of dealing with whatever problems might come out. In the book Peter Lehmann and I did,[8] there's a woman from Germany—Regina Bellion—who talks about how she arranges to have several of her friends take turns sitting on her for a few days instead of taking drugs. They call it a Ulysses contract; they prefer to be tied down than to be drugged.

Farber: Yes, they had to tie Ulysses to the mast. There are not enough of the alternative mad patient groups. I mean if you're in Oregon you can go to David Oaks's Mind Freedom, if you're in Northampton you can go to the Freedom Center, but these places don't exist across the country except in virtual reality on the Internet.

Dr. Stastny: The Internet in the end doesn't really help people enough. You're going to find it takes a group of very committed and courageous people that are willing to spend a couple of days and nights with someone who is in a really bad way. What's amazing is that it really helps, but it is something not many people are prepared to do, or even trained to do. We need places like Soteria for the person who is going crazy or flipping out. Hopefully your book will encourage more people to put effort into creating self-help alternatives.

Farber: They can get more specific ideas from reading your book *Alternatives beyond Psychiatry*. What's amazing to me is that if you do that in the beginning you can deflect the person from being inducted into what would have been a lifelong career (to quote Erving Goffman) as a chronic mental patient—just by a strong intervention. By strong I mean sometimes just by telling them, "Look do not let the psychiatrists and your parents convince you that you're mentally ill. You'll be okay. You need to gradually get off the drugs." Often that was enough. I've experienced this before: I was blacklisted in mental health clinics because I often deflected persons from getting entangled in the system.

Dr. Stastny: I've heard many stories like that where people in the beginning are deflected. In Vienna, I worked once in a pediatric adolescent medicine ward where kids would come for a variety of reasons—including some kids who were sent there from a poison center where they were detoxed after they had taken an overdose. Instead of sending them to the mental hospital up the hill they sent them to us. So basically, they were not put on medication and instead given some therapy—individual and family—and they didn't become labeled. They didn't have to be associated with other people who were labeled as mentally ill, and they did very well. One woman is grateful to me till this day that I spared her admission to a psychiatric hospital at the age of fifteen. I don't know what would have happened to her if she had a different experience.

We do the opposite here in America; we send kids to hospitals so easily, and the children's hospitals are generally worse than adult hospitals. I see kids coming out of there, and some of them are really damaged, but others throw all their pills away, and they sort of become basically normal five or six years or ten years later—and they were labeled with every freaking diagnosis in the book. It would be very interesting to do a study on people who have been through this, just like the study that Courtney Harding did in Vermont. She found after thirty years a whole bunch of people were living happily without medication. We might find that same thing with these kids you know, the ones who escaped, so to speak.

Farber: Can you say a little about Soteria?

Dr. Stastny: There are Soteria houses based on the original model right now only in Switzerland, and Alaska has a recently opened one. There might be a small one in Germany, and in Scandinavia there's a small one. Basically, it's a place where people can go when they're having an acute "psychotic" episode where they're really not in touch with reality or they're scared or maybe hallucinating and whatever. There's a small community of people who work there, and some of them might have had similar experiences in the past. It's an intense environment where people are supported through these experiences and usually come out of them within a matter of days without medication, although sometimes they don't.

The interesting thing about the original Soteria is that they weren't doing any therapy. It's not a therapeutic model; it's a community that functions as a community because people need to eat, they need to use the bathroom, they need to clean up, they need to live, and they want to come back from wherever they are in these states of whatever you want to call it—madness, craziness, or freak-out. The original Soteria was a study for people who would have been diagnosed with first episode of schizophrenia. It turns out—we know this from follow-ups—that many of those people later on no longer met those criteria.[9]

Farber: You're referring to the research they did which was published, which of course is revolutionary because psychiatrists claim schizophrenia is incurable and that the patient will deteriorate without "medication." No one's done any studies like that since then. It was pretty conclusive, was it not?

Dr. Stastny: Yeah, I mean if you read John Boles's work, he's published several articles of meta-analysis. It's very powerful and very definitive that it's basically safe to withhold medication from people for a period of several weeks.

Farber: You're saying he went back and looked at Mosher's research and confirmed it?

Dr. Stastny: Yes, and he also looked at a lot of the Scandinavian studies, which were based on the Soteria model, and found they worked. The difference between Soteria and what's done in Scandinavia today is that

Soteria was a residence for people to go to live—a building, a community—and now in Scandinavia they mostly have therapists living with the families. They work with people wherever they are, they found they did not need to move people to a different environment. Here in this country we always say, "Let's find you a place, either a hospital or some other place to stay so you can go through your madness." In Scandinavia or in England people generally stay with family.[10] The families there, I would think, are not as problematic as here, which is interesting.

Farber: Anyway, Mosher showed in the seventies that the Soteria non-drug treatment was actually superior to treatment with drugs—even in terms of less hospitalizations.

Dr. Stastny: Well, it was superior in the long run and it was equal in the short run, which was really interesting, you know. One could argue that if you give psychosocial treatment over a period of time and you do a variety of things, that people will get better. It worked just as well as the hospital in the short run—without giving patients psychiatric drugs and without locking anyone up.

Farber: How did you come to adopt this unconventional point of view? You had conventional psychiatric training, right?

Dr. Stastny: My unconventional point of view began before I had any formal psychiatric training, because I was exposed to the Italian democratic psychiatry movement while I was in medical school. The Italian psychiatrist Franco Basaglia and his group impressed me because whatever I learned about psychiatry, even as a general medical student, seemed to prove to me that institutions were really not about helping people.

I was involved in the anti-institutional movement before I even learned anything about psychiatry. The fact that I became a psychiatrist was a bit of a fluke: I was looking for other medical specializations, like cardiology, but I started to realize that in medicine and cardiology the person is always treated as an object—left out of the equation. That bothered me, and so I figured in psychiatry that would be a place where people are included, since it's about talking to people. I came here from Germany and did my residency under the leadership of Joel Kovel; he was my director of residency. He was a Marxist and Freudian.

Farber: Joel is a friend of mine, but I did not know that.

Dr. Stastny: He did not want to deal with people with more severe troubles, but still he had a different perspective than most psychiatrists. I was exposed to some pretty interesting people during my training at Einstein,* such as people who believed in systemic work and family therapy, as you talked about. After that I actually went to work at Bronx State; today is an interesting day because I have been associated with that hospital for thirty years, and today I finally quit. I resigned after all these years.

Farber: Did you do it for any principle?

Dr. Stastny: No, I resigned because my work doesn't really mean anything there anymore, and I worked there only four hours a week now. When I went to work there I never wanted to work in an inpatient unit, but they gave me the opportunity to work with the people that were trapped in the hospital—meaning that they had nowhere else to go, they were essentially homeless. I said, "I'll work under one condition: the doors are open, nobody is forced to do anything, and anybody can leave when they want to." That was my condition, and they agreed. The funny thing is that when we had the open doors, almost nobody left—as opposed to from the locked ward where people constantly tried to run away. We called the open ward the hotel ward.

We did a lot of stuff that was interesting: we encouraged people to become friends, to make plans together, to get out together, to live together, and to work together. In the process of that atmosphere people felt freer to come up with their own ideas. I learned from the people that were hospitalized that we—the staff—are really secondary: 90 percent of the time we stand in the way of people. So I concluded that what we need to learn is (a), get out of the way and (b), facilitate people's recovery. I don't like to call it "recovery." I prefer to say people's opportunities in the world. My interest wasn't in therapy. My interest was very social: it was about giving people opportunities to be creative, to make a living, and to start organizations. I really believe it doesn't matter what diagnosis people have; what's important is how people live

*The Albert Einstein College of Medicine, in Bronx, New York

and what kind of chances they have in life. If you support that, people go beyond the expectations that are created by their "diagnoses."

Farber: And it actually worked?

Dr. Stastny: We did great stuff. We had a federal grant and we developed the first business run by ex-patients, which started in a state hospital in New York, although you could start it pretty much anywhere.

Farber: Thank you. I think it will be surprising for many who read this book to discover that there are psychiatrists like you in America. And they can go to INTAR's website at www.intar.org.

2

The Mind Freedom Hunger Strike

In July of 2003 David Oaks and seven other psychiatric survivors (former mental patients) went on a hunger strike for "an indefinite period of time" to protest the abuses of the psychiatric profession and to hopefully attract public attention to their claim that the psychiatric profession has been deceiving and poisoning (with psychiatric drugs) the American public. According to Oaks, the psychiatric profession has no proof that emotional distress or mental illnesses are caused by brain disorders or biochemical imbalances. In order to demonstrate this, Oaks and the hunger-strikers posed a series of questions to the American Psychiatric Association. Oaks also recruited a team of the leading critics of psychiatry to back up the strikers. The result was one of the most interesting public exchanges in the history of modern psychiatry. One might call this intellectual battle "Mental Patients Liberation versus the Psychiatric Establishment."

To understand the significance of the hunger strike, it is helpful to place it in historical context. By the late 1980s the biopsychiatric model had eclipsed psychoanalysis as the dominant model in the mental health field.*

---

*Biopsychiatry is the name given to the school that holds that all "'mental illnesses" are caused by disorders of the brain.

An editorial in the *Archives for Psychiatry and Nervous Diseases* opined, "Psychiatry has undergone a transformation in relation to the rest of medicine. This transformation rests principally on the realization that patients with so-called mental illnesses are really individuals with illnesses of the nerves and the brain."[1]

This editorial aptly describes the change that psychiatry has undergone in the last few decades—but it was not written, as readers might imagine, in 1997, but in 1867! My point is that this is not the first time that psychiatry has "realized" that what it has called mental illnesses are really brain disorders. (In modern terms it has realized that mental illnesses are *caused* by biological disorders of the brain.) The public does not know that dominant models of madness fall in and out of favor and that biopsychiatry had once before been dominant—in the nineteenth century until Freud's appearance in the early twentieth century led to the captivation of the popular imagination by psychoanalysis.

The modern Freudian or psychoanalytic effort that spanned most of the twentieth century and attempted to prove that mental illnesses were caused by childhood traumas has now been deemed a failure by most psychiatrists and many, if not most, psychologists. Freudianism was finally undermined by numerous factors: the failure to provide more than anecdotal evidence for its theories; the increasing evidence that people, even children, were more resilient than psychoanalysis allowed; and the exposures of Freud's own personal and theoretical failings (particularly Freud's effort to cover up sexual abuse of children by adults). All of these factors left psychoanalysis vulnerable when biopsychiatry became (once more) the rising star by the 1990s—and one that offered psychiatry considerably greater economic advantages. Thus mental health professionals, particularly psychiatrists, routinely tell their patients that their mental illnesses are caused by genuine biological brain disorders or biochemical imbalances of the brain. However, the fact is that psychiatry does not have the evidence to back up its claim. The 1867 editorial represents a *hope* on the part of psychiatry or, as a review article by Guy Boysen in *The Journal of Mind and Behavior* terms it, "an empty biological *promise* . . . that has never been fulfilled."[2]

The American public has been convinced by a massive advertising effort undertaken by the psychiatric-pharmaceutical complex in the 1990s "proving" that mental illnesses are caused by biological abnormalities. However, as Boysen aptly puts it "[t]he plain, cold, hard fact is that there are almost no mental disorders for which a specific biological cause can be pinpointed."[3] (The exceptions that Boysen mentions, e.g., Alzheimer's, are not generally considered mental disorders.) Privately, as we will see, the American Psychiatric Association (APA) acknowledges this cold hard fact.

The biopsychiatric model is appealing to psychiatrists for a number of reasons—not least of which are its obvious financial advantages. It is the biopsychiatric model that provides the foundation for the symbiotic relationship between Psychiatry and the pharmaceutical companies that developed in the last few decades. Psychiatrist Peter Breggin has chronicled the formative phase of this relationship in the late 1970s and 1980s, which led to the creation of the psychiatric-pharmaceutical complex. As Dr. Breggin puts it, "In the early 1970s [the] American Psychiatric Association was in financial trouble. It was losing members and its total income was $2 to $4 million per year"—as compared to its 2003 income of over $38 million dollars.[4]

Why was Psychiatry in such hot water in the 1970s? Primarily because the idea of solving problems with psychotherapy—trumpeted by Freud and his followers—had become rooted in the imagination of the American public. In the countercultural 1960s all kinds of new schools of psychotherapy had sprouted and bloomed. Thus it is not surprising that by the mid-1970s "psychiatry was losing badly in the competition with psychologists, social workers, counselors, family therapists and other non-medical professionals who charged lower fees than psychiatrists for psychotherapy patients. Psychiatric journals and newspapers were filled with gloom, lamenting that psychiatrists could no longer easily fill their work weeks."[5] At the same time, the image of psychiatry had been tarnished by a wave of criticisms from within and without that reached a peak in the early 1970s—as exemplified most powerfully by the movie *One Flew Over the Cuckoo's Nest* (based on Ken Kesey's classic book of the same title).

A small group within the psychiatric profession throughout the 1970s believed that psychiatry needed to raise its own ethical standards. Some members of the APA's board of trustees felt—according to the *American Journal of Psychiatry* in 1974—that the APA's relationship with the pharmaceutical companies was going "beyond the bounds of professionalism" and compromising the APA's ethical principles.[6] The APA appointed a "Task Force to Study the Impact of the Potential Loss of Pharmaceutical Support." The task force concluded that the loss of support of the drug companies would be catastrophic. Thus the decision was made to continue to collaborate with the multibillion-dollar drug companies.

Dr. Breggin wrote, "The floodgates of drug company influence were open and would grow wider each year." This was only the beginning: in 1980 the APA board of directors decided to "throw ethical caution to the winds"[7] and solicit drug company support for major professional and cultural activities. Psychiatrists who criticized these new developments were ignored by the leadership of the APA, and the collaboration between psychiatry and the drug companies was extended to the political sphere—to influencing congressional legislation. Dr. Breggin wrote, "Whatever function APA had ever fulfilled as a professional organization was now superseded by its function as a political advocate for the advancement of psychiatric and pharmaceutical interests."[8]

What is most important to understand is that in order to protect and advance these interests, Psychiatry *must* promote the biopsychiatric model; it must assert that mental illnesses are caused by biological dysfunctions—*and* that these dysfunctions can only be corrected by psychiatric drugs. Psychiatry realized that it needed to embrace the biopsychiatric model to survive and prosper in the marketplace. The APA continually reiterated in its in-house publications that "only a medical or biological image can enable the APA to compete economically."[9] A major effort was undertaken throughout the 1990s to prove that mental illnesses (the problems of living) are caused by biological disorders; the public has been deceived into believing that this effort has succeeded. The research that psychiatrists undertake today is not disinterested scientific inquiry. It is mostly financed by the pharmaceutical companies, and it is designed to promote the joint interests of psychiatrists and the drug companies: selling the biopsychiatric model, selling drugs, and buttressing the image of the psychiatrist as the medical specialist most qualified to treat people's emotional problems—by prescribing the correct medications.

While the majority of psychiatrists accept the biopsychiatric model and proclaim that there has been remarkable scientific progress within the last two decades, there are still heretics. Thomas Szasz, now in his nineties, continues to denounce the myth of mental illness. In Szasz's view, as Roy Porter wrote, "The entire history of psychiatry is an obdurate and pitiless defense of a fantasy."[10] Szasz denies that there has been any psychiatric progress at all. He writes, "When I was a young psychiatrist, there were but a handful of psychiatric diagnoses/diseases. Now there are more than three hundred. Not one was discovered. All were invented. In the absence of empirically verifiable discoveries, they had to be."[11]

Szasz and the various other critics of biopsychiatry agree on this one point: there have been no empirically verifiable discoveries of biological (brain) disorders. If there had been such discoveries, diagnoses today would be confirmed by laboratory tests, just as they are for physical diseases. Psychiatric drugs were not designed to treat diseases that had been discovered. Szasz cogently argues that the diseases were invented to justify the "treatments" (the medications). He notes that the textbook most widely used in medical school lists approximately three hundred "psychotherapeutic drugs" considered appropriate for the treatment of these disorders. Szasz pithily comments, "This plethora of drugs reflects the psychiatric view . . . that the vexations of life are due to mental diseases caused by chemical imbalances in the brain, and that these can be effectively treated by a balancing of the chemicals."[12] But, Szasz argues, no one has demonstrated the existence of diseases of the "mind" much less of the "chemical imbalances" that were allegedly causing them.[13]

While the propaganda machine continues to proclaim that mental illness is a product of a brain disorder, privately the search for the physical defect of the brain continues quietly, with Psychiatry assuring its in-house critics that it is only a matter of time before the defect is identified. I agree with most of the critics of biopsychiatry that the very idea of a disorder of the mind or of the brain persists partially because of the propaganda of the psychiatric-pharmaceutical complex. In addition, I would argue that the public was susceptible to this theory from the start, despite the lack of real evidence, because it is rooted in the collective imagination: the idea that there is something wrong with the mind has been the abiding obsession of Western culture for centuries.

In the age of religion, Western civilization was convinced that our souls were diseased, flawed, and damaged because of original sin. In the age of science—when few people believe we have souls—it was first the mind and now the brain that is ostensibly diseased (and not just in a few people but in a rapidly growing proportion of the population). In both cases we are possessed by the idea that the core of our being is flawed or tainted. This idea originally was presented in Christian terms; it derives from Augustine and from the Protestant Reformation (Luther had been an Augustinian monk)—but not from Jesus, and not from the gospels. It was Augustine who first claimed that our souls were all irreparably damaged, "totally depraved" (in Calvin's words) as a result of original sin.[14]

Jesus was a radical in the tradition of the great Jewish prophets: he believed that the human soul was whole, holy, and that despite the ubiquity of human sinfulness, the soul retained it likeness to God—in whose image it was created. It was the idea of the sacred worth of every human soul that provided the philosophical basis for a democratic society; thus the early church was an egalitarian organization.[15] However, Jesus's democratic ideas were inconvenient for the fledgling Christian church in the fourth century when it decided to become allies with the Roman Empire, and thus the idea that the human soul has no worth took hold of Western Christianity, and thus of Western civilization.[16]

For most of the twentieth century we believed we were flawed as a result of the Oedipal complex or maternal deprivation—the "original sins" of the parents according to Freud. Now we are convinced that the problem is defects in the brain. The embarrassment for Psychiatry today—now that it has asserted that it is this physical (brain) defect that is at the root of mental illness—is that it has been unable to find hard evidence. Despite years of searching and numerous "scientific" studies published, Psychiatry cannot demonstrate the existence of a brain defect or chemical imbalance. Nevertheless, Psychiatry continues to reassure the public that mental suffering is due to biochemical imbalances and gets irritated when its critics point to the failures of this assertion.

None of the critics of the medical model argue that human unhappiness does not exist, but most of them are convinced that "problems of living," as Szasz termed them, must be faced by human beings—not avoided by attributing them fatalistically to biological defects. By the end of the 1990s as is evidenced here, resistance was mounting against the massive drugging of America. Psychologist John Breeding and neurologist Fred Baughman teamed up to protest the psychiatric drugging of children. They both asserted that "attention deficit disorder" was a bogus disease used to rationalize the massive drugging of children.[17]

In 1998 Dr. Loren Mosher wrote a long letter (that was later published in *Psychology Today*) resigning from the APA after thirty-five years. Mosher, who had been a founder of the Soteria Project and director of the studies of schizophrenia at the National Institute of Mental Health from 1969 to 1980, wrote that the reason for his resignation was that the American Psychiatric Association had actually become "the American Psychopharmacological Association." Mosher went on to say prophetically, "At this point in history, in my view, psychiatry has been almost completely bought out by the drug companies. The APA could not continue without the pharmaceutical company support of meetings, symposia, workshops, journal advertising, grand rounds luncheons, unrestricted educational grants etc. etc. Psychiatrists have become the minions of drug company promotions. . . . It seems clear that we are headed toward a situation in which, except for academics, most psychiatric practitioners will have no real relationships—so vital to the healing process—with the disturbed and disturbing persons they treat. Their sole role will be that of prescription writers."[18]

The adversaries of the psychiatric-industrial complex include dissident psychiatrists and other mental health professionals, as well as those who are active in the psychiatric survivors' or the Mad Pride movements. The largest organization of psychiatric survivors today (see chapter 3) is Mind Freedom International (formerly Support Coalition International), both of which were founded by David Oaks.

Oaks has spent most of his adult life attempting to demonstrate to the public that the biopsychiatric model is a fraud; psychiatry has not proven that the "mentally ill" have brain defects or diseases. Mind Freedom International is both an activists' organization that sponsors protests and lobbying efforts as well as a self-help forum (see chapter 1) in which those who have been assigned to the role of chronic mental patients are provided the opportunity to make a transition from that social identity to another: activists working collectively for the liberation of other psychiatric survivors. This transition from patient to activist is a radical psychological transformation—a fact that is unacknowledged by the psychiatrists and their supporters, who have both vilified ex-patient activists as enemies of science (as discussed later in this chapter) and ignored the fact that their self-transformation proves that biopsychiatry's position on madness is wrong. If the dominant position were correct, these activists would be chronically disabled and dependent on psychiatric drugs instead of high-functioning activists who have found they can handle life's challenges and their own moods without resorting to the routine use of psychiatric drugs. (I say "routine" because it is possible that they take a sleeping pill every now and then.)

The basic intellectual framework of Mind Freedom International's leading activists is a rejection of biological Psychiatry—a conviction that psychiatric drugs are harmful—and above all, a commitment to oppose all involuntary psychiatric treatments. Since the organization is pro-choice it is of course open to all persons who oppose involuntary treatment, even those who take psychiatric drugs.

As we will see in chapter 3 the mental health system attempted to induct Oaks into the role of a chronic mental patient, but instead of being incorporated into the psychiatric metanarrative, Oaks—like the other psychiatric survivors in the movement against psychiatric coercion and misinformation—developed a "resistant identity."[19] What made Oaks and the other subjects in this book become resistant, how and why they differed from those who accepted the role of chronic patients and its discrediting consequences, is a matter that cannot be adequately discussed here. I think long-time activist and former mental patient George Ebert aptly described his decision to resist when he said to me, "If I had accepted that I was so-called mentally ill, I would not have been able to accept myself."

From the psychiatric perspective Oaks met all the criteria for the diagnosis of "mentally ill." He did not become a chronic patient because the diagnosis is a self-fulfilling prophecy—and David rejected the diagnoisis. The important fact is that the more patients become aware of stories like Oaks's, the more they tend to resist being inducted into the role of chronic patient and the more attracted they become to the idea of assuming the identity of a creatively maladjusted activist like Oaks. Once Oaks became an activist, he set out to debunk the very idea that he and other former patients had brain defects—the current psychiatric dogma. It is my contention that psychiatry has not been able to find brain defects in the so called "mentally ill" because they are not defective—not because psychiatry has not invented yet the right instruments.

Oaks and his comrades in his organization Mind Freedom also knew that psychiatrists had no real evidence of brain defects; this is why they came up with the idea of the hunger strike, which they initiated in July 2003. The strike received media attention and captured the interest and ire of the APA. The rest of this chapter will present several documents, which include those from mainstream media sources as well as excerpts from the original statement by the strikers and the responses from the APA.

The following *Washington Post* article by Kimberly Edds, dated August 29, 2003, reports on the hunger strike, which was already under way.

California Hunger Strike Challenges Use of Antidepressants

After two weeks, four mental health advocates are still on a hunger strike, protesting the widespread use of prescription drugs to treat mental illnesses and challenging psychiatrists to document their rationale for prescribing them. Over the last few decades, doctors have embraced the view that depression, schizophrenia and other mental illnesses result from imbalances in brain chemistry, and they have treated such illnesses with drugs intended to rebalance that chemistry. In recent years, the use of antidepressant drugs has grown dramatically in the United States, with the number of prescriptions nearly doubling since 1998, according to the pharmaceutical consulting company IMS Health.

As more people turn to antidepressants, mental health experts and patient advocates are beginning to raise questions about side effects and the potential for addiction.

The strikers are calling on some of the strongest voices in the psychiatric profession, including the American Psychiatric Association and the National Alliance for the Mentally Ill, to provide concrete evidence that mental illnesses are the result of brain chemistry imbalances. They also want to call attention to alternative treatments.

"Millions of people are signing up for these prescriptions because they are convinced they have a chemical imbalance. But there is not one piece of evidence that can back that up," said David Oaks, executive director of Mind Freedom

Support Coalition International, or SCI, an organization of current and former psychiatric patients that organized the strike.

A spokesman for the American Psychiatric Association referred a reporter to a letter the association's medical director, James H. Scully, wrote to Oaks on Aug. 12. "In recent years, there has been substantial progress in understanding the neuroscientific basis of many mental illnesses," it said. "Research offers hope and must continue."

The National Alliance for the Mentally Ill (NAMI) did not respond to several requests to comment, but Oaks made available an e-mail he received today from Rick Birkel, NAMI's national executive director.

"NAMI has never stated to my knowledge that 'mental disorders are caused exclusively by biological factors,'" it said. "Instead, we are saying that biological or genetic vulnerability appears to be pre-requisite to serious mental disorder." Birkel added that mental disorders result from complex interactions of many factors, including environmental forces, stress, personality, social support, illness and injury.

Birkel's e-mail reflects a growing consensus in the psychiatric establishment. Most psychiatrists say that complex mental disorders are like arthritis and other chronic physical ailments—no less real because they cannot be spotted with laboratory tests.

The hunger strikers, who include three former mental patients, said that the responses were not satisfactory and that they wanted a study and a diagnostic lab test that proves the connection. Until then, they plan to continue their protest.

They began with six hunger strikers, but two, including Oaks, left because of health difficulties. The remaining four have been downing daily a dark red brew of juices from garlic, beets, kale and carrots, and spending their time answering supporters' e-mails and making phone calls to media outlets.

Hunger striker David Gonzalez said he spent two years confined in an inpatient facility after being diagnosed with major depression and, later, manic depression, and that he was forcibly drugged during that time. He said the drugs impaired his eyesight and memory.

"When someone has cancer, they don't lock the door behind them, and they show them the tests," Gonzalez said. "But when someone has a mental illness, they lock the door behind them and show them no tests. When they lock that door behind me, I want to know why."

Oaks said he, too, had been confined in institutions and forcibly drugged for what was diagnosed as schizophrenia. He recovered, he said, through the love and support of his family, rather than drugs.

"People do not know what it's like to be on these drugs," Oaks said. "If you want to take it and it obliterates your pain, that's one thing, but when you are pushed to be on it, it's like a wrecking ball to your thoughts and feelings."

Studies have shown that daily exercise, psychotherapy and even changes in diet and nutrition are as effective as, if not more effective than, prescription drugs, said Stuart Shipko, a Pasadena psychiatrist and panic disorder specialist who serves on an SCI scientific panel. But there is not widespread support for such treatments.

"We're overdiagnosing. How many of these supposed mental illnesses are really just problems in your family life? They're anxious, and they're being put in a chemical straitjacket," Shipko said.[20]

Before beginning to fast, the hunger strikers released this July 28, 2003, statement outlining their grievances with the psychiatric-pharmaceutical complex and requesting clear information regarding the use of psychiatric drugs.

Original Statement by Hunger Strikers to Psychiatric Association, National Alliance for the Mentally Ill and the U.S. Office of the Surgeon General

1. A Hunger Strike to Challenge International Domination by Biopsychiatry. This fast is about human rights in mental health. The psychiatric pharmaceutical complex is heedless of its oath to "first do no harm."

Psychiatrists are able with impunity to:

*** Incarcerate citizens who have committed crimes against neither persons nor property.

*** Impose diagnostic labels on people that stigmatize and defame them.

*** Induce proven neurological damage by force and coercion with powerful psychotropic drugs.

*** Stimulate violence and suicide with drugs promoted as able to control these activities.

*** Destroy brain cells and memories with an increasing use of electroshock (also known as electro-convulsive therapy).

*** Employ restraint and solitary confinement—which frequently cause severe emotional trauma, humiliation, physical harm, and even death—in preference to patience and understanding.

*** Humiliate individuals already damaged by traumatizing assaults to their self-esteem.

These human rights violations and crimes against human decency must end. While the history of psychiatry offers little hope that change will arrive quickly, initial steps can and must be taken.

At the very least, the public has the right to know IMMEDIATELY the evidence upon which psychiatry bases its spurious claims and treatments, and upon which it has gained and betrayed the trust and confidence of the courts, the media, and the public.[21]

I have excerpted additional relevant passages from the statement below.

Why We Fast

There are many different ways to help people experiencing severe mental and emotional crises. People labeled with a psychiatric disability deserve to be able to choose from a wide variety of these empowering alternatives. However, choice in the mental health field is severely limited. One approach dominates, and that is a belief in chemical imbalances, genetic determinism and psychiatric drugs as the treatment of choice. This medical model is sometimes termed "biopsychiatry." Far too often, this limited choice has been exceedingly harmful to both the body and the spirit.

Governments and the mental health industry use extensive taxpayer funding, judicial edicts, and repressive laws to enforce a biopsychiatric approach. The mental health system rarely offers options other than psychiatric drugs, and still more rarely offers people full, accurate information about the hazards of psychiatric drugs. The mental health system is coercing increasing numbers of people to take psychiatric drugs against their will, even on an outpatient basis in their own homes. Electroshock, even forced electroshock, is quietly making a comeback.

Biopsychiatry is now one of the most profitable of all industries and its power is globalizing rapidly. The World Health Organization and the World Bank have multibillion dollar plans to spread biopsychiatry to developing nations.

Given all these facts, citizens have a right to ask:

"Has science established, beyond a reasonable doubt, that so-called 'major mental illnesses' are biological diseases of the brain?"

"Does the government have compelling evidence to justify the way it singles out for its primary support this one theory of the origin of emotional distress and of pharmaceutical remedies for its relief?"

Both public and personal health and safety are dependent on the answers to these questions.

This fast is not about judging individuals who choose to employ biopsychiatric approaches in an effort to seek relief. We respect the right of people to choose the option of prescribed psychiatric drugs. Some of us have made this personal choice.

We must act in the nonviolent tradition of Cesar Chavez and Mahatma Gandhi by saying "No!" to oppression with our bodies and spirits through fasting, while affirming the humanity of those people to whom we make our demands.

"If you see injustice and say nothing, you have taken the side of the oppressor." —Desmond Tutu

WE THE UNDERSIGNED WILL REFUSE ALL SOLID FOOD for an indefinite period of time as we await our challenge to be met by the following:

1. American Psychiatric Association (APA)
2. National Alliance for the Mentally Ill (NAMI)
3. Office of the Surgeon General of the United States

WE ASK THAT YOU PRODUCE scientifically-valid evidence for the following, or you publicly admit to media, government officials and the general public that you are unable to do so:

1. EVIDENCE THAT CLEARLY ESTABLISHES the validity of "schizophrenia," "depression" or other "major mental illnesses" as biologically-based brain diseases.
2. EVIDENCE FOR A PHYSICAL DIAGNOSTIC EXAM—such as a scan or test of the brain, blood, urine, genes, etc.—that can reliably distinguish individuals with these diagnoses (prior to treatment with psychiatric drugs), from individuals without these diagnoses.
3. EVIDENCE FOR A BASE-LINE STANDARD of a neurochemically-

balanced "normal" personality, against which a neurochemical "imbalance" can be measured and corrected by pharmaceutical means.

4.　EVIDENCE THAT ANY PSYCHOTROPIC DRUG can correct a "chemical imbalance" attributed to a psychiatric diagnosis, and is anything more than a non-specific alterer of brain physiology.

5.　EVIDENCE THAT ANY PSYCHOTROPIC DRUG can reliably decrease the likelihood of violence or suicide.

6.　EVIDENCE THAT PSYCHOTROPIC DRUGS do not in fact increase the overall likelihood of violence and suicide.

7.　FINALLY, that you reveal publicly evidence published in mainstream medical journals, but unreported in mainstream media, that links use of some psychiatric drugs to structural brain changes.

Until the above demands are met to the satisfaction of an internationally respected panel of scientists and mental health professionals, we plan to drink only liquids and to refuse solid food for an indefinite period of time.

Signed by Fast for Freedom Participants:

Initial core group committed to fasting:

Vince Boehm, Krista Erickson, David Gonzalez, David Oaks, Dawn Rider, Hiromi Sayama, Mickey Weinberg, LCSW

Initial scientific panel to review evidence:

Fred Baughman, M.D.; Peter Breggin, M.D.; Mary Boyle, Ph.D.; David Cohen, Ph.D.; Ty Colbert, Ph.D.; Pat Deegan, Ph.D.; Al Galves, Ph.D.; Thomas Greening, Ph.D.; David Jacobs, Ph.D.; Jay Joseph, Psy.D.; Jonathan Leo, Ph.D.; Bruce Levine, Ph.D.; Loren Mosher, M.D.; Stuart Shipko, M.D.[22]

The APA responded to the hunger strikers: the following letter was sent to Oaks, through Dr. Shipko, on August 12, 2003.

Response from APA

Dear Mr. Oaks:

I am acceding to your request that I send my response to your letter of July 28, 2003 to Dr. Stuart Shipko.

The mission of the American Psychiatric Association is to promote the highest quality care for individuals with mental illness and substance abuse disorders and their families. In recent years, there has been substantial progress in understanding the neuroscientific basis of many mental illnesses. Research offers hope and must continue.

The answers to your questions are widely available in the scientific literature, and have been for years. I suggest you begin your review with Surgeon General David Satcher's report, "Mental Health: A Report of the Surgeon General." In addition, I recommend the Introductory Textbook of Psychiatry (3rd edition), edited by Andreasen and Black. This is a "user-friendly" textbook for persons just being introduced to the field of psychiatry.

A more substantial and advanced series would include The American Psychiatric Publishing, Inc.'s "Textbook of Clinical Psychiatry (4th edition)," edited by Hales and Yodofsky. For the latest science, of course, there are the American Journal of Psychiatry and Archives of General Psychiatry, among many other journals which are available in both printed and on-line versions.

These are but a few of the extensive number of scientific publications that answer your questions.

I share the concern of Rick Berkel [sic] of NAMI that your proposed activities are ill-considered and invite you to join NAMI to help improve the care of our fellow citizens who suffer from serious mental illnesses.

Sincerely,

James H. Scully, Jr., M. D., Sc.D. Medical Director[23]

The panel of dissident mental health professionals responded to the APA with a letter of their own, which follows below. In brief they noted that, "*In the judgment of the panel members, your reply fails to produce or cite any specific evidence of any specific pathophysiology underlying any "mental disorder."* The reason the APA failed to do so is because there is no evidence that there are brain disorders underlying "mental illness": there is not a single study that provides valid and reliable evidence for the "biological basis of mental illness."

I would add that in the absence of discernible brain pathology, there is no basis for any kind of claim of "mental illness"—or mental disorders. Yet the APA diagnostic manual used in every mental health clinic claims to be a manual of mental disorders, and the term *the mentally ill* is routinely used by mental health professionals and journalists. The term *mental illness* is a misleading metaphor: in the 1990s the psychiatric establishment had decided that those previously labeled mentally ill were not merely ill in a nonphysical sense (whatever that means), but they had brain disorders. As we see from the following letter, dated August 22, 2003, *there is no evidence for that claim.* The diagnosis of mental illness is based exclusively on deviant behavior: the mentally ill person acts strange—her behavior is disturbed or disturbing to other persons. This is a value judgment. But there is no objective basis, no biological evidence, that the behavior troubling to the psychiatrist is caused by a defect in the brain.

Scientific Panel Addresses APA Claims

Dear Dr. Scully:

David Oaks, Executive Director of Mind Freedom, has forwarded to us your reply dated 12 August 2003 to the hunger strikers involved in a "Fast for Freedom in Mental Health." We are a panel of 14 academics and clinicians who have agreed to review any such reply for scientific validity.

The hunger strikers asked your organization, as well as the Surgeon General of the United States, and the National Alliance for the Mentally Ill, to provide:

1. evidence that establishes the validity of "schizophrenia," "depression" or other "major mental illnesses" as "biologically-based brain diseases";

2. evidence for a physical diagnostic exam that can reliably distinguish individuals with these diagnoses (prior to treatment with psychiatric drugs) from individuals without these diagnoses;

3. evidence for a baseline standard of a neurochemically-balanced "normal" individual, against which a neurochemical "imbalance" can be measured;

4. evidence that any psychotropic drug can correct any "chemical imbalance" attributed to a psychiatric diagnosis;

5. evidence that any psychotropic drug can reliably decrease the likelihood of violence or suicide.

In your reply, no specific studies of any kind were cited with reference to any of the questions above. You cited three general sources, including the recent Surgeon General's report on mental health and two textbooks of psychiatry.

In examining each of these sources, we found numerous statements that invalidate suggestions that behaviors referred to as "mental illnesses" have specific biological bases.

Mental Health: A Report of the Surgeon General (1999) is explicit about the absence of any findings of specific pathophysiology:

> p. 44: "The diagnosis of mental disorders is often believed to be more difficult than diagnosis of somatic, or general medical, disorders, since there is no definitive lesion, laboratory test, or abnormality in brain tissue that can identify the illness."

> p. 48: "It is not always easy to establish a threshold for a mental disorder, particularly in light of how common symptoms of mental distress are and the lack of objective, physical symptoms."

> p. 49: "The precise causes (etiology) of mental disorders are not known."

> p. 51: "All too frequently a biological change in the brain (a lesion) is purported to be the 'cause' of a mental disorder . . . [but] the fact is that any simple association—or correlation—cannot and does not, by itself, mean causation."

> p. 102: "Few lesions or physiologic abnormalities define the mental disorders, and for the most part their causes remain unknown."

In the third edition of Textbook of Clinical Psychiatry (1999), we find similar statements:

> p. 43: "Although reliable criteria have been constructed for many psychiatric disorders, validation of the diagnostic categories as specific entities has not been established."

> p. 51: "Most of these [genetic studies] examine candidate genes in the serotonergic pathways, and have not found convincing evidence of an association."

In Andreasen and Black's (2001) Introductory Textbook of Psychiatry, we find, in the chapter on schizophrenia:

> p. 23. "In the areas of pathophysiology and etiology, psychiatry has more uncharted territory than the rest of medicine. . . . Much of the current investigative research in psychiatry is directed toward the goal of identifying the pathophysiology and etiology of major mental illnesses, but this goal has been achieved for only a few disorders (Alzheimer's disease, multi-infarct

dementia, Huntington's disease, and substance-induced syndromes such as amphetamine-related psychosis or Wernicke-Korsakoff syndrome)."

p. 231: "In the absence of visible lesions and known pathogens, investigators have turned to the exploration of models that could explain the diversity of symptoms through a single cognitive mechanism."

p. 450: "Many candidate regions [of the brain] have been explored [for schizophrenia] but none have been confirmed."

As you are no doubt familiar with these textbooks you cited, you will agree that such statements invalidate claims for specific, reliable biological causes or signs of "mental illnesses." In the judgment of the panel members, your reply fails to produce or cite any specific evidence of any specific pathophysiology underlying any "mental disorder."

You have also referred us to 60 volumes of *Archives of General Psychiatry* and 160 volumes of *The American Journal of Psychiatry*. The 28 July 2003 cover letter from the hunger strikers and panelists that they sent to you by certified mail stated:

> "We are aware that research studies can run to thousands of pages. Therefore, please respond only with those studies that you consider the best available in support of your claims and theories in a timely way. When responding with evidence, please send citations for the original publications or copies of the publications you are citing."

Like you, we are familiar with the material found in these journals. It is understandable why you did not provide any citations. There is not a single study that provides valid and reliable evidence for the "biological basis of mental illness."

The members of the panel wish to make some further observations which we hope will assist the American Psychiatric Association to present an honest scientific stance with respect to the hunger strikers' questions. In the panel's view, the questions posed by the hunger strikers are serious and fair. These questions are legitimate questions that any patient or family member or interested person might ask of any psychiatrist, or a student might ask of a professor. The panel was therefore quite dismayed that you, as Medical Director of the world's largest, wealthiest, and most resourceful psychiatric association, could not provide a more specific or substantial response than the equivalent of, "See our textbook."

If, as you state in your letter, "the answers to [the above] questions are widely available in the scientific literature, and have been for years," then it behooves your organization to make these answers and their specific sources—

if they differ from the quotes we present in this letter—available promptly.

The panel members could not help but notice the contrast between the hunger strikers, who ask clear questions about the science of psychiatry and consciously take risks in the name of protecting the well-being of users of psychiatry, and the American Psychiatric Association, which evades revealing what actual scientific evidence justifies its authority. By not giving specific answers to the questions posed by the hunger strikers, you appear to be affirming the very reason for the hunger strike.

Sincerely,

Fred Baughman, M.D.; Mary Boyle, Ph.D.; Peter Breggin, M.D.; David Cohen, Ph.D.; Ty Colbert, Ph.D.; Pat Deegan, Ph.D.; Al Galves, Ph.D.; Thomas Greening, Ph.D.; David Jacobs, Ph.D.; Jay Joseph, Psy.D.; Jonathan Leo, Ph.D.; Bruce Levine, Ph.D.; Loren Mosher, M.D.; Stuart Shipko, M.D.

At the end of the letter it stated, "The hunger strikers endorse the scientific panel's statement."[24]

A month passed. There was no answer to the dissidents' letter. The hunger strike ended.

Then on September 26, 2003, the APA put out a press release—clearly an attempt to counter any negative publicity provoked by the former "mental patients' hunger strike." In the press release, which follows, it is revealing that the APA is obviously extremely annoyed by its critics. One would expect that legitimate scientists would welcome critics; this after all is how scientific progress is made. One would expect that they would be curious about how former mental patients with severe mental illnesses were able to recover from their illnesses and function effectively without taking psychiatric drugs. Genuine scientists would be interested in investigating these unusual people and trying to determine how they were able to recover.

Instead, the APA—acting like the medieval church denouncing heretics—asserted that the hunger strikers were enemies of science itself! The APA states, "It is unfortunate that in the face of this remarkable scientific and clinical progress [in successfully treating "severe" mental disorders], a small number of individuals and groups [who were themselves diagnosed as severely mentally ill—the APA neglects to mention] persist in questioning the reality and *clinical legitimacy* of disorders that affect the mind, brain, and behavior" (my emphasis).

The APA felt threatened. Here were the pesky ex-mental patients who were exposing to the public that the emperor had no clothes. Their franchise was being attacked, their facade was being torn off, and like any imperialists the APA lashed out against the enemies of the empire.

The term *clinical legitimacy* is revealing. It is a term that is intimidating but means nothing—or to be more precise it means that the problems of living that sometimes overwhelm people can only be treated by "clinicians"; "clinical" disorders by definition "belong" to psychiatrists. It is reflective of the debasement of the public discourse that the term *clinical depression* is often used as if it were a term with a referent different from those denoted by *despondent, sad, anguished,* and the like. But as Boysen notes, "The plain, cold, hard fact is that there are almost no mental disorders for which a specific biological cause can be pinpointed."[25]

Therefore instead of "clinical disorders," I contend there are only problems of living—problems that cause unhappiness and fear or despair. However, as becomes evident in the following letter, the APA does not agree. (If readers find the technical language in the document confusing, I suggest they skip forward and read first the more lucid response to this letter by the dissident professionals.)*

American Psychiatric Association Statement on "Diagnosis and Treatment of Mental Disorders"

Over the past five years, the Nation has more than doubled its investment in the study of the human brain and behavior, leading to a vastly expanded understanding of disorders that afflict and are mediated by the brain. This effort, undertaken by both the public and private research sectors, as well as by diverse professional organizations that are dedicated to moving new information about mental disorders into clinical applications, has greatly improved

---

*On one point I am in disagreement with both the APA and the dissidents. With the APA I think there very well may be a genetically influenced predisposition to become "psychotic." However, a genetic loading does not imply pathology. There are many character traits that have a genetic component, from intelligence to sexual orientation. (See discussion of transliminality in chapter 11.)

our ability to treat severe, frequently disabling mental and behavioral disorders effectively. Improved treatments dramatically improve the quality of health care and, in turn, the quality of life for millions of Americans who themselves have a mental disorder as well as for countless families in which a family member has a severe mental or behavioral disorder.

It is unfortunate that in the face of this remarkable scientific and clinical progress, a small number of individuals and groups persist in questioning the reality and clinical legitimacy of disorders that affect the mind, brain, and behavior. One recent challenge contended that the lack of a diagnostic laboratory test capable of confirming the presence of a mental disorder constituted evidence that these disorders are not medically valid conditions.

While the membership of the American Psychiatric Association (APA) respects the right of individuals to express their impatience with the pace of science, we note that the human brain is the most complex and challenging object of study in the history of human science. Conditions termed "mental disorders" that affect or are mediated by the brain represent dysfunctions of the highest integrative functions of the human brain including cognition, or thought; emotional regulation; and executive function, or the ability of the brain to plan and organize behavior.

Research has shown that serious neurobiological disorders such as schizophrenia reveal reproducible abnormalities of brain structure (such as ventricular enlargement) and function. Compelling evidence exists that disorders including schizophrenia, bipolar disorder, and autism to name a few have a strong genetic component. Still, brain science has not advanced to the point where scientists or clinicians can point to readily discernible pathologic lesions or genetic abnormalities that in and of themselves serve as reliable or predictive biomarkers of a given mental disorder or mental disorders as a group. Ultimately, no gross anatomical lesion such as a tumor may ever be found; rather, mental disorders will likely be proven to represent disorders of intercellular communication; or of disrupted neural circuitry. Research already has elucidated some of the mechanisms of action of medications that are effective for depression, schizophrenia, anxiety, attention deficit, and cognitive disorders such as Alzheimer's disease. These medications clearly exert influence on specific neurotransmitters, naturally occurring brain chemicals that effect, or regulate, communication between neurons in regions of the brain that control mood, complex reasoning, anxiety, and cognition. In 1970, The Nobel Prize was awarded to Julius Axelrod,

Ph.D., of the National Institute of Mental Health, for his discovery of how antidepressant medications regulate the availability of neurotransmitters such as norepinephrine in the synapses, or gaps, between nerve cells.

In the absence of one or more biological markers for mental disorders, these conditions are defined by a variety of concepts. These include the distress experienced and reported by a person who has a mental disorder; the level of disability associated with a particular condition; patterns of behavior; and statistical deviation from population-based norms for cognitive processes, mood regulation, or other indices of thought, emotion, and behavior.

As noted in the Diagnostic and Statistical Manual of Mental Disorders, which is published by the APA, the lack of a laboratory-based diagnostic test is not unique to mental and behavioral disorders. The identification of migraine headache is based on symptom presentation, and the presence of hypertension is detected through a measure of deviance from a physiological norm, or standard. The definition of "high" cholesterol has moved downward in recent years as more has been learned about the role of low-density lipoprotein (LDL) cholesterol as a risk factor for cardiovascular disease and as medications highly effective in reducing LDL cholesterol have been refined and increasingly available.

The mapping of the human genome already is spurring the search for genes and gene variants that singly or in combination may confer risk for the onset of a mental disorder. It is highly likely that the maladaptive expression of a risk gene will be shown to require "triggering" by certain adverse environmental influences. Here, "environment" may refer to traumatic events, prenatal/obstetric complications, or other phenomena that act on and interact with the brain. Thus, mental disorders may well be shown to be emergent properties of multiple systems that have gone subtly awry.

The lack of a laboratory-based diagnostic test for mental disorders does not diminish the irrefutable evidence that mental and behavioral disorders exact devastating emotional and financial tolls on individuals, families, communities, and our Nation. The National Institute of Mental Health estimates the direct (clinical treatment and services) and indirect (lost/diminished productivity and premature mortality) cost of mental disorders to be some $160 billion annually in the United States. And the landmark Global Burden of Disease study, conducted by Harvard University scientists under the sponsorship of the World Health Organization and the World Bank, found mental disorders, including suicide, to rank second in societal burden, behind only cardiovascular conditions, in established market economies such as the U.S.

Growing public awareness of the burden and costs of mental illness and of the gains being made through research are contributing to increasingly enlightened policies for the organization and financing of mental health care. Last year, President Bush identified three obstacles that prevent Americans from getting the mental health care that they need—stigma, unfair treatment limitations and financial requirements under health insurance plans, and a fragmented mental health service delivery program. In April, the President's New Freedom Commission on Mental Health recommended strategies for redressing these and other barriers to high quality, appropriate mental health care for all Americans who need it. The APA was privileged to participate in the development of the report and strongly endorses the call of the President's New Freedom Commission ". . . to protect and enhance the rights of people with mental illness."

In the months and years ahead, the APA, along with the National Alliance for the Mentally Ill, the Nation's mental health research and clinical communities, and the public at large will strive to achieve the President's New Freedom Mental Health vision, and will not be distracted by those who would deny that serious mental disorders are real medical conditions that can be diagnosed accurately and treated effectively.

The American Psychiatric Association is a national medical specialty society, founded in 1844, whose 35,000 physician members specialize in the diagnosis, treatment and prevention of mental illnesses including substance use disorders. For more information, visit the APA Web site at www.psych.org.[26]

The response of the panel (below) of dissident professionals to the APA statement speaks for itself: it is a scathing critique of biological psychiatry and of the medical model of human psychology. The medical model obscures the roots of human suffering. The emphases in italics are my own, intended to call readers' attention to the most significant points.

Scientific Panel Replies to APA statement

Dear Dr. Scully:

We believe that the above-mentioned APA Statement was released in response to the questions posed last summer to the American Psychiatric Association, the National Alliance for the Mentally Ill, and the Surgeon General of the United States by the Fast for Freedom in Mental Health based in Pasadena, California.

The scientific panel convened by the hunger strikers has written the present letter to respond to this APA Statement. We have paired the contents of the 11-paragraph APA Statement to the strikers' original questions and also added our own comments about some issues the APA Statement raises.

The Fast for Freedom in Mental Health wrote on 28 July 2003:

"WE ASK THAT YOU PRODUCE scientifically-valid evidence for the following, or that you publicly admit to media, government officials and the general public that you are unable to do so:

1. EVIDENCE THAT CLEARLY ESTABLISHES the validity of 'schizophrenia,' 'depression' or other 'major mental illnesses' as biologically-based brain diseases.

2. EVIDENCE FOR A PHYSICAL DIAGNOSTIC EXAM—such as a scan or test of the brain, blood, urine, genes, etc.—that can reliably distinguish individuals with these diagnoses (prior to treatment with psychiatric drugs), from individuals without these diagnoses."

The APA Statement's fourth paragraph states:

"Research has shown that neurobiological disorders like schizophrenia reveal reproducible abnormalities of brain structure. . . ." Without any citations, these statements cannot be supported, qualified, or rejected.

However, in the fifth, sixth, and eighth paragraphs, the APA Statement admits to the absence of "discernible pathological lesions or genetic abnormalities" in mental disorders. This admission contradicts the previous assertion of "reproducible abnormalities."

Without evidence of brain pathology no basis exists to call emotional distress, disturbing behavior, or unusual thoughts or perceptions "neurobiological disorders." This and similar terms negate the sufferer's distress as reaction, protest, or adaptation to his/her position in the personally relevant social context. A person is understood in terms of personal history and social circumstances. A neurobiological disorder is understood differently. The choice of labels is of great consequence.

Moreover, finding reliable biological markers would be only a first step toward concluding that mental disorders are essentially neurobiological. For example, blushing, an obviously physical reaction, is not biologically caused. Its effective cause is acute embarrassment. Biological processes make blushing possible but they do not cause blushing.

Even total congruence between biological processes and psychological events does not show that the former cause the latter. In other words, just because the is a correlation does not mean there is causation. Psychiatric research is far from showing any reliable connections between mental disorders and biological measurements, much less revealing anything definitive about the nature of mental disorders.

Aware of this shortcoming, the APA cites migraine headache and hypertension to illustrate that the lack of biological markers (and thus of physical diagnostic tests) is not unique to mental and behavioral disorders. It is true that medicine has yet to find the biological cause for these two disorders, though it has developed a very reliable physical measurement for blood pressure.

However, *in other branches of medicine such disorders are exceptions. In psychiatry they are the norm. Psychiatry is the sole medical specialty that treats only disorders with no biological markers.*

Moreover, hypertension is regarded as a symptom of physical disease because hypertension can degenerate into frank physical disease, even death. No such parallel exists in psychiatry. For example, people diagnosed with schizophrenia or major depressive disorder often are physically healthy: unless their social circumstances and neglect interfere negatively, they may live long lives and die of the same physical causes as other people.

The APA confirms in paragraph six that, in the absence of biological markers, mental disorders are defined by "a variety of concepts": "distress experienced and reported," "level of disability," "patterns of behavior," and "statistical deviation from population-based norms." Precisely. The APA should therefore explain how such sociological concepts—which easily define conditions such as poverty, discrimination, or war—substantiate the existence of "neurobiological disorders."

The Fast for Freedom in Mental Health also requested:

"3. EVIDENCE FOR A BASELINE STANDARD of a neurochemically-balanced 'normal' personality, against which a neurochemical 'imbalance' can be measured and corrected by pharmaceutical means."

These issues were not addressed in the APA Statement.

The APA Statement could have replied accurately that neuroscientists have not established any normal baseline quantity for any known neurotransmitter (no measurements even remotely parallel to blood pressure to diagnose hypertension exist), nor have they shown any chemical imbalance to correlate with mental disorders diagnosed in un-medicated individuals (Breggin, 1991; Healy, 1997; Valenstein, 1998).

The Fast for Freedom in Mental Health also requested:

"4. EVIDENCE THAT ANY PSYCHOTROPIC DRUG can correct a 'chemical imbalance' attributed to a psychiatric diagnosis, and is anything more than a non-specific alterer of brain physiology."

The APA Statement merely states what has been known for at least 50 years, that "medications clearly exert influence on specific neurotransmitters. . . ." This response states the obvious: all mind and mood altering drugs have effects on the brain. This includes illegal mind and mood altering drugs, though no one has suggested that they correct chemical imbalances in the brain.

Given the Food and Drug Administration's impotent exercise of its mandate to protect consumers from false advertising, *pharmaceutical companies recklessly advertise cartoons showing neurotransmitter "imbalances" corrected by drugs. However, in the absence of scientific proof to substantiate such claims, it is ethically and medically reprehensible for doctors to convey such messages to justify prescribing drugs, and for the APA's own journals to publish such advertisements.*

And finally, the Fast for Freedom in Mental Health also requested:

"5. EVIDENCE THAT ANY PSYCHOTROPIC DRUG can reliably decrease the likelihood of violence or suicide."

Not addressed in the APA statement.

"6. EVIDENCE THAT PSYCHOTROPIC DRUGS do not in fact increase the overall likelihood of violence or suicide."

Not addressed in the APA statement.

"7. FINALLY, that you reveal publicly evidence published in mainstream medical journals, but unreported in mainstream media, that links use of some psychiatric drugs to structural brain changes."

Not addressed in the APA statement.

Despite its use of terms such as "compelling evidence" and "research shows," the APA Statement provides no citations to any scientific literature. This was also the case in the first letter that Dr. Scully addressed to the scientific panel on 12 August 2003.

Associations devoted to research and treatment of genuine diseases readily provide consumers with scientific references on the pathological basis of these diseases. The APA is a 35,000-member organization, with an annual budget exceeding $38 million. With a handful of allies, it shapes mental health practice and policy in this country and has convinced taxpayers to spend billions to support its claim that psychiatrists treat "neurobiological disorders."

The APA should be able to provide a one-page list of published scientific studies to support this claim. Yet, the APA only speculates on future findings: "Mental disorders will likely be proven to represent disorders of intercellular communication; or of disrupted neural circuitry." (This sentence is yet another de facto acknowledgement that neuropathology cannot be shown in mental disorders.)

The APA uses terms like "complex," "emergent properties," and "subtle" when describing people's overwhelming mental and emotional crises. It states: "the human brain is the most complex . . . object of study in the history of human science." Yet this language about complexity is completely at odds with the biological model that reduces the human mind to a machine. Since the discovery of the infectious cause of neurosyphilis nearly a century ago, this model has failed to explain the cause of a single mental disorder. Yet this model dominates the mental health system.

Aware of this utter failure to find causes, the APA claims that money spent by the public and private sector "has greatly improved our ability to treat severe, frequently disabling mental and behavioral disorders effectively." However, relevant indicators show the exact opposite.

For schizophrenia, worsened relapse rates and increased numbers of people on disability status characterize outcomes over the last 50 years (Hegarty, Baldessarini, Tohen, Waternaux, and Oepen, 1994; Whitaker, 2002). For depression, increased incidence and prevalence are reported. Indeed, the APA Statement cites that mental disorders "rank second in societal burden, behind only cardiovascular conditions" in modern societies.

Perhaps the treatment is worsening the disorder. At best, the treatment is not helping: researchers now recognize that the most popular psychiatric drugs, the SSRI antidepressants, rate only slightly better than inert placebos (Kirsch, Scoboria, and Moore, 2002; Kirsch, Moore, Scoboria, and Nicholls, 2002). In addition, negative research findings (sponsored by industry) are commonly suppressed, and adverse drug effects are massively under-reported in psychiatric journals and to the Food and Drug Administration. These dubious but tolerated practices create an enormously misleading view of the actual impact of drug treatments.

Rather than acknowledge the lack of progress despite the huge expenditure of public and private funds, the APA dismisses its critics as denying the reality of suffering and impatient with the "pace of science." A genuine science states hypotheses in ways that allow them to be proven true or false. For a century now psychiatry has put forth hypothesis after hypothesis that is not falsifiable.

Today, despite no biological causes, no discernible biological markers or abnormalities, no diagnostic tests, no accurate predictions of treatment response and outcome, the APA still continues to claim that emotional disorders are genuine neurobiological disorders . . . with causes too subtle to detect at present! This is hardly an advance over earlier unfalsifiable ideas such as the Oedipal complex.

In sum, the APA's statements reflect less the "pace of science" than the pace of commerce: they blur with the pharmaceutical advertising themes saturating our media. This is because the APA is not an independent organization. One third of its operating budget comes from the drug industry. Drug companies dominate its professional meetings to advertise drugs. In addition, the drug industry funds, directs, and analyzes many drug studies (Healy, 2003), and psychiatric journals publish so-called scientific reports of these drug studies that are ghost-written by industry employees or marketing firms. Psychiatric drug experts with no significant ties to industry can hardly be found. Industry largesse binds many psychiatric practitioners to the industry (Editorial, 2002).

The hunger strikers asked the APA for the "evidence base" that justifies the biomedical model's stranglehold on the mental health system. The APA has not supplied any such evidence, which compels the scientific panel to ask one final question: on what basis does society justify the authority granted psychiatrists, as medical doctors, to force psychoactive drugs or electroconvulsive treatment upon unwilling individuals, or to incarcerate persons who may or may not have committed criminal acts? For, clearly, it is solely on the basis of trust in the claim that their professional acts and advice are founded on medical science that society grants psychiatrists such extraordinary authority.

We urge members of the public, journalists, advocates, and officials reading this exchange to ask for straightforward answers to our questions from the APA. We also ask Congress to investigate the mass deception that the "diagnosis and treatment of mental disorders," as promoted by bodies such as the APA and its powerful allies, represents in America today.

Signed:

Scientific Panel for the Fast for Freedom in Mental Health: Fred Baughman, M.D.; Mary Boyle, Ph.D.; Peter Breggin, M.D.; David Cohen, Ph.D.; Ty Colbert, Ph.D.; Pat Deegan, Ph.D.; Al Galves, Ph.D.; Thomas Greening, Ph.D.; David Jacobs, Ph.D.; Jay Joseph, Psy.D.; Jonathan Leo, Ph.D.; Bruce Levine, Ph.D.; Loren Mosher, M.D.; Stuart Shipko, M.D.[27]

One of the psychiatrists on the hunger strikers' team of experts was Dr. Loren Mosher, whose career in psychiatry exemplifies the sad story of the forces of change in the mental health system. As a young psychiatrist in the early 1970s, Mosher was a supporter of the mental patients' liberation movement and a student and friend of R. D. Laing. By the end of the 1970s Mosher was appointed head of the National Institute of Mental Health. In this role he procured funding for and did the pioneering research for the Soteria Project, a very successful model of a largely drug-free alternative treatment for "psychotics." Soteria's funding was cut in the mid-1980s, and Mosher was removed from NIMH. In spite of assiduous efforts, he was never again able to get funding for a drug-free alternative to standard treatment. He died one year after the hunger strike at the age of seventy-one.

Today in 2012, the words of Mosher's resignation letter to the APA ring truer than ever: "The major reason for this action is my belief that I am actually resigning from the American Psychopharmacological Association. At this point in history, in my view, psychiatry has been almost completely bought out by the drug companies. . . . Psychiatrists have become the minions of drug company promotions."

3

Interview with David Oaks

From Harvard to the Psychiatric Survivors' Movement

*D*avid Oaks is the director of Mind Freedom International. As described in the story below,* Oaks had become involved with the mental patients' liberation movement in the late 1970s. In 1985 Oaks began writing, editing, and publishing *Dendron,* a magazine for psychiatric survivors who were critical of the mental health system. In 1990 Oaks formed Support Coalition International (SCI) after meeting with representatives from thirteen other groups opposed to psychiatric oppression. In 2005, SCI changed its name to Mind Freedom International (MFI). (The website is www.mindfreedom.org.) MFI currently unites one hundred grassroots sponsors and affiliate groups to campaign for human rights in the mental health field.[1]

MFI is an accomplished organization and is the only group of its kind to have accreditation by the United Nations as a nongovernmental

---

*Solveig Wilder came up with some of the questions for this interview and participated in the interview process.

organization (NGO). Its status as an NGO enabled it to work with disability advocates from all over the world to produce the Convention on the Rights of Persons with Disabilities (CRPD) that was officially passed by the United Nations. As Oaks wrote me on October 13, 2011, "The CRPD is a stepping stone that is helping to change the paradigm in mental disability and liberty. Headed by our board president Celia Brown, our own team was able to mix in with these leaders, and build a lot of great relationships."

An MFI human rights e-mail alert network reaches more than ten thousand people who take action and complain to governmental authorities about abuse. Several of these campaigns have resulted in liberating individuals from forced psychiatric treatment. MFI has numerous accomplishments: it negotiated an internationally binding treaty about disability and human rights; it conducted a number of successful campaigns, including the hunger strike described in the previous chapter (see chapter 2); and it coordinates Mad Pride cultural events and guerrilla theater in more than six countries, including Ghana (described in the interview below). MFI activism against forced electroshock treatments (ECT) persuaded the World Health Organization to endorse a ban of involuntary ECT. An MFI campaign on behalf of Haitian political activist and psychiatric survivor Paul Henri Thomas led to his release from a state mental hospital. Similar campaigns resulted in the release of others.[2]

I first met Oaks in 1990 in New York; we were both involved in protesting the annual meting of the American Psychiatric Association. I interviewed him at the time for the book I was writing—*Madness, Heresy, and the Rumor of Angels.* On the basis of my interview I reconstructed an account of his "psychotic episodes" in the late 1970s when he was an undergraduate at Harvard and included it as a chapter in the book; it is reprinted in the extract titled "David's Story" in this chapter.

The psychiatrists had told Oaks that he was a chronic schizophrenic and that he would need to take "antipsychotic medication" for the rest of his life. By the time I first interviewed him, he had proved that they were wrong. As of this recent interview (2008) Oaks has been off psychiatric drugs for thirty years. Oaks is an example of a "creatively maladjusted" person. Clearly his organization, website, and numerous campaigns have helped inspire thousands of psychiatric survivors.

Farber: It's been a long time since the first interview I did with you. In the meantime—despite the psychiatrists' claim that you were schizophrenic or bipolar—you have not been locked up again or had any kind of breakdown.

David Oaks: No, I haven't. I haven't used the psych system for thirty years, since I got out of it my senior year of college. If I am upset about something I rely upon peer support. For example, I'm in a men's group that started in the spring of 1989. We've been meeting for nineteen years now, and we're good friends who support each other.

Farber: Is this a group of psychiatric survivors?

David Oaks: They don't really identify as activists in the mental health consumer or psychiatric survivor movement. Most of my friends don't identify as mental health consumer psychiatric survivors. I know a lot of my friends through the peace movement or the environmental movement. I know some people live, eat, breathe, and drink [the psychiatric survivors' movement], and you know all their friends are consumer survivors. That is not the case for me.

Farber: We know broadly about some of the accomplishments of MFI. What does this mean for you day-to-day? What is a typical busy day for you?

David Oaks: I tend to work weekdays, nine to five. I come down here to the Mind Freedom office. We're seeing people—there are three of us here—and I work answering clients and going to meetings, speaking out, speaking to media, and then going home. It's kind of close to normal.

Farber: Does Mind Freedom offer any services to psychiatric survivors like peer support?

David Oaks: Mind Freedom itself does not offer direct services. Through human rights groups that we promote, we support and we encourage a whole variety of alternatives, but we ourselves are not providers. We feel that it might be a conflict of interest to be an activist group also promoting one particular approach over others.

Farber: Psychiatry claims that anyone who has a "breakdown" or "psychotic episode" is chronically mentally ill and/or biochemically imbalanced. They tend to discount people like you who don't conform to their self-fulfilling prophecies; they claim in hindsight that you were not really schizophrenic, that you were misdiagnosed.

David Oaks: A lot of mental health professionals who label people and who deny recovery actually have severe mental problems themselves. One of these problems is hopelessness. What we're finding is that mental health professionals who are very embedded in the mental health system will sometimes have an extreme problem of what might be called pessimism or hopelessness. They will say, "Oh no, you can never recover." And what it is—that's a sign of their own mental/emotional problems. Certainly people can and do recover all the time from extreme mental and emotional problems, and a lot of our members prove that.

Farber: When did you get involved with the Mad Pride idea? How has it developed?

David Oaks: That was started by some folks in England in 1999. Specifically, there are two people who are considered coconceivers of it. One of them was Pete Shaughnessy. He and someone else saw a Gay Pride event in London, and they said, "Hey what about Mad Pride? Why don't we do some Mad Pride events?" So that's how we heard about it. And as a community organizer you really want to encourage leadership by other people. When somebody has a great idea and is doing something really great like that, we love to encourage and help out, and that's what we did. So Mind Freedom took that on as a way to support it. I helped link it up with Bastille Day. Mad Pride events can be held any time of the year, but they have tended to be in July, around Bastille Day, or May, or October, which is the Mental Health Month.*[3]

---

*In 2010, many Mad Pride events involved poetry readings, cabaret, and public performances based on the theme that normality is insane and oblivious to the destruction of the planet. As they put it, "Eco Madness!!! Or, Humans Are Killing the Planet and I Feel Fine."

So I would say that what I added to Mad Pride was some level of international organized support and encouragement. One of the founders, one of the earlier organizers of Mad Pride—when I told him about this he said, "Oh I'm not sure we should be organized."

What we helped provide was recognizing that we can affirm Mad Pride but use rationality in planning and organization and leadership to promote it. So Mind Freedom combined the idea of Mad Pride with an organized approach. We have an international committee with leaders. We have teleconferences, planning, publicity, and a website. We encourage people to do Mad Pride, we help coordinate between them. So that's what we brought to the mix. Even with that, it's still very slow to take off in a huge way.

The main Mad Pride event, which we call an anchor event, tends to be about a dozen actual events: art galleries, theater events, campouts, and things like that, and fairs and festivals. So right now we're trying to move it to the next level where lots and lots of people will be part of Mad Pride where lots of people can celebrate—even in their own homes, or with a few people, a small group, or individually—that it's a human thing to celebrate our uniqueness, our difference. That's why we connected up with the idea for International Association for the Advancement of Creative Maladjustment [IAACM]. Martin Luther King used that name more than ten times, including in front of the American Psychological Association on September 1, 1967. It was a laugh line in his speech—instead of the NAACP—but he was serious about the idea. So we incorporated the IAACM in Oregon. I think we're the first ones to consciously and overtly create an IAACM. I've written to MLK's son, who has a psych label, and said, "Hey, we're forming this." I didn't hear back. So as far as I know, we're the first. Patch Adams is our honorary chair.

The International Association for the Advancement of Creative Maladjustment, it sounds funny, but it's a serious thing to organize something intentionally. Like, many people still think Rosa Parks did what she did because her feet were tired, but she was an activist from the NAACP. That was a conscious act that she did; when she sat on that bus she was consciously advancing creative maladjustment. So Mad Pride is similar; for this thing to take off, we really need to consciously support it. It's very challenging, and I'm proud that we've gotten as far as we've gotten—that Mind Freedom has boosted Mad Pride.

Farber: Are you saying that both Mad Pride activities and civil disobedience are forms of creative maladjustment?

David Oaks: Yes. Mad Pride is in the realm of art at the moment. It's more like an idea, a concept. I would love to see Mad Pride develop art to such an extent that the general public does creative maladjustment activities. Martin Luther King and Rosa Parks did what was called civil disobedience. So we had a mass civil disobedience movement during the civil rights movement and again during the war in Vietnam. Our Mind Freedom hunger strike was in that spirit.

I would add, also there is cultural disobedience, and that's how I see Mad Pride. A group singing on a busy street corner and revealing their heart's feelings—to such an extent that maybe some of them weep or open themselves up to say what they really think or feel—is utterly inappropriate in our society. There's a frame of normality; you can't do that. You can't stand up in the theater before the movie starts, as a group, and say what you really think. Why not? We don't realize how the norms we follow limit us—prevent the development of a sense of community. We need to depart from business as usual: in a crowded restaurant, tap on the glass—you'd be considered obnoxious and all these things, of course—or go to a mall and throw new dollar bills over the railing people tend not to do that. I would like to see more civil disobedience where we do go to jail. But I'd like to see all kinds of non-violent, creative strangeness in the name of challenging, like the climate crisis. Let's show people that there's a crisis going on in the world. Let's make it visible. Why don't we see it?

Farber: You are advocating creative maladjustment. Would you say that normal society is itself insane?

David Oaks: No, I don't use the word *insane*. I'd say normal society is certainly what any mental health professional would call insane— current society would fit that criterion—but I myself don't like to use the word *insane*. What's called normal is the worst mental and emotional distress in the history of the planet, and the climate scientists are showing that what's been called normal is wrecking the planet. Our members, labeled schizophrenic, are not threatening to tear apart the ecological fabric of our planet. It's the people labeled normal that are wrecking the basic infrastructure of our planet. So that is violence. You know, what we define as violence is very revealing.

Farber: What does Mad Pride mean to you then?

David Oaks: We are all mad, and I defy an individual to prove to me differently. Being mad is a part of ourselves we should all accept. It's not like there is one perspective that is objectively true. Science now knows; no one has a grip on reality. It may be impossible to get a grip on reality. This is from complexity theory, quantum theory, particle physics, string theory, and all the cutting-edge sciences. Neurosciences are showing that we don't have this grip on reality.

Farber: Does the word *mad* have any meaning for you?

David Oaks: It's just culturally relative. The word *deviant* simply means "off of the path." In our society, if you're not—quote—normal then you're considered mad and deviant. So like this guy was on a bus in Canada a few months ago, and he suddenly killed the guy next to him, began eating his ear, and cut off his head and held it up in the air. Obviously almost everybody in our society says, "Oh my God, that is clearly madness." Okay? Well, what made it mad was it was utterly unexplainable and utterly unjustifiable, different. This is just so "out there" that it's called psychotic.

But different does not have to be destructive. It could be creative. That's why Martin Luther King Jr. advocated *creative* maladjustment. We don't see what Rosa Parks did on that bus as psychotic, but she was breaking free of normality. She was doing something that was nonnormal. So if we use the word *madness* to mean something utterly and totally different and nonnormal, she was, by that definition, mad. Of course, we won't call her that. But the word origin of *madness* simply means "changed." So that is very revealing. So that's why I say one can be proud to be mad. Our movement wants to explore this idea, crazy and proud, like Howie the Harp's song "Crazy and Proud."

Our society needs to break out of the mold of normality because what is called normal, let me repeat it, is like one of the best mental health movies out now: *An Inconvenient Truth.* Normality is a state of denying inconvenient truths.

Farber: Mad Pride means then an effort to wake people up by dramatically calling attention to the crisis of humanity?

David Oaks: Yes. Two things have always been a touchstone for me. One thing that psychiatric survivors can bring to the table is how we can use things like peer support and other alternatives to keep the human spirit alive, to keep it refreshed and renourished. We all suffer, all of us, but survivors have been through a lot of hell, a lot of them, so they have something to offer the planet. Survivors know to go through remarkable states, like suicide attempts, and come back and support each other and have something to offer society. So peer support, how to support one another, is one thing this movement has to offer.

The other thing is what Martin Luther King called creative maladjustment. He said the salvation of the world lies in the hands of the creatively maladjusted. Definitely thinking outside of the box—like Rosa Parks, not like the guy in Canada who chopped off his neighbor's head—but *creative* maladjustment. What the guy in Canada did was a negative maladjustment. We're talking about the Rosa Parks–style creative maladjustment. So those are our two things, mutual support and thinking outside the box.

Farber: You said in the 1990 interview that when you had your breakdown you were experiencing "new aspects" of yourself, "spiritual, emotional, and mystical," and that you wished there was someone "to help in the process of birth." Do you still think looking back that your "psychotic" experiences in the 1970s were features of spiritual rebirth?

David Oaks: Yes, I do. I want to say first that I think that the word *psychotic* in mental health is like the "N" word in racism. It's one of the worst things that people could be called. I'd say it depends on the individual, but for me, yes, there are spiritual aspects of everything. I think that when I went through my experience—when I was labeled psychotic—I got a taste of what saints, mystics, prophets, and shamans experience. Every cell in my body was certainly involved in the experience. It wasn't just like a theoretical—you know—"Let us pray." It was actually like, "I'm having a vision. I'm in an ecstatic state. I'm in an overwhelmed state."

So I think that definitely it not only is a spiritual experience, but I got a taste of what those who came up with our various religions went through. I would not compare the quality of my experience to what Muhammad went through, but when Muhammad began to recite the Qur'an, I feel that I got a little tiny taste, a hint, a whiff, of what it was like to enter into that state. I really appreciate that. I would definitely consider that spiritual. There are other words for it . . .

Farber: You said in 1990 you had developed the ability to be centered and lucid and "still be in an altered state of consciousness." You said, "Now I am capable of being in a so-called psychotic state without freaking out. I can go back and forth." Is this still true?

David Oaks: I would say that I can experience what is called psychosis and be peaceful and functioning and return to do the work that needs to be done, so there you go. I can experience strong and overwhelming mental and emotional feelings—and unusual beliefs and states—without getting overwhelmed by what is called or what would be considered psychosis. I think that everybody's in that state at times. In fact, we came up with a new acronym, pronounced "pumpkin": People Mistakenly Considered Normal, PMCN. There are labeled people, and there are PMCNs. We're all in the same mad boat, you know?

Farber: You were brought up Christian; you considered yourself an atheist at Harvard. Are you still an atheist now, Christian, or—?

David Oaks: I went to a Catholic church, but I became kind of an agnostic slash atheist. From early on, like in grade school, I would say I went through spiritual experiences. I don't consider myself an atheist. I would consider myself, if you had to label me, an agnostic/pagan.

Farber: Do you think others who have been labeled quote unquote mentally ill—for all of them there's a spiritual element? Are they potential mystics?

David Oaks: Well, I really take this whole pro-choice thing real strongly. So I wouldn't at all take it upon myself to in any way describe other people's experiences. Judi Chamberlin is an atheist.[*4] What she went through, she defines in her own way. Other members might define it in a spiritual way. Mind Freedom's approach, and my approach for trying to get interfaced spiritually, is where we try to bring together the different perspectives, and that can include people that don't believe at all. What I mean by interface is that you bring together a Jungian psychologist, an orthomolecular therapist, an acupuncturist, a peer support person, a housing expert, and each one of them may have a different perspective on what The Answer is—you know, capital T, capital A.

I think we need interfaces and many answers. We need to give people choices; are they being offered full information and support alternatives? That might include housing and vitamins, it might include peer support, it might include exercise and spirituality. The top few main alternatives to psychiatry are orthomolecular therapy, counseling, and spirituality, and each one of them has to be careful that it doesn't become like the current system. With the current model, the medical model, the problem isn't only the model, it's the bullying behind it. I call it the bullying model.

Very easily a spiritual model could replace it and could become the same way; if somebody said, "Well, The Answer is this one form of prayer, this one kind of religion, this one type of exorcism," that's the problem as well as The Answer. If it became the dominant mode, we would question that Answer too. It wouldn't mean that we're anti-spirituality, but that we're pro-choice. So I cannot say if madness is a spiritual experience for other people. It was for me.

Farber: You don't think that people who get labeled, who have breakdowns, may be more spiritually inclined or more sensitive? Are they just the same as the average Joe or Jane?

David Oaks: Certainly a major issue is the trauma of being labeled. Being officially "othered" in our society is inherently a traumatizing act.

---

*Judi Chamberlin was one of the leading activists in the mental patients' liberation movement. Her book *On Our Own* became a classic among people in the movement. She died in 2010 at only sixty-five years of age of terminal pulmonary disease.

Being labeled is just like being black in our society. If you quiz people about black and white, antiracist experts will point out several things. First of all, there's no clear scientific differentiation between white and black. There is more variation within a race than there is between races. So there's no easy scientific definition of who's white or black.

But further than that, African-American activists tend not to be saying, "Oh, there's no difference between people." What they're saying is, "There are lots of differences, based on all kinds of things. All kinds of mysterious things, all kinds of cultural things." We ought to explore those differences, celebrate differences. So no, I'm not saying that there's not any difference.

Here's a quick insight into what I'm saying: it's okay to have lines in our society between, let's say, this group and that group. It's okay to have distinctions, but they should be smart. The more you dive into that subject, you're not going to find some absolutely clear dividing line. It comes down to the fact that we all are in the same boat. Nobody has a grip on reality. Therefore, we need everybody's heart and mind onboard in making decisions together. Therefore, we need to be really careful and as nonviolent as possible.

Farber: So when you think of the people you've met who've been labeled mentally ill, do you think there might be similarities between these people—they might be more aware or sensitive than so-called normal people? Is there something distinctive that could be a source of Mad Pride?

David Oaks: I would say that, if you take a group of people that have been labeled mentally ill and you take another group that hasn't been labeled, there may be—there certainly would be some differences but there's no way to truly distinguish them. I would say that I am proud of what I call the mad movement. I've never organized strictly on labels. Everybody is welcome to join in and identify themselves as a psychiatric survivor.

I think everybody on the planet has experienced, has been harmed by the psychiatric system and its repression and so forth. So I think everybody can identify themselves as a psychiatric survivor. I think everybody can identify as someone who's had severe mental and emotional problems. In fact, if you claim that you've never had severe mental and emotional problems, that is a good sign that you definitely have a severe mental and emotional problem. If you haven't noticed that there's a climate crisis or that we humans are all struggling on the planet or that you love people and then people you love die, if you haven't come to grips with your mortality—I mean, if you haven't experienced (or are unaware of any of that)—then you probably have some kind of cognitive problem, injury, or mental condition. I mean, it's okay that you do, but you do. You're in denial: we're all in the same boat.

I think Psychiatry uses labels to divide us. In terms of the label *consumer*, why is it that the government has succeeded in defining a mental health consumer as somebody who uses official health system-licensed professionals? Those who see themselves as psychiatric consumers buy into it. The fact is that every entity, every living being, and every animal utilizes mental and emotional support constantly. If you take a monkey away from its mom and put it in a cage, it will wither. It might not die, but its brain will be smaller, it will be smaller, and nothing—no pill, no Jungian therapy, nothing—is going to make up for that. We are all interdependent, not just the people who get labeled mentally ill or consumer or survivor—everyone. The Psychiatry distinctions obscure our commonalities.

So in sum, I would definitely argue against making absolute, sweeping statements about anybody; that's how bigotry and prejudice get started. That said, it's okay to be proud of our community, and I'm proud to be a person who's been labeled and who has made my career working in this field. I'm proud of being part of that community. There are amazing, vibrant, creative people I know who've been labeled and been through that.

I gave a speech in Vancouver recently. I concluded it by saying, "We're the people who survived forced drugging and electroshock, labeling, and we persevered and we kept going, a lot of us, those that lived. A lot of us have kept on going, and there's something very special about that; I like to describe it as 'been on the front seat of watching the human spirit come back.'"

We've found in ancient archaeological digs evidence of human sacrifice. How can you explain that? There's no rational explanation. And anybody who comes along and says they have a bumper sticker slogan as the answer or they have a magic pill—no. Don't believe them. The answer is going to be everybody working all together, just like Martin Luther King talked about.

It's about being human and remembering our humanity. It's about that special, unique identity of the human. This is really about Human Pride. One of my so-called psychotic visions was about being a human being and having pride in being a human being and how we relate to the rest of the universe: we have a very unique planet and a very complex ecology. We human beings have something to bring to the table of the universe itself. So I think that has always been a touchstone for me, that so-called psychotic experience. Anyone could have that experience, and that, for me, is Mad Pride—Human Pride.

The following is reprinted from *Madness, Heresy, and the Rumor of Angels*. I interviewed Oaks for that book, on which I had just begun working. The year was 1990. I had just met Oaks for the first time. The narrative below, based on my interview, tells the story of Oaks's breakdown. It had many strong spiritual elements. Together these pieces present a picture of Oaks's life from youth to middle age. The reader can see for herself that Oaks was psychotic by the standards of Psychiatry.

One question is, how do people who know our society is insane tolerate it? Joseph Campbell—the famous mythologist and Jungian philosopher—had counseled "young people" to "follow your bliss," to pursue what interests you passionately. It may well be that the only way Oaks could have stayed stable and happy was to find a niche in which he had an opportunity to contribute to the good of society, to its salvation, or in other words, not to adjust but to live in a state of tension with society, a state of creative maladjustment. Oaks had a degree with honors from Harvard, but he wasn't the kind of person who could be content making lots of money working for a large corporation. And yet if he really had a defective brain he could not have been as successful as he was and he would have ended up on a psychiatric ward again over the years.

David's Story*

David Oaks is the editor of the magazine *Dendron,* a forum for individuals in the mental patients' liberation movement. He has been active in that movement since his senior year at Harvard in 1977. He makes a living as a peace and environmental activist. Despite five incarcerations in mental hospitals due to emotional distress during the time when he attended Harvard, he graduated cum laude in the typical four-year period. He was given various diagnoses such as "schizophrenic" and "manic-depressive." In other words David is supposed to be "chronically mentally ill" and able to function at a minimal level with the help of "medication." He has taken no psychiatric drugs, nor been in a mental hospital, since 1977.

A Difficult Transition

Going to Harvard represented a major transition for David. "I came from a working-class background. I went to an all-male, Jesuit high school and then went with a union scholarship to Harvard." Harvard represented making it, and his parents wanted to help him "mainstream."

The summer before he started school he had two part-time jobs as an office worker. "When I got to Harvard that freshman year I was totally exhausted and out of it. And I didn't have clothes that made me feel as if I fit in. I had these clothes that were really awkward."

The culture was different from the one to which he was accustomed. His high school was competitive in an overt and obvious way. "People were very into competition and cutting each other down; the brutal insult kind of thing." David's father worked as a clerk for Penn Central Railroad; he had little formal education, but he spent much of his time reading. David's mother was a housewife who also loved the written word. They lived in Chicago.

The Jesuit high school he went to was preparing students for college. It was oppressively all male. It was intellectually stimulating, highly

---

*This section on David Oaks is based on an interview conducted with him in 1990 and appeared in my previous 1993 book *Madness, Heresy, and the Rumor of Angels: The Revolt against the Mental Health System* (printed with the permission of Open Court Press).

structured, and competitive but in a way that was familiar to him. "Harvard is an elitist place. It is extremely competitive, and it puts you down emotionally." The students there seemed very fraternal and "comfortable" with themselves. "But deep down there was a kind of elitist competitiveness." Would he make it? Would he fit in? "I came from a working-class background, and I was going to Harvard, and people don't understand how that kind of thing affects you to the very cells of your being."

He had the opportunity to be socially confirmed and credentialed as being a member of "the best and brightest." "Harvard mainly offers a mentality of elitism. Your ego gets pumped up. But in this society where we are beaten down so much that's quite a commodity to get, isn't it? They're pumping air into people's heads there."

The opportunity to succeed was paired with the omnipresent threat of failure, a threat that transformed David's sojourn at Harvard into a prolonged identity crisis, which explained in part the moments of acute distress that led to his incarcerations in mental hospitals.

Going to Harvard also represented to David the opportunity of transcending the limitations of the environment in which he grew up and that had influenced him to some extent. It was a first step to becoming a leader in the movement for social change in this country. The South Side neighborhood that David grew up in was ethnic blue-collar and racist. "The Nazi party had a headquarters only about ten blocks from my house."

He felt that he had internalized some racial animosity. Away from his old community, he became aware of this and transcended it during his years at Harvard. "Martin Luther King came to my neighborhood, and he said he saw more hatred there than he did in any part of the country. I read later after I finished college that he felt almost hopeless. The only hope was if a few of the young people got out and went to college. And I thought, that's a message for me."

The threat of not making it haunted David throughout the four years he was at Harvard, and the memory of it still occasionally disturbs him now, thirteen years later. "I actually still have nightmares in which I'll experience this enormous, almost cloud-like, megalithic feeling of being encompassed by this intellectual womb, which I take to be Harvard. I'm in a class, and I'm not prepared for an exam. I had never even gone to the classes for it. This is a common nightmare. But in mine, I am returning from a break. I can't concentrate or remember."

The pressure for David was intensified after his first hospitalization. The authorities attempted to confer on him the degraded social identity of a person who was "mentally ill." In the process of climbing the mountain back to stability he slipped and risked being hurled into the abyss of nonpersonhood ("the chronically mentally ill") from which many individuals never escape. "Always, in this nightmare, I had left Harvard, and I've flipped out, and I'm coming back to Harvard, and I'm looking at the exam, or trying to find my way around campus. I can't read. Just like the first time after I was hospitalized and I couldn't read. I can't think. And I'm trying to piece together what's happening. And it's hard and I'm making mistakes."

Religious Experiences

Harvard was an impersonal environment. "You don't have that much personal attention from people. You rarely interact with the professor. You have huge classes with sections led by graduate students who are a few years older than you." It was not until his sophomore year that he "flipped out."

"It was strange because I began having a Christian religious-based experience and for years I had defined myself as an atheist. . . . The images and beliefs that I had learned in high school in terms of saints and the Holy Spirit came flooding back, and I experienced what I thought was the Holy Spirit; it led me into kind of a dangerous Boston neighborhood. . . . I had not slept in days and I was very tired, so I turned into a Jesuit school and I asked to speak with a priest. He was no help. He called my friends, who took me to the psychiatric unit at Stillman Infirmary, which is right in Harvard Square. . . . I saw a woman psychiatrist, and I had remembered seeing a poster around Cambridge criticizing psychiatric drugs and psychiatry so I was suspicious and told her what she wanted to hear."

He was released. He went back to the dormitory, but he was still in a state of distress. David's distress distressed his friends, which distressed David more. His friends took him back to Stillman. One girl said as she was about to leave him at Stillman, "Dave, you're in a lot of trouble." "Those were her last words before leaving, which scared the hell out of me. Not a smart thing to tell a person—and this was my friend."

He was placed in a room. They came to administer drugs. He refused to take them. "I began panicking that because I had done this, gone to the priest and so forth, that Harvard was going to put me on trial, and I'd be thrown out." The element of truth in his "delusion" was the realistic possibility of not "making it" at Harvard, the threat of failure that haunted this working-class boy throughout his four-year initiation at this elite institution.

There were positive aspects to his experience. "I felt I could see a pattern of an angel in a door, and I felt the Holy Spirit had guided me." His friends had brought him the huge book, *Lives of the Saints*. "I began identifying with the saints." He decided that he could lessen the threat of retribution by taking the drugs, so he reluctantly decided to do that. He was given a combination of Thorazine and Stelazine.

"The neuroleptics made me feel like a zombie. . . . I remember my parents had flown out to see me, and I tried to reassure them that I was physically okay. I started to do some push-ups. I did a few and then I began to bite my tongue. I tried to open my mouth and I couldn't and my whole body was in paroxysms. My parents got a doctor and they're watching me, this total writhing thing, and they put me onto the bed. Then a whole bunch of medical personnel showed up, and they administered an emergency dose of some kind of real tranquilizers that put me to sleep."

He got out of Stillman about two weeks later and tried to go back to school, but he couldn't concentrate. He went home to Chicago for a few weeks. He was in an altered state of consciousness, but he felt he was in a safe, supportive environment and was able to enjoy many of the unusual experiences he had. "I felt a third eye in the middle of my forehead." At that time he had only in passing read the Indian literature that described the existence of a "third eye," whose power could be developed, enabling one to attain clairvoyant vision. "It felt as if someone was trying to place a diamond in my third eye."

David felt at times that the TV was personally communicating with him. He explains this experience now as partly a self-generated attempt to compensate for the spiritual vacuity of modern society. "In Native

American cultures, in Earth-based religious cultures, people speak freely about relating directly to nature. And they believe that nature gives them messages. The belief that nature directly communicates to you is common in these Earth-based religions. We now live in an era where we are enclosed in a glass sphere, a bubble, of technology. So my way of restoring the sense of a dialogue with my environment was believing that the TV was personally sending messages to me."

His family was supportive. His grandparents on both sides grew up in Lithuania. David felt that Lithuania had an "ancient" culture and belief system that validated the kinds of experiences that would be viewed as symptoms of mental illnesses in our culture.

His uncle was particularly helpful. David remembered one time he expressed to his uncle his fear that the wall in the house would fall. His uncle pressed up against the wall and said, "Don't worry. I'll just hold up the wall." "My uncle was actually willing to give credence to my experience. He was very interested in ESP and parapsychology. . . . So when he was there I was able to calm down. Once, I stared at a TV antenna as a kind of meditation technique to help me to focus so that I could be centered and lucid and still be in an altered state of consciousness but not panicking."

He described an experience with his brother that was both reassuring and inspiring. "I was waiting in the car. I saw my brother go into McDonald's, and I saw this kind of macho guy walk in after him with what looked like a board in his hand. I felt the guy's hostility. My brother walked back out, cheerful and tough at the same time. Something about his air of independence protected him. Seeing my brother come out safe in the most dangerous areas, I realized that I could also. I could walk through this wall of flame, and if I had support I could remain calm and lucid. It took me a while to develop that ability, but now I am capable of being in a so-called psychotic state without freaking out. I can go back and forth."

After several weeks at home life returned to normal and David went back to school. He made up for lost time so that by the end of the summer he was caught up with his schoolwork.

In his junior year David started once again to have ecstatic mystical experiences. He cultivated these states because he felt that it was part of a process of becoming a more whole person. David gave a Jungian explanation for this: it was as if his unconscious mind was attempting to round out his psyche, to help him grow spiritually and to expand his potential as a person. Jung called this the individuation process. David had a tendency—he believed in hindsight—to be too analytical, controlling, hierarchical, distancing, overcompetitive, and linear. Now his psyche was pushing him away from a "left-brained" mode of experiencing the world because it limited his potential as a human being. He feels that Theodore Roszak's book *The Making of a Counter Culture* explains his attitude then: creativity transcending the technocratic state.

At that time he was appointed publisher of a poetry magazine for Harvard students called *padam aram*, which means "stairway to heaven" or "Jacob's ladder." Serendipitously or synchronistically the building that Harvard gave the poets to use as an office had a ladder that went up to the roof.

David was a bit "flipped out" one day; he had not gotten much sleep and had smoked a little marijuana. At dawn, he walked up the ladder to the top and he looked at the gym and the ivy across the way and he noticed that there was a flock of birds in the ivy. "I believed they were sending me messages. They were passing messages on from other flocks of birds. I realized that they had a global communications network. I was ecstatic. . . . We're talking pure ecstasy."

I asked him what the message was.

"I don't remember specifically. But it had something to do with telling me that what I was doing was okay, was meaningful, was part of a greater plan."

This reminded him as we were talking of an experience he had ten years later as an environmental protection activist. "There was a train carrying hydrogen bombs. They call it the White Train. We blocked it in the northwest three times. I was in front of it all three times. I felt the same sense of purity as when I saw the birds. You know you're in the right place, and you're loving it, and you're feeling connected."

Incarceration and Chemical Torture

Pressures mounted and David continued to be plagued by a sense of insecurity. His behavior was sufficiently eccentric, although not in the least dangerous, that he was committed to McLean's Hospital in Belmont, Massachusetts, against his will. "It's Harvard's teaching hospital. . . . It looks like a country club from the outside, but it's all connected by tunnels inside, you seldom see the outside. . . . I was put into the hospital, put into my bedroom, and I sat down and they came in with the Thorazine. And they said, 'Okay, take this,' and I said, 'No, thank you.' I was in there singing to myself, and I had a top-of-the-world kind of feeling."

"You really felt good?"

"I did. Yes. And they kept pushing the cup of Thorazine toward me, so I poured it on the ground. For that crime they immediately came in and brought me to solitary confinement and forcibly injected me. Then they made me go back after a day or two in there and mop up the Thorazine on the floor. You know, they took me to solitary, they held me down and pulled down my clothes and gave me the injection. I felt as if I had been raped. I wiped up the Thorazine with my hair to outrage them with my 'submissiveness.'

"The drugs caused me all kinds of problems. I couldn't see. I could not read my music or see across the room. I thought my eyes were going bad. The subjective feeling is actually one of disturbance. It's important for people to know that it's not a tranquilizing effect at all. What you feel is a sense of inner turmoil. Viewed from the outside you may look less agitated because you're all mixed up and you're not going to make much noise or show any spirit.

"I had difficulty thinking. I remember once trying to make a list of the books I needed from class and not being able to finish the list. I had difficulty moving my tongue, which I really resent because I still have residual effects today. I felt like the rats who were given Thorazine in 1950. Thorazine was first tried on rats in December 1950. The French researchers were looking at a range of chemicals, trying out different ones, looking to find one that would cause 'maximal behavioral disruption.' They had a rat trained to climb a rope for food. They finally tried Thorazine—they did not have a name for it yet—but they gave this chemical to the rat, and the rat would go to the rope and would not be able to decide whether to climb the rope for the food. It would panic. It was immobilized. Then they decided, 'This is the one we will use.' They were using it supposedly for other medical purposes . . . but within a year or two it was being given to mental patients. That's one reason why so many people who continue to take these drugs when they get out of the hospital seem to lack the motivation to do things. They will not even climb the rope for the food, metaphorically speaking.

"A psychiatrist tried it on herself in the early 1950s, and she said she felt as though she was dying; she couldn't get angry at anything. That's how I felt. A few years ago two Israeli psychiatrists took Haldol [a similar neuroleptic drug], and they reported they were unable to work, to think, to even answer a telephone."

David said that forcible druggings were routine and were not restricted to occasions when the "patient" was agitated or threatened violence. "You see a pattern in all three of my hospitalizations. Any display of spirit was considered to be the enemy, and they just looked for that." For example, one time David was attending a "patient government" meeting. A patient complained that one of the staff members had promised to take him for an ice cream and then defaulted on the promise. David went to find the staff member. He said, "John, Joe would like you to come to the meeting to find out why you did not go for ice cream." John ignored David, who then became angry and said, "Go to the meeting now." John handed David a cookie. David crumbled it in his hand. "Immediately they started to get mental health workers all over the place. I said, 'Wait a minute, just because I crumbled a cookie? I'll put it in the garbage.' Which I did. But it was too late. It turned into another forced drugging."

David described another demeaning experience he had. "I needed a dime for the pay phone, and a nurse came by, and I asked her for a dime, which she gave me. And I was trying to be cheerful even though I was on drugs. A psychiatrist was walking by and said, 'Excuse me, what are you going to be giving that nurse in return for the dime?' And I said, 'A smile!' And he said, 'That's the sickest thing I ever heard.' And that hurt me . . . and it helped me to realize their game: either through drugs or words they break you down."

In his senior year David learned about the mental patients' liberation movement that had formed in Cambridge. "I went to Phillips Brooks House, which is a social service agency for Harvard students. I said, 'Look, you should have something about mental patients' rights in here.

It's terrible in those places.' One of the women said, 'Let's meet for lunch,' which we did and she told me about the Mental Patients' Liberation Front [MPLF] in Cambridge." David joined the organization, went to meetings, gave legal advice to people who called the office, went to demonstrations, and helped to start a drop-in center for former mental patients.

Rebel with a Cause

The mental health experts told David that he was schizophrenic and needed to stay on medication for the rest of his life. Each time he was released from the hospital he stopped taking the drugs. Harvard required him to take psychiatric drugs to attend. He graduated from Harvard cum laude in 1977. He beat the system.

The possibility of making the kind of major life transition represented by Harvard activated David's fears of failure. The working-class boy who made it big, made it to Harvard, and "flipped out" suddenly found himself facing the worst threat of all: the destruction of all his dreams and reduction to the status of nonperson by the mental health establishment.

David did not capitulate. He was too strong a spirit to be inducted into the role of chronic mental patient. He did exactly what therapists like Jay Haley recommend: as soon as he got out of the hospital he went back to "normal" life.

I asked David if at any point they had persuaded him he was mentally ill. "I never really, internally, bought the diagnosis. And I never have. My parents would say, 'You know, you really just have to trust somebody.' I was not being supported by the mental health system. I was experiencing new aspects of myself—spiritual, emotional, mystical—but this was happening in a rapid and unassisted way. The help I wanted did not mean someone to stuff it back in, but to help in the process of birth."

David's independence of spirit was a trait he possessed for a long time and helped him to lead others. "I was a rebel with a cause since I was a kid. I published a radical newspaper when I was nine years old, and again at twelve years old, that was censored by my local grade school." In high school he was in the student-empowerment movement and in the anti-Vietnam war movement. In college he remained critical of the "power system," including Harvard, corporate dominance of America, and authoritarian social relationships.

David's sense of self is defined in broader terms than being a Harvard graduate. "I'm not going to totally reject the accomplishment of getting in there, but I recognized it now as a very narrow aspect of my being. Although of course it is a very unusual thing to graduate in four years with five so-called hospitalizations."

When he finished college, MPLF supplied a great deal of his support. David continued to go to support group meetings and on MPLF wilderness hikes, and he became romantically involved with a woman activist in the movement who helped him improve his nutrition; he became a vegetarian. He has worked as a volunteer and as a worker for a variety of social causes since 1974. After several years in Boston, supporting himself through office work, David travelled for two years.

In 1982 he helped to organize the International Conference on Human Rights and against Psychiatric Oppression, which took place in Toronto. After the conference he was excited and had gone without sleep for several days. He began to feel distressed. He was staying in a friend's loft. "I decided that I would take care of myself. I would lie in bed until I slept. I felt calmer after some sleep, but I was in an altered state. I'd go outside, and I'd see construction workers, and I'd think these are human beings dressed as construction workers, like actors playing out this experience. Despite this I realized I would be a calm person. I called myself 'the Calm Lithuanian.' I would experience these bizarre thoughts and not panic. And there's a grain of truth here: just because someone is wearing a little plastic cap and has a little sign on their back does not mean that's their identity. I was looking at the person as a whole person, and it struck me as funny that they're also playing this little game by digging in the ground and wearing this hat. I have the skill now to experience these things without panicking or getting carried away."

In 1983 David moved to Eugene, Oregon. He continues to edit *Dendron* and to make a salary as an organizer for the movement against nuclear weapons and nuclear power plants. He has been active in the movement to protect the wilderness old-growth areas in Oregon: "These old-growth wilderness areas are being rampantly cut down. They are Douglas old-growth—Douglas fir—with incredible diversity of species, more living matter per square foot than anywhere on the Earth. The ancient forest evokes feelings very similar to the nonlinear states Psychiatry is attempting to destroy. Cutting all the old-growth down is a violation against nature. I am connected to nature. It's a violation against me. People trying to preserve their natural areas is a very important struggle."

David envisions a global nonviolent revolution. He sees people coming together.

> As long as we're alone we can be numbed by the destruction of the planet's ecosystem, by poverty, racism, sexism. We're like deer with the headlights in our eyes. We can't run off the road. But if we organize and support each other our spirits will be lifted so we'll have the strength to fight back. The mental liberation movement can assist overall societal transformation—a nonviolent revolution—in two ways. Two of these are by fighting the tyranny of normality and teaching the skills of empowering ourselves to lift our own emotions. With all due respect, I feel a vital part of the human spirit is the Fool. I love this part of ourselves. Our essence of foolishness is a key lesson of the environmental movement: that humans are interrelated with all of nature in such complexity, we should therefore walk as gently and humbly as possible. When a macho businessperson arrogantly tinkers with nature by, for instance, building a nuclear power plant and ignoring its waste, they deny the foolish essence of their humanity, ironically making themselves more foolish, but also more dangerous. They act as death clowns, if you will. How easily their self-interest bends their logic. Unfortunately, their so-called delusion is far more dangerous than those of us actually labeled "psychotic."

Today, the unwritten rules that weave our social fabric catalyze a mass adaptation to this death clown behavior. The crime of our century has in fact been obedience, not deviance. Those who violate the very core of behavioral fascism, as many in our movement do, can contribute to overthrowing this tyranny of normality.

Our movement also shows people that even a survivor of terrible spirit-destroying economic, social, and psychiatric oppression can still overcome. One method we have explored is user-owned mutual support. The idea that individuals can get together as equals and consciously affect—uplift—each other's emotions, lives, and even their biochemistry is heresy. In fact, that was one reason witches were burned: they formed groups of wise women, linked to the wildness of nature, who, through ritual, gained power over their own minds and feelings.

The hierarchical, technocratic state we live in has been useful at times. But now it is deadly to Earth itself. Our movement is part of the transformation by pointing out the unspoken, superpowerful, absurd dictatorship of an enforced sanity. And we can help nurture nonviolent revolution by showing that everyone has the power to transcend numbness and despair and keep creative, democratic spirits strong. Through humility and mutual support, humanity can gain the confidence to creatively overcome the dominant worldview, hopefully nonviolently if at all conceivably possible.

Commentary on David's Story and Interview

David Oaks's story as described in the above interview and in the account of his hospitalizations and rebellion provides confirmation for my own Mad Pride theory. I am arguing that mad people tend to have a distinctive mad temperament that puts them at odds with normal society and that makes them more prone to having visionary ("psychotic") experiences. Once the mad are liberated from psychiatric serfdom (both from overt psychiatric control and from internalized images of themselves as mental defectives), once they begin to view their "psychotic" experiences as revelations or crises rather than symptoms, then they will be free to develop the capacity to act as catalysts of social transformation in our insane society; the mad will be free to join with other kindred spirits to constitute the vanguard of a new cultural/spiritual order.

Oaks has been very influenced by Martin Luther King Jr., who said many times, "Human salvation lies in the hands of the creatively maladjusted." King was not referring to mad people; at that time there was no resistance movement of former mental patients. However, it makes sense that those who have trouble adjusting and end up getting labeled "mentally ill" or "defective" by psychiatrists would include persons who have the greatest yearning for a different kind of society. The mad are often the most aware (often unconsciously) and most disturbed by the harm we are inflicting on each other and on the Earth. A "normal" person might be intellectually aware but not as inclined to feel the suffering of others. It makes sense that many of them would realize that our society is itself insane and that instead of endeavoring to be normal they would rebel and aspire toward creative maladjustment.

Oaks agrees with one of the major contentions of Mad Pride (see the section Insanity and Madness in the introduction), that adjustment to society does not constitute a legitimate criterion of "mental health" or spiritual well-being—or sanity—because our society is itself "biologically dysfunctional" or existentially off course, as Laing put it (see chapter 5).

Society is insane. Oaks was reluctant to phrase it that way—evidently for the same reason I felt it was necessary to invent and utilize a semantic distinction between "insanity" and "madness." I suspect that a number of people, including many Mad Pride activists, believe as I do and Laing did, that the term *insanity* is indispensable; it is necessary in order to convey accurately the state of spiritual derangement and moral inversion of normal society. Consider: our (normal) society is insane. This premise changes our view of the "mental health system" since "mental health" by definition entails the adjustment to society!

Those who are in the Mad Pride movement have typically undergone madness. As did Oaks. (Some never were "psychotic"; they might have been labeled depressed or ADHD.) The mad experience is typically what John Weir Perry called a visionary experience; the "psychotic" is plunged into the myth world, the collective unconscious, into the deeper nonrational levels of the psyche. If the mad person is able to weather the crises of madness, he or she could become (as those in Mad Pride and in this book prove) a shaman, a mystic, a prophet—or an ordinary nonconformist. For what is the difference between "psychosis" and mysticism? Joseph Campbell (see chapter 5) had used a striking analogy; he stated that the mad person and the mystic are immersed in the same ocean of beatitude, but the mystic is swimming while the mad person is drowning.

When Oaks first had his mad experience he felt like he was drowning. The psychiatric system wanted to rescue Oaks, to pull him out of the ocean and transform him into a chronic mental patient. He resisted and broke away, and then he learned to swim in the ocean of the inner world. As he stated in 1990 and in his story and reiterated in our recent interview in this chapter, he now is able to have mad experiences—what the psychiatrists would consider psychotic episodes—and remain calm and lucid. Many authorities on various forms of mysticism would say that the ability to have altered states of consciousness and remain calm is the salient feature that distinguishes the mystic from the lunatic.

One of the Mad Pride movement's important goals, as I see it, should be to help the mad to swim in this ocean. The first step is for the mad to become aware that it can be done—that madness represents not a meaningless biochemical aberration but a potential opportunity to discover new dimensions of existence.

But why, the reader may ask, do I refer to Oaks as "mad"? Is he not simply a mystic? Why seek to subsume potential mystics under the banner of Mad Pride? What does it mean to be mad? Of course the term *mad* is relative. For some persons the mystic herself at best *is* mad; her sanity is questionable by the standards of society. A prophet himself (e.g., Jesus) has typically been declared mad; he is a threat to the guardians of the status quo. The establishment (whether religious or scientific) has frequently attempted to disqualify the mystic, the prophet, or the non-conformist as a heretic, if not a mentally ill person.

In fact the use of term *heresy* is revealing. It was originally a stigma used by the religious establishment during the Inquisitions to denote those with "deviant" religious views who were thus deemed threats—and often demonic—to the religious establishment, the social order, and potentially to God. Today the term *heretic* typically connotes courageous nonconformity, that is, the word has been transformed and positively valued in the last century. It's not considered an insult; holding nonconformist views is more highly valued today. Einstein for example was a scientific "heretic" when he proclaimed his theory of special relativity, thus refuting the "ether" theory. The term *heretic* was transformed.

Mad Pride could similarly transform the cultural meaning of the term *madness* and its cognates—*madman,* and *mad woman.* That is the main reason why I think it is valuable to use the word *mad,* and *Mad Pride*—to sanction those altered, often mystical states of consciousness that are invalidated in this society. It could be used to apply to all those who have had or have altered states of consciousness—whether these be deemed "psychosis" or "mysticism" by the establishment.

The Icarus Project transvalues the phenomenon of being mad when it states madness consists of "dangerous gifts." Mad people are today owning and valorizing the experience of madness, just as dissidents have owned the intellectual deviance of heresy instead of repudiating the word *heretic* and trying to redefine their heresy as nonthreatening to the establishment. Mad Pride activists want those who are labeled "psychotic" to realize that although they may be different from the norm, although their experiences may be frightening to them and threatening to the mental health professions that regard normality as normative, their brains are neither diseased nor defective; on the contrary madness is a gift. The mad person is a potential mystic, a potential prophet; she is at the nascent phase of her growth, and she will grow spiritually if her phase of madness is not aborted by psychiatric treatment and psychiatric drugs. As Oaks's story illustrates, the "psychotic" or the mad person can learn to swim in the ocean; he can learn to have so-called psychotic experiences and remain calm. Such a person would then be a mystic, not "psychotic," not mentally ill.

Once the person learns to "swim," would she then cease to be mad? Would she be a *pure* mystic? Or would she be a mad mystic? From the Mad Pride perspective these questions are irrelevant. By affirming the value of madness—transvaluing the meaning of the term *mad*—Mad Pride makes it easier for the mad to accept and affirm the positive aspects of what society deems "psychosis"—madness—and to realize their kinship or identity with the mystic and the prophet. Then they can to learn how, as Oaks did, to have "psychotic" experiences and remain calm—instead of suppressing their unusual states or accepting the self-fulfilling psychiatric prophecy that they are chronically "mentally ill."

Not only did Oaks become a mystic, he also developed or strengthened his prophetic sensibility; he became a full-time social activist and spokesperson for social change. Oaks did not resolve his psychosis by becoming well-adjusted to society; rather he resolved it by becoming creatively *maladjusted,* and his life is proof that others can become so as well. One cannot help but wonder, *could* Oaks have adjusted to normal society? It is very possible that had Oaks not created a niche that enabled him to financially support himself at the same time as acting as an agent of social change, he would *not* have been able to adjust to the world; he would have been depressed or unstable or profoundly discontented. Perhaps he is one of those persons who can only find his equilibrium by being creatively maladjusted. Perhaps there are many people like this, people for whom Mad Pride can offer an alternative.

Another way of saying Oaks is creatively *maladjusted* is to say that he is "adjusted" to the future, not to the present; in Laing's terms he is "ontologically on course," he is adjusted to the new world, the new order ("New Age," as many would call it) that is he is helping to bring into existence.

Now the question of "madness" again arises: Is not adjustment to the *new* order the essence of true sanity? Yes, from the viewpoint I present here, accepted by all my interlocutors, it is. *Is* this new world also mad? These questions are unanswerable; the terms are relative. However, such an order is *beyond* sanity as we know it, as it is currently defined. The fundamental reality is not what we are living in now. St. Paul said we see "through a glass darkly." The Hindu sage says we are living in a state of metaphysical "ignorance," which distorts our experience itself. All mystics agree that it is difficult if not impossible to use words to describe the world or being when viewed from a "higher," more "real" perspective. Therefore, we can infer that the new order is as different from ordinary perception as madness itself is different. The Zen master claims that the fundamental reality eludes thought. In a speech I gave to a conference of former "mental patients" I stated, "[T]he new order that is seeking to come into existence *is* mad when judged by the limited standards of the enfeebled imagination that reigns now in the name of reality." Furthermore, "The new order we are creating will lie between the realm of dream and reality, of sanity and madness. . . . It will have the vibrancy and intensity of madness, the magical quality of a dream, but the fierceness of madness will be restrained by the firm but gentle power of love, which will ensure that the imagination is bound but not weakened by the task of maintaining our unity as a species."[5]

It is my contention that the future—the new order—is breaking through the boundaries of the present social order under the guise of madness, of "psychosis." It is breaking through in the psyche of the mad person. *What we call madness is not a sickness; it is the future itself seeking to be born, to be incarnated in the "real world."*

Readers will notice that ironically Oaks's theory of "mad pride" is not about madness but about catalyzing social change—using imaginative forms of street theater and art to stretch society's acceptance of what is "deviant" and culturally expressive behavior and to push society to overcome their denial of inconvenient truths that threaten the survival of humanity.

Oaks skirts the issue of madness—"psychosis"—as a potentially regenerative experience, and while he certainly values social diversity and each individual's contribution to diversity, *he denies that there are any genuine differences between mad people as a group and normal people.* To claim that there are differences, Oaks fears, would be to obscure our common humanity. As he put it, ". . . I think everybody can identify themselves as a psychiatric survivor. I think everybody can identify as someone who's had severe mental and emotional problems. In fact, if you claim that you've never had severe mental and emotional problems, that is a good sign that you definitely have . . . . If you haven't noticed that there's a climate crisis or that we humans are all struggling on the planet or that you love people and then people you love die, if you haven't come to grips with your mortality—I mean, if you haven't experienced (or are unaware of any of that) . . . you're in denial: we're all in the same boat. . . . The answer is going to be, everybody working all together, just like Martin Luther King talked about."

Certainly Oaks's point is well taken, and his formulation is poignant. As human beings we are all existentially equal in worth. There is no escaping the human plight; if we are going to save the planet we will all have to work together. Oaks articulate this central insight repeatedly and eloquently. However, we are not all equal in abilities. Some people, for example, are smarter than others. Some are better engineers. Some are more spiritually aware. The ethical challenge every individual faces is to use her talents to help struggling humanity.

The temptation is to use one's gifts to enhance one's own power or financial wealth or that of one's tribe or country or family, oblivious to the effect one is having on the human species, on the planet. The early Christians yielded to the temptation of power in the fourth century when they gave up their vows of poverty and nonviolence and accepted the offer of Emperor Constantine to be the priesthood of the new imperial

Christianity, the religion of the Roman Empire. Throughout history idealists have repeatedly succumbed to the temptation of power. Evangelical Christianity in America has largely (tragically) been transformed into a cult of the American military war machine, if not into a completely un-Christian effort to foster wars in order to bring on the Armageddon. In the name of Jesus, it has abjured the nonviolence, humanitarianism, and love of the enemy that was the essence of the teachings of Jesus. All human beings, no matter how gifted—*particularly* those who are gifted—are faced with this temptation of succumbing to power.

But whatever the genuine dangers, I believe that there is a rationale for Mad Pride—for affirming that the mad *are* gifted, spiritually more aware than the "average" person. It is, after all arguably, true. As Laing wrote in 1967, "If the human race survives future men will look back on our enlightened epoch as a veritable Age of Darkness. . . . They will see that what we call 'schizophrenia' was one of the forms in which, often through quite ordinary people, the light began to break in the cracks in our all-too-closed minds." Jesus himself said the "last" shall be the first—that social pariahs would be most ready to enter into the kingdom of God. After centuries of being told that they are mentally defective, what harm can result from asserting that mad people have certain assets, certain "dangerous gifts," as Mad Pride activist Sascha DuBrul called them, which can and should be cultivated?

If I am correct, as I have argued in the introduction, the empowerment of the mad will lead to the emergence of prophetic voices and revitalize the dormant counterculture that arose in the 1960s. As society continues to persist in practices that are destroying the Earth (despite the warning signs, from global warming to nuclear proliferation)—as America continues to build bombs and start wars—it is imperative that we protect our visionaries from psychiatric destruction so they can help to save *us*. Among the mad are many who are mad enough to believe that there is an alternative, mad enough to believe (as did most American Christians—and Reform Jews, as well—in the late seventeenth and eighteenth centuries, before evangelicals reverted to reactionary Calvinistic fatalism and premillennialism) that the ancient messianic aspirations of humankind—the realization of the kingdom of heaven on Earth, the kingdom of God on Earth—can be realized. The alternative is the destruction of humanity—and of life on Earth.

Part Two

The Intellectual
Background
of Mad Pride

4

Mental Patients' Liberation

*I*n 1961 Thomas Szasz's book *The Myth of Mental Illness* was published. Szasz launched an intellectual revolution with his argument that the idea of mental illness is a myth. The mind is not a material entity; therefore, unlike the body or brain it cannot be diseased. Szasz's book was written decades before the theory of biochemical brain disorders rose to favor and replaced the psychoanalytical theory that "mental illnesses" were caused by emotional traumas. (Despite the change in theory mental health professionals still use the term *mental illness* today; in fact it is enshrined in the diagnostic catalogue *Diagnostic and Statistical Manual for Mental Disorders*, or "DSM," used by all mental health professionals, which classifies *all* emotional problems as "mental disorders.") The sense of identity of psychiatrists hinges on the idea that they are medical specialists—with all the prestige doctors possess in modern society—engaged in a valiant and steadily advancing battle against the epidemic of mental illness. Szasz debunked this idea with his argument that "mental illnesses" were really just "problems of living"; furthermore his corollary was that psychiatric treatments were a form of scapegoating and social control aimed at those individuals who deviated from social norms.[1]

The psychiatric establishment was outraged at Szasz. The head psychiatrists of the Department of Medicine at the State University of New York Medical School, where Szasz taught, tried to silence him in the early 1960s. Supporters of the status quo in the mental health field wrote reams of articles attempting to refute him. Over the past half century Szasz continued to defend and expound his theories and to rebut his critics in over thirty books and countless articles. Szasz is not entirely alone: his work has inspired a handful of leading mavericks within the mental health field—including Peter Breggin—who have come to share his belief that mental illness is a myth or at least an inadequate paradigm.[2]

Without the books of Szasz there would have been no mental patients' liberation movement. Szasz's deconstruction of the concept of mental illness made it possible for "the mentally ill" who read him—or were aware of his ideas—to think of themselves in new terms and to resist the psychiatric definition of their identities: they were not persons with chronic "mentally diseased" minds, incapable of making rational decisions for themselves. Instead, they were free moral agents who were victims of a punitively paternalistic psychiatric establishment that denied their status as moral agents, which is the basis for full citizenship. The definition of a person as mentally ill is not a "medical diagnosis," it is a "moral verdict"—as two of Szasz's colleagues aptly put it.[3] Diagnosis is, according to Szasz, the first step in the process of depriving persons who deviate from cultural norms of their constitutional right as citizens to liberty and subjecting them to involuntary psychiatric treatment.

Although Szasz's work was the essential stepping stone that made possible a revolutionary redefinition of the so-called mentally ill, it stopped short from the perspective of recent developments; it did not provide a basis for Mad Pride, for a positive interpretation of madness. In fact, Szasz doesn't believe in the existence of madness; he thinks the mad are pretending to be mad and they are acting in bad faith. Szasz wrote recently, "All mental illness is malingering (or may be said to be a kind of malingering)."[4] Laing, on the other hand, believed what the psychiatrist calls "mental illness" is actually an emotional or spiritual crisis characterized by an altered state of consciousness.

In the last few years Szasz has decided that madness is as much of a "myth" as is mental illness.

It was Laing, more than any other figure, whose writings provided a basis for the mad to affirm their madness, to assert it as a spiritual gift and to question the sanity of normal society. For one reason or another Laing's works were virtually ignored by the mental patients' liberation movement (except for a brief time in the early 1970s), and the psychiatric survivors' movement remains steadfastly secular in orientation—ironically so, considering the fact that the overwhelming majority of former mental patients are unusually and intensely spiritual. Unlike Szasz, who was venerated by radical activists in the ex-mental patients' movement, Laing's work was rarely read by ex-patients and less rarely cited. I am not sure why this is the case; perhaps it was because Laing remained aloof from the patients' activism. Perhaps it was because from the start, some of the *leaders* of the movement (e.g., Judi Chamberlin) were secular in orientation. Perhaps Laing's theories seemed too "far-out" to people who were trying to demonstrate they were really rational just like "normal" people and thus deserved the same rights. Perhaps this was an inevitable product of the youthfulness of the movement. (I mean of the movement as a whole, not of the activists.)

A few years after *The Myth of Mental Illness,* Laing's most controversial book, *The Politics of Experience* (1967), was published. Laing startled the world anew with the claim that the mad were mystics and that schizophrenics were saner than normal people, including psychiatrists. Here was a basis for Mad Pride. Laing even said that schizophrenia may be the result, not of a genetic flaw, but of a genetic asset. He explained, "Our society may itself have become biologically dysfunctional, and some forms of schizophrenic alienation from the alienation of our society may have a sociobiological function that we have not recognized."[5]

He wrote, "The condition of alienation, of being asleep, of being unconscious, of being out of one's mind, is the condition of the normal man. Society highly values its normal man. It educates children to lose themselves and to become absurd, and thus to be normal. Normal men have killed perhaps 100,000,000 of their fellow normal men in the last fifty years." Madness may be a way of healing "our appalling state of alienation called normality."[6]

Psychiatrists were aghast. Many psychiatrists said that Laing himself was crazy. Rumors persisted for years—of no substance—that Laing had gone off the deep end and been locked up in a mental hospital. According to Laing's critics, then and today, his ideas were unsound—irrational products of the feverish 1960s' counterculture.[7] In the 1970s the psychiatric establishment launched a massive campaign to discredit him; it was said that Laing was a kook who "romanticized" mental illness. It was implied that Laing believed that "schizophrenics" were happy as larks. This is nonsense, as a careful reading of Laing would demonstrate: the fact is, Laing was a mystic in the Romantic tradition who believed the mad were frequently "on to something," but he had also worked for years as a therapist with the mad, and he did not view them—nor normal people—through rose-colored glasses. He knew the mad person—entering a new unfamiliar world—is often "completely lost and terrified."[8]

Like Szasz, Laing believed that people labeled "mentally ill" were experiencing problems of living. But he parted company with Szasz where Szasz denied the existence of madness.* Laing believed that madness was an altered state of consciousness, madness was a "journey" in the inner world; psychotics were pioneer explorers of the inner world. He also argued in *The Politics of Experience* that madness was (often) a natural process of spiritual death and rebirth. These two *complementary* themes run throughout Laing's book—madness as exploration of the inner world and madness as a process of death and rebirth.

It was Laing's firm conviction that mad persons and madness should be taken seriously—not treated as specimens of mental disease. Laing wrote, "We respect the voyager, the explorer, the climber, the space man." Why is it we do not respect the mad who are often exploring "the inner space and time of consciousness?"[9]

Normal people, Laing stated, are so out of touch with this realm that "many people now argue that it does not exist."[10] "Our time has been distinguished, more than by anything else, by a drive to control the external world . . . and by an almost total forgetfulness of the internal world."[11]

---

*There was certainly a kernel of truth in Szasz's argument: in some cases madness consists of an act or acts of self-deception.

"The outer divorced from any illumination from the inner is in a state of darkness."[12] By "inner world" Laing means fantasies, dreams, spiritual experiences, and the experience of God.[13] Laing regarded this denial of the spiritual inner realm as insanity—the form of insanity, alienation, that is most characteristic of the modern world, the normal world (see the introduction).

Laing is clear that the person labeled mentally ill may be creatively maladjusted. Laing illustrates this with an illuminating analogy. A plane may be *out* of formation but *on course*. "The whole formation may be off course." "If the formation is itself off course, then the man who is ready to get 'on course' must leave the formation" to do so.[14] The person who is out of formation may be "mentally ill"—socially devalued in the eyes of others and Psychiatry—but she may be trying to find the way to get *on course*.

Many of the mad were pioneers venturing into unknown or forgotten realms. We should "learn to accord to so-called schizophrenics who have come back to us [from their voyage into inner space] . . . no less respect than the often no less lost explorers of the Renaissance."[15] We know Columbus was lost, Laing writes, yet we still admire him; after all, even though he was disoriented, he still stumbled on America.

Laing believed that madness was a potential death-rebirth experience. Madness constitutes a descent into the primordial chaos of the inner world, which makes possible a reconstruction of the self. If this experience was not aborted by psychiatry the mad person might be spiritually reborn as a mystic or a prophet; she might transcend normality and attain a new self attuned to God, to the cosmos, a self that was truly sane. As Laing eloquently wrote, "True sanity entails the dissolution of the normal ego, that false self completely adjusted to our alienated social reality . . . and through this death a rebirth . . . and the eventual re-establishment of a new kind of ego-functioning, the ego now being the servant of the divine, no longer its betrayer."[16]

Throughout Laing's life (and after his untimely death in 1989) the psychiatric establishment ridiculed his theories, refused to acknowledge the value of madness, and continued to insist that the mad were "mentally ill," and thus treated them with disdain and pity, often disguised as compassion. In 1987, looking back on his career, Laing said he was "disheartened" by the fact that his writings were continuously misinterpreted and that he had had so little effect on changing the system despite his celebrity in the 1960s and 1970s. It was as if, after all his explanations and clarifications, his message had fallen largely on deaf ears.*[17]

Laing's critics say he "romanticized" the mad. They don't understand that Laing *was* a Romantic who believed that the experience of madness had spiritual value and that people in normal society must reconnect with our own inner worlds in order to overcome the alienation that is driving us out of our minds. *Laing believed that madness could be the path back to sanity—not normality, but true sanity, a higher sanity.* But his work raised a vexing question for those who are critics of society; if the person becomes sane, how can she tolerate living in an insane society? Laing never addressed this question. He did not know how we could change society or if we could.[†]

Psychiatry does not have this problem of how to help the awakened person to live in this society. Its goal is to adjust the person troubled by the insanity of the world to the normal world at all costs. Better to drug him back to sleep. How could it be otherwise? Psychiatry is part of this normal world—even more so today than when Laing wrote (prior to the takeover of Psychiatry by the pharmaceutical companies). If the adult—or child or teenager—becomes maladjusted despite her education for normality, then the task of the psychiatrist, like that of the educator, is to use his tools (from drugs to indoctrination to electroshock) to help the deviant *re*adjust to normal society and return to her state of obliviousness to the horrors of the world.

Despite the lacunae in his work, Laing's perspective provides a philosophical basis for Mad Pride. It buttresses the idea expressed in DuBrul's writings (see chapter 9) that the personality

---

*In a 1989 conversation with Robert Mullan (see *Mad To Be Normal: Conversations with R. D. Laing*), Laing responds, "My work has not made the slightest difference [in Psychiatry]—in fact, it's only entrenched them." Laing was correct; ten years later (after his death), his name was virtually unknown among mental health professionals. If he is mentioned it is to assert (inaccurately) that his theories have now been proven wrong by biopsychiatry.

†Laing said this in seminars I attended and in a discussion I had with him in 1987.

traits that predispose one toward having mad experiences give rise to mystical and transpersonal experiences. The mad have spiritual proclivities—"dangerous gifts"—that reflect an unusual capacity for spiritual experience that should be developed and treated with "care."

Laing's analysis provides a basis for Mad Pride in another sense: *normative standards of spiritual well-being (which include contributing to society and to saving life on Earth) need to be created, which are not based on normality.* A paradigm for spiritual growth is required, which is based on the realization that normality is a condition of alienation, of insanity, that must be transcended if humanity is to survive, if humanity (in the words of The Icarus Project) is to "tap into the true potential that lies between brilliance and madness." Mad Pride is based on the same premise as Laing's books: helping the mad does not mean drugging and coaxing them into a state of "adjustment," but rather appreciating the state of madness for what it is: an existential clearing in the jungle of our insane modern society that potentially leads into the realm of true sanity, which, in the world today, means a state of creative maladjustment.

5

R. D. Laing, John Weir Perry, and the Sanctuary for Visionaries

Laing's ideas on madness were remarkably similar to those of psychiatrist John Weir Perry. Perry was a Jungian psychiatrist and a visionary. Perry did not have Laing's penchant for provocative declarations, and thus he did not become a famous icon of the 1960s' counterculture like Laing or a fierce warrior against Psychiatry like Szasz. Like Laing, Perry was convinced that madness—psychosis—is a natural *process* of spiritual renewal, of psychic reorganization, of spiritual death and rebirth. Perry argued the mad need understanding and sanctuary in order to successfully complete this process.

As the director of an alternative sanctuary for psychotics in the 1970s (called Diabasis) and a therapist who had worked with psychotics for decades, Perry had the evidence to back up his claim that madness was a renewal process. (Laing of course had set up an alternative asylum in London in the 1960s, but due to extraneous conditions the reports of its efficacy were mixed.)[1] Perry and the staff at Diabasis helped successfully guide many psychotics through the inner "journey" of madness. At Diabasis, and at a kindred project—the Laingian-inspired Soteria House—the clients were placed on minimal or no psychiatric drugs, and as a result of this type of support they got better; they did not become chronic patients. Perry found that 85 percent of the clients at Diabasis resolved their "schizophrenic episodes" within two or three months (without medication) and "went on growing" after leaving Diabasis.[2] They did not necessarily become normal, but they did become sane. Perry, quoting Theodore Roszak, described this attainment as a "higher sanity" based on "the knowledge of many realities," not just the one "narrow reality" of normal life but also the realities of the inner world and of supernatural realms.[3]

In 1979 the funding of Diabasis was abruptly terminated. The principle on which Diabasis was based is anathema to psychiatry today—that madness, "psychosis," is not an illness but a natural process that fosters the spiritual evolution of the individual. This principle was succinctly formulated in a short "message" written by Perry and given to every new resident at Diabasis upon admission: "This is not a disease, illness or psychopathology. It is a rich inner experience in a visionary state that may be turbulent and scary at times, sometimes nightmarish and sometimes sublime, yet that's all tending to move toward a goal that is favorable for a better life. We're here to help you with it."[4]

The psychiatric establishment ended *all* funding for facilities based on alternative models in the 1980s.[5] Psychiatrists were no longer going to support sanctuaries for psychotics that were based on the idea that madness was a growth crisis, and they were certainly not going to support residences where patients were not forced to take psychiatric drugs—no matter how much more effective they were than traditional psychiatric treatment.[6] The days of experimentation were over.

The psychiatric establishment was now in effect saying to the kind of troubled young people whom Diabasis had helped, "If you want our help you must accept you are mentally ill, take your medication, and recognize that your 'visions' are hallucinations and symptoms of your mental illness." Innovators like Perry were told that there was no place for them within the public mental health system.

But one of Perry's legacies to the Mad Pride movement was his demonstration that sanctuaries for the mad are viable; they work. Patients from the sanctuaries would get better, even "weller than well" (to borrow a phrase attributed to psychiatrist Karl Menninger). There are, in fact, at least two ideas of Perry's with which most Mad Pride activists agree. First, the experience of madness has value, and second, there should be sanctuaries for people undergoing madness. These sanctuaries, like Perry's, are where madness—the "psychotic episode" as the psychiatric establishment calls it—is treated as a growth experience and where persons are not forcibly drugged.

Ashley McNamara, a writer, Mad Pride activist, and cofounder of The Icarus Project (see chapter 8), wrote that "we live in a society that does not provide any guidance when we're flying or allow any crash space when we're coming back down. . . , a society that will punish us by evicting or incarcerating us if we get too far from the one sanctioned reality: working life."[7] Mad Pride activists like McNamara are encouraging the mad to establish their own self-help groups—to provide guidance and "crash space" for each other. But, of course, they realize that their task is difficult without social and financial support. Nevertheless, successful Mad Pride self-help groups and communities are proliferating all over the world[8] as it becomes clear that Psychiatry is the problem, not the solution.

Perry and Laing both believed that the psychotic episode is not a disease; to the contrary it is a healing or growth process. Laing and Perry believed that psychiatric practices result in aborting the regenerative process and, further, that psychiatric practices induct the patients into "careers" as chronic mental patients.[9] Why does this breakdown/ breakthrough process happen to some people and not to others? For most of his career, Perry theorized that the prepsychotic ego was more impaired, more "pathological," than that of the normal person, and because of this pathology the unconscious attempts to heal the ego by bringing about the regenerative process of psychosis. By the 1990s Perry had revised his theory; now he believes that the self of the "schizophrenic" was not more impaired but more sensitive; her greater "sensitivity" to the pain of others made her more likely to become imbalanced and to undergo a breakdown/breakthrough, to experience the regenerative process of madness.*[10, 11]

Laing also went through a trajectory similar to that of Perry. At first he thought the self of the mad person was more seriously impaired than that of the normal person and thus in greater need of healing,[12] but by the time he wrote *The Politics of Experience* he had come, like Perry did later, to believe that the mad person was more sensitive. Further, the mad person typically had less of a capacity to tolerate the dishonesty and pretense that are endemic to modern life. It is extraordinary that these two psychiatrists had independently undergone a similar evolution in their views and that, furthermore, they both reached the conclusion that it was the mad person's spiritual superiority in certain respects that made her more likely to be launched on a regenerative process (see the discussion in chapter 11).

Laing went further than Perry. Perry stopped just short of Laing's assertion in *The Politics of Experience* that mad persons constituted a spiritual vanguard. Laing repeats this affirmation several times in *The Politics of Experience* (although in his subsequent work he abandoned the theme, as if he feared triggering another storm of controversy). Although I cited this passage earlier, it is worth repeating here. He wrote, "If the human race survives, future men will, I suspect, look back on our enlightened epoch as a veritable Age of Darkness. . . . The laugh's on us. They will see that what we call 'schizophrenia' was one of the forms in which, often through quite ordinary people, the light began to break in the cracks in our all-too-closed minds."[13]

The implication was of course that this process could be of value to everyone and that the mad were charting a way forward that we must follow (though hopefully with less pain and confusion) if we are to overcome the alienation that has driven us to kill each other (under the "legal" guise of war) and to destroy the Earth. (Laing lived in the days

---

*Perry writes revealingly that the persons most apt to undergo a psychotic episode are "usually endowed with a highly sensitive make-up, so that in childhood they were inclined to perceive falseness, defensiveness, and hidden emotions more than others." The family "accustomed to denial" of course did not welcome this perceptiveness and these sensitive individuals were "made to feel in an awkward position."

before global warming and ecocide, but the cold war created an omnipresent threat of mutual nuclear annihilation.)

In Laing as in Perry we find the same two ideas with which most Mad Pride activists, as stated above, would agree. First, the experience of madness has value, and second, there should be sanctuaries for people undergoing madness, sanctuaries where madness—the "psychotic episode" as the psychiatric establishment calls it—is treated as a growth experience and where persons are not forcibly drugged. (These two ideas were convictions that Laing held his entire life; in fact, not only had he run an alternative sanctuary for several years, but he spent his whole life trying—with little success—to get funding to create and maintain other sanctuaries for the mad.[14])

As cited earlier, Joseph Campbell came up with an apt metaphor and analogy—inspired by the work of Perry, with whom he became friends. He wrote that the mad person and the mystic are all in the same ocean, the same "beatific ocean deep," but the mystic and the saint are swimming, while the mad person is drowning.*[15] The reason for the difference, as Campbell saw it, is that mystics (or those who become mystics) are prepared for the ocean; they have usually been raised in or studied a spiritual tradition (whether it be Buddhism or Hinduism or Christianity). They know about the ocean before they venture into it, while mad persons (those who become "psychotic") have no preparation or guidance; in most cases they are not even aware of the ocean's existence until they find themselves immersed in it.

But more and more mad people are learning how to swim in this ocean—the ocean of the "inner world." Psychiatrists try to drag them out, drug them up, and warn them never to go near the water; then they tell them they are incurably mentally ill. "What do we do with our visionaries?" Perry asked in dismay. "When the divine madness takes over them to the point of distress . . . we pull them out of it with isolation and medication to squelch by every means this process."[16]

By creating self-help alternatives to Psychiatry, Mad Pride will

---

*Most, if not all, Mad Pride activists would agree with Campbell that the experiences of madness are often similar if not identical to those of the mystic—that there is something "spiritual" about them.

provide an environment in which the mad can learn to swim. Mad Pride affirms that madness is an "extreme" state, not a state of pathology; it is not a pathological aberration from the natural order, from the benevolent guardianship of nature. It is natural—not pathological— to be maladjusted to this society, Laing asserted. The fact that the mad are maladjusted to society does not mean they are maladjusted to nature, or to the underlying basis of the cosmos.

Mad Pride wants to give the mad the freedom to be themselves, to be maladjusted to an insane world. Many Mad Pride activists feel better merely by working with others to change society; this in itself often enables them to attain a state of creative maladjustment. For many mad people, adjustment to the status quo may not be feasible. It may well be that the only way they can achieve a state of emotional equilibrium is to become the prophets, activists, and spiritual leaders who will endeavor to bring the world closer to the visions they have had and to attempt to help humanity to make the transition to a higher stage of consciousness beyond the status quo.

6

Interview with Chaya Grossberg

Spiritually Informed Social Activism

Chaya Grossberg was a twenty-eight-year-old yoga teacher, poet, writer, and Mad Pride activist when I interviewed her in 2009. She had been one of the leading organizers of Freedom Center for six years, where she ran a yoga group and taught creative writing. In the summer of 2009 she moved to the Bay Area of California, where she got a job at the Alternatives to Med Center helping people withdraw from psychiatric drugs and opiates. After a year the center moved across the state. Grossberg did not want to move; she works now as an intuitive reader, or psychic, and a massage healer. In a letter to me in January 2011 she described her life: "I have been mostly living a simple life in a small studio in the woods and studying my environment and wild herbalism and foraging, as well as [performing in] theater and [doing] creative writing. I am healthy and happy. . . . I spend time every day meditating and writing and eat wild foods almost daily." Her website is http://chayagrossberg.weebly.com.

In the course of our conversation she affirmed most of the

contentions that I listed as explicit or tacit beliefs of Mad Pride movement activists. She seemed to agree with my theory—although she had not thought it out fully—that we are involved in a process of spiritual evolution and that we are currently in an acute evolutionary crisis where the role of the Mad Pride movement is to act as a catalyst for making the transition to a new stage of human development. Like all the activists in this book, Grossberg is one of the creatively maladjusted. Her process of spiritual development can serve as a model for other psychiatric survivors who have not broken out of the psychiatric net and not discovered their identities.

Excerpt from Chaya Grossberg's Keynote Address to National Association for Rights Protection and Advocacy (NARPA), 2005.[1]

I recently went to a training for [patients' rights advocates] that ended with a talent show. I realized that if everyone in the room took their talent and ran with it, we'd have a room full of artists, musicians, and craftspeople rather than people who identify as ADD, manic depressive, and "mentally ill." We could have a roomful of people who know they have gifts and need to nurture their health through exercise, good nutrition, and less toxins. Instead we had a roomful of people on one two or three psych drugs each (with a few exceptions), who smoke a pack a day, and drink a few Cokes and a few coffees. I could see the unresolved hurt under the layers of psych drugs, nicotine, and caffeine. As people worked to speak through the layers, I could tell that their brains were not functioning optimally. When there are problems, do we want to see more or less clearly? This is a question that needs to be asked directly before getting hooked on psych drugs. I know because I have been on those drugs. I know that difficulty. In fact, being on neuroleptics was the only time I identified as having a mental illness. I was unable to think clearly.

To drug people into stability is to take away their essential humanity. Imagine if someone found chemicals that could keep the sky stable—free from too much rain, free from too much sun. Or if the Earth were stabilized so there were no mountains, no deserts, no valleys, no large bodies of water. Just as there is order in the natural world, there is an order in my life, and yours. There are natural forces that I see as spiritual forces, which keep me on track. They keep me in line with my destiny—they guide me to heal myself and others with love and brilliance. I make space for these possibilities. I treat my life as a garden. I must fertilize it, water it, I must take care of it. The bulbs I planted long ago will grow and I plant new ones all the time. Wildflowers grow too—ones I never expected. The whole thing looks messy sometimes.

You cannot afford to withhold your brilliance from the world, even if it is labeled madness. Whatever society calls it, and people will find all different names and explanations, it is your gift and the world needs it. This is what we can think of as passing the torch—taking the risks to show your brilliance and inspire others. For the future generation of activists, that's us. We have a mental health system gone haywire that appears to be capturing people faster than they can be born. When you take the chance and offer your gifts, it is a huge leap of faith. I say this as someone who, like you, is able to take the leaps sometimes. I have much farther to go with sharing my own gifts. And so do you, that is why you are here. I must say "I love you" to myself and to G-d numerous times everyday, and take the leap. I have met many young activists, around the country, and I sense that faith is one of our strongest points.

Grossberg is also a gifted poet. Here is a poem she wrote when she was undergoing the crisis described in the interview. She believes it was a premonition.

Want

Now things are well.
They want to know about my journey.
"Were there rocks?
Were there diamonds?
How did you sleep on the slants of hills?"

All I have in my pockets is quiet, I say
and open my hand to their ear, to their footsteps.

They want to eat chocolate with me,
and dance.
They don't know what these things
mean to me.

If you step on a rock, get a degree in diamonds,
You must hold their weight strong in your ear, in your
　　foot steps.

The world is full of brown and retreat,
purple and history,
clear and mystery.
The world is full of Snickers bars and ballerinas,
hospital potatoes, wheelchairs,
writing and waiting
and watching people work
with the wonton of
Want.

It's been called a wrestle
and wonderful.

I haven't been waiting.
I haven't been watching.
I wrinkle at the wonders,
which has been called a withdrawal.

I call it a wrap, a wash.

CHAYA GROSSBERG

Farber: When you were eight or nine years old, you went to therapy. Your parents—you said in the *Madness Radio* interview broadcast in 2007—were getting a divorce. That was the occasion that made you or your parents decide therapy would be a good idea, right?

Chaya Grossberg: Yes. My mom's a social worker; she believes in therapy; she's very therapy oriented.

Farber: And you basically liked it at first, the therapist and the therapy?

Chaya Grossberg: Yeah. I grew up in New York City and . . .

Farber: (Laughs.) So did I, and I know therapy is a religion here.

Chaya Grossberg: And it's like there's not that much community there. I mean, it's not like growing up in the country or even in the suburbs where people have time. . . . And I think for me having therapy was just having somebody I could just talk to, and that was a really big deal, so it started out being something very positive for me.

Farber: Were you unhappy?

Chaya Grossberg: In some ways I was. My parent's divorce was really hard. And I had a younger brother: it was really hard for him. And me being the older sister, it was also even doubly hard to see it being hard for my younger brother whom I felt really close to, and I felt very protective of him. For me, I wasn't really struggling in terms of school. I always did really well in school.

Farber: It wasn't a particularly acrimonious divorce, was it? They weren't battling for custody over you?

Chaya Grossberg: Well, they weren't battling for custody, because they both wanted joint custody. They both wanted to be part of our lives. Their divorce was *not* pretty. It took a long time. There was a lot of fighting. . . .

Farber: They both thought it was be best for the kids to have joint custody.

Chaya Grossberg: Yes, and they both wanted it for themselves, too. Neither of them wanted the kids all the time. They were both in the same neighborhood, and neither of them had any desire to leave that neighborhood, so my father just moved a few blocks away, and then we went back and forth.

Farber: So you got to high school, and then your therapist persuaded you to take an antidepressant. Was that Prozac, you said, at the beginning?

Chaya Grossberg: Yes.

Farber: And you didn't mind taking it at first.

Chaya Grossberg: Actually I did. I *really* didn't want to at first.

Farber: You said in your interview on *Madness Radio* that it enabled you to socialize more.

Chaya Grossberg: Well, that was *after* I was on it for a while. At first I didn't even want to talk about it. When my therapist suggested it, I would get very upset . . . and my mother wasn't into meds, either.

Farber: You said it was a stigma still at that time.

Chaya Grossberg: Yes, it wasn't the way it is today where like all the kids are all on meds. The main thing was I just had an intrinsic sense that it just wasn't the right thing for me. It just felt to me like it wasn't addressing anything.

Farber: And the thing that you thought needed addressing was the relationship between your parents or between you and your parents?

Chaya Grossberg: Yes, but I didn't think that was the only thing.

Farber: And what did you think was the other part of the problem?

Chaya Grossberg: I was really good in school. So I got into a competitive high school in New York City.

Farber: Which one?

Chaya Grossberg: Stuyvesant. I did not like the competitiveness, and I was also very sensitive socially. I've always been like very sensitive in every way basically. So I guess there's a lot of things that contributed to it.

Farber: You say that now you have a different view of what made you unhappy then than you had at the time?

Chaya Grossberg: I also have even more holistic awareness, so I could say my diet wasn't really that great.

Farber: There were a number of things that were contributing to make you unhappy, so you went on Prozac. You were on it until senior year in high school, right? How would you overall . . .

Chaya Grossberg: Well, what I was saying is when I first took it, it made me kind of manic, like constantly socializing. And it also made me nicer on the surface and just more agreeable with everything. And it also made me less empathetic with other people and very impulsive.

Farber: You must have read Peter Breggin, right?

Chaya Grossberg: Yes.

Farber: I think you referred to him, didn't you, somewhere? Peter Breggin said, about Prozac, it cuts you off from your feelings.

Chaya Grossberg: Yes, it did. I would just say things without thinking, insensitive things to other people, and it gave me more acne.

Farber: And there must have been some feeling of stigma as long as you're on the drug.

Chaya Grossberg: At that time in my high school, there was this underlying sense that everyone had that if you were doing stuff like cutting a wrist—which I never did—you had to keep it a secret or the guidance counselors would find out and make you take meds. (Laughs.) So there was definitely that sense already of "madness" being something that people had to hide and there being a system that would force you into something that you didn't want or hospitalize you.

Farber: That's a little bit different from what I was thinking. . . . Was there any sense that it undermined your self-esteem just taking the drug? That it made you feel you were defective or mentally ill or anything like that?

Chaya Grossberg: I don't think I really felt that way. Partly because it *was* already kind of "in fashion"; you know the way they advertise things, they make them somehow "in fashion." So Prozac was already "cool" or something.

Farber: So the fact that you were on a psychiatric drug wasn't something that made you feel bad about yourself per se?

Chaya Grossberg: Not really; I had a few moments and situations. I got off it in senior year in high school without any problem—on my own. I didn't tell my father that I was on it for a while, a long while. I didn't want my father to know that I was on it or that I had been on it. . . .

Farber: Because. . . ?

Chaya Grossberg: I don't know. I just didn't feel comfortable talking to him about any of my feelings.

Farber: So you were still having a strained relationship with one or both of your parents at this time?

Chaya Grossberg: Yes. My relationships with my parents were strained. There were definitely good parts of them, but they were difficult for me and still can be sometimes.

Farber: Was this through the divorce period?

Chaya Grossberg: Yes. Both my parents were then single parents, living in Park Slope, working full-time. They were very busy, very stressed out, not a lot of support living in a city. . . .

Farber: So then you went off to college. When I knew people going to Hampshire in the seventies, it was sort of a hippie college. Did it have that reputation when you went there?

Chaya Grossberg: Yes.

Farber: Similar to Evergreen?

Chaya Grossberg: Uh-hmm.

Farber: Your first year, you weren't happy. . . .

Chaya Grossberg: Well, at first I wasn't, but then I was. In the middle of my first year of college—this is also a spiritual turning point for me, a mystical awakening. I had already started to become very spiritual in high school. I was into yoga, meditation, and writing, and poetry. I was always very spiritually oriented.

Farber: When you say "yoga" you mean hatha yoga—body stretching. . . .

Chaya Grossberg: Yeah.

Farber: What kind of meditations and things were you reading?

Chaya Grossberg: In high school I was reading books on yoga and meditation, and I also had a class in school called metaphysics, which was an English elective at Stuyvesant. And we meditated every day and talked about all the different types of meditation.

Farber: Did it alter your perception of the world?

Chaya Grossberg: Well, when I did yoga, it did. I definitely entered into blissed-out states from yoga.

Farber: Euphoria?

Chaya Grossberg: Yes, and also writing poetry. That was another really big thing for me, because I've always been a poet. So that also pushed me into mystical states, my poetry. And also I did a *little* bit of psychedelics. I smoked a little pot, and I did mushrooms.

Farber: Did the idea of God enter into this picture at all?

Chaya Grossberg: I think I prayed to God, mostly just when I was in a crisis or something. (Laughs.) At other times too—to give thanks. It was more in my own way; it wasn't in a religious way.

Farber: So it wasn't part of your whole mystical awakening, the idea of God or loving God or providential God or anything?

Chaya Grossberg: I think it was later—in college.

Farber: How did these mystical experiences make the world seem different to you than before—in high school?

Chaya Grossberg: Right. Well, I think it gave me this sense that, first of all that there was something I could do that would make my reality different. With yoga, it was like, "Wow, I can go to this yoga class and then afterward feel entirely different, feel totally blissed out."

Farber: Did the universe seem more mysterious?

Chaya Grossberg: Well, I think the world always seemed kind of mysterious to me: the way that I'm rooted, the way that I'm wired. I think I've always had this kind of sense of faith. Even when things were really bad with my parents, something would happen, some kind of amazing coincidence like a sign from God. Or even, my relationship with my best friend in high school felt like this very spiritual thing, but me and my best friend were really in love with each other.

Farber: You don't mean in a sexual way?

Chaya Grossberg: No. There was a *little* bit of that feeling. It was more like just friendship and loving each other as people. She had a very stable family—she lived right nearby—and whenever my mom would start flipping out at me or something, I would go over to her house, and we'd go for a walk, and I felt this sense of love with her, and we would talk about spiritual things. We'd even talk about psychiatry a lot and debate in our minds or discuss our feelings. We had the same kinds of feelings that I have now about psychiatry, this instinctive sense that it's just not right. (Laughs.) And then the whole poetry thing was a really huge opening for me, because it also made me aware that I had this psychic ability, slightly. It just started to open up in high school, when I would write poetry and this stream of consciousness—images and words—would come into my head out of nowhere.

Farber: Like you were channeling or something?

Chaya Grossberg: Yeah, kind of like that, and even now when I read back on the poetry I wrote in high school, I think I was definitely already getting into these states, mystical states. (Laughs.) It was very *real*. Not real . . . it *was* mystical.

Farber: Okay, let's skip ahead to the college thing. At first you were happy because you met new people, I suppose, and you were away from home.

Chaya Grossberg: I'll tell you about my first year of Hampshire: I met a lot of people, and some of them I resonated with, although the crowd that I got involved with in the beginning of college was not really the right crowd for me. They were the partiers . . . people who are a lot less sensitive than me. They were more into drinking and hooking up with each other and having fun. Then in the middle of my first year of college, I got into a car accident. I wasn't driving, and I wasn't hurt seriously, but the other people in the car were. One or two of them were hurt somewhat seriously. That gave me for some reason this wake-up call: just the experience of being strapped to this stretcher and being lifted up through the sky and being really out of control of everything when that happens.

Farber: When you were on a stretcher, it must have gone through your head that you might die?

Chaya Grossberg: I knew that I was totally unhurt.

Farber: Even when the car was crashing, you didn't have a fear that flashed through your head that something may happen, that you might not live?

Chaya Grossberg: I don't think so. It felt more like a wake-up call. I thought about how one *could* die at any moment, anything *could* happen. I wasn't in that situation that I really could have died. . . . I mean, I *could* have. But since I was wearing a seatbelt in the back seat, there was no fear that I was going to die in that situation. But for some reason it made me feel as if my life wasn't really on the right track.

Farber: After this happened?

Chaya Grossberg: Yes. I started to think twice about things. Okay, well, who are my *real* friends, who do I *really* want to be spending my time with, what do I *really* want to be doing? And why am I wasting my time with these people who aren't my real friends, who are just having fun and being young and partying and having sex with each other. It felt like all of a sudden I lost interest. I lost interest in being popular and fitting in and being part of this group of people that I had been trying to be part of. Then I started to meditate every day and do yoga more.

Farber: What kind of meditation at that time?

Chaya Grossberg: Actually, there was a mantra. I took this class at my college . . . in meditation and yoga. Basically, I just sat. There's a mantra, but I think what I started to do was just sit every day on my own in the morning, just sit in my room for twenty minutes or whatever, just sit and breathe and just focus on my breath. And sometimes I would do it even twice a day, for twenty or thirty minutes.

Farber: And this was before your Buddhist connection?

Chaya Grossberg: This was before I went to that Buddhist center. And just that simple act of meditating every day really transformed me. I became a lot happier and less concerned with . . .

Farber: Did you become detached from the negative thoughts and more able to feel some distance from the kind of thoughts that used to disturb you?

Chaya Grossberg: Yes. Yes.

Farber: Did you know what you were going to do then, or things didn't really gel until you discovered this Buddhist center the following year?

Chaya Grossberg: What do you mean, did I know what I was going to do?

Farber: Well, you said before that you realized you were hanging out with the wrong people and you were on the wrong path.

Chaya Grossberg: Yes, I started to seek out different types of people, different types of friends. I sought out more quiet people, people who seemed more spiritual to me, and also I sought out some people who were involved in activist stuff, because they seemed to care about something besides . . .

Farber: Political, antiwar activism? What year was this?

Chaya Grossberg: It was Hampshire, so all the activists were in the same clique.

Farber: What year was this? Obviously it was before Bush.

Chaya Grossberg: It was '98. I wasn't myself an activist at that time. Like I said, Hampshire's a very small school, so there was probably just a small group of people who were really into activism, and they were all friends of each other. I became more interested in people who seemed to be doing something that had a broader purpose than just themselves.

Farber: Was there anything in particular that you were drawn to changing or bothered by about the world?

Chaya Grossberg: Yeah, there were. But my focus was more on changing things via spirituality as opposed to just via . . .

Farber: Changing things through changing people? Starting through changing the individual?

Chaya Grossberg: Yes, exactly. There was a big Free Tibet group—there were some people who were into Buddhism—it was kind of a cross between being into activism and being into Buddhism, and they would get monks to come to the school and visit. I started to hang out with some of these people; I mostly developed individual friendships with some of these people.

Farber: So you felt better, more of a sense of belonging.

Chaya Grossberg: Yeah, definitely. I became more able to focus on the people that I actually felt connections to and less on the people that I didn't. And also I was still writing a lot, poetry and just writing for school. I always felt very comfortable writing; writing has always been something that has felt natural.

Farber: So the first year of college you had begun the process of finding yourself. What happened the second year? Then you went to the Buddhist center?

Chaya Grossberg: That summer I went to the center—before the second year.

Farber: So was that a major turning point, then?

Chaya Grossberg: Yes.

Farber: In the interview, you said it was amazing at first.

Chaya Grossberg: Yeah, it was. We would meditate for so long each day.

Farber: What kind of meditation?

Chaya Grossberg: It was very simple, like following your breath.

Farber: I did that—Vipassana meditation—years ago, in the seventies. I found that incredibly boring. (Laughs.)

Chaya Grossberg: We would sit and meditate for hours, like three hours a day.

Farber: Was it connected to the Tibetan Buddhists, around Chogyam Trungpa?

Chaya Grossberg: Yeah, that's what it was.

Farber: What was it called?

Chaya Grossberg: Karmê Chöling.

Farber: What year was this now?

Chaya Grossberg: Ninety-nine.

Farber: Yeah, I used to go to that group in New York in the midseventies for about a year. They would talk about how you had to get used to the boredom, sitting for hours watching your breath, but for you it wasn't boring, even at first, right?

Chaya Grossberg: No, I really liked it. I would get into states that were meditative, very blissed-out states of mind, where I was in total peace.

Farber: So just by getting away from your own thoughts you were getting into transcendental states.

Chaya Grossberg: Yeah. Like sitting, just sitting and breathing and my energies would just open up, and I would feel very full and just very much at peace and able to concentrate on my breath really deeply.

Farber: So you were feeling peaceful and happy, and so-called reality seemed different.

Chaya Grossberg: And it was also that I was surrounded by a lot of other people who were doing this in the center, and it was a fascinating summer for me. Also, we were eating all locally grown organic food from the garden. It was just like a fantasy summer. I met this boy there and had this romance. It was also being in the country, being in the country versus the city. . . .

Farber: You felt that you were connected to nature.

Chaya Grossberg: Oh yes, especially because the center was in rural Vermont. There was nothing around us besides gardens and forests.

Farber: Was your conception of life changing as well?

Chaya Grossberg: Oh yes. You see I was brought up Jewish, but I wasn't brought up religiously.

Farber: You said you were culturally Jewish.

Chaya Grossberg: Yes. My parents were very Jewish, but they weren't very religious, and they weren't pushy. They didn't try to push any religion on me or anything. I had decided on my own to have a bas mitzvah. I think that was also part of my spiritual sense that this felt important. But with the Buddhism, my parents thought it was a cult that I was at that summer. (Laughs.) And it did have certain cultlike qualities, in terms of everybody trying to study the same thing and being "Buddhists." (Laughs.) But not real Buddhists, you know, like Americanized Buddhists. It had a lot of positives, but it also led me away from my roots entirely. And another thing, in terms of Judaism: growing up in New York you don't even really realize that you're Jewish and that you're in a minority.

Farber: Yes, I know.

Chaya Grossberg: And out here, there's definitely a good amount of Jews where I am now in western Massachusetts, but you'll definitely encounter people here who've never heard of Yom Kippur or who have never heard of Passover.

Farber: That's amazing.

Chaya Grossberg: There are people who live here who grew up in places where they only knew one Jewish person.

Farber: Wow.

Chaya Grossberg: Yeah, totally. So it's definitely a culture difference, and I didn't really realize that. Since I never had a Jewish identity to begin with, I didn't even think it mattered. I never had a Jewish identity, but now I do. Here in Massachusetts I feel a sense of having to preserve my culture and my religion, and I definitely identify as Jewish.

Farber: In a spiritual way, as well as a cultural way?

Chaya Grossberg: Yeah, totally. And it feels important. And I notice that with some of the other Jews around here—Jews who are not very religious. But basically for me at that time I was totally disinterested in Judaism.

Farber: Well, Buddhists are atheists, right? God doesn't figure in their religious metaphysics.

Chaya Grossberg: That's a good point, because that was actually part of the thing that sort of drove me crazy.

Farber: Really?

Chaya Grossberg: Yeah, because everything was about your own responsibility over your mind. In Buddhism, everything is about how you have to take responsibility. . . . Actually, in real Buddhism that's not true, but in Americanized Buddhism, in the Buddhism that people from America take and decide what they want to take and what they want to leave, it becomes that. I mean, it depends. Some American Buddhist might be worshipping different deities. . . .

Farber: Yes, sometimes Buddha sits in for God in some of the Buddhist groups.

Chaya Grossberg: Right, or there are different deities and different masters. . . .

Farber: Well, of course the major difference is between Mahayana and Theravada or what Mahayanas call Hinayana. Mahayana is more supernatural, and in some of the schools, Buddha is like God. That wasn't something that you studied at the time?

Chaya Grossberg: Well, I did, but for me for some reason the way that I interpreted the religion—the parts that I took from it—were mostly that I had to take responsibility for my mind.

Farber: Right, and you think this is a Westernized version of Buddhism?

Chaya Grossberg: When you take a religion out of its culture, it's dangerous because a lot of religion is culture and there's tradition. For me it was dangerous, because I just took the parts that I took, and then there were other parts that weren't as prevalent or whatever, or I just didn't resonate with as much or something. Even though there were these deities that you could pray to, something about it, I can't quite explain, but something about it—it wasn't *my* religion. I think part of it was that it helped me to feel that I could escape from the difficulties of my life, that had been in my life before.

Farber: Well, I know often when you meditate, these things that seem so difficult become dwarfed, and they seem like trivial. You're supposed to become more "detached" from it. Did you feel you were getting a sense of detachment then?

Chaya Grossberg: Yes.

Farber: That could be therapeutic. Was it then or later that you felt that God was missing from the whole Buddhist picture as you learned it?

Chaya Grossberg: Well, I think the following year, the following summer. So I actually did a one-month meditation retreat that winter. . . .

Farber: Oh, that was the one. You talked quite a lot about that in the interview on *Madness Radio,* about being frightened of doing it and there being the teachers—the monks—who were nervous about you doing it, but they finally allowed you to do it.

Chaya Grossberg: Yeah. So that was a really hard experience for me physically, because I was sick; I was physically sick at that time. I had lost some weight, and for me, thin as I am, losing weight is not an option. (Laughs.) I think partly it was that I was in Vermont, it was the winter, and it was freezing cold out; I spent the entire month just sitting doing nothing inside. (Laughs.) My appetite got lower from just not doing anything, and also the way I was thinking about things: at that time, I was really disconnected from people. I felt so detached, so different, and like I was in another world from other people. My parents had agreed to paid for the retreat for me, even though they didn't really want to. It was another factor, I think, that my parents had a lot of money, and they always basically gave me money. They have always been very generous, and I suppose, like everything parents do, it has had mixed effects on me.

Farber: You talked about before, how the meditation gave you a feeling of happiness and ecstasy. Did you have that during the retreat?

Chaya Grossberg: I think I had moments of it, but for the most part I was struggling a lot. I was not healthy; I had the flu for the entire time. I was struggling just to even be there, just to even stay. Then I got back to college; this is actually when my interface began with the mental health system, when I got back. People could tell when I got back to college that I was really out of it, really not present and not healthy. I would lie on the floor of my dorm feeling I wasn't in my body, so I went to the guidance counselor, finally, because I just felt so scared. I was having panic attacks, and I felt dissociated and terrified. Terrified. I didn't trust anyone. Because in a way I had felt like I was on this path, but then all of a sudden it was like, I didn't trust anyone, I didn't trust any of the people . . .

Farber: The people on the Buddhist path, you mean?

Chaya Grossberg: Yeah, I had felt like I was on this path with Buddhism. I think I felt betrayed by it, because I realized even these Buddhists who are so-called spiritual don't really have any rock-bottom sense of faith or they don't know what to do when somebody is having a really hard time. So, I ended up at the University of Massachusetts psychiatric ward, where I was put on antidepressants. I was disillusioned when everybody at the Buddhist center got scared because I was having a hard time; they didn't have a sense of faith in me, and they didn't have any real wisdom to give me. They just got scared. (Laughs.)

Farber: You had expected them to have more of a sense of faith in you?

Chaya Grossberg: Well, I felt like the spirituality they were practicing didn't have a rock-bottom quality about it. If it did they would have been able to handle my fear. And I started to see the flaws in the whole system that they were following. I don't say that it's wrong for everybody, but I realized it wasn't for me. It wasn't really my path ultimately.

Farber: What were the flaws?

Chaya Grossberg: I think what I had to realize, and actually kind of what you were asking before, was that I had to find God again. Because the Buddhists didn't talk about God. . . . I mean, they did have their sense of protectors and stuff like that, but that stuff was not really resonating with me. It doesn't have to be about anything in particular, in terms of meditating a certain way, for instance, or even thinking a certain way. It just has to be about having faith in my life overall, which for me is more like having faith in God and also not feeling like it was all my responsibility or all *anybody's* responsibility. To me, having faith in God means that I don't have to put all my faith in any other person or in myself or in a guru or in my friends. It's more like an all-encompassing faith that's in just life itself.

Farber: Is it kind of like a Providence that has some kind of role in designing your path or your destiny?

Chaya Grossberg: Yes, totally. I definitely believe that I have a destiny, that my life has a path, that I can't get off of it, and that I couldn't get off of it even if I tried. (Laughs.) And that it's not all my responsibility. . . . I feel like I'm interwoven into the world. . . .

Farber: Let me go back to another question. When you were on the Buddhist path, did you have an idea of where you thought it was going to lead or where you wanted it to lead?

Chaya Grossberg: I guess I just thought that I was going to become enlightened.

Farber: So you had the idea that you would reach the state of enlightenment and that was where you were hoping it would go?

Chaya Grossberg: I kind of felt like I already was enlightened, and I just needed to keep meditating to sustain it. (Laughs.)

Farber: And did it have to do with other people becoming enlightened, too? You know the boddhisattva ideal . . .

Chaya Grossberg: For me at that time it didn't.

Farber: So God didn't come in at that point—when you were taken to the University of Massachusetts and they gave you antidepressants? You weren't thinking then, feeling then the absence of God? That's something you thought about later?

Chaya Grossberg: Yeah, I wasn't thinking about that then, but I was thinking then that these counselors were really insensitive and didn't really know what was going on in terms of the whole Psychiatry thing.

Farber: Did you think maybe psychiatrists knew something that the Buddhists didn't know?

Chaya Grossberg: I went to the counselor at my school because my friend suggested it, because I felt that my life was falling apart. I was having a really hard time, even just concentrating in school or just functioning on a basic level, because I was really dissociated at that time. I was kind of hoping for someone to talk to.

Farber: And how was that?

Chaya Grossberg: Well, the thing was, because I had lost some weight and I was really skinny, I was *really* skinny,—not that I was like anorexic or anything; I wasn't *trying* to lose weight—they were really worried about me. The counselors and therapists just reacted with fear, and I guess I had wanted them to react with kindness and caring about me, but for them it was just fear: "You have to resolve this instantly." I thought they were being impatient and kind of impulsive, which in a way could be understandable, since I was somewhat dangerous and unhealthy, but . . .

Farber: Dangerous to yourself?

Chaya Grossberg: Especially with my weight.

Farber: But you weren't anorexic, you said?

Chaya Grossberg: No. I've never been anorexic in the sense of wanting to lose weight, but I have the type of constitution where if I get overwhelmed or if anything happens that causes me to not eat enough, I lose weight very quickly. And for me, losing five or ten pounds is dangerous!

Farber: You had some kind of an emotional/spiritual crisis that the authorities wanted to "diagnose" as a chronic mental illness." Was that how it was?

Chaya Grossberg: I got different things from different people, different psychiatrists and stuff. But yeah, they basically told me that I was going to need to take drugs for the rest of my life.

Farber: That must have been upsetting?

Chaya Grossberg: No, because I didn't take it seriously.

Farber: Oh, you didn't. (Laughs.)

Chaya Grossberg: I knew at that point that they didn't know what they were talking about. (Laughs.) But I didn't believe in drugs; I never did.

Farber: You mean psychiatric drugs?

Chaya Grossberg: Yes.

Farber: Had you read anything critical of drugs before this happened to you?

Chaya Grossberg: Not that much, no. I was a very natural person. I never liked to take any kind of drug medicine. I've always found that natural things helped better for me. I had a very strong intuitive sense that the drugs would just do me harm.

Farber: You agree that you were having some kind of crisis at the time?

Chaya Grossberg: Yes.

Farber: What were some of the factors that you think were provoking it, besides your disappointment with Buddhism?

Chaya Grossberg: Family stuff and spirituality and more culture shock.

Farber: The culture shock from being at Hampshire?

Chaya Grossberg: Yeah, a little bit. I think that if I had grown up in the country, it might have been easier to me because I was opening up to a lot of things at once—things that I had never really been able to open up to before. Growing up in New York City I didn't have that much connection to the natural world, so even that was kind of a big thing for me. I think mostly though, it was a big spiritual opening, and some of it had to do with a desire to reconnect with Judaism, but not really knowing how. I think as a woman it's hard to understand how to reconnect since most organized religions are pretty much designed by and for men.

Farber: Well, that's particularly true of Orthodox Judaism, right?

Chaya Grossberg: Yes, and I had one friend at Hampshire who had became Hasidic. He grew up Reform, but he . . . became a Lubavitcher. And I really liked him. He was smart and really sensitive and very spiritual. So I would talk to him a lot because he was the only person I knew who identified as being Jewish and was also very spiritual.

Farber: Even during your Buddhist phase you talked to him a lot?

Chaya Grossberg: Well, it was kind of at the turning point that I started talking to him a lot. He was going through a transformation too, because he was slowly but surely becoming really religious. I think he understood my confusion and the struggle I was going through, but not entirely. I knew that, at that time, that it didn't feel like my path, becoming Hasidic. At the same time, I just felt so drawn in, like on the holidays sometimes I would feel this really strong presence of God with me, for so long. I would feel so peaceful and so connected to God that I was practically dysfunctional. I just couldn't bring myself to go to my classes or do schoolwork stuff, because it suddenly seemed like it was kind of pointless. At Hampshire, it's not that structured. Everybody I know that went there really has the sense of not like, "I'm going to conform to the world," but, "I'm going to decide what to do in the world and it will conform to me," kind of thing, you know?

Farber: Yes.

Chaya Grossberg: It fosters a sense of self-direction and autonomy. Which is amazing, but it's also, I think, really hard at that age.

Farber: So did you start praying to God at that point, or what?

Chaya Grossberg: Well, like I said, I always prayed. . . . Not probably at that point, but a little bit later; I had a prayer book, so I would read my prayer book pretty frequently at a certain time. I would just read the prayers as a way of connecting with God.

Farber: So you saw God as creator.

Chaya Grossberg: I think the way that I relate with God is kind of like a guide, a guiding force that's in charge of my life—a guiding force that's in charge of the whole universe, not just my life. Something that's beyond my comprehension. In terms of the creator, there's the phrase from the beginning of the Torah, "In the beginning, God created heaven and earth." But in the real translation, if you look at the Hebrew, there's no separation between God, the beginning, and heaven and Earth. God is both the creator and the creation and the act of creating. So there's no dualism in terms of God creating. . . .

Farber: Oh! You find the same thing in the Hindu scriptures. In Christian mystical thought also, God creates the world out of *himself.* There's not a dualism because there's nothing existing apart from God.

Chaya Grossberg: Right.

Farber: Everything is God. That's a more mystical conception.

Chaya Grossberg: I've always been a mystic. And I think that another thing about the Jewish tradition is this act of questioning and talking about things, as opposed to just taking things verbatim. A lot of the Jewish tradition is about debating different ways of looking at the text.

Farber: Like the Talmud.

Chaya Grossberg: What my friends and I do a lot, my Jewish friends and I, is that—not to say that all my friends are Jewish—we discuss things from our perspective, so I guess in that sense, it's pretty Reform. In western Massachusetts I started to connect with other Jews from different places and developed a Jewish identity. We share a common heritage. For those Jews who were oppressed by the Holocaust, which some of my family was, there are certain common experiences, traumas that get passed down through the generations. Growing up in New York City I did not identify as coming from an oppressed minority group with a traumatic history. Part of it is that we celebrate holidays together, and since we are a minority, it is more "special," we have to make more effort, and there is a need to speak up and preserve our traditions, or who will? But it's mostly on the holidays that our group gets together.

Farber: When you pray do you refer to God as he or she? The Reform books have "he" and "she" now, don't they? Reform *siddur* (prayer books).

Chaya Grossberg: I don't think that God really has a gender at all.

Farber: How would you pray?

Chaya Grossberg: I would never say "he."

Farber: You wouldn't?

Chaya Grossberg: I might by accident. But if I was really thinking about it, I would never say "he." I think if I was writing, I would probably write "HIR," like to represent him/her, but to me God is like a spirit, and there's no real place for gender in that. It's just like God is everything. It's not gender. It's like asking what color God's hair is or if God has a big nose or a small one. It just seems ridiculous. . .

Farber: Although, the Hindus worship God alternatively as father and Divine Mother—just as often as Mother. So this is a daily practice with you?

Chaya Grossberg: Now?

Farber: Yes.

Chaya Grossberg: Prayer, you mean?

Farber: Yes, and whatever other rituals you do.

Chaya Grossberg: I don't do any daily practice right now that's specifically Jewish. I would say I pray almost every day, but it's in different ways, and I don't think any of them are specifically Jewish. Most of them are just my own personal prayer, my own personal connection to God. At this point I don't really bring that much Judaism into it.

Farber: You were taught Hebrew when you were growing up?

Chaya Grossberg: I was taught how to read it. I know what the prayers mean, but I couldn't have a conversation.

Farber: How often do you celebrate the Sabbath?

Chaya Grossberg: There were times when I did celebrate it every week. I celebrate it in my own way every week. I have to work on Saturday mornings . . . but I usually take Saturday afternoons and just do nothing, rest, kind of like do nothing, and that's part of my way of celebrating.

Farber: Do you think there's anything distinctive about Judaism as a religion that differentiates it from Christianity or Buddhism—from Buddhism I think is pretty obvious, but other religions?

Chaya Grossberg: Well, I think there is, but I don't think that's really my expertise. I've studied some other religions. But I don't know that much about Islam or Christianity.

Farber: And how did you come to be shaped? How many people do you meet with on the holidays?

Chaya Grossberg: It totally varies. It's not like a set number or anything. Sometimes if there aren't enough I'll go to synagogue.

Farber: Where you live now, up in Massachusetts?

Chaya Grossberg: Yes.

Farber: Which synagogue? Reform or Orthodox?

Chaya Grossberg: There's a Conservative one in Northampton that I go to sometimes. There's a Reform one in Amherst and another Reform nearby that I go to sometimes. But the interesting thing is that here, since it's not like New York—say, there's one synagogue in each . . . there's not *even* one synagogue in each town—so actually at the Conservative synagogue, there are Orthodox people and there are Reform people. So the Orthodox people have their own room. There's not that much segregation here; all Jews feel that they have a common bond around here, even the Hasidic Jews feel connected to the other Jews.

Farber: Oh, that's different!

Chaya Grossberg: So yeah, it's not like New York, it's very different, and that actually enabled me to learn a lot about Hasidism.

Farber: Did you learn about the Baal Shem Tov and Reb Nachman and Martin Buber?

Chaya Grossberg: Yes. I read some about those people.

Farber: Let's go back to your other run-ins with the mental health system.

The summer before Grossberg's third year in college she had another crisis. She did not want to go back home, but due to financial pressures she ended up back in Brooklyn with her parents. She said in the *Madness Radio* interview that she "had a crisis in the New York City subway station." She ran into a friend who noticed Grossberg was acting strange and "out of it." The friend called Grossberg's family. When she got home, both her father and mother confronted her and told her she needed help.

Chaya Grossberg: I wanted everything to be between me and God. My mom asked me if I wanted to go to the hospital, and I said, "Tomorrow."

The next day when Grossberg refused to go, her mother called the police. Since she was uncooperative, the police put her in handcuffs and escorted her by ambulance to a hospital two blocks away. She was not suicidal. In the hospital she was "shot up" with "major tranquilizers" ("antipsychotics") that made her sleep continuously. After a few days her mother had her transferred to a hospital in upstate New York called Four Winds, which had a backyard and was much nicer.

Chaya Grossberg: In Brooklyn I was treated like a prisoner. At Four Winds it was looser.

Farber: By the way, what were the psychiatric "diagnoses" they gave you?

Chaya Grossberg: I was labeled with various other things from different psychiatrists. In college they said "chronic depressive disorder" or "dissociative identity disorder," and at the hospital they said "schizophrenia" and "obsessive compulsive disorder."

Farber: Yes, there is no reliability to their diagnoses. That is a basic requirement for any scientific validity—reliability, meaning agreement. Those are such demeaning epithets to use to describe a sensitive young woman going through a spiritual identity crisis. Of course, it seems each time they released you, though, they told you to stay on at least one "antipsychotic," and they told you that you would have to be on "medication" for the rest of your life.

At Four Winds there were a lot of people like Grossberg who believed what they were going through was a spiritual experience.

Chaya Grossberg: At Four Winds, there was one guy about seventeen years old who said repeatedly, "It's not a mental illness, it's a spiritual thing," and we talked about God and I forget what else, but lots of our spiritual experiences. He and I and another girl there would chat a lot about how we were not mentally ill but in spiritual transition. Another guy, I sensed he was psychic, and I asked him to write what he thought my job would be in society, and he wrote, "Transformation and healing, guidance and healing. You must walk the path in order to show the way." This guy hardly knew me! I believe a lot of patients' issues stem from problems and lack of communication in the family, and one person gets labeled as the "sick one," and the psychiatrists continue this process of labeling.

At Four Winds they increased the "antipsychotic," Risperdal, Grossberg was taking.

Chaya Grossberg: They always say, "Take your medication." Always "*your* medication," like it defines you.

She decided to stop taking the drugs, "her medications." She said, "This was the beginning of an intense experience. . . . They decided that they wanted to keep me in the hospital and that they had to force me to take medication. So I was going to have a court hearing to battle for my right to refuse psychiatric drugs."

Grossberg was challenging the basis of the system. A patient who refuses to take medication is considered to be "treatment resistant." This makes it impossible for the patient to assert her rights, unless she agrees to do what the doctors command. The assertion of the legal right to refuse treatment is defined as a symptom of mental illness. A patient's refusal to take "medication" could cause financial problems for the hospital: since "medication" is the primary "treatment," hospitals have a difficult time getting reimbursement from the insurance companies if the patient is not undergoing *treatment,* which means taking "her medication." Thus the psychiatrists have a vested interest in pushing the drugs. Grossberg had little chance of winning the hearing because the lower court judges typically defer to the hospital psychiatrists' argument that the patient's reluctance to take medication is a sign that she is too ill and incompetent to make her own medical decisions. This is the ludicrous catch-22. Psychiatrists are convinced that *any* patient who does not want to take her medication is ipso facto "treatment resistant" and thus *incapable* of making competent medical decisions about her body.

Chaya Grossberg: I did not want to live on medication. I wanted to show it's important to fight for your rights.

Grossberg's mother realized if her daughter lost the case she could spend a long time in a state mental hospital, so she went to the hospital, signed her out, and drove her back home. Most patients do not have parents who could or would rescue them. In spite of Grossberg's discontent with her parents, they acted in this instance in an appropriately protective manner. On the other hand, it was Grossberg's determination to fight for her rights that obviously prompted her mother to remove her from the hospital.

Grossberg went back to live at her father's. She wanted to move into her own apartment, but her parents insisted she was not well enough.

Thus they all decided that the following January Grossberg would go to Windhorse, an expensive alternative Buddhist treatment facility ($40,000 a year) where clients are placed with housemates and supervised by a team of therapists. I was not surprised by what she revealed (later this chapter) about the Buddhist "alternative" because I had read the book by its founder Ed Podvoll, *The Seduction of Madness,*[2] and was disappointed to discover that he was as committed to the idea of mental illness (psychopathology) as Freudians were.

Podvoll's approach was antithetical to that of Laing and Perry (see chapter 5), who believed "psychosis" was a natural healing process. He failed to appreciate the potential value of madness as a life crisis that fostered a process of spiritual growth; he saw it only in pejorative terms. Podvoll used Buddhist terminology but was convinced that madness was essentially a state of mental illness. (One often finds a prejudice in Buddhism against visionary states, which are seen as obstacles to enlightenment.) He did, however, believe it was possible to recover from "psychosis," to get off medication, and thus his approach constituted an alternative to standard treatment.

At Windhorse, Grossberg was placed once again on three psychiatric drugs plus a sleeping pill, Ambien. She said that she felt the therapists there were always talking to her parents behind her back. She felt tired and fuzzy and had a fever for three months—due to the drugs, she realized later, but at the time she thought she had "chronic fatigue syndrome," an autoimmune disease. At this point Grossberg had a dream that she believed was a message to her to get off the drugs, particularly Risperdal, an "antipsychotic"; she does not remember the specifics of the dream. She had a second dream that indicated she should get off the Risperdal gradually. (All of the critics of the use of "antipsychotics" believe withdrawal should always be gradual.)[3]

She started to reduce the Risperdal until she was off it and the fatigue symptoms had faded, but she still thought she needed the antidepressant and that she would have to be on it her entire life. "I was convinced at Windhorse that I was mentally ill."

It was at this time that a critical event occurred in Grossberg's life. She was walking in the street one afternoon in Northampton, and she happened to pass a Freedom Center "speakout" against psychiatric oppression. Grossberg stopped to listen, and she talked to a woman who told her that she had been on twelve psychiatric drugs and that now she was completely free of them. Grossberg knew if this woman could get off twelve drugs, she could get off a few. The dreams and the meeting with the people from Freedom Center marked a turning point in Grossberg's life—the transition from "mental patient" to social activist and spiritual teacher.

Grossberg "knew" she had to go back to Hampshire the following fall. She knew she had to get off the drugs to do well in school. Grossberg finished at Hampshire in several months and received her degree, but it was a struggle to do well in school while she was still reducing the drugs and could not think clearly a lot of the time.

Chaya Grossberg: Over time I got off every single drug I had ever been on. It took about eight months to get off of everything and was very difficult. Risperdal, Xanax, and Effexor were the hardest. Prozac and Buspar were the easiest for me. Ambien was hard too; I went over a week without getting a full night's sleep while I was reducing some of these. The Risperdal withdrawal made me feel more insane than anything else ever has. The Effexor withdrawal made me lose my appetite, feel nauseated, and basically be unable to get out of bed for days. But most of the withdrawal was acute and short-lived. I was surprised to feel fairly sane, energized, and "normal" once they got out of my system after a week or two. Freedom Center people helped a lot, especially in offering a sense of community after I had been isolated for so long.

By the following spring I was very involved with Freedom Center. Freedom Center was the bridge for me, and I knew my story could help other people, and that made me feel good. Also I was doing a lot of writing because I finally had my mind back. My parents became very supportive. My father is practically a Freedom Center activist. He reads their website almost every day.

Farber: You said in the *Madness Radio* interview there's a danger in trying to deny the past. What do you mean? Well, you're not trying to deny the past anymore, right?

Chaya Grossberg: Well, maybe I was trying to forget the past. Now I don't really try to deny or forget the past. My brother and I sometimes talk about our past, our childhood.

Farber: Does he agree it was difficult?

Chaya Grossberg: Yeah, actually, he talks about it in a much more exaggerated way than I do.

Farber: Is it any more resolved today than in the past?

Chaya Grossberg: Sometimes I have conversations with my mom about the past. We had one this week that was pretty good, but it's hard to tell. She can be really understanding and kind and compassionate one day, and then the next day it seems to upset and scare her so much, or she just isn't open to it and perhaps I am not either. I don't always feel I have the skills to talk with them about it in a way that doesn't upset me. With my dad, I don't think I've ever really been able to talk to him about the past; I guess I've always been too scared. Right now, I'm financially independent from my parents. My parents have a lot of money and—it has had its plusses and minuses. If I were to say I am not grateful for it, that would be a lie, but right now, I don't accept any money from them, and that helps me to be freer.

Farber: Maybe he's less controlling than he would have been when you were eighteen or nineteen or whatever? Neither of them remarried?

Chaya Grossberg: My mom's about to get remarried. My dad—I would say, he's probably with the person that he'll be with.

Farber: So he has a girlfriend.

Chaya Grossberg: Yeah. They've been together for a while, I think they'll probably . . .

Farber: But that hasn't improved your relationship with them, them recoupling with other people? It sounds like it's somewhat more resolved now, no?

Chaya Grossberg: It's hard to say "resolved." Yeah, I don't think it will ever be 100 percent resolved. I don't even know what that would be. But

I feel like in terms of the mental health stuff, it's resolved. They don't think I'm mentally ill.

Farber: And they did for most of this period of time, right?

Chaya Grossberg: Yes.

Farber: That's a big change. You spend a lot of your time now with Freedom Center, trying to save people from getting involved in psychiatric hospitals, getting involved in the mental—I call it the "mental death system." Keeping people out of hospitals, getting them off of drugs, things like that?

Chaya Grossberg: Well, there are different things we do. A lot of the stuff that I do is educational. I speak at conferences, sharing my story and sharing my perspective.

Farber: Yes.

Chaya Grossberg: Everybody in the Freedom Center has their own little piece of it that they take on, and that's the part that I like the most: speaking to large audiences of people about what it's really like and what happened to me and what I've seen. I find that to be the best role for me. We also do organizing events with speakers and a lot of other things.

Farber: So then what do you think are the most destructive things that are done in hospitals; what should be done?

Chaya Grossberg: In my experience, hospitals have always forced or coerced me into taking many drugs that destroyed my health and made me tired and apathetic so I could be easily controlled. Also, the hospital environments were loud and stressful, populated with very highly drugged and traumatized people, and staff were disinterested in anything but control of the environment.

I would like to go to a hospital, if I were distressed perhaps and if it were a very different kind of hospital. I would go to one where there were many options for treatment, none forced, but all available—a hospital that offered lots of time in nature; fresh food of very high nutritional value; meditation groups; writing groups; art groups; one-on-one talks with kind, loving counselors who are spiritually oriented; massage, yoga, and exercise opportunities; acupuncture; nutritional counseling with supplements available; herbalist consultations with herbal preparations available; prayer groups; and quiet time to rest whenever needed. I would go to a hospital where others who have been through a breakdown/extreme states/trauma/spiritual transformation and are now living highly healthy lives made up much of the staff. I would go to a hospital that, of course, let me talk to friends and family on the phone and have visitors. I would go to a hospital that I could check out of when I felt ready to.

Farber: Do you believe in a messiah? Judaism was the first Western religion to envision the resolution of the suffering of humanity and the Earth in a messianic age of cosmic harmony. There has always been a prophetic tradition in Judaism that said the Jews could help—through righteous deeds, through *tikkun*—to create the conditions for the messianic age or the return of the Messiah. Is that part of being Jewish for you?

Chaya Grossberg: As for the messianic era, it reminds me of what other traditions call the Golden Age or even the end of the world, like the 2012 prophesies. In a way, total harmony would be heaven, and it is hard to imagine what one would do in a world without any problems. The words *paradox* and *parabola* come to mind. *Paradox* because everyone wants peace and to be free from strife and suffering, but when I think of life that way I wonder what my purpose would be, or anyone's. And *parabola:* like we get closer and closer to perfect peace but never quite reach it? In a way that seems more heavenly since it does not equal the end of the world. But I am also open to the idea that eventually we will all be ready to let go of the world as it is and enter into a mystical, harmonious musical reality where everything flows in ease and beauty forevermore. In a world like this there is no duality whatsoever in anyone's consciousness, so all is one and there can be no "righteous deeds" for everything is already right. In the world right now, I feel that spiritual people, and even less spiritually aware people, have a vision or guiding force in their lives toward this ideal.

Grossberg's story is a powerful invalidation of the narratives scripted by the mental health establishment. Had Grossberg not had such strong inner convictions she would be a chronic mental patient today, hooked on psychiatric drugs and convinced that she had a "bipolar" or "schizoaffective disorder." (Since she is educated she probably would not have been given the most stigmatizing of all diagnoses, "schizophrenic.") Instead, she is a teacher and a striking example of a person who is creatively maladjusted.

From the beginning of her transition, Grossberg felt she was on a path and that she was "guided" by a higher power. If so, it seems to be that she was guided to a state of creative maladjustment. She is not one of those persons who can easily fit into society the way it is. When she first got to college, it did not take her long to sense she did not "belong" with those students who only wanted to party and have fun. She was drawn both to spirituality and to social activism.

This is a hallmark of many of the emerging leaders in the Mad Pride movement. They reject the idea of a dichotomy (or a conflict) between social activism and spiritual self-transformation. There are exceptions, of course. Caty Simon (see chapter 7) tended to see "spirituality" as a form of escapism. Most of the "leaders" of Mad Pride—Sascha DuBrul, David Oaks, Chaya Grossberg, Will Hall[4]—differ from those on the secular left who think spirituality is escapism, as well as from some associated with the "New Age" movement who think any form of protest, of contestation of the power structure, is an expression of "negative thinking." Increasingly, Mad Pride leaders are fusing social activism and spirituality.

Grossberg underwent some kind of transition after she went off to college that led to multiple hospitalizations. Since I know her account only, the list of "symptoms" in the story above is short. (I do not know the psychiatrists' version or her parents' version.) However, it is clear from Grossberg's account that she underwent acute anxiety that became panic at times and that many of the psychiatrists and other mental health professionals who saw her regarded her as "psychotic"—although she did not report any "hallucinations." We know that at the time she was and still is intensely interested in spiritual issues. Psychiatrists usually consider a keen interest in spirituality in and of itself as a danger signal of psychosis.[5] I would guess that Grossberg also exhibited some forms of bizarre and unusual behavior in addition to what she described. Why is she not a chronic mental patient today? Why is she not dependent on psychiatric drugs in order to function? Virtually every psychiatrist she saw, including the ones at Windhorse, told her she would need to be on medication for the rest of her life. This in itself is a damning indictment of the system.

What caused Grossberg's problems? What caused her recovery? Clearly there were multiple factors. On the one hand Grossberg was going away to college, she was leaving home in an existential as well as literal sense; this is a critical and often difficult phase in the life cycle.[6] During this phase if there are problems from the past they often resurface. This is a time when many young people have breakdowns, "psychotic episodes." If they resolve their problems and successfully complete this phase of the life cycle—if they make a break*through*— they will have established a basis for a robust sense of personal identity.[7]

Many young people do not complete the transition because at the time of the breakdown they are placed in the mental health system, where they are inducted into careers as chronic mental patients. Many young people are unconsciously scapegoated at this time by parents who fear their children's independence. This scapegoating would usually not succeed without the help of the mental health system. In Grossberg's case whatever tendency her parents felt to scapegoat her was resisted, due partially to Grossberg's own persistence (despite her pitfalls) in persevering and establishing her own identity—despite the efforts of the mental health system to incorporate her into their own narrative of a chronically defective person.[8] Despite Grossberg's criticism of her parents and despite lingering conflicts, they ultimately supported her independence. They supported her in becoming her own person. This is rare among parents of young people who have been psychiatrically labeled; they usually follow the lead of the psychiatrists, who, as stated, are intent on transforming the person into a patient.

The process of becoming independent probably would have been smoother and easier for Grossberg had there been genuine family therapists to help her and her parents communicate to each other and negotiate their conflicts. I was trained as a family therapist by Salvador Minuchin and Jay Haley, and I know how family therapy can work to correct family "dysfunctions" while reversing the scapegoating of the most sensitive member as "mentally ill."[9] However, by the late 1990s when Grossberg was hospitalized, genuine family therapy had been replaced by the so-called psycho-educational model of family therapy that is based on teaching the entire family, including the patient, to accept and cope with the patient's putative "mental illness." This, of course, reinforces the scapegoating process by disguising it as a benevolent paternalism, and it inculcates the family with the sense of the importance of uniting to take care of the "sick" patient. Thus the family's own "dysfunctionality"—its danger of splitting—is suppressed by the focus on the patient. This usually enables the family to survive while suppressing an awareness or resolution of its conflicts.[10]

In the lives of persons who escape from Psychiatry there is often a fortuitous or synchronistic encounter. David Oaks encountered the Mental Patients' Liberation Front in Cambridge. Grossberg encountered Freedom House at an even more critical point in her life. It enabled her to complete her transition and find support in taking that last decisive step—of getting off psychiatric drugs and trading the identity of a mental patient for that of a social activist and spiritual teacher. As we will see in the next chapter, for Caty Simon the encounter with Freedom House was also serendipitous.

Grossberg's resolution of her crisis also involved her redefinition of her spiritual identity. The "New Age" Judaism she embraced provided a culture, a community, and a spiritual practice that gave direction and stability to her life. It provided her life with a sense of spiritual gravity, of "bedrock faith" (to use Grossberg's term from the interview above), and a relationship to the infinite, which is essential for those who are not philosophically satisfied with the glib materialism of modern society or with the various secular philosophies of those modernists or postmodernists who believe that the only authentic philosophical stance is based on a metaphysical defiance of all "external" authority, including "God"—on atheism.

However, atheism does not provide a strong foundation for faith in life because it—typically at least—answers the "fundamental question" of Einstein ("Is the universe friendly?") with the assertion that the universe is a mere accident, an absurdity, and it thus becomes a self-fulfilling prophecy. Grossberg's embrace of Judaism helped her to cultivate awareness of the "trans-sensible" (beyond the senses) reality of the Infinite, the reality of the Transcendent, of the holy and loving God of which the world of perception is a pale, albeit sacred, reflection.

7

Interview with Caty Simon

The Communitarian Vision

aty Simon is a twenty-eight-year-old activist in the Mad Pride
movement. She has been affiliated with Freedom Center
since 2003.

She wrote in 2005:

Freedom Center is the area's only group run by and for people
labeled with "severe mental illnesses." We call for compassion,
human rights, self-determination, and holistic alternatives. One
can't say enough about what a difference it makes to work through
one's problems among peers rather than trying to solve them within
a hierarchical model.

None of these [therapists], even the best of them, helped me
get better, ultimately, because not only did therapy undermine me
in the myriad ways listed above, it was simply ineffective. What I
needed was a community of concerned, socially active people to
become engaged with and learn how to relate to, whereas therapy

locked me in a room with one bourgeois professional with whom I had a totally artificial relationship who wanted me to become more socially *adjusted*. Members of the Freedom Center support group see each other every week. Every week, we listen to each other's problems, and offer support, humor, and advice. We do each other little favors the way every interdependent community does. We celebrate each other's successes and mourn each other's losses.

In this way, people labeled with severe "mental illnesses" who are used to nothing but isolation, get to experience what being a part of a vibrant, living community is like, that is, what being truly cared about is like.[1]

Although Simon was diagnosed as "psychotic" she did not have any visionary or mystical experiences, unlike the other activists interviewed. She did not see angels or feel a sense of God. She stated, "I'm as close as an agnostic could be to being an atheist." She was keenly aware that most people in the Mad Pride movement do have a spiritual worldview, but she said, paraphrasing Marx, "I don't really seem to align with that. It quickly becomes an opiate of the people—any mystical tendencies." (Of course, it is a thesis of this book that mystical experiences do not necessarily undermine social activism but, to the contrary, can predispose persons toward embracing a vision of radical social-spiritual transformation.) Unlike the other interviewees, Simon did not believe her emotional conflicts had initiatory significance.

Yet Simon is certainly not unrepresentative of Mad Pride activists, some of whom like her have no interest in spirituality and have had no mystical experiences. Based on my experience with Mad Pride activists as well ex-mental patients over the past twenty years, I believe that secular activists are a minority within the Mad Pride movement. Of the six mad persons I interviewed, one is secular and the others are intensely spiritual—two were not actively involved in the movement. This is probably typical of the composition of the population of former "mental patients."

Because Simon is a rebel and was a victim of Psychiatry, she identifies with the mad and with outsiders in general. Despite her secularism there *is* a messianic strain in her thought: she consistently defines herself as an "anarcho-communist," and she eloquently describes her vision of community in terms antithetical to a capitalist society based on the apotheosis of competition. The kind of competition prevalent in normal society is unrestrained by a sense of the unity of humanity and/or the interconnectedness of all life and is leading to the destruction of the fabric of social life and of the ecosystems of the Earth. When I asked Simon how she expected this ideal could be achieved, she acknowledged that she had no idea. (I did not include this exchange in the interview below.)

I think Simon's story is exemplary because it illustrates very clearly two of the contentions of this book: first, the superiority of collective self-help to therapy, and second, that there is no "need" for any person to take the more powerful psychotropic "medications" (e.g., "antipsychotics") on a regular basis; these drugs, particularly when taken over the long term, are harmful. Simon corroborates Dr. Stastny's point: the drugs are part of a "package deal" (see chapter 1). Thus not only was Simon debilitated by the drugs, but she spent critical years of her youth convinced her problems were a result of mental illness. This severely undermined her self-esteem.

Psychiatric drugs are necessary for those who believe in them—as I try to show in my analysis of Sascha DuBrul (see chapter 9). This is because just as they function as a placebo, so does giving them up activate fears and expectations of going crazy. That can become a self-fulfilling prophecy. Furthermore, as Dr. Stastny points out, the longer one stays on these drugs the more difficult it is to give them up—the more debilitating are the withdrawal effects. On the other hand, my interviews show that even the most severely troubled patients were able to break the habit—if they stopped before they had been on the drugs for years. Those I interviewed who got off the drugs were those who were skeptical about them in the first place.

Like everyone I've met in the Mad Pride movement Simon believes that society is insane. She agreed that those who get labeled psychotic tend to be persons who find it more difficult than others to adjust to normal society. Like every activist in this book, Simon is one of the creatively maladjusted.

Caty Simon: I was diagnosed when I had a very typical situational breakdown caused by a lot of pressures of adolescence. I was a daughter of an immigrant family—a Russian Jewish family—who immigrated in 1981, the year I was born. Basically, like a lot of immigrant families, there was a lot of pressure to succeed in the new world.

Farber: Both your parents were Russian Jews?

Caty Simon: Both my parents were Russian Jews, and as with many Jewish families, of course there was a really huge focus on academia and academic success; also, my parents had belonged to the Russian intelligentsia, a class that very much emphasized academic success as one of the few markers of basic personhood—of success as a person.

Farber: When you say Russian intelligentsia, you mean your parents were artists and writers?

Caty Simon: My father was an engineer and my mother was a journalist, and they both had master's degrees from very good schools. They would have gone to the best schools had anti-Semitism not blocked them from admission in Russia. My mother had become very interested in reconnecting with her religious history and origins, and she became an Orthodox Jew. So typically, she then sent my brother and I to a private Orthodox Jewish high school. It was a great school in many ways; it was from the Modern Orthodox Jewish sect, which meant that there was equal focus on learning Jewish texts and on secular curriculum. It was a ten-hour school day. It was also a school that was very much focused on academic excellence as well, and it sent a really high proportion of graduates to the Ivy Leagues. The problem was, here I was, this budding—I was a bisexual . . .

Farber: How old were you at the time you were identifying as bisexual?

Caty Simon: I was in that school from the time I was in fifth grade, but as I got into middle school, then I was a bisexual, human-rights-oriented feminist, in a misogynistic, homophobic environment.

Farber: How did you become a bisexual human-rights feminist?

Caty Simon: Well . . . I was a feminist basically from consciousness. I remember Russian culture, although it allows women more freedom in terms of their careers, it can also be very misogynistic, and I think I reacted badly to that very early on. So I had feminist leanings from the earliest that I can remember. It was the same thing in terms of the human rights movement.

Farber: When did you start thinking?

Caty Simon: I always kind of gravitated towards those things, and in terms of coming out to myself as bisexual that was around fourteen or fifteen, although I probably had stirrings about that earlier. But I remember even as early as thirteen—this was the kind of place it was—I was dragged into the principal's office to talk about, and this was the word he used, my "heterodox" beliefs and how they were threatening to the school.

Farber: What in his opinion did heterodox beliefs consist of?

Caty Simon: Probably just questioning certain religious tenets. I don't really remember everything, but it was also that they wouldn't have treated me this way if I hadn't been the relatively poor daughter of a Russian Jew.

Farber: There was prejudice among the American Jews?

Caty Simon: There was definitely prejudice toward people who had come later toward religion and definitely classism disguised as religious snobbishness.

Farber: So was this upsetting when you were taken before the principal?

Caty Simon: Yeah, it was pretty upsetting because in general I was kind of an outcast there.

Farber: How old were you when your mother put you in this school?

Caty Simon: I was in fifth grade.

Farber: So before that you more or less got along?

Caty Simon: Before that I was kind of a geekish, bookish nerd, but I never felt ostracized in particular. I just stayed to myself more often because I liked reading books at recess and picking my nose.

Farber: Were you reading adult books in fifth grade?

Caty Simon: I read all sorts of books from a very early age. I was a pretty precocious kid.

Farber: So it was traumatizing being placed in this new school.

Caty Simon: I don't know if I would used as strong a word as traumatizing, but certainly ultra-shock and it was difficult. I'm just building up to the things that kind of came to a head when I was fifteen years old—the time that I got my psychiatric diagnosis. It was a ten-hour school day and one of the ways that I could redeem myself from being a Russian-Jewish scholarship kid was to get all A's. My parents wanted me to achieve academically, but I found that my values were in harsh contrast to the school, so I had to get away a lot. I sought out these artistic, booky kids from the public school nearby, and I had this huge social life outside of school, and I also had these kind of Virginia Woolf-esque aspirations to be a writer and I forced myself to write a thousand words a day. . . .

Farber: Was Virginia Woolf a person you'd read or you were modeling yourself on?

Caty Simon: One of the people, certainly, and it was important in another context because I was reading a lot of modernist fiction and I was getting all these messages about how, in order to be a true artist and/or writer and/or genius, you had to have a touch of madness. If you weren't like Virginia Woolf and didn't hear the birds singing in Greek, you weren't truly brilliant.

Farber: Where were you getting this, and from whom?

Caty Simon: Just from reading, from reading about Byron, Woolf, all writers that had gone mad; madness seemed to be an inextricable part of being this writer that I wanted to be. Also, I was in this slightly sexually abusive relationship with—starting from that time that I was twelve to the time that I was fifteen—a guy that was eighteen when I was twelve because I guess I was really lonely and he took me seriously intellectually. A lot of times that is what a precocious teenager will want more than anything else. I was putting my energy into so many different places—in order to get all A's and to continue this relationship and to have a social life outside of school and to write a thousand words a day. I guess I made the immature teenage decision that in order to fit this all in, I had to dispense with sleep: to do this ten-hour school day and four hours of homework and then everything else. Of course we've seen in studies that sleep deprivation causes all the symptoms that the DSM labels mania—especially in a conflicted, young, developing teenager.

Farber: Were you also conflicted about sexuality or not?

Caty Simon: Well, I was conflicted about my sexuality's place in my religion, and even though I was really in violent kind of disagreement with a lot of the tenets of the religion I was in, it was the only community that I really knew. So owning up totally to my queerness and to my feminism was then to force myself outside of the only belonging that I had. So all of those things kind of came to a head, and I made a number of flimsy, very by-the-book suicidal ideation cries for help kinds of things—though I never actually made a serious suicide attempt. I would swallow a few pills of aspirin and drink a few sips of vodka and then say I had ingested much more than that. I didn't actually think that they would send me to the hospital; if I had known a way to talk to authority figures or just someone who could guide me about what was really bothering me, then maybe I wouldn't have done any of those things, but what happened was then I got sent to these juvenile wards.

Farber: Juvenile psychiatric wards?

Caty Simon: Yes, because they thought I was suicidal and because the doctors didn't particularly like arguing with a pedantic, precocious, argumentative teenager.

Farber: Were these doctors in the hospital, or did they take you somewhere?

Caty Simon: Yeah. It was in-patient first of all, after these suicidal calls for help.

Farber: Just the pills?

Caty Simon: I took pills, but like I told you I would take a few pills and drink a few sips of vodka and pretend that I'd taken the entire bottle. I didn't realize I'd be put into this brutal, oppressive . . .

Farber: Were you able to articulate to the psychiatrist, like you're articulating now?

Caty Simon: Well, I didn't totally realize—a lot of those things were subconscious—the conflicts that I was having. What I was able to articulate was this strong defiance—that I wasn't crazy—which obviously irritated them to no end, and obviously I could cogitate fairly quickly, and with the manic symptoms that were provoked by extreme sleep deprivation my thoughts pretty much raced too, and because I argued with them, they immediately said something like, "Well she's either paranoid schizophrenic or has bipolar disorder, but it's too soon to tell." I stayed in three different juvenile wards for a period of a week each.

Farber: In which hospitals?

Caty Simon: Once in Charles River Hospital that no longer exists, and the second two times I went to Westwood Lodge in Westwood, Massachusetts. Charles River I think was in one of the suburbs of Boston. In Charles River I was immediately put on Zyprexa, and I noticed that every single kid there regardless of their diagnosis was put on Zyprexa. Zyprexa dulled my thinking and deadened my intellect, and that was what I'd been taught to see as the core part of myself.

Farber: Did they put you on Haldol or . . . ?

Caty Simon: No, but an atypical antipsychotic was enough, and I think they did shoot me up with Thorazine one time as a disciplinary measure; that was always in the background as a threat. In Charles River Hospital I think it was the first time that I realized that in certain situations people could have absolute power over you and could hurt you and there was nothing you could do about it; as a minor I had no rights.

Farber: Did they think you were really suicidal?

Caty Simon: Sure they did, but the worst thing was I saw a twelve-year-old girl get raped by another inmate, a seventeen-year-old boy. Witnessing that rape wasn't the worst thing; it was the staff's response to it. They took us into a room and started lecturing us about personal contact and about not letting our desires get a hold of us, and they didn't seem to acknowledge that it was rape. The twelve-year-old girl was sitting in the corner crying, and finally a staff member said, "If you can't stop acting out and behaving inappropriately, then you're going to have to be limited to your room." It seemed like their huge concern was of her being pregnant; they immediately sent her for a pregnancy test. They had absolutely no concern about the trauma she might have suffered, at all. Everything we did was because we were just misbehaving, horrible children or our diseases were controlling us like demonic possession. Everything that happened was both our fault *and* everything was a symptom of our illness . . . so even if we were victims, we were to blame.

Farber: Yes, I see, you were both sick and bad, both mad and bad.

Caty Simon: Yeah, exactly. It's not like our sickness removed us from responsibility or from blame. So the twelve-year-old girl was being blamed for not being able to control herself, for not being able to stop a perfectly reasonable reaction to having been violated.

Farber: And this was what year, in the '90s?

Caty Simon: It was 1996.

Farber: Supposedly a more liberal and enlightened time.

Caty Simon: Yeah, and this was not a state hospital, it was a private hospital; my parents' insurance paid for it.

Farber: Did you tell your parents about this incident?

Caty Simon: No, I didn't. At the time I just felt betrayed by them, and I didn't feel that I could reach out to them.

Farber: But you're saying that had you told them, they would have at least been shocked by what you said and angered at the hospital?

Caty Simon: I honestly don't know. I don't know how the hospital would have spun it, and they had the weight of authority and I didn't. I was just one teenage girl who was diagnosed as defective, and they were a system that had all sorts of PR-spun reasons for what they did.

Farber: This was one of the most traumatizing features of being in the hospital, the rape?

Caty Simon: Yeah, that and just the general sense of being totally discredited, having no rights, and being chemically imprisoned.

Farber: It sounded like you didn't believe . . . the diagnosis?

Caty Simon: I fought the diagnosis at first, but again, I was just one teenage girl against this whole system. . . .

Farber: First you were afraid that you were mentally ill in a serious way?

Caty Simon: No, no. At first I fought the diagnosis, but then I changed. I succumbed to this idea that there was something inherently wrong with me.

Farber: At first you fought it.

Caty Simon: Right, at first I fought it, and that's what gave me an even worse diagnosis, because they saw my fighting as denial. . . .

Farber: Yes, they call that noncompliance with treatment, which they see as part of the illness. . . .

Caty Simon: But then, like I said, I was just one teenage girl against not only a system that bought into this biomedical model, but an entire culture. Around that time, Prozac was seen as the nectar of the gods.

Farber: Yes, exactly. That was around the time the book *Listening to Prozac* by the psychiatrist Peter Kramer was published, and he gushed over Prozac like it was going to usher in the millennium.

Caty Simon: Yeah, that's around when it came out, and it was just scary; everybody saw mental illness this way, and nobody would have listened to me, even outside of the psychiatric system.

Farber: You mean, you couldn't have gone to anyone you knew and said this is too much pressure for me at this school?

Caty Simon: I couldn't have said that because I didn't know that I wanted to leave the school; it was the only community I knew. Like I said, a lot of these things are subconscious. Otherwise I think I could have just articulated what my problems were without staging these fake suicide attempts.

Farber: And you might have been successful and found a counselor who understood without being put on psychiatric drugs?

Caty Simon: Right. It *could* have happened, certainly.

Farber: Did you believe in God at that time also?

Caty Simon: I tried to make myself believe in God, so I could fit in, so I could stay in this place. On the one hand it was really intoxicating for an intellectual teenager: you got a chance to study the Torah, which was much more sophisticated than any secular stuff that was offered to teenagers, and it was the only community I knew. I thought that it was me, that something was wrong with me and that I needed to force-fit into the school, and I wish I could learn how to do that. I didn't know that I needed to leave the school, until of course I got expelled—for not doing my schoolwork.

Farber: What was the timing of this?

Caty Simon: I was locked up for a week each time: three times between the ages of fifteen-and-a-half and sixteen. Then I was expelled the last year of school.

Farber: And at the end of it you believed you were manic-depressive?

Caty Simon: Yes, I believed that I was "bipolar," the label that they finally decided to stick on me.

Farber: Did that upset you?

Caty Simon: Sure. Now I thought that there was something that was going to be wrong with me for the rest of my life, that I couldn't achieve everything that I wanted to achieve, and worst of all was being chemically incarcerated. A lot of people at Freedom Center say that they'd rather—having experienced both—be in prison than in the mental hospital, because at least in prison you get control of your own mind. I didn't even have control of my own mind anymore. . . .

Farber: You were taking Zyprexa?

Caty Simon: Zyprexa, then they gave me Depakote, and most of the medication acted as a depressant for me and made me feel even worse, and I felt like they halved my IQ, and I couldn't do what I used to be able to do because I didn't have the same agility of mind, and that was what I valued most in myself. So I was just being snowed by all this propaganda and being told over and over again by these powerful authority figures that there was something wrong with me.

Farber: They told you it was a disease like diabetes?

Caty Simon: Exactly. Then I had these antidepressant medications take hold of me so I couldn't do my work, so that, for example, senior year of high school I could hardly get out of bed; I was so depressed because of the medications.

Farber: And they told you that if you went off your medication, you would crack up and . . .

Caty Simon: And then it seemed that it was self-fulfilling, that now I had gone through my manic cycle and now I was going through my depressive cycle, depressive phase rather. It was horrible: I felt paralyzed emotionally, and just in terms of my productivity, I started my first two years of high school with all A's and I ended hardly being able to attend school.

Farber: Do you attribute this to drugs or to the psychological impact of being labeled?

Caty Simon: Mostly to the drugs, but the psychological impact certainly didn't help. Being told that you couldn't do things and that your depression was crippling and chronic—it was a self-fulfilling prophecy.

Farber: Were there conversations that they had about you, or with you, where it was impressed upon you that you were mentally ill?

Caty Simon: Not to me. About me—in front of me—more like. I'd go to the psychiatrist with my parents, and they would decide together what to put in my body. I had no say.

Farber: So as you said you ended up thinking that you had a chronic disease like diabetes?

Caty Simon: In the same model as diabetes, but worse because I ended up believing that this bipolar illness ate up the most basic things that I valued most about myself.

Farber: Such as?

Caty Simon: Such as my intellect, my ability to achieve, my ability to articulate, for instance.

Farber: But in reality it was the psychiatric drugs you took that were doing this to you?

Caty Simon: Yes, I believe that now, but I didn't know it then. I thought I was going through my depressive phase of my bipolar illness. That's what they kept telling me. . . .

Farber: What did they tell you would happen if you didn't take your meds? They must have given you their typical warning?

Caty Simon: Yeah, sure they gave me that one, that I would have a relapse, that my current depression would get worse and/or I would be manic or out of control, that I'd be rehospitalized. My mania had never really been out of control—my sleep-deprived mania.

Farber: Was any of the mania euphoric?

Caty Simon: Euphoric, maybe. I would do amazing work under its influence. It wasn't just through the filter of grandiosity that I saw this. It was well-done work: both fiction and papers that I would send in to my professors. One of my religious studies papers got published in an adult journal.

Farber: What was it about?

Caty Simon: It was about the book of Exodus, sort of hermeneutics in the book of Exodus, it was really interesting. I knew Hebrew and Aramaic and could write in those languages as well, so . . .

Farber: At some point after this you were seeing a therapist? A Freudian?

Caty Simon: She was kind of cognitive-behavioral.

Farber: Because you wrote that you were supposed to talk about your mother and your father and early childhood and all that stuff.

Caty Simon: They're still very into developmental stuff. Talk therapists are still very much into that. That's still a holdover from those days. It was difficult because it was such a narrow-minded view of . . .

Farber: I think they must have been somewhat psychoanalytic if they thought everything was your mother and your father and the early years.

Caty Simon: Not everything. Obviously there's still influence by psychoanalysis, but she was also into something that I think was somewhat positive, which was changing one's mental tapes.

Farber: Was this the same woman?

Caty Simon: I did go to several different psychologists at first, but the woman I was with most of the time, she did kind of emphasize changing your self-talk.

Farber: Well, yeah, that's cognitive. And this was the one that told you that the borderline personality disorder diagnosis was bullshit?

Caty Simon: Yes. Have you read *Making Us Crazy*? It shows how psychologists and psychiatrists will often diagnose a patient with borderline personality disorder when she is not meeting their expectations of what a patient should do. It's like their bruised ego compels them to label them that way. There's even a joke: "How do you treat someone with BPD?* You refer them."

Farber: Right. The term really expresses contempt. I witnessed that in the 1980s when I worked in a clinic with psychoanalysts. It was the patient they did not like—for whatever reason—who got labeled BPD.

Caty Simon: Basically I think that I got that diagnosis in the beginning because the doctor just didn't like a powerful woman's voice, and he

---

*BPD is the acronym for "borderline personality disorder"—considered by psychoanalysts who named the "disorder" to be a chronic disorder of the "personality" and thus intractable, if not incurable.

didn't like the fact that I was unashamed about my sexuality. One of the first doctors that I had who gave me that diagnosis basically called me a slut. I think that my sexuality combined with my assertiveness was threatening to him, coming from a young teenage girl.

Farber: You said you first got the label "bipolar" when you were in the hospital, right? And you were also labeled "borderline."

Caty Simon: Right. There's always another axis that they can add onto, right?

Farber: So they said you were bipolar with a borderline personality disorder.

Caty Simon: Yes, double-damned, basically.

Farber: After going through this hospital experience there was this sense of malaise that was lingering from everything that had happened to you.

Caty Simon: I'd call it iatrogenic depression, basically. I was taking Zyprexa, Prozac, and Depakote, and then just Depakote and Prozac, and the Depakote just knocked me out. It took all the energy out of me and just made me incredibly depressed, so I went from being a straight-A student to basically failing. Let me explain the dynamics. There was this period where I was supposedly being "manic"—but my mania was caused by sleep deprivation and the situation that led me to deprive myself of sleep was that I was not getting enough work done because I was depressed by the so-called medications. The mania was followed by me being depressed when I came down, and I would say that that further convinced me that something was inherently wrong with me, which completely undermined my self-esteem and gave me this feeling that I was doomed for life.

There is considerable evidence that the drugs Simon was taking do in fact often produce a state of profound apathy and depression.[2] Psychiatrist Peter Breggin has argued, based on extensive documentation, that antipsychotics—including newer "atypicals" like Zyprexa—blunt the emotions, producing a "chemical lobotomy and a chemical straitjacket."[3]

Simon was prescribed multiple psychiatric drugs. The interaction of multiple drugs has a negative synergistic stress reaction, which may result in maladaptive body changes that psychiatrist Grace Jackson has termed an "allostatic load."[4] Since (as Dr. Stastny noted in chapter 1) the prescription and ingestion of multiple drugs became the norm in the 1990s (for financial reasons), patients are now suffering from an increased allostatic load, which accounts for the kind of feelings Simon described. Furthermore, the psychological effect of being labeled mentally ill usually produces a state of lowered self-esteem and depression.

The theory that Simon suffered from a biochemical imbalance is completely unnecessary to account for her depression. Furthermore, this theory is particularly unpersuasive due to the fact that contrary to the propaganda of psychiatrists and drug companies, no evidence has ever been presented that those labeled mentally ill have brain abnormalities (see chapter 2). Those who know the psychiatric literature realize the claim that biochemical imbalances account for "pathological" behavior is an unproven theory and an article of faith among psychiatrists. Most psychiatric patients believe this claim for the very reasons Simon had explained: it is repeatedly impressed on them by experts with the full weight of the highest authority.

A third source of Simon's unhappiness could be postulated: she never resolved the conflict that led to her "cry for help"—the conflict between her desire to succeed and excel and the resentment at the toll this constant pressure was exerting on her ability to relax and enjoy life. Fueling this conflict was the idea instilled in Simon that in order be a person of worth one must continually compete to maintain and aggrandize one's social status in the academic marketplace. It is easy to see how one could become lured by the rewards of success, and even more potent is the fear of failure. As Jules Henry wrote, "To be successful in our culture one must learn to dream of failure."[5] In school, failure often becomes the occasion for public humiliation, and thus "the . . . nightmare is internalized for life." This is how we are socialized to become part of the "rat race" of "normal" society in which every other human being is viewed as a competitor; although, as Simon noted, there is a sense of self-esteem that one gains from belonging to the academic elite. This was the ethos that Simon had internalized, which as Jules Henry documented, is taught in the family and in the schools.[6]

It was the internal conflict generated by this ideology, this ethos, that had led to what Simon called her cries for help, but this conflict was never addressed by any of the experts she saw. How *could* they have addressed it? They too had internalized this paradigm, they were part of the rat-race society, and they saw it as natural. Instead of addressing it they loaded her body with psychiatric drugs and told her she was mentally defective. Assuming—reluctantly—the role of chronic patient relieved Simon of the pressure to compete, but at the cost of her sense of self-worth and of her capacity for autonomous creativity. She needed guidance, someone to help her attain balance. The mental health system has only two products to offer—psychiatric diagnoses and psychiatric drugs.

Years later Simon found a "cure" for her "illness" when she discovered a community based on mutual aid—Freedom House—a community that encouraged individual initiative in the service of the community, not individual self-aggrandizement. Simon's "cure" included repudiating the ideology of competitive capitalism and affirming the vision of a society based on cooperation. This vision was not based on the idea of the subordination of the individual to the collective, as in the theory of Soviet-style communism, nor was it based on the exaltation of individual freedom regardless of its effects on others, as in American capitalism. It was based on an awareness of the unity of all—and thus the reconciliation of the happiness of the individual with the good of society. It was the ideal not of traditional communism but of anarcho-communism.

Farber: So by the time you get to Labor Day of 2003 and you go to the Freedom Center, how much later is that?

Caty Simon: I spent the years that I was sixteen, seventeen, eighteen, and nineteen just depressed and barely functional. I did get into Bryn Mawr, but based on my prior grades and on a lot of teachers writing great recommendations for me. I went to Bryn Mawr, and the whole time, even though I had come to believe that I was mentally ill, I instinctually despised the drugs. I knew that they were doing something bad to me, and I think that there was still some kind of base of integrity about my sense of identity deep down, this kind of core part, and I knew that there was something wrong with the drugs. As soon as I got to Bryn Mawr at eighteen and nineteen and was on my own, I stopped taking the drugs cold turkey. But I had no information about how to withdraw from drugs, and I wasn't in therapy anymore.

Farber: How was that experience?

Caty Simon: Horrible. It confirmed this idea that I was mentally ill.

Farber: Yeah, you thought it was your illness coming back. You obviously hadn't read the psychiatrist Peter Breggin at that point, right? Of course Breggin shows that psychiatric drugs are highly addictive and produce powerful states of withdrawal, which are typically seen as the illness returning. The withdrawal effects according to Breggin can include hallucinations and panic.

As Grace Jackson writes, "Far from reflecting the faulty genes of the patient, or the return of the underlying illness, [as patients are constantly told] withdrawal symptoms have been repeatedly investigated and explained by predictable drug induced transformations in the body—many of which persist for weeks or months."[7]

Caty Simon: It wasn't totally a breakdown; I just went from being mostly depressed most of the time to a minute-by-minute kind of physical agony where I couldn't stand to be in my own skin. Akathisia, it's called.

Farber: Were you pacing a lot then?

Caty Simon: Yeah, but I couldn't really tell what my natural state was, because as soon as I started feeling these things, I started smoking weed every day; I didn't really like weed particularly, but I thought that it was the only drug available to me. I'd never really taken illicit drugs before.

Farber: You could have taken alcohol.

Caty Simon: I really hate alcohol. It makes me stupid, and it makes me feel bad. I started smoking weed just because I felt I needed to have my state of mind altered to anything else.

Farber: This was when you were completely off the psychiatric drugs. Did it work at all?

Caty Simon: It put me into another state, but—I had been encouraged as a career mental patient to constantly monitor my own moods for so long, and that creates its own problems—it hurts to be totally self-centered.

Farber: Yeah, that's a good point. I think a lot people decide they're bipolar on the basis of that continuous self-monitoring of their moods. One no longer has spontaneous moods when one is worriedly self-examining oneself.

Caty Simon: Right. And I just didn't know any real coping skills, so even though the weed provided a kind of respite—you know how potheads have kind of tangential thinking . . .

Farber: You mean they go off on digressions?

Caty Simon: Right. So these kinds of thoughts would constantly lead back to self-hatred or self-loathing because I'm so used to focusing totally on myself, but the weed dampened the feeling I had of severe withdrawal from those medications, which I had no idea was occurring.

Farber: No one who gave you the drugs ever warned you of that?

Caty Simon: No. Firstly because nobody ever expected me to go off of them, right? Nobody would ever have encouraged me to do so . . .

Farber: They all told you that you needed them.

Caty Simon: . . . and secondly, because in the '90s when I was first prescribed them they were still trying to hide the fact that coming off of psychiatric drugs would lead to withdrawal. They would try to refer to it by other euphemistic names in certain literature, something like "discontinuation syndrome" or anything other than the actual word *withdrawal*. But I wasn't even exposed to that particular literature that explained there were withdrawal effects. So anyway, I just thought that it was my old illness coming back in some way, and although part of me kept on doggedly denying that I was mentally ill, the only other alternative way that I could explain the past few years to myself was that I had some sort of horrible defect of character—that I was lazy and wrong and bad.

Farber: But you were off the drugs, and you were passing classes at Bryn Mawr?

Caty Simon: No, I wasn't. That's the thing. I was deeply involved in my classes, but since I was smoking weed all the time I couldn't really pay attention or complete tasks, or I would get so caught up in the literature we were reading that I would just read it further instead of writing the paper or . . .

Farber: Yeah, that would happen to anyone on marijuana.

Caty Simon: Right. I remember this particularly ludicrous period where I was smoking so much weed and reading *Das Kapital,* and instead of reading that one little section that they assigned me, I was reading as much of it as I could through the blur and not writing the paper about it at all, or reading Hegel to get some background on it and just being totally captivated by that work. I was exercising myself intellectually, but not in the way that would help me pass classes. Then of course when I didn't pass classes I would continue to be self-recriminating, and it would just make the whole thing worse.

Farber: How long did that go on for?

Caty Simon: A while, and not just because the withdrawal continued for so long but because after the withdrawal I got into doing drugs of different kinds and that certainly didn't help my productivity. Nobody in therapy or nobody in the hospital or nobody anywhere had really taught me how to achieve and produce without being on drugs.

Farber: What year did you start Bryn Mawr?

Caty Simon: I don't really remember, 2001? I took a year between because I didn't finish high school my senior year, and so I had to take some classes at the state college to finish up. Also I was volunteering at a rape crisis shelter, but I was still really disturbed.

Farber: But at the end of the year you had flunked your classes?

Caty Simon: Yes.

Farber: So what happened the next year?

Caty Simon: I also just hated the place. I was kind of this naive little girl who thought that going to a Seven Sisters school meant that I would enter this anarcho-feminist utopia, but instead, Bryn Mawr was just basically a made-over debutante school.

Farber: So you considered yourself a leftist by this time, an anarcho-syndicalist, did you say?

Caty Simon: I'm an anarcho-communist . . . in the Emma Goldman style. I wouldn't really consider myself an anarcho-syndicalist. I think my school of thought is sometimes referred to as social libertarian as in, I have a lot of socialist beliefs but I also don't believe in the state. Although nowadays, most leftists in my circle seem to be more anarchist than socialist.

Farber: Nowadays, though, when I run into someone who calls himself an anarchist I get the feeling they just mean run in the street and engage in direct action or throw rocks in windows or something. I didn't have any feeling that it necessarily meant that they were theoretical anarchists; I think the term is used pretty loosely, isn't it?

Caty Simon: It's used more loosely, but you're talking about Black Block kind of thinking. I mean it in the sense that my utopia consists, like I said, of a stateless world in which a community makes decisions but doesn't impose them through violence and things are structured on a small community-based level rather than on a large, centralized scale, using self-determination. I think a lot of people see it that way. Direct action is part of the tradition. The Icarus Project itself is kind of anarchistic, it's self-management. . . . Anyway, I did consider myself a leftist and to see women whose horses cost as much as my father's salary in a year was kind of disgusting, and to see women who thought that feminism meant that women could be CEOs too. This place was so monoculture—as Sascha would put it—that I used to joke that even the lesbians were straight and even the Asian girls were WASPs. It was a pretty awful place for me to be in, especially when even the supposed liberal democrats in the Democratic Party were moving more toward the right.

Farber: Including the ones on your campus?

Caty Simon: Yeah. They were all about entering the corporate system and doing well for number one. They weren't even really intellectually interested in what they were studying, only its utility to them and their careers.

Farber: So by the end of the first year you were disgusted with it.

Caty Simon: I was disgusted with it, and even if I hadn't been disgusted with it, I wouldn't have been in a frame of mind where I could really achieve there anyway.

Farber: But you did remain off the psychiatric drugs without having to be rehospitalized?

Caty Simon: Yes, and I wasn't rehospitalized because my weeks at the hospital were some of the most traumatizing times of my life, maybe *the* most traumatizing times of my life because I'd never had authority so brutally imposed on me so indifferently. They would threaten, "If you don't take your meds then we're going to shoot it up your ass." Although I'd been in paternalistic places like the Orthodox Jewish school, I'd never been in a place where the exercise of power was so naked and brutal. So I did everything I could to appear right on the outside and to never get into a situation where I could get hospitalized.

Farber: So you've already proved them wrong, you'd already been a year off the drugs that they said that you needed to keep from going insane.

Caty Simon: Yeah, but I didn't really quite come to that conclusion because I was still doing so horribly according to my own ideals of what I should be able to accomplish.

Farber: So what happened with the second year?

Caty Simon: I left Bryn Mawr, and I followed a rich boyfriend to upstate New York.

Farber: Was he a leftist?

Caty Simon: He was malleable. He was mostly apolitical, but I kind of pushed him to the left a lot. And then I left him when I was twenty and moved to Northampton and started becoming economically self-sufficient and became more involved in the human rights movement.

Farber: Was this what you were referring to when you said you had these new left-wing friends and they agreed with you about everything except the psychiatric issue?

Caty Simon: Right. I was doing low-income rights work, I was doing sex worker rights work; I was doing all sorts of things. I was finally doing the kind of work I advocated, instead of just theorizing about it. I was finally putting my money where my mouth was and doing the kind of activism that I never could elsewhere, and that really started my recovery. I think just doing the things that I believed in took me outside of the endless ruminations about the self and this endless self-monitoring and put me in a place where I was just focused on doing what I needed to do for the organizations I was in. So suddenly, without my even noticing it, I started becoming more "functional." A lot of it also was I just started to relearn these habits that I had allowed to sink in when I was told that I was just a walking array of symptoms. I really focused on trying to be responsible in my relationships with other people, because before I would be really needy and dramatic and manipulative—I thought there wasn't anything I could do about it because I was just BPD—but I began to counter that actively with, "Yes, there is something I can do about it," and that I owe something to my friends and I owe something to my community to behave in a responsible and caring manner toward others and toward the work that I was doing. That was part of my recovery. I think that when you talk about a spiritual recovery, mine was an existential-spiritual recovery in the sense that I was accountable for my own voice, rather than being these effects of my supposedly defective chemical makeup, just a pawn of my broken brain. So I think that was the major step for me, saying that I'm an actor, a moral agent, not an object.

Farber: That is something Laing emphasized, you know. He got it from Sartre—the idea that our actions are praxis, not a process. They are intentional, goal-directed, not mere effects of biology or psychology. So your transformation had to do with a number of things but not therapy. And getting off psychiatric drugs was critical.

Caty Simon: Well, for me, even talk therapy was out. The psychotherapy I encountered always labeled me the sick person in the room in need of guidance. Therapy didn't work for me because it immediately put me in this submissive state.

Farber: Yeah, that was one of family therapy's critiques of traditional psychoanalytic therapy, that it did that—it put the so-called patient in a one-down position. There is this idea of the identified patient—because if anyone is acting crazy it means the entire family is dysfunctional—but only one person becomes the family scapegoat.[8]

Caty Simon: Right, exactly. I was constantly the identified patient. But even if you pathologize an entire family, you still have the psychologist, the therapist who is the supposed source of sanity and salvation, and I really didn't appreciate that. My therapist was always asking me why or what I felt, but we never did anything about what I *did,* which was most important, as it turned out.

What I really needed was peer support where people all put themselves on an equal level saying that, "No, we're not all crazy, but some people who are struggling may be unhappy to some greater degree than others." Nobody can place themselves as being the center of sanity while other people are identified as somehow defective in the way that they behave or are. Placed in that environment I think really finally sealed my recovery.

Farber: So you were pretty much out of the sick role and empowered before you even got to Freedom Center.

Caty Simon: I was pretty much empowered, but I think Freedom Center really sealed the deal by allowing me to get into peer support.

Farber: To help other people?

Caty Simon: I did a lot of facilitating certainly, but still even the facilitators spoke about their troubles. Nobody ever held themselves above or was this visibly impersonal figure in this emotionally volatile group. We all put ourselves into it, we all put what was actually going on in all our lives into it. The facilitators shared about their lives as well.

Farber: That would have helped you even if you'd never been labeled a mental patient. . . .

Caty Simon: I'm sure it would have.

Farber: It's a community that helps people deal with what Szasz calls the problems of life?

Caty Simon: Right. So half of my recovery was an individual thing on my part. I took responsibility for my individual actions. The other half was a community aspect of realizing that my problems weren't so unique or extreme and that other people were experiencing similar things or had experienced similar things but were now happier because they were doing the kinds of things they wanted in their lives.

Farber: So today you've been off these drugs for years, and you never went back on the drugs they told you needed for your bipolar illness?

Caty Simon: No. I think I still swing back and forth, and I still lead a very unstructured life. I do all this work for these organizations on a volunteer basis, and I support myself through black market means, and I do structure a lot of my time myself, so it isn't the traditional life. I still don't have a nine-to-five existence, so there are still times where I fuck up or I'm not as "functional" as I want to be, and there are still times when I kind of retreat into this maybe depressive space, but I know how to cope with it. I know not to hate myself for falling short of the perfectionism of my youth, and I know that because a project of mine failed it doesn't mean that I am a failure. It doesn't all fall back on labeling my entire identity or entire being as somehow lacking, which is what a diagnosis did.

Farber: Did you read Kate Millett's book *The Loony-Bin Trip*?[9] She talks about the self-loathing induced in her by being labeled manic-depressive.

Caty Simon: Right, I love that book, and then I loved the way that it portrayed how the people that we love the most can buy into this dogma and think that they're doing the best they can for us when they deliver us into the hands of the mental health system.

Farber: Exactly. So one of the ways you deal with your depression, you go to a group at Freedom Center?

Caty Simon: Sometimes. I think that the support group's utility in my life, the phase for that ended. Eventually I became kind of emotionally overwhelmed by the work of being a facilitator. I don't attend a support group much anymore, but I appreciate how it helped me—and how it can help others—to realize that they are not alone in the human experience and that what we call mental illness is simply part of the continuum of the human experience.

Farber: You referred to being so-called manic at certain points. You agreed that there were some positive aspects of it. Do you think that there are some ways in which your temperament is not defective, but distinctive?

Caty Simon: I don't think it's inherently distinctive. I think I was brought up in such a way, I had a ten-hour school day, I had so many conflicting interests, and I just learned to push myself really hard into this state of continuous productivity, which led to what they call the manic state. I don't really believe in the whole Icarus Project ideology of mad people having dangerous gifts—at least not in my case. Nobody's born with a specifically differing temperament; I think we all get that way through developmental, cultural influences.

Farber: So there's no biological component.

Caty Simon: I don't believe so, and I don't think that we're especially sensitive or talented, although maybe talented people are prone to be misunderstood and labeled. What I've seen the psychiatric industry do is label marginalized people of whatever kind or people who just act in ways that are more extreme than the implicit social covenant that we have to behave ourselves in a certain way. So you get queer teenagers who are labeled, you get people of color who are labeled; you know that there is a study done with psychiatrists, and the only thing that they change is the fact that the person is a person of color, and a white middle-class person gets a diagnosis of major depression, while the person of color who's poor gets a diagnosis of schizophrenia.

Farber: Let's control then for class factors. Don't you think among middle-class people that people who tend to get labeled schizophrenic and bipolar seem to be more creative and more sensitive than people who don't get labeled?

Caty Simon: I know plenty of people who are creative and sensitive who never get labeled. It's partly that maybe there's not enough room for the different ways that people behave when they're creative and talented.

Farber: So you agree that people who are creative and talented might in fact be *more* likely to be labeled in the first place?

Caty Simon: Sure. I think anyone who challenges the status quo is likely to get labeled. Anyone whose expression of emotion is too intense for our society to bear.

Farber: So you do agree that people who get labeled tend to be distinctive in a number of different ways, but you don't think there is any biology involved?

Caty Simon: Right.

Farber: What about people who say they are having spiritual states, like Sascha?

Caty Simon: If that's their subjective reality, then I'm not going to judge it or critique it. If that's the model they use to promote their recovery that's fine, and that's why the Freedom Center is mostly agnostic about what mental illness is.

Farber: Do you have a viewpoint just as a person, not a Freedom Center rep, about that? How do you account for the many people, like Sascha, Ashley, and people before that from my first book? I have an unusual number of so-called psychotics who believe they had spiritual experiences.

Caty Simon: I'm simply just not going to judge it because I don't know. For me, spirituality just isn't a really comfortable school of thought.

Farber: For philosophical or ideological reasons, or political reasons?

Caty Simon: Basically, I'm as close as an agnostic can come to being an atheist. I think that for me, I focus on the here and now rather than the transcendental, the community and socio-economic problems of the community. To me sometimes, spiritual ways of thought don't really seem to align with that. It quickly becomes an opiate of the people, because it always is the idea that the material doesn't matter. Well, the material does, and I think a lot of people don't realize their privilege in these supposed spiritual explorations, and if they were hungry and deprived they wouldn't have all this time and energy to play around with these ideas.

Farber: I don't know if anyone that I know would disagree with you.

Caty Simon: People who aren't middle-class don't get to pretend to be shamans, or they don't get access to all of these alternative spiritualities.

Farber: If they're black, they're likely to believe in a spiritual or religious viewpoint anyway, though.

Caty Simon: Sure, but it's not spirituality, it's not like an individualized form of thinking about the transcendental; it's a cultural, religious influence. It's about the spiritual thought of the community, not the spiritual thought of the individual. A lot of times when we talk about these people who are pathologized and middle-class, when they recast their experience as a spiritual one, it's about their own "individual spiritual journey." I'm sorry, but I don't want to talk about all African-Americans as a whole because I don't think you can generalize this to what most African-Americans believe. I want to be centered on the community rather than on my own emotional quirks that I can turn into a spiritual journey. I want to be deeply politicized, and most of these people at some point or another see a constant politicization of the world you experience as some sort of attachment that you need to let go of or as not seeing the broader picture. Well, the broader picture for me is that human suffering still exists on a huge scale because of basic social-economic problems.

Farber: What about American Indian societies? Clearly religious or spiritual rituals play an important part in them. The original shamans obviously were not privileged middle-class white people.

Caty Simon: As a white Jewish immigrant child I have no right to talk about something I know so little about, a community I've never been in. I think you should see all my statements in the context of my talking about the culture that I'm familiar with, which is middle-class white people or middle-class people of color.

Farber: So when you described being very productive and artistic when you were in some of your manic phases, do you have an explanation for that?

Caty Simon: Sure, because if you have more hours in the day and sleep deprivation is causing your body to have—it's kind of the same thing that happens chemically when you take cocaine or speed. At first it seems like you're more productive for a while because you simply have more hours to the day, because you're not sleeping and you have this kind of super-focused attention and concentration, but eventually your body burns out.

Farber: So you think it could happen to anyone?

Caty Simon: Right, I really do. If someone were as determined to do what they were doing as I was, and if someone were to put themselves into a manic state by not sleeping, yeah, anyone could do it.

Farber: And they could have what they felt was a more creative frame of mind?

Caty Simon: Yeah, sure.

Farber: So it's not necessarily a bad state. It has some social value perhaps?

Caty Simon: Right, and I think people have accomplished things in these kinds of states; talk about journalists who stay up for a deadline. There are a lot of professions that seem to work around people denying themselves sleep and working in this hyperintense kind of way, but its value is temporary, and it can't really fit into long-term fulfillment. For me, I'm slowly, humbly learning even now a way to achieve and to be creative and to do the work of my movement in a way that's not about burning my reserves really quickly, but in a sustainable fashion.

One could say that we live in a hyperactive or "manic" society. I read recently that we have the most work hours of any first-world country. It's interesting that caffeine is the country's most used legitimate drug. I think that from the 1950s, or even earlier, we're a society that's focused on speed and production at all costs, and I think that's why maybe we're seeing so many people who are being diagnosed as bipolar, because people push themselves and push themselves and push themselves for short-term results.

Farber: Do you have any feelings about places like the Soteria Project, in which the idea is that when people are having these extreme states of consciousness they should be allowed to go through them?

Caty Simon: It depends. I've read about the Soteria Project. The whole Laingian idea of allowing someone to go into the extreme state, it depends on whether it seems to be going well for the person. I've seen people who have these extreme states, breaks with reality that they want to go through it and it's necessary, but I've also seen people who just want to be able to dampen it. It depends on what works best for that person.

Farber: Well, that's what they claim they did at places like Soteria House.

Caty Simon: Right. I'm totally for the idea of safe houses and non-coercive sanctuaries for people, and I wish we had the funds and the support behind our movement to create . . .

Farber: It won't be funded because of the pharmaceutical companies.

Caty Simon: Yeah, of course. Because of the fact that it's the sixth or seventh largest industry in the world and because those ideas threaten that system, we don't get funding. The biopharmaceutical model dominates all thought about people who are experiencing extreme states in society, and we don't even get a hearing about these kinds of things. Although, it's a little bit more widespread in Europe: they have more safe houses there, runaway houses and things like that. I just think that the Laingian idea that somebody should just go through that state and it's always productive and helpful to the person, I think that should be questioned as well. We should listen to the person about how they want to be helped.

Farber: So you think if someone says, "I want to take a lot of psychiatric drugs," they should be given all the psychiatric drugs they want, right?

Caty Simon: Well, in the Freedom Center what we're going for is informed consent on that issue. If there was true informed consent, if everybody knew how unhelpful and deeply damaging these psychiatric drugs were then there would be far, far fewer people who would choose to take them, but as for the people who did, that's their choice as long as they knew what they were doing. The fact is there can be no true informed consent when the pharmaceutical industry hides the horrible side effects of their drugs, like adult-onset diabetes, for decades.

Farber: They fund, create, manufacture all the research nowadays. I think it was Merck Corporation that was subsidizing a psychiatric journal, and people thought it was an independent journal. Did you see that?

Caty Simon: Yeah, there are a lot of different cases of that, and it's frightening.

Farber: Here's one other radical idea said by Laing that I think most people actually agree with, even from David Oaks to Sascha DuBrul, though they might change the wording. Laing said normal society itself is insane and therefore provides no normative standard such that one could say adjustment to it is desirable.

Caty Simon: That's absolutely true. It is insane. And that's the other thing: sometimes there are people who just find it difficult to adapt to a ridiculous capitalist system, in which we are all so isolated from each other, in which what we're supposed to achieve is so ultimately meaningless. Some people just find it harder to fit these insane standards.

Farber: But couldn't you say their temperament is more sensitive so they find it harder to fit this competitive society?

Caty Simon: I just don't want to glorify those of us who experience extremes as the artists and the thinkers. I think it could happen to anyone; any particular person could say this is crazy. Anyone's emotions could just come out, and even if they can't intellectually understand that the world they're being forced to conform to is crazy, everything inside them is screaming that it is. Some people still have their right minds, that's all. It's just common sense or integrity of people's identities.

Farber: Integrity that enables or forces them to go crazy, go mad?

Caty Simon: Right. Going mad could be a sane response to an insane situation. Whether you're a middle-class artist or have all the creative impulses of a mechanic, there are some people that just—the integrity of their identity screams out that they are not going to fit into a crazy world. I don't think that us mad activists are special, I think it's because society is just so insane.

Farber: So why do some people remain normal and adjust and go to work every day and work for not only pharmaceuticals but go off to war and are good soldiers and others won't take it?

Caty Simon: I don't know why. I wish I did.

Farber: Adjustment to society is not a sign of mental health or well-being. So what's the solution?

Caty Simon: I do not know. But I know mad people are not the only ones who rebel against conformity. Plenty of people rebel against conformity but find some way to do it without disintegrating, but some of us just break down before we can find an answer for ourselves.

Farber: I would say that what you are talking about is what David Oaks, following Martin Luther King Jr., calls creative maladjustment. Not adjusting to normality but being able to creatively function. That's what I'm hoping to make more available to people—particularly mad people—as an option, and you are one example of creative maladjustment.

Part Three

Dangerous Gifts

8

The Roots of The Icarus Project

There Arjuna could see, within the midst of the armies of both parties, his fathers, grandfathers, teachers, maternal uncles, brothers, sons, grandsons, friends, and also his fathers-in-law and well-wishers. . . . Arjuna, . . . cast aside his bow and arrows and sat down on the chariot, his mind overwhelmed with grief.

THE *BHAGAVAD GITA*[1]

The object of the Gita is to show "the most excellent way to attain self realization" and "this can be achieved by desireless action; by renouncing fruits of action; by dedicating all activities to God, i.e., by surrendering oneself to Him body and soul."

MAHATMA GANDHI ON THE *BHAGAVAD GITA*[2]

True sanity entails the dissolution of the normal ego, that false self completely adjusted to our alienated social reality . . . and through this death a rebirth, and the eventual

200

*re-establishment of a new kind of ego-functioning, the ego
now being the servant of the divine, no longer its betrayer.*

R. D. LAING[3]

*I saw the best minds of my generation destroyed by madness,
starving hysterical naked . . . angel-headed hipsters burning
for the ancient heavenly connection to the starry dynamo in
the machinery of night. . . .*

ALLEN GINSBERG, *HOWL*[4]

In September of 2002 Sascha DuBrul wrote an article that was published in the *San Francisco Bay Guardian* under the title of "The Bipolar World."[5] Ashley McNamara read the article, contacted DuBrul, and together they formed a website called The Icarus Project. In 2004 they published a booklet titled *Navigating the Space between Brilliance and Madness:* it consisted of insightful social criticism; stories of love and loss, anguish and madness; trenchant critiques of society; explorations of the link between madness and mysticism; and gifted creative writings by DuBrul, McNamara, and a number of other "bipolar" people. The theme animating The Icarus Project is expressed in the project's mission statement, posted on their website: "We believe we have mad gifts to be cultivated and taken care of, rather than diseases or disorders to be suppressed or eliminated. By joining together as individuals and as a community, the intertwined threads of madness and creativity can inspire hope and transformation in an oppressive and damaged world."[6]

The booklet immediately sold the thousand copies that had been printed and went through five more editions. It was an inspired work, and it demonstrated that the so-called mentally ill were grappling with serious questions about the nature of our world. Included in this anthology were writings of some of the "best minds" of their generation, but unlike Allen Ginsberg's peers who were destroyed by madness, these folks were determined to take care of their "mad gifts" and contribute to the world. The Icarus Project itself grew rapidly. DuBrul and McNamara could honestly say by 2006, "We bring the Icarus vision to reality through a national staff collective and a grassroots network of autonomous local groups." Icarus groups met in New York, Minneapolis, Portland, Philadelphia, and spread every year.[7]

The mission statement of The Icarus Project was a bold and radical attack on the medical model of so-called mental illness. It stated, "While we respect whatever treatment decisions people make, we do not define ourselves as essentially diseased, disordered, broken, faulty, and existing within the bounds of DSM-IV diagnosis. We are exploring unknown territory and don't steer by the default maps outlined by docs and pharma companies. We're making new maps." This affirmation that the so-called mentally ill were not (really) ill and that the psychiatric paradigm was useless and misleading placed The Icarus Project on the radical wing of the mental patients' rights movement. Furthermore, although all psychiatric users and survivors were welcome to join "whether you take psychiatric drugs or not and whether you describe yourself with diagnostic categories or not," DuBrul and McNamara pledged "[t]o ensure we remain honest and untamed, we do not accept funding from pharmaceutical companies." They even adopted a Laingian concept of madness, although neither (as I learned) had read Laing. "We recognize that we live in a crazy world, and insist that our sensitivities, visions, and inspirations are not necessarily symptoms of illness. Sometimes breakdown can be the entrance to breakthrough."[8]

Thus a radical new organization was launched, an organization that would prove to be on the vanguard of the Mad Pride movement. No one could have predicted reading DuBrul's propsychiatric article in 2002 that he would become the cofounder of this organization, but the Mad Pride movement in the United States has not emerged from the minds of its founders with its sense of identity fully formed. Rather it is in process—with one foot in the past and one foot in the future. No one embodies this contradiction more starkly than DuBrul, arguably for a brief time the most prescient and influential leader (before he reduced his activism in 2009 in order to simultaneously pursue other educational goals) of the new generation of Mad Pride activists—although The Icarus Project staff denies attribution of leadership to any individual and disdains "heroic individual narratives" (see the introduction to this book).

DuBrul's own life journey has been rocky. His 2002 article was written after his third hospitalization in 2001. (His first hospitalization was when he was eighteen, and his second took place six years later.) Although DuBrul expressed ambivalence in the article about Psychiatry, there was nothing particularly critical of the mental health professions; he did not, for example, express the kind of highly critical stance taken by David Oaks immediately after his hospitalizations. Even today, despite the radical mission statement of The Icarus Project, DuBrul is not entirely critical of Psychiatry or of psychiatric drugs, as I discovered when we met in 2007 and when I interviewed him recently. However, it is characteristic of DuBrul's temperament that despite the emotional turmoil in his life, he is self-confident enough to respond to criticism without becoming defensive or hostile. When he agreed to let me interview him he knew that although I was impressed by The Icarus Project I would be critical of him for taking too tolerant a view toward Psychiatry. Yet he agreed to be interviewed and displayed the kind of affable and generous attitude that is constitutive of responsible leadership.

The Crack Up and Birth of a Movement

When reading DuBrul's 2002 article,[9] "The Bipolar World," I wondered to myself if there had been any life events that led to DuBrul's first breakdown. He did not look backward—as others did (e.g., Grossberg)—and attempt to discover the events and relationships that may have been the cause of the stress that precipitated his breakdown. Later, reading his blog online, I discovered how difficult his adolescence was. He wrote, "My parents were always fighting. And my Dad was slowly and painfully dying in front of me; hooked up to machines in the hospital" (May 15, 2008, Sascha/Scatter blog).[10] The article did not mention any of this; he accepts the psychiatric explanation that he has a biochemical disorder.

Nonetheless it is a dramatic account of his breakdowns and unwittingly reveals how he was inducted into the psychiatric system and why he still has mixed feelings about Psychiatry. At the very beginning DuBrul was convinced the drugs had saved him, and in the article he disparaged as extremists those who criticized the pharmaceutical industry. On the other hand, Psychiatry did not have all the answers.

The nightmare began when DuBrul was eighteen.

> I was eighteen years old the first time they locked me up in a psych ward. The police found me walking on the subway tracks in New York City, and I was convinced the world was about to end and I was being broadcast live on primetime TV on all the channels. I hadn't slept for months, and I thought there were microscopic transmitters under my skin that were making me itch and recording everything I was saying for some top-secret branch of the CIA. After I'd walked the tracks through three stations, the cops wrestled me to the ground, arrested me, and brought me to an underground jail cell and then to the emergency room of Bellevue psychiatric hospital, where they strapped me to a bed. Once they managed to track down my terrified mother, she signed some papers, a nurse shot me up with some hardcore antipsychotic drugs, and I woke up two weeks later in the "quiet room" of a public mental hospital upstate.

In the article it is clear that DuBrul accepted as scientific (initially and at the time he wrote the article) the psychiatric diagnosis eventually given to him: "bipolar disorder," or "manic depression" as it was termed previously. If he had any objections to the rough and insensitive way he was treated in the hospital, he did not mention them. The article poignantly conveys the sense of despair he felt when he was given his diagnosis; at that point DuBrul had no awareness of the critics of Psychiatry, no basis on which to question its pronouncements. He realized he had been given a sentence of neverending torment, if not doom, and he accepted it as his fate. This is typical for most patients today, for whom the prognosis becomes a self-fulfilling prophecy.

> After I'd been in the psych ward for a while, the doctors diagnosed me with something called bipolar disorder (otherwise known as manic depression) and gave me a mood-stabilizing drug called Depakote. They told my mom to get used to the idea that I had a serious mental disorder I was going to be grappling with for the rest of my life and that I was going to require daily doses of medication to be able to function healthily in the outside world.

Furthermore he was evidently informed later (I'm sure that the doctors told his mother at the time) or read later that there was a high risk that he might kill himself.

> I didn't realize it at the time, but I, like millions of other Americans, would spend years wrestling with the implications of that diagnosis. Manic depression kills tens of thousands of people, mostly young people, every year. Statistically, one out of every five people diagnosed with the disease eventually commits suicide. But I wasn't convinced, to say the least, that gulping down a handful of pills every day would make me sane.

This is a psychiatric lie. Bipolar disorder does not kill tens of thousands of people every year: Psychiatry does. There may be a correlation between bipolar disorder and suicide but it is a fundamental principle of scientific research that correlation does not entail causation. The higher suicide rate among "bipolars" is a result not of having a so-called bipolar disorder, *but rather of the psychiatric treatment* of the "disorder": the sentence of doom, the feelings of unworthiness engendered by the diagnosis, the brain-disabling iatrogenic "side effects" of the psychiatric drugs. (Furthermore, teenagers who are suicidal are more likely to attract attention and thus be labeled "bipolar.") In fact, studies show that antidepressants (SSRIs)—usually given to all hospitalized patients—increase the risk of "suicidality."[11]

I had been friends with two different women who were given this diagnosis who *did* kill themselves in the early 1990s. Both of these women, in their late thirties or early forties, were devastated by their diagnosis. Their sense of worth was profoundly undermined by the label. They became convinced they were defective. One of the women, the sister of a famous American actor, had called me from California. She felt better every time I told her she was merely going through a crisis. She was devastated when her Chinese husband left her shortly after she was given the label. She was upset because her brother, whom she adored, would not talk to her once she was labeled psychotic, or so she said.

I advised her to try to get off the drugs (gradually) but she was emotionally dependent upon her psychiatrist who told her she needed the drugs. She begged me to move from New York to California to counsel her. Several months passed and I had not heard from her. One day a mutual friend told me she had killed herself. Once she was labeled she felt like "damaged goods." And her loved ones seemed to agree—they shunned her.

In Robert Whitaker's 2010 book, he shows that "bipolars" are put on and "maintained" on a "cocktail" of psychiatric drugs, prescribed by psychiatrists, which over time have a deleterious effect on them, preventing them from recovering their "pre-morbid" level of functioning. In the predrug era, the overwhelming majority of "bipolars" (then called "manic-depressives") had recovered entirely within two years after their first episode. Today the majority tend to have a chronic condition. The drugs prevent them from recovering![12]

From my perspective there is no "bipolar disorder" [see chapter 2], although I believe there is evidence that those labeled "bipolars" tend to be more sensitive than most people, have a more expansive awareness, and are thus more emotionally vulnerable. Like all diagnoses, the diagnosis of "bipolar disorder" often masks ongoing life issues that are never acknowledged or resolved once they are attributed to the alleged brain disorder.

Those labeled "bipolar" may be more psychic. Some of the experiences DuBrul had seem prescient.

DuBrul described his experiences in the months before his hospitalization.

> I started to think the radio was talking to me, and I started reading all these really deep meanings in the billboards downtown and on the highways that no one else was seeing. I was convinced there were subliminal messages everywhere trying to tell a small amount of people that the world was about to go through drastic changes and we needed to be ready for it. People would talk to me and I was obsessed with the idea that there was this whole other language underneath what we thought we were saying that everyone was using without even realizing it.

In this article DuBrul repeats the psychiatric propaganda as if there is no doubt about its veracity. The psychiatrists convinced him that he had a genetic disease and that his instability was a result of a biological abnormality. DuBrul himself astutely observes that his sympathy to the psychiatric establishment seemed to conflict with his background and philosophical outlook.

> I was raised by parents with pretty radical leftist politics who taught me to question everything and always be skeptical of big business and capitalism. I spent my teenage years growing up in a punk scene that glorified craziness and disrespect for authority. . . . My worldview didn't leave any room for the possibility that my instability and volatility might actually have something to do with biology.

But this is not as unusual as DuBrul thought. As Kate Millett had learned, even radical leftists and feminists tend to lean toward credulity when it comes to Psychiatry. DuBrul ended up back in the psychiatric system six years later. He does not describe what environmental factors might have led to this development since at the time he wrote the article he had become convinced he had a biological disorder.

> When I was 24, I ended up back in the same program, out in the New York suburbs, that my mom had put me in as a teenager. I was miserable and lonely. The doctors weren't quite sure what I had, so they diagnosed me with something called schizoaffective disorder. They gave me an antidepressant called Celexa and an atypical antipsychotic called Zyprexa. I was in group therapy every day. There was an organic farm to work on down the road from the halfway house, and after a couple weeks they let me volunteer there a few hours a day sowing seeds and potting plants in the greenhouse. Eventually I convinced them to let me live there, and I moved out of the halfway house and came for outpatient care just a couple of times a week.

Soon after this DuBrul realized that despite his previous doubts, the drugs were "working." It is at this point that DuBrul first became an ambivalent convert to the biological model of Psychiatry.

It took a few months, but for the first time I could see that the drugs were actually working for me. It was more than the circumstances, it actually felt chemical. Slowly all the horrible noise and thoughts faded and I started to feel good again. I remember watching an early summer sunset over the fields at the farm and realizing I was happy for the first time in months and months. Once I moved onto the farm full-time, I would come into the city on the weekends to work at the farmers' market and hang out with my friends. As obvious as it was that the drugs were helping me, I really just saw them as a temporary solution. They made me gain a bunch of weight. I always had a hard time waking up in the morning. My mouth was always dry. They were relatively new drugs, and not even the doctors knew about the long-term side effects of taking them. Besides which, the whole idea just made me feel really uncomfortable. How would I talk to my friends about it? What if there were some global economic crisis and instead of running around with my crew torching banks and tearing up the concrete I was withdrawing from some drug I suddenly didn't have access to anymore? I didn't want to be dependent on the drugs of the Man.

But were the drugs really responsible for DuBrul's sudden happiness? It is impossible to be sure, but I do not believe it. DuBrul's certainty is belied by story he tells—by the radically positive changes in his environment and by what we know about the placebo effect. DuBrul felt better, but it is more likely that his happiness was a result of his change of environment—of getting out of the city and suburbs and working on a farm, of sowing seeds and potting plants and watching sunsets. And, most importantly, of being part of a community. It is significant that at first DuBrul was "miserable and lonely" in the halfway house, but he was able to get out of sick role—to move out of the halfway house and live on an organic farm, no doubt with a group of people ("hippies" they might have been called in another era, or self-reliant Americans in the age of Emerson) whose philosophical affinities were similar to his.

Added to this is the powerful impact of the placebo effect itself. Let me emphasize that it is clear that both placebo effects and environmental changes can induce actual chemical changes as powerful as that of any drug. DuBrul's conclusion that his happiness "was more than circumstances, it actually felt chemical" was undoubtedly true. But that does not mean his emotional change was caused by the psychiatric drugs. What is significant and unfortunate is that DuBrul became convinced that the psychiatric drugs had saved him. In addition to the placebo effect induced by the drug itself, one must take into account the expression of concern by the treating psychiatrist (usually included in the placebo effect). One would expect that a young man who had tragically lost his father at such a young age would be responsive to the psychiatrist's paternal (or maternal) concern and to the magic pills the psychiatrist told him would help him.

In this article DuBrul overlooks all these environmental factors, these privileges he had that are not available—although they should be—to the typical patient less resourceful than he was, and he attributed his improvements solely to psychiatric drugs. It is revealing that the witless psychiatrists did not even give him the diagnosis that he had been given on the previous occasion—"bipolar disorder"—but instead labeled him "schizoaffective" and put him on an antidepressant and an "antipsychotic." Later he would decide he was bipolar and attribute his recovery to lithium.

Would DuBrul have felt the same uplifting feelings had he been taking the drugs but in a less idyllic place—had he stayed in the city in an apartment with his mother? Would he have experienced the same recovery had he been stuck in the halfway house like the other patients? In my experience as a psychologist, halfway houses and day treatment have a discouraging and demeaning effect on persons; they convert persons in crisis into chronic patients with "low self-esteem."[13] It is depressing just to visit these grim places.

DuBrul himself tells us that he was "miserable and lonely" at the halfway house he was placed in. DuBrul tells us that he "convinced" the people with the organic farm to let him live there, rather than the halfway house. One can infer that DuBrul felt an aversion to the halfway house, and he obviously did not find his daily group therapy very helpful as, once he moved into the organic farm, he went for outpatient care "*just* a couple times a week" (my emphasis), instead of daily. The fact is, DuBrul designed his own "milieu therapy" and improved in spite of the "therapeutic treatment" of the doctors, which he resourcefully got out of.

The "illness" recurred again in 2001. And this time he was diagnosed as being bipolar, as he had been the first time.

> The police picked me up wandering the streets of Los Angeles on New Year's Day 2001. I'd been smashing church windows with my bare fists and running through traffic scaring the hell out of people screaming the lyrics to punk songs, convinced that the world had ended and I was the center of the universe. They locked me up in the psych unit of the L.A. County Jail, and that's where I spent the next month, talking to the flickering fluorescent lightbulbs and waiting for my friends to come break me out. I was quickly given the diagnosis of bipolar disorder again and loaded down with meds.

DuBrul spent a month in jail before he was sent to the psychiatric ward and given the diagnosis of bipolar. One imagines that even the grimmest psych ward would look pretty good compared to being crazy in a prison cell in L.A. This incident may be one source of the positive feelings DuBrul still had for psychiatrists. For reasons DuBrul leaves to our imagination he did not call home. One phone call to his mother would no doubt have gotten him transferred expeditiously to a hospital. After the hospital he spent another four months in a halfway house for the "severely mentally ill." Finally he moved back into his "old collective House" in Oakland.

At home he continued to take lithium and Wellbutrin (an antidepressant). Nowadays he would have been prescribed and told to take at least five drugs—a drug "cocktail" (see chapter 1). And then he started doing research.

> And that's when I finally started doing the research I'd been putting off for so long. After a year of not being able to read, I started to pick up some books I'd collected about manic depression. And that's when I really began the internal and external dialogue about my condition, when I began to put the puzzle together and to make sense of it all so it wasn't just a bunch of isolated pieces that didn't fit together. I started talking to friends really openly and using the column I had in a punk rock magazine as a forum to talk about madness and manic

depression. And I started coming to terms with the paradox that, however much contempt I feel toward the pharmaceutical industry for making a profit from manic-depressive people's misery and however much I aspire to be living outside the system, the drugs help keep me alive, and in the end I'm so thankful for them.

But judging from DuBrul's reading list, his research was incomplete. He may not have realized it, but he only read those authors who accepted the standard psychiatric model of emotional problems—of bipolar disorder as a disease caused by faulty chemistry. Missing from his list were the three most prominent psychiatric critics of Psychiatry in the twentieth century: Thomas Szasz, R. D. Laing, and Peter Breggin. Dr. Breggin has done more than any person to debunk the myths behind biopsychiatry and to expose the harmfulness of psychiatric drugs.

Probably at this time DuBrul had not heard of any of these critics; we can assume their books were certainly not recommended by the psychiatrists who were treating him. But for some reason he did not seem to be aware of their writing when I spoke to him later—after he had become critical of psychiatry and after he had learned who they were. He read Kay Jamison, a psychologist and fervent apostle of the biopsychiatric model who was herself "bipolar"; her book (*The Unquiet Mind*) was recommended by his doctors and was, as DuBrul notes "the standard reading of the time, the book all the doctors recommended." He never read Kate Millett, who tells the story of how she escaped after thirteen years of spiritual captivity to lithium and Psychiatry. Millett has described how (this was *after* she had become a celebrated author) her sense of self was diminished—rendered inarticulate—not by her alleged "chronic manic-depression," but by the chronicity of her degradation by psychiatrists, of being continually told her mind was defective. She felt taking the lithium was a ritual reenactment of her own inadequacy and the legitimacy of the psychiatric narrative. And she describes at the end of the book how she heroically broke free and got off lithium.[14] Thus the results of DuBrul's research were to bolster the myth that he had a bipolar disorder that could be controlled by psychiatric drugs. But he also derived from the writings of Kay Jamison a different idea that began to germinate in his mind—the idea that there was a link between creativity and "manic-depressive illness."

Nowhere in the 2002 article does DuBrul discuss the destructive side effects of psychiatric drugs, particularly of the nephrotoxic drug he was taking—lithium. He became more aware of these by the time he wrote his blog (see The Revolt against the Monoculture in this chapter). These are discussed in detail in the works of Breggin. I have found many people who take lithium do not realize that the reason their blood level is tested regularly is because if their level is too high it could cause severe harm.

The effects of lithium were discovered in 1949 when John Cade injected two guinea pigs in his lab in Australia. He noted that after two hours the animals became "lethargic and non-responsive to stimuli." It was not long before lithium was being given to human beings, not because it corrects an imbalance but because it has a general subduing effect on patients. The tremor typically caused by lithium (see the section titled The Revolt against the Monoculture in this chapter) is a result of its toxic effect on the brain and nervous system. DuBrul confesses that although he does not trust capitalism, he has in fact learned that psychiatric drugs have helped him. On the other hand, he says in the next paragraph, clinical language does not fit his own experience. He's looking for others who have had similar experiences and presumably share his ambivalence. A few weeks later he was contacted by McNamara.

> In the end, what it comes down to for me is that I desperately feel the need to connect with other folks like myself so I can validate my experiences and not feel so damn alone in the world, so I can pass along the lessons I've learned to help make it easier for other people struggling like myself. By my nature and the way I was raised, I don't trust mainstream medicine or corporate culture, but the fact that I'm sitting here writing this essay right now is proof that their drugs are helping me. And I'm looking for others out there with similar experiences.
>
> But I feel so alienated sometimes. . . . Words like "disorder," "disease," and "dysfunction" just seem so very hollow and so crude.

DuBrul ends the article with the affirmation that he is a moderate who is neither "for" nor "against" the mental health system—and yet he still feels there is something artificial about psychiatric language.

> Our society still seems to be in the early stages of the dialogue where you're either "for" or "against" the mental health system. Like either you swallow the antidepressant ads on television as modern-day gospel and start giving your dog Prozac, or you're convinced we're living in Brave New World and all the psych drugs are just part of a big conspiracy to keep us from being self-reliant and realizing our true potential. I think it's really about time we start carving some more of the middle ground with stories from outside the mainstream and creating a new language for ourselves that reflects all the complexity and brilliance that we hold inside.

DuBrul is far more critical of the pharmaceutical companies today, even after his "retreat" from his radical views in 2007 (see chapter 9). He realizes that the pharmaceutical companies *do* conspire with psychiatrists to increase their sales and to discourage patients' self-reliance. On April 18, 2010, he posted an article that he had written on the Icarus website. The article was titled "Unraveling the Biopsychiatric Knot: the Future History of the Radical Mental Health Movement." The article discuses the hegemony of the pharmaceutical companies, within the economic context of neoliberal capitalism. For example, he wrote:

> The pharmaceutical industry sponsors much of the clinical research on depression. Industry-academic collaborations are becoming an increasing source of funding for universities, academic medical centers, and hospitals. Never before has this "biopsychiatric" culture, which defines our health and happiness in terms of brain chemistry, been so heavily promoted through the mass media, become embedded in central institutions, and embraced by policy makers.

In 2002 he would have disparaged this kind of analysis as "extremist" and as simplistic.

McNamara was one of forty or so people who read the *San Francisco Bay Guardian* article and wrote to DuBrul. She felt his experiences were similar to hers. She shared his confusion and his desire to reach out to people and to create something new. Their meeting was to result in one of the most productive collaborations in the history of the patients' liberation movement: the two of them gave birth to The Icarus Project. Two years after their meeting they had both edited, wrote, and produced on their own The Icarus Project's first book, described above—*Navigating the Space between Brilliance and Madness*. They took off in a truck together, with a thousand copies of the booklet to distribute to colleges and clinics, with the determination to build a new Mad Pride movement and to preach their message to the world: madness is not all breakdown, it can also be breakthrough. Mad people are not mentally ill or psychiatrically disabled. On the contrary they are gifted; you are gifted. You have mad but dangerous gifts, like the wax wings of Icarus in the myth. You, the mad, have a responsibility to cultivate your gifts and to use them for the benefit of the world.

The transformation of DuBrul from a brilliant but confused young seeker who had placed his faith in Psychiatry into a leader who placed his faith in the mad was extraordinary. It was as if DuBrul was channeling something bigger than himself, a new myth, a new zeitgeist seeking to be born. And so the young man who had been indoctrinated by Psychiatry, who expressed how very "grateful" he was to lithium and Zyprexa and Eli Lilly for saving his life became—perhaps to his own surprise—a founder and leader of the first Mad Pride organization in the country. His journey, as we will see, led him not only over the mountains, but also into deep valleys.

The Revolt against the Monoculture

In 2007 I had first discovered The Icarus Project and was fascinated by what I read on the website—scintillating, highly intelligent, and often brilliantly perceptive online conversations between many psychiatric survivors regarding madness and spirituality, corporate capitalism, and the soullessness of modern society, to name just a few topics. I had been particularly impressed by some of the online articles written by the cofounder of The Icarus Project, McNamara. I wrote DuBrul that I was planning to write a book on the Mad Pride movement and would like to meet him sometime since he was located in New York. Since he had not read my first book, I wanted to give him a copy.

We met a few weeks later at a local coffee shop. I was impressed by his maturity (he was twenty-nine) and his personable manner. He was thin, pleasant looking, casually attired, with an appealing air of self-confidence and enthusiasm. (I should add that he did not conform to the stereotype of the ex-mental patient—displaying a bizarre manner created by high dosages of psychiatric drugs—but in appearance and manner seemed like other social activists I knew in the various antiwar movements over the years.) I told him I was impressed by The Icarus Project's exploration of the connection between madness and spirituality, but I wondered why he did not more explicitly repudiate the mental illness construct.

He responded that he thought it was irrelevant. I was disappointed when I discovered that DuBrul had not read any of my favorite critics of "the myth of mental illness": not Szasz, not Laing, not Peter Breggin. At this time I had not read his 2002 article in *The San Francisco Chronicle,* so I was taken aback when he told me that he was "grateful" to lithium since it had "saved his life." "But why do you feel a need to take lithium now?" I asked. He responded, "What if I told you I take it to control my superpowers, which otherwise could overwhelm me?" I was baffled. I asked him if he was aware of the harmful "side effects" of lithium. He was. He said he had been on the radio with David Oaks, and he suspected my ideas were similar to Oaks's; nonetheless, he had not read Oaks's mentor, Dr. Breggin, whose writings had steeled Oaks's resolve to stay off psychiatric drugs. He shrugged when I wondered how it is that one of the leaders in the Mad Pride movement, an intellectual who reads many books, avoids reading the critics of mainstream Psychiatry!

I took out a copy of my book *Madness, Heresy, and the Rumor of Angels,* quickly inscribed it to him as a comrade in the movement, and then gave it to him. (I discovered later that he never read my book either—at least not a couple years after our meeting.) Before we parted he warmly invited me to not just visit the Icarus website but to introduce myself and post on it. I said I would.

I noticed DuBrul's ideas became surprisingly far more radical in the course of the next year—from 2007 to 2008.[15] I was surprised when I read some assertions on his blog indicating he was reassessing the whole mental health system. I think he was moving closer to a consistent critique of Psychiatry and developing an alternative way of interpreting madness. His original position, as I stated above, was inconsistent: on the one hand, The Icarus Project asserted that the disease model was misleading and did not do justice to the human soul and its quest for meaning, while on the other hand, he claimed he suffered from a biological defect, a biochemical imbalance that was corrected by the daily ingestion of lithium.

Thus on June 15, 2008, about a year after DuBrul had told me that he was grateful for lithium and ten months after he had written to me in a open letter on The Icarus Project website that if it were not for the lithium he was given he might be dead, he wrote on his blog:

> So I don't profess to really understand what's going on, but I've come to believe that somehow I, like a bunch of the other people who have gravitated to The Icarus Project, have the ability to cross back and forth between different "realms" of reality that most people do not have access to and usually don't even know exist. I am very aware that this makes me "crazy" in the eyes of the society we live in. Nonetheless, I believe that I crossed over to the other side of reality for the first time when I was eighteen and I didn't know how to handle it and there was no one around to help me figure it out. *I also believe really strongly that if I, and the other people around me, had had different language to talk about what I was going through back then—possibly a language of "spirits" and "possession"—that I never would have gotten locked up in the psych hospital and stuck on all those drugs in the first place.*

I was stunned. DuBrul had not read Laing, he had not even read the book I gave him, but he was now expressing ideas similar to Laing's. According to Laing the "psychotic" was thrust into a different realm, the "inner world," a realm equally as "real" as that of the normal world. The suffering and confusion of the "psychotic" arose not because he was in a different realm but because (as DuBrul put it) he "didn't know how to handle it" and because (as Laing put it) there were no guides. DuBrul said that "there was no one around to help [him] figure it out." Furthermore, DuBrul goes on to state that *had* there been a different model available to render intelligible what he was going through, he would not have needed to be hospitalized or placed on psychiatric drugs.

The spiritual nature of what DuBrul had gone through was of course not recognized by the psychiatric establishment. As they saw it his strange experiences were symptoms of illnesses, and DuBrul had believed them, partially. He equivocated, but in this blog in 2008 he says that the psychiatrists have missed the most important part of what occurred to him. When DuBrul had his first breakdown he had an intuition of this spiritual realm. "With enough psych drugs they reintegrated me into society and convinced me that I was *just* bipolar" (my emphasis added). When it happened again "the drugs and time in the hospital allowed me to reintegrate." By "reintegrate" DuBrul means to readjust—that was the purpose of the hospitalization and the drugs. However, DuBrul's goal was creative *mal*adjustment, and now he was even critical of lithium. As a result of eight years on lithium, "I still shake like an old man at thirty-three. I hope the shaking stops when I kick the lithium. It's such a deal with the devil."

DuBrul had finally rejected the biopsychiatric model he had embraced in 2002 and finally rejected the diagnosis he had clung to for so long. How did this happen? Because of the support he received from the mad community. He explained (May 15, 2008):

> To really delve into this "spiritual" stuff, especially after being raised the way I was [as an atheist] and diagnosed by the Western medical system as having "Bipolar I with Psychotic Features—a serious and persistent mental illness," has taken some real faith in myself, not in small part because of the success of this incredible mad community of ours. The recent collective victories of The Icarus Project have given me a whole lot more faith in the power of big dreams and the power of the "mad ones" to shape the material realm and the

public dialog around us. All of you people who have come together to tell your stories like I'm telling mine right now, and the formal and informal support networks that are clearly growing because of our group work—all of what we are doing together is giving us the ability to truly rewrite our Collective History. And more people are starting to listen to us because what we're saying is not only interesting, but seems to be helping lots of struggling folks who aren't being helped by the mainstream medical system. There is an incredible amount of visionary power in this mad little community of ours.

The community of mad people had given him the courage he lacked in 2002. DuBrul was no longer sitting on the fence. He rejected the idea that he had a psychiatric disability, and he was decreasing the drugs he was taking. He would not have been on the drugs in the first place had there been people around who could place what he was going through in a different nonpsychiatric model—as he put it if they had had a "different language to *talk about what I was going through*" (my emphasis). He clearly believed that once he learned to "swim" in the inner world, the spiritual world, he would not need the drugs at all. DuBrul had adumbrated a new Mad Pride theory with all the seven aspects I delineated in the introduction. He studied shamanism and learned to meditate. He wrote (May 15, 2008), "[I]n the last couple years, in different ways, I've been studying Shamanism and Mysticism, catching up on all the interesting stuff I always wrote off as being New Age . . . hippy crap: learning how to meditate and control my dreams, listening to the voices in my head and getting them to talk to each other rather than taking drugs to try and make them go away. *I still take psych drugs though at lesser doses . . .*" (my emphasis).

The affirmation of the reality of a different spiritual realm is integral to shamanism—to which DuBrul frequently referred. Many groups in the Western esoteric tradition (e.g., the Theosophists) have also attested to the existence of an "astral realm" that human beings can enter through various meditative exercises—or spontaneously after death. The body in the astral plane is similar in form to the physical body, but it has different properties and abilities.[16]

Unlike David Oaks, DuBrul believed that mad people were more inclined than "normal" people to experience these nonordinary states. This explains The Icarus Project's frequent use of the term *dangerous gifts*. Mad people had a responsibility to "cultivate" and "take care" of these gifts. The mad had a distinctive sensibility that made them more sensitive, made it harder for them to adjust to normal society, to the insanity of *"the monoculture."*

Allen Ginsberg argued in the 1950s that the mad were revolting against the violence and materialism of normal society—symbolized for him by "Moloch." Ken Kesey believed the mad were rebelling against the repressive authoritarian conformist order of normal society, which he called "the Combine." Millett had seen through and denounced the coercive rationality of those who sought—in the name of sanity—to constrain the unfettered imagination and to drug the mad into oblivion. DuBrul also now believed that the mad were rebelling instinctively against the homogeneity of normal society; it responds to this revolt by labeling them ill and seeking to silence them.

DuBrul drew an analogy between monoculture in agriculture and mass culture in modern society. On March 31, 2008, he wrote in his blog:

You can see it all from the highway: enormous monocrops of identical corn plants that reach for miles bordered by an endless sea of strip malls, parking lots, and tract housing. You can see it on our kitchen counters and in our classrooms: the same can of soda on the table in Cairo and Kentucky, the same definitions of "progress" and "freedom" in textbooks around the world. Monoculture: the practice of replicating a single plant, product or idea over a huge area, is about the most unstable, unsustainable, unimaginative form of organization that exists, but in the short term it keeps the system running smoothly and keeps the power in the hands of a small number of people. In the logic of our modern world, whether it's in the farmer's field or in the high school classroom, diversity is inefficient and hard to manage.

In the book without a date written by The Icarus Project, *Friends Make the Best Medicine,* it is stated that mad people have a hard time tolerating the monoculture, the insanity of normal society—and they have visions of an alternative society that is actually more sane.

> We believe that people do not belong in grids and boxes of rootless lonely monoculture. Humans are adaptable creatures, and while a lot of people learn to adapt, some of us can't handle the modern world, no matter how many psych drugs or years of school or behavior modification programs we've been put through. . . . There are so many of us out here who feel the world with thin skin and heavy hearts, who get called crazy because we are too full of fire and pain, who know that other worlds exist, and who are not comfortable with this version of reality. . . . We've been busting up out of sidewalks and blooming all kinds of misfit flowers for as long as people have been walking on this earth. . . . You could think of us like dandelion roots that gather minerals from hidden layers of the soil that other plants don't reach. If we're lucky we share them with everyone on the surface. . . . A lot of us have visions about how things could be different, why they need to be different, and it's painful to keep them silent. Sometimes we get called sick and sometimes we get called sacred, but no matter how you label us we are a vital part of making this planet whole. We need to recover our dreams and scheme up ways to make them happen.[17]

It was an expression of a messianic-redemptive yearning.

By May 2008 DuBrul was even more explicit about the potentiality of "the mad ones" to make a decisive contribution to a radical transformation of society. As he wrote (quoted above), "The recent collective victories of The Icarus Project have given me a whole lot more faith in the power of big dreams and the power of the 'mad ones' to shape the material realm and the public dialog around us." The mad then had increased his faith in humanity's ability to attain high ideals. "I think it's important for us to understand that on some level people like us really are dangerous to the system because we don't believe in its future and we actually listen to the voices in our heads. And that's 'mad.' In the eyes of the State we're the equivalent of Islamic Fundamentalists. . . . Maybe just call it The Spirit of the Times." The mad are not committed to the status quo but believe in the possibility of realizing their visions: "I have faith in the power of the mad ones because they're the only ones that are crazy enough to think they can change the world and have the outlandish visions and drive to be able to do it" (March 31, 2008). DuBrul made the point that we have to imagine a new possibility before we can realize it. "[A] strategic relationship to the mass is essential for large scale social change. What would mass change look like if it was positive? Can we even imagine it? We have to be able to imagine it if we want it to happen" (March 19, 2008).

DuBrul argues that there is strategic value in using the term *mad* as a way of eradicating stigma and building a movement that encompasses different social classes and ethnicities. He writes on April 6, 2008 (emphasis mine):

> If we're really going to be breaking down stigma we need a term that is going to bring together everyone from the middle-age homeless schizophrenic black man that has chronic tardive dyskinesia from too much thorazine to the rich white girl who's cutting herself because she can't feel anything in her sheltered suburban life. And everyone in between. There are a lot of us out here. And clearly we need to be reframing the conversation to talk about community mental health—not individual mental illness. Somewhere in this vision are beautiful mad maps of many shapes and colors and styles, the excuses for us to talk in groups about the hard stuff, about how we can support one another individually and collectively amidst it all. Somewhere in there is an understanding that some people are really sensitive and good at crossing boundaries and we need spaces to cultivate those skills. Somewhere in there are collectively developed skills and spaces that feel safe to talk about power and privilege and shame and can build the bridges and networks that will hold together a growing movement. *Maybe "mad" isn't a term that everyone is going to relate to. But I think it's worth adding to the mix.*

Mad Pride is creating space for those who have been silenced for centuries; they can finally speak and hopefully be heard. As DuBrul writes on May 15, 2008, "[I]t really does all feel like a riddle to me, and as weird as it sounds I think part of the answer to the riddle has to do with the Mad Ones, the sensitive ones, the ones that feel injustice and power struggles like knives under their skin, the ones who aren't only struggling for decent living conditions but are viscerally fucking haunted by the ghosts of slavery and genocide and the mass rape of women and the Earth. It seems like it's our responsibility to carve some space for those voices, not just drug them into silence."

9

Interview with Sascha DuBrul

The Reluctant Warrior, May 2009

*D*uBrul is speaking by phone from the ashram where he has been living for several months. In 2008 he had an unexpected "psychotic episode" and was put in Bellevue by the police (see chapter 10). After he was released he decided to go into a retreat at a Hindu farm in upstate New York. Most of his waking hours are spent working outside on the grounds, in collective meditation, worshipping, and chanting.

Farber: You are now at Swami Sivananda's ashram. You said you were raised an atheist.

Sascha DuBrul: I was raised an atheist. I was raised by a man who was beaten by nuns in Catholic school in the '50s in Queens. I remember very clearly being six years old and asking my dad if there was a God, and he said "No." That answer satisfied me for a long time.

Farber: Were you still an atheist when you founded The Icarus Project?

Sascha DuBrul: Yes. I dropped out of college when I was twenty, and I started traveling. Shortly thereafter I had some intense spiritual experiences—I definitely wouldn't have used the word *God*.

Farber: You were a punk-anarchist for a number of years. You said the punk-anarchist thing was pretty atheistic, except Hakim Bey (Peter Lamborn Wilson) was an anarchist and Sufi.[1]

Sascha DuBrul: I know it. And we were all so inspired by Hakim Bey. Even amongst the anarchists there is a craving for transcendence and communion. I hope, I feel like we're doing something similar with The Icarus Project. The Icarus Project has its roots in the anarchist, punk rock social milieu, and it's a very spiritual project; you look at the discussions on the forum and there's a mix of people talking about spirituality. . . .

Farber: Well, I've noticed that for years, not just on the forums, but people in mental hospitals are definitely more "preoccupied" with spiritual issues. Shrinks consider that pathological.

Sascha DuBrul: Sure, sure.

Farber: You must have noticed that at Icarus. You're saying the same thing right? There's more preoccupation with these issues than among the average population?

Sascha DuBrul: Sure, yeah. We're the ones having the experiences.

Farber: So when you refer to spiritual experiences in your twenties, you weren't referring to the experiences that got labeled psychotic?

Sascha DuBrul: No, I was just talking about stuff that happened after that. But before my first hospitalization when I was eighteen, I definitely had "spiritual" visions. I had this vision that the world was going to end, but somehow we were all going to live on, on some other kind of world that was like television. I came out of that experience and didn't know what the fuck to think of it. I mean I was scared.*

---

*Will Hall, another Icarus staff member, later interpreted this vision as a premonition of the social interaction that now takes place on the Internet.

Farber: Could you say that it was like a kind of modern-day messianic vision?

Sascha DuBrul: Well, I was walking on the subway tracks with my arms outstretched, thinking that I was some kind of messianic figure, that the world was going to end and that I somehow represented the end of time, and that I was going to die and was going to be resurrected in this other reality. I wasn't raised a Christian, so I didn't even have that. . . . I was just raised in this culture and I just kind of absorbed . . .

Farber: In a secular culture in New York?

Sascha DuBrul: Yeah, a very secular culture. One thing I've realized about being at the ashram here, we are praying to all these Hindu deities. All of the equivalents of these Hindu deities were in the comic books I read when I was a kid. The comic books are totally the secular version of all these same stories that we're learning from.

Farber: So you think the comic books were written by some kind of psychedelic-type heads or something?

Sascha DuBrul: I don't think so. I think they were probably written by really straight people; I think it's just woven into the collective unconscious.

Farber: Oh, so it wasn't like dope smoking hipsters writing *Mad* magazine in the 1950s?

Sascha DuBrul: I don't think so. I don't think Spiderman and Batman and Superman . . .

Farber: One of the things about madness that interests me the most is the kind of messianic aspects and visions that frequently are associated with it. You know John Weir Perry wrote about this?

Sascha DuBrul: I have a thought on the messianic thing that maybe you'll find interesting. Because it affects me so personally, I've had to do a lot of thinking about it. It's all fine and good to think it's really fascinating, but it's actually very disruptive for our social lives. Who wants to hang out with someone whose ego is swelled to the size of a God? It's not fun—it's really not—and go to a mental institution where you're around a number of people like that and it's horrible. So one of the aspects of the yogic traditions that's been really helpful for me is the understanding—the importance—of really letting go or basically killing our egos and the importance of selfless service and the importance of basically not thinking about yourself. Actually, the night that Ashley and I met, she pulled this book off her shelf by Ram Dass called *Be Here Now*.*[2] There's a quote in there about people who end up going up to heaven and then getting kicked back down because they have their egos on, and we both really related to that. That's what ends up happening to people who think they're Jesus, who think they're the Messiah; they're tapping in to something, clearly, but they have ego issues.

Farber: Yes, but the shrinks—even the more spiritual shrinks, the New Age ones—want to create a kind of barrier between the mystic and the schizophrenic, like they are two qualitatively different things. Then there are other people, Joseph Campbell or Perry, who see the boundary as more fluid. So as I see it, schizophrenics are mystics in the embryonic stage of development.

Sascha DuBrul: Okay, we got that down already; we're on the same page about that one. I agree that a schizophrenic is a mystic who hasn't learned to swim, as you wrote me; what I'm saying is that here's the path that you take, that there are actually spiritual paths that people take to be able to swim and that people have been doing it for a very long time and that's the yogic traditions. That's what people are doing here, and there are tons of people, and this is what I was writing you—my contention with you about the strategicness of using *mad*—of calling the movement the Mad Pride movement. Living in these two ashrams for the last six months, I've met tons of people who struggle just as intensely as I do; mad is not what they want to call themselves; they're really working on being actually quite the opposite of what's thought of as mad, very focused and very disciplined.

Farber: Were these people who were labeled schizophrenic at one point?

---

*A bestselling book among young people in the 1970s, its influence led it to be characterized as a "countercultural bible."

Sascha DuBrul: No, these are just people who believe in the spiritual path.

Farber: Yeah, but they share the common cultural prejudices then, right? Against the so-called mentally ill, and they want to say, "Well, we mystics aren't like the sick people, et cetera . . ." because it's such a stigma being schizophrenic or bipolar.

Sascha DuBrul: Any movement that defines itself as victims and then starts rising up and saying, "We're not victims"—that's a step forward. So the idea of Mad Pride had its place, I agree, but what I'm saying is that there's a lot of people who struggle—who I would say are not any different from me, except that I've had the experience of being locked up.

Farber: You mean they would have been labeled psychotic by the shrink establishment had they come to their attention?

Sascha DuBrul: Yeah, totally. The swami at the ashram I was living on, for the stuff he was saying would be labeled psychotic.

Farber: That's support for my theory though. That there is such an overlap between those labeled bipolar or schizo and the *very small* group of people (they're not the cultural norm, either) devoted to spending all their days for months or years worshipping on a Hindu ashram in America. I mean, you're an example.

Sascha DuBrul: Totally. But what I'm saying is that, yeah, the shrinks are so off-target, that's not even a question. But, what I'm saying is that as far as movement building, I'm really interested in the whole generation of kids that have been put on psych drugs and that have been given psychiatric labels, and I want to help get them off of their drugs and I want to help. . . .

Farber: Oh, you're more into that now, the getting off the drugs, the . . .

Sascha DuBrul: If it's appropriate to get off their drugs. For me, I'm taking my psychiatric drugs, and at the moment I'm happy taking my drugs. I'm not across-the-board saying everyone should get off their drugs. What I'm saying is that, I think that there's all of these kids—

how are we going to empower them? Is identifying them with madness what's going to empower them? I kind of see Mad Pride as a transition step, like I was saying . . . in the end identifying as mad is really ambiguous. I still feel I'm part of the emerging Mad Pride movement.

Farber: You're not going to, say, disassociate yourself from it because of your reservations about the name?

Sascha DuBrul: Yeah, of course not, how can I do that? No, no, I want to be helpful, but I'll tell you on a very practical level, it's all fine and good to read the theory—it's really important what you're doing, writing an intellectual basis for the movement—but on a day-to-day, on-the-ground level, being able to actually organize with people on the basis that we're mad is a really hard thing to do. Especially without any kind of spiritual grounding that's solid. I don't really want to do that, and I don't want other people to get hurt. When I think of Mad Pride, I can't help but think of what's happened to similar movements in the past: high ideals but they deteriorated.

Farber: Let me contextualize it somewhat because the psychiatric idea originally—the Freudian idea—was that people who were schizophrenic were pathological, and their belief that they had some kind of religious mission was said by the shrinks to be a compensation for a sense of very low self-esteem. They called it a "reaction formation," and they claimed the structure of their ego was very brittle—and that they had to stay away from spirituality and religion because their egos were so weak that it could implode and the so-called schizophrenics or bipolars would then have no defenses and become acutely psychotic again. Psychosis was seen as a regression to the primitive infantile state before the formation of the ego. Now Joseph Campbell, *on the other hand,* says the madman, the schizophrenic, and the mystic are in the *same* ocean—it's beyond the infantile state—but the mystic is swimming, and the psychotic is drowning.[3]

The psychiatric warning to the patient was, "Stay away from the ocean." Actually, they didn't even acknowledge that the ocean—this spiritual reality—existed other than as hallucination because their idea of consensual reality is very limited. So their idea was to keep psychotics on drugs, prevent them from getting into any spiritual thing whatsoever, because that would be very dangerous for their weak egos. Now Anton Boisen was a chaplain who had had a breakdown in the 1920s, he wrote about in the 1920s and 1930s (see chapter 13). He said there's an element of truth in these messianic feelings compared to the kind of idea—prevalent then and now among many philosophers—that we're all just a collection of atoms in a meaningless universe. On the other hand, you have spiritual traditions—Hindu, that says we are all God, or Russian Christianity, that says men and women could become Gods. So if a schizophrenic or bipolar says, "I'm God," or "I'm the Messiah," is he or she any further from the truth or closer to the truth than the psychiatric establishment, which says that we're just accidental aggregates of atoms and molecules swirling around space? [Pause.] You yourself said the mad ones were maybe the only ones who had the outlandish visions that could take us beyond. [Pause.]

Sascha DuBrul: Yeah, well they might be the ones who have the outlandish visions, but for things to actually happen, it takes people who actually are grounded enough in reality to be able to talk to everyone else. I think that there's a really important need for people who have the ability to walk between the worlds—this world and the world of spirits—and go from one side to the other and come back, and that is the distinction between the shaman and the schizophrenic, right? The schizophrenic doesn't know how to come back.

Farber: But he can learn. At least he knows the other world *exists.* Here are these two things that I said that I thought were kind of implicit or explicit assertions of Mad Pride. I have six, but the first two are: one, that there is a distinctive mad sensibility different from that of the normal person, and two, that this sensibility is potentially an asset and provides a basis for Mad Pride. Those are the first two. Would you agree with them?

Sascha DuBrul: I've just got to say that I don't. There are such different experiences that people have. What about people who end up getting locked up in the hospital because they're poor and don't fall into that category here? Drawing distinctions between the mad and the normal seems tricky.

Farber: It's a distinction you were drawing frequently in your writings in 2008.

Sascha DuBrul: Yeah, I know, I know.

Farber: "The mad ones" was the term you used. You remember that, right?

Sascha DuBrul: Of course I do. I don't know if you're familiar with the yoga sutras of Pantanjali?

Farber: A bit, I haven't read them. I'm more familiar with the Vedas.

Sascha DuBrul: It's one of the classic sacred yogic texts. It's four chapters, and the third chapter is all about the superpowers that you get once you achieve the level of concentration: you can become invisible, and it talks about being able to read people's minds. When I read that, it was such a relief, because I was like, "Oh, okay, I'm not crazy." And here's a manual for this, there's a path, a spiritual path that people have carved and learned. So what I wonder is, is the knowledge that I've gained from being mad any different from the knowledge of the person who is not mad, but who has a really disciplined meditation practice and the lessons that they gain from that? I guess that's what I'm saying, when it comes down to it. I think that spiritual knowledge, spiritual truths can be reached be people who aren't mad.

Farber: Of course. As Ramakrishna said, the goal is one, the paths are many. But madness is one path—a difficult one. It's not chosen, it just happens to some people. Using the term *madness* is a way of validating experiences that shrinks denigrate as "mental illness." Ashley [the cofounder of The Icarus Project] wrote in one of her essays that she achieved access to visions in a few weeks of mania that it took many people years of meditation to reach. What is called "mania" could be like a quick opening to a higher state designed by God, but, of course, it's dangerous if someone does not have support, which he doesn't in this society.

Sascha DuBrul: Yes, there are different paths, but it's actually quite presumptuous to say the mad ones are the ones who are going to lead.

Farber: So you're saying it was a presumptuous kind of thing you said about a year ago?

Sascha DuBrul: Yeah, I was making leaps that today I wouldn't make in the same way. Do I think it still sounds really sexy? Yeah, come on, you know, and can you quote me saying that stuff? Yes, you can, as long as you say something of what I'm saying now just to temper it, because I feel good about everything I've said, I just don't totally agree with it anymore.

Farber: Would you still say that there are many of the people who tend to get labeled mentally ill who are having spiritual experiences that are difficult to handle—as you said a year ago? Or are you unusual among that group?

Sascha DuBrul: No, there are quite a lot of mad people who fit what you say, but I'm not going to speak for everyone. I also think that it starts getting very subjective when you start talking about normal people and mad people. At some point I'm not sure where to go with that.

Farber: Do you still think society is insane?

Sascha DuBrul: That goes without saying. Listen, I've got to go into the temple.

We finished the interview two weeks later. DuBrul was visiting his mother in New York City and agreed to stop at my apartment. He was in a less relaxed mood than when he was at the ashram.

Sascha DuBrul: Let's get away from the idea that it's the mad ones who are the vanguard or the ones who are going to lead the charge or something.

Farber: Last year you sounded very radical in your writings on Mad Pride, the mad as forerunners.

Sascha DuBrul: Yeah, and then I got my ass locked up, my collective of people got sick of me because I was acting egotistical and messianic, and it was a good lesson in the downfalls of that philosophy. You see, I tried to go off my lithium, and I was really manic.

It seems he's reluctant to talk about this, so I change the topic.

Farber: You wrote that during your first breakdown that you were possessed by the spirit of your deceased father.

Sascha DuBrul: I think it's something more like there's a larger force that wasn't my father. My father was a mortal man, but I think there was a spirit inside of him, and I think when he died it entered me. Something like that—I wish I understood it more. There's definitely something in biology though. Biologically, we can look at the lithium levels in my blood and see it was way lower than it had been, and that had a big impact on me feeling spirit much stronger because so much more was coming in. That's biological. . . .

Farber: But this is a myth! There is absolutely no evidence that manic people have lower levels of lithium than "normal" people.

Sascha DuBrul: I wasn't talking about that—about a group. I'm talking about the fact that I take lithium every day, regardless of whether I'm normal or abnormal. I take lithium every day, and it has an effect on me.

Farber: Why do you take it?

Sascha DuBrul: Because if I don't take it, I'm really sensitive and can have a hard time being in the world.

Farber: Why don't you at least take some of the newer stuff they use, with less harmful side effects?

Sascha DuBrul: I figure I'll be on the new stuff at some point. I figure at some point I'll get off the lithium train before it does too much damage, and I'll move on to—what is it—I don't even remember, but there's a drug that seems it would probably work pretty well for some people.

Farber: You'd rather sleep with the devil you know?

Sascha DuBrul: Lithium has been very helpful to me. And the thing that they say, as far as this stuff goes, is that if the drugs work for you, you're lucky. If they work, if they don't fuck you up and they're actually doing their job, then you're lucky! And I know that from experience.

Farber: Lithium has terrible side effects, which you wrote about. Are you're saying you'd rather stick with a drug that worked than try a new drug that might not work?

Sascha DuBrul: Yeah, at some point I'll do it, but there are these levels of stability. My life has been unstable. I aspire to be able to hold down a job and support myself, and I have had a hard time doing that over the course of my adult life. It's like you talking about having a whole bunch of people read your book and then being affected by it positively. I was in a place where I was really well respected and all these people were looking at me and read my writing and thought I was just cool. There were all these young people who were inspired, and my ego started getting the best of me, and I started thinking that I was really cool. In doing that I separated myself from the other people around me and ended up—because it's my natural inclination to be—a guy alone in a room with a bunch of books. That's my natural inclination. I actually want to have relationships with people that are challenging, that actually force me to change and to grow rather than getting into my own mind-set.

I can totally see that you want to write this book: you see the importance of what you have in mind that can connect the dots—that this is really important for the movement—but I'm sure that a part of you also is like, "I want the movement. I want the movement, I want the people, I want to be a part of the movement that doesn't exist yet, and I'm trying to create it." I'm maybe reminding you of what you already know. It is all around us, and that's something that you tune into, it's a frequency that you tune into, that universal love story where it's like you and God, and here we are in our universal love story . . . but don't let ego get in the way. That's my natural inclination. I actually want to have relationships with people that are challenging, that actually force me to change and to grow rather than getting into my own mind-set.

Farber: What's the ego? The ego is no big deal when you have a vision of the infinite bliss, the infinite happiness that God wills for us all. You are overwhelmed by it, and the ego shrivels up. It's only when the vision is lacking that the pride of the ego seems important, but when you have an awareness of the infinite you are just spontaneously humbled. The problem is most people do not have that vision . . . or they forget it, or they dismiss it as illness. How did you come to be worshipping God? Most young Americans who reject their own traditions because they've become anemic or narrow-minded choose to become Buddhists because they have a hard time worshipping God—they think it's authoritarian—but you're worshipping Krishna.

Sascha DuBrul: I'm just kind of worshipping Krishna because that's the God that's in front of me right now. I'm worshipping the Creator. We worship the Creator by being really present and joyful. I think it's about gratitude, just continually feeling grateful and not just intellectually feeling gratitude, but the emotion of gratitude. Gratitude opens you up and allows you to feel joy, and if you can feel joy then that joy transforms into the ability to be present.

Farber: Did you not have to overcome any barriers that said worshipping God is just superstition?

Sascha DuBrul: Sure I have. What happened to me when I was eighteen years old was that I had a spiritual awakening that my rational mind and the rational society around me wouldn't—couldn't—accept it, so I just buried it, and then it came back. I think I was just different. I think if I had been born in a religious society, a spiritual society, I would have been very spiritual from a young age, and they would have picked me out, and it would have been clear that I was different, but because that didn't happen, it took an extra long time to happen. If you believe in God, then you realize that everything happens for a reason, and everything happens in its due time. So I feel like I'm here to be a bridge-builder between the secular and the spiritual worlds.

Farber: Did your belief in God arise out of what was labeled a psychotic experience?

Sascha DuBrul: Definitely. Definitely. Well, for me the way it manifested itself was that I had this vision as an eighteen-year-old. I was in Reed College in Portland, Oregon, reading Plato and Aristotle. I'd taken mescaline a couple of times and was smoking a lot of West Coast weed and drinking a lot of coffee. I had this experience that was like the classic story of Plato's allegory of the cave; the person walks out of the cave and realizes that everything they've been seeing is just shadows of the real, and then he walks back in and tries to tell people about it, and they say he's crazy.

Farber: Did you have the experience of God then as a loving . . .

Sascha DuBrul: I think it was actually more sinister than that; I wasn't paranoid, but I felt really powerful myself. I felt, because of my leftist upbringing I'm sure, like the billboards I saw on the highway that had secret messages implanted in them—I saw the secret messages in them that no one else was seeing—so it seemed really clear that something was afoot, and I had this vision that the world was going to end, but somehow we were all going to live on, but the way that I saw it was that we were all going to live on, on television. I didn't know what it meant, but that's how I saw it. I wasn't using the word *God* for sure because I just didn't have any of that language then, which was probably good, it probably made my psychosis more interesting, but the unity of all things—I was feeling that really intensely. So that happened to me when I was eighteen.

When I was twenty I dropped out of college, and I started traveling, and I remember going into the desert for the first time in northern Arizona and just seeing the entire sky and feeling this incredible sense of spirit and feeling connected to something much larger than myself and feeling that I was so obviously in the right place at the right time— for the first time in my life. That had been after I'd gotten out of the psych hospital after being there for months because back then they held people longer. I was in the hospital for two-and-a-half months, and I was in a private psych hospital for another two-and-a-half months, and then I got out and was trying to go to college—Columbia University; I was trying to play the part, and it didn't work.

So going out to the desert traveling, I felt spirit, but I didn't call it God; I just felt that everything was connected to everything else and that there was some kind of flow and you could tap into that flow. Then it just—honestly, man, and I never thought about this before— but there's this way that there was always a kind of ego-filled, messianic quality to my spirituality, where I thought that I was chosen to do things, and that went on for years, and The Icarus Project played right into that dynamic.

It wasn't until I got to the ashram and started understanding that this spirit that we're talking about, that everyone has it and it's everywhere and that actually the spiritual path is about letting go of the ego. The ego is what gets you into trouble, and that's when I started using the word *God,* actually, that's when I started realizing that the path to spirit is one of relinquishing control to God. To get back to where we started when you asked the question, yes, does that fly in the face of the leftist ideologies and philosophies I was raised with—it sure does, but that doesn't bother me. I'm very excited, because I feel like I'm still in the process. I've known since I was young that I wanted to be part of a mass movement, and being around spiritual people makes me feel that I'm part of it.

The ashram does not make me feel like these are my people worshipping Krishna and Vishnu and Shiva, that's not my calling, but the spiritual path in itself and using it as a vehicle for organizing, that has a whole new dimension to me. I go back and look at the Icarus materials and I feel like I'm in a process of translation, my own translation right now, where I don't really know exactly where I stand with everything, but I'm very open.

Farber: When you took up the yogic path did you say, "Screw the movement. I'm just going to be here now, and I don't want to be part of a cause."

Sascha DuBrul: I did that for a little while because I feel like that's part of the deal. Now I'm in a process of synthesis, and I'm looking for other people who are somehow combining the worlds.

Farber: East and West?

Sascha DuBrul: East and West, and radical social political movements with Eastern philosophy. I'm saying that there are all these traps in the West that we get into and that it's really important to let go.

Farber: Let me read you a quote from Anton Boisen. He had a breakdown in the 1920s and recovered—which was unheard of then—and he became a chaplain and worked in a psych ward. This is from *The Exploration of the Inner World.*[4] He noticed of course that many schizophrenics thought they were the Messiah, but so did Jesus. He writes that we will never be able to understand Jesus unless we realize that "Jesus had the same set of ideas we have found to be characteristic of our acutely disturbed patients." Boisen holds with Albert Schweitzer that Jesus thought he was the Messiah, he thought he was going to usher in the kingdom of God. But Jesus was wrong. So how is Jesus different from any patient in a hospital who thinks he's the Messiah?

Sascha DuBrul: That's a very provocative question, and I think, not being a Christian, it's not appropriate for me to be talking about Jesus so much, but I feel like the question of messianic . . . the thing about the Messiah is there's only one.

Farber: No, there is the concept of the cosmic Christ and the Christ consciousness in all of us, and you know in Kabbalah there is the idea that all the Jews have to liberate the divine spark within their souls. Many forms of esoteric Christianity posit that human beings are the Messiah. The idea that there is one is incidental. You have this idea in Sri Aurobindo that it is going to take more than one person. What is essential is the messianic process. The key would be to awaken the messianic consciousness within each person—within as many people as possible. The idea of there being only one messiah is a remnant from the age of monarchy—when there was only one king.

Sascha DuBrul: Once again, it gets back to the ego and our relationships to the ego. The ego wants to usurp power. But you know if you think you're the Messiah that's basically a sign that you're not.

Farber: This is how Boisen answers the question. When he points out Jesus was wrong about the timing he was not trying to say Jesus is as screwed up as a mental patient but rather the mental patient was on to something, just like Jesus was! He says, "Even the hospital schizophrenic who thinks of himself as Christ may not be wholly mistaken. [Jesus] exemplifies the truth which the acutely disturbed hospital patient is grasping after, that man is made in the image of God." So when the schizophrenic says he's the Messiah there is an element of truth.

Sascha DuBrul: That's really beautiful, and once again, let's talk about day-to-day relationships. These people that think they're the Messiah, what's their relationship like with their mom, with other people in their lives?

Farber: That's another issue—for everyone. I think Boisen had the answer to it, which is similar to the teaching in the *Bhagavad Gita:* you give yourself over to the messianic task while sacrificing the ego. He writes, "We may affirm furthermore that the heart of Jesus' message is ever to be found in his doctrine of the cross. Through him there comes to us the imperious summons to assume the same responsibility he assumed and to give ourselves completely to the sacrificial task of bringing in the new world which ought to be." So the heart of Jesus's message is to assume the messianic task as Jesus did. Don't throw away the baby with the bathwater. The baby is the messianic vision—the new world we want to bring into existence. That doesn't entail an individual messiah; it's a group of people or a movement.

Sascha DuBrul: What do you mean by a messianic movement? When I think of messianic, I think of messiahs; who would be the messiahs?

Farber: But that's the old fashioned, traditionalist way—now it's fundamentalist. I'd say it's more like the Aquarian Conspiracy, as Marilyn Ferguson called it. It starts with a few people and it gets larger.

Sascha DuBrul: So everyone's a messiah? Have you read Eckhart Tolle? You should read *The New World,* that's his whole thing.

Farber: Do you still want to be part of Mad Pride?

Sascha DuBrul: Yeah, I want to be a part of it; read *The New Earth,* man, see what Eckhart Tolle has to say about who are the people, because the people who are enlightened, by definition, they're not mad.

Farber: But your swami and Jesus were mad, psychotic *by the standards of psychiatry;* we already agreed.

Sascha DuBrul: I guess this is at the crux of my contention with your term *mad.* You're using it to define yourself in opposition to normal and the world of Psychiatry. In the end that's a duality; it may be a way to catalyze people and get people excited, but it's not the movement. The movement I want to see is actually happening right now, and I think that we play a part in it.

Farber: What movement?

Sascha DuBrul: The spiritually based movement I've been inspired by when I read Joseph Campbell and he talks about the new religion.

Farber: Does this the movement include The Icarus Project?

Sascha DuBrul: Sure it does, but I don't have the audacity to think that we're that important. We have a role to play, but I don't think we're that important. I think the Icarus myth is a tragedy, the original myth, and eventually that story is going to birth new stuff, but it's a chapter—and dude, if I were you, that's how I would frame what you're doing. Rather than proclaiming that this is the way and this is the path, I would say this is a step to how we're getting to where we're going. You want to do something so people reading Eckhart Tolle—and there are a lot of them—will feel connected to it and want to be a part of it.

The Icarus Project can be a supportive first step in finding other people who are like you and knowing you're not alone, but it's not a long-term way of growing. You can't hang out with mad people all the time; you'd go crazy. You have to hang out with people who are structured and have it together. The mad movement has its place, but I don't think it's a vanguard force like you do. I hope that I've made myself clear—that my perspective is such that I think that we have a definite role to play, but we're tiny. To even use the terms *messianic* or *mad* is too problematic.

Farber: But my book is about the Mad Pride movement.

Sascha DuBrul: Yeah, clearly you have to use the term *mad*, that's what your book is about. You do what you've got to do and write your book, and I'm glad you're nudging things in our direction; I'm in a process of exploration where I'm seeing what else is out there.

10

The Warrior In Retreat

In my interview with DuBrul he was reluctant to discuss his more recent breakdown, so in trying to make sense of it as something other than an unpredictable purely random effect of aberrant biochemistry, I was forced to speculate.* Just as I provided in chapter 8 a nonpsychiatric explanation for his "miraculous recovery" from his misery and loneliness when he moved to the organic farm when he was twenty-four, so I could, drawing on my experience as a family therapist (see chapter 5), explain without any reference to psychiatric drugs what happened that led to him finding himself in Bellevue in 2008.

The purpose of this speculation is to present readers with more options *for themselves,* to give them an alternative frame of reference for their own unusual experiences so they don't fall prey to the self-fulfilling prophecy of the psychiatrist: "If you don't take your drugs your illness will come back." People are not victims of aberrant brains; their experience usually is intelligible when considered in the context of their environment. People who are "bipolar" may well be more sensitive and more vulnerable, but that is not a flaw. So with apologies to DuBrul for speculating about his life on the basis of insufficient facts, for the benefit of other psychiatrically labeled readers, I will try to give a brief nonmedical explanation for his breakdown.

---

*Chapter 11 contains a written statement that DuBrul gave me two years after the interview in chapter 9, and shortly before this book's publication (see pages 250–53). It suggests an alternative explanation for his hospitalization, one that is complementary to my own.

In September 2008 DuBrul had a "psychotic episode" (his first in seven years) and was taken to Bellevue. He was picked up by the police on top of a building in Manhattan. He was "barefooted and disheveled" (in the words of the hospital summary; see Scatter blog, October 16, 2008) "smashing a satellite dish because he thought it was broadcasting alien signals." In his blog DuBrul related his action to "fantasies that creep up periodically that the world is going to turn upside down . . . and all of a sudden it's going to be obvious that things have become incredibly fucked up and will never be the same again."

What happened?

DuBrul evidently has mixed feelings about lithium. Although in 2007 DuBrul thought he did not need lithium, on many occasions he has reiterated the canard that lithium corrects an imbalance in one's biochemistry. (In the statement written in 2011 he finally abandoned this canard; see this section, below.) As discussed in chapter 2, there is no evidence to support this theory. According to *The Comprehensive Textbook of Psychiatry*, "There is no evidence that bipolar mood disorder is a lithium deficiency state or that lithium works by correcting such a deficiency."

Revealingly, the *Textbook* acknowledges and sanctions the fact that patients are in effect lied to by psychiatrists. "Patients are often told it corrects a biochemical imbalance, and, for many, this explanation suffices." Furthermore, there are only a relatively small percentage of people who respond positively to lithium, despite the books by celebrities hailing it as a miracle drug. For most people lithium does not work—particularly in the long run. As author and British psychiatrist Joanne Moncrieff put it in 1997, "There are indications that it is ineffective in the long-term outlook of bi-polar disorders, and it is associated with various forms of harm."[1]

Many patients are afraid to get off psychiatric drugs. They have been told that if they do so their "illness will return." As Dr. Breggin notes, "Drug withdrawal presents a potentially frightening challenge to live your life differently without a guarantee you'll be up to the task. This natural, almost inevitable fear may be worsened by years of being told that you have an incurable disease caused by biochemical imbalances that must be corrected with modern medical panaceas."[2]

Just as there is a positive placebo effect, so there is what I term an inverse or negative placebo effect: the expectation that something will go wrong without the psychiatric drugs for support, the idea that one needs a drug or drugs to correct one's alleged "imbalance," and the fear that one will go crazy without them. The negative placebo creates *a psychological dependence* on psychiatric drugs. Those who believe in Psychiatry will be more likely to experience the placebo effect, both positive and negative.

The faith in Psychiatry is tenacious in our society; even "revolutionaries," rebels, Marxists, feminists, those who challenge every hegemonic institution, are likely to place their faith in modern Psychiatry. In our secular scientific age, Psychiatry, like medicine in general, is God. Psychiatrists have wrapped themselves in the shroud of science since the 1990s, which was dubbed by the U.S. Congress and President George H. W. Bush "the decade of the brain."[3]

As a psychologist and writer I have studied and talked to many people about getting off of psychiatric drugs. If they are succeeding and they "trip up" there is invariably some factor in the environment that explains it—not decreasing the drug itself. DuBrul had been decreasing the lithium with positive effect for months, judging from his own reports on his blog. (I should add that the longer patients have been on a drug and the more drugs patients are taking, the stronger the withdrawal symptoms will be.) I suspect DuBrul was wisely withdrawing gradually.

DuBrul mentioned conflicts he was having with his friends and housemates. He blamed the conflicts solely on himself, on his egocentricity, but I'm not sure the problem was not a group problem, as conflicts often are. In such situations one needs either family therapy or group mediation or, if those are not available, one needs to get away, one needs "space." The solution is simple, but often implementing it is difficult. Finding space can be a problem for those who are not wealthy; some people end up getting themselves taken to a psychiatric ward just to get away. When DuBrul was twenty-four, as we saw, he found an organic farm to live on down the road from the dreary halfway house where he had been placed.

I had a client (later a friend), Lisa G., who was so determined to get off psychiatric drugs that she created her own emotional space. She was living with her mother and could not afford to live elsewhere. She was twenty-seven and had various "diagnoses," from "bipolar" to "schizophrenic." Fortunately, she had only been on the drugs, the "antipsychotics," for a few years. She stopped taking the drugs (gradually), but she told her propsychiatric mother she was taking them. Only I knew the truth. What's more, she acted, she told me, as she would have acted had she still been on the drugs. She acted listless, unemotional, slow. She found this situation very unpleasant. She put on a facade for over a year; by then she had saved up enough money to move in with a roommate. (Such a solution is courageous and admirable, but of course not always feasible.) Twenty years later, she has not taken any psychiatric drugs.

If one person decreases her dosage of psychiatric drugs it can alter the group's dynamics. For example, perhaps DuBrul became more emotional when he reduced the lithium he was taking. Maybe his friends—even other activists—became frightened of his emotionality, knowing he had reduced his intake of the drug. This could have set up a vicious cycle, with his fear feeding off their fear. This is what happened to Kate Millett when she first tried to withdraw from lithium—although she was living with feminists and nonconformists. It is a common scenario.*[4] "Get enough sleep, have faith, and *tell no one*," Millett was finally advised by an activist in the psychiatric survivors' movement. She did, and despite seventeen years of using lithium, after spending six months in 1988 and 1989 decreasing her dosage, she stopped for good, with no ill effects.[5]

Staying on psychiatric drugs for a lifetime can be very harmful.† Robert Whitaker has demonstrated in his recent book (see this section, p. 246) the deleterious and often tragic effects of psychiatric drugs;

---

*As a trained family therapist I know that, as stated earlier, it is common in conflicted or "dysfunctional" families for one person to become psychotic—as documented by Laing and family therapists. One person gets the label, but it is the family or group unit that is having difficulty dealing with change.

†I have one friend who had been on "antipsychotic" drugs, as well as several other drugs, for twenty-five years before I met her. She had never heard anyone critical of psychiatry until she met me—and this was in New York City. Now, ten years after we met, she realizes the drugs have ruined her health and impaired her life, but she has been on them too long to get off. She did finally find a psychiatrist who was willing to reduce her dosage.

244 •• Dangerous Gifts

some psychiatric drugs are worse than others (see discussion with Dr. Stastny in chapter 1). It is difficult to get a psychiatrist to prescribe a mild tranquilizer without a cocktail of others drugs. But as Dr. Stastny points out in chapter 1, a benzodiazepine used cautiously in emergency situations could actually help one cope with acute stress and avoid hospitalization. Many times a "psychotic" episode is triggered because of lack of sleep. Yet that could be remedied with a mild tranquilizer or prescription sleeping pill. Instead millions of patients are put on the most toxic drugs, allegedly to treat their "affective disorders." In fact, Whitaker shows the drugs used create the very symptoms attributed to the psychiatric disorders!

The Mad Pride movement wisely respects patients' right to choose to take or not take psychiatric drugs, but in light of Whitaker's revelations discussed below and the power of the pharmaceutical companies, I think more thought should be given to the issue: How can there be legitimate informed choices made by patients when there is a major "cover-up" occurring about the effects of these drugs?

There ought to be Soteria-type asylums (see Dr. Stastny's description in chapter 1 and the discussion of Diabasis in chapter 5), sanctuaries for people undergoing crises. (In his most recent statement included below, DuBrul implies also that there ought to be resources to help persons deal with trauma.) Had there been such a place, I think DuBrul would have gone there when he had the conflict with his friends in order to get "space." The fact that he felt he was receiving "alien signals" is revealing: he felt estranged, "alienated," from his friends. In a Soteria-type alternative, DuBrul would have been presented with the opportunity to finally get off psychiatric drugs. Considering there are no such sanctuaries in America anymore and DuBrul's conflict with his friends was not being mediated, it is not surprising he ended up in Bellevue. He had no other way to get away, to get space.

DuBrul was not in as dire a situation as most "bipolar patients," on psychiatric drugs. As far as I know he was taking only one drug—lithium. Most patients are placed on several drugs. However, when DuBrul was at Bellevue he was undoubtedly given higher dosages of drugs than he had been taking—this is the routine on psychiatric wards—and unfortunately when he was released he was more convinced than ever that he *needed* lithium. After her first unpleasant experience of trying to get off lithium, Kate Millett also became more convinced she needed it. Only later did she realize in hindsight the role the environment (i.e., her friends) played in making it impossible for her to withdraw from lithium.

After he was released from Bellevue, DuBrul wisely *did* go to an alternative environment to recover—to the ashram mentioned above—but by this point he had no desire to wean himself off psychiatric drugs. Several months before his episode he had been planning to get off of psychiatric drugs. Now he was convinced again that he could not live without lithium. Very few people labeled bipolar are on only one drug, as I believe DuBrul was; most are on a "cocktail." Fortunately DuBrul's hopes of getting off drugs were revived again later. Yet apart from the potential physical harm caused by the drug, would taking the one drug undermine DuBrul's self-confidence in the long run? I don't know. For many persons, it certainly would. They are told they are mentally defective or disabled, and they believe it. They believe it until they have a chance—if they take it—to prove to themselves that their minds are *not* afflicted by a mental disability. Kate Millett, already a renowned writer, said she had to get off lithium to prove to herself that her mind was not flawed.

Study after study has shown in the long run those patients who are not treated with drugs do much better in terms of numerous criteria, but many patients will not take this leap because they suffer from the negative placebo effect. As we saw above, DuBrul's original conclusion, expressed in *The San Francisco Bay Guardian,* that the "drugs were working" was based on his lack of knowledge about the power of placebo and the effects of a change in environment. Many "patients" are not even aware that the placebo effect of psychiatric drugs in general is so high; usually about 50 percent of depressed persons respond to a placebo, which is the same as those who respond to the drug.

In other words, the placebo effect accounts for the positive effects of the "medication." Furthermore, it is the negative placebo—that is, the *psychological* dependence on psychiatric drugs engendered by the fear of getting off the drugs—that keeps most patients on psychiatric drugs for years. The consequence of this long-term drug use is at least comparable in magnitude of harm to that of tobacco-caused cancer in America in the era before most Americans stopped smoking.

As Robert Whitaker has meticulously shown, the mental illness epidemic is almost entirely iatrogenic. In 1955 there were 12,750 people hospitalized with bipolar disorder (then called "manic depression"). Today there are close to six million adults with this diagnosis, and according to John Hopkins School of Public Health, 83 percent of these six million are severely impaired.[6] Prior to the drug era, the famous German psychiatrist Emil Kraepelin and others reported that only one-third of "manic-depressives" suffered more than three episodes in their entire lives. In other words, those in the United States who had more than three episodes amounted at most to several thousand people. Studies done by NIMH and others show that "manic" and "depressive" episodes are now frequent. The increase in the number is partially due to the enormous expansion of the criteria for the diagnosis of bipolar, but now we also know that psychiatric drugs cause chronic impairment, including continuous up-and-down cycles, which mental health professionals attribute to the alleged disorder.[7] Let me reformulate: most people who think they are "disabled" or limited by "bipolar disorder" are, in fact, disabled by the medications they are taking to treat this supposed disorder.

Whitaker shows through a survey of the scientific literature that the antidepressants have a particularly adverse effect on "bipolars." Those on antidepressants were four times more likely to develop "rapid cycling" and twice as likely to have multiple manic or depressive episodes.[8] Also, as Dr. Stastny testifies in chapter 1, the custom now—largely for financial reasons—is to put people on multiple drugs, or "drug cocktails." A patient labeled bipolar is likely to be maintained on *at least* four drugs. Thus, they end up suffering from what Whitaker calls "polypharmacy psychiatric drug illness."[9]

This syndrome includes cognitive deficits, obesity, diabetes, cardiovascular problems, and thyroid dysfunction.[10] In the predrug era, 85 percent of manic-depressive patients recovered and returned to work. Today only one-third of patients achieve "full functional social and occupational recovery to their own premorbid levels," according to a review of the research published in a psychiatric journal in 2007. In typical psychiatric fashion the reviewer concluded that whereas the prognosis for bipolar used to be favorable, "contemporary findings suggest that disability and poor outcomes are prevalent, despite major therapeutic advances."[11] The reviewer makes no effort to reconcile his mindless acceptance of Psychiatry's claim to have made "major therapeutic advances" (i.e., psychiatric drugs) with the deterioration in outcomes the studies document. *The logical conclusion is there have not been any therapeutic advances: to the contrary, the drugs are harming people.*

Psychiatrists are living in an Alice in Wonderland world. They have to be: on the one hand, they make their living today as psychiatric drug pushers, while on the other hand, they still think of themselves as legitimate doctors. Millions of persons' lives are destroyed by the iatrogenic epidemic of "mental illness"—and virtually none of the psychiatric patients realize that they are suffering not from a brain defect, nor from a psychiatric disability, nor from a genetic disorder, but from the emotional ravages that are caused by months or years of ingesting toxic, mind-disabling psychiatric drugs! Consider also that today the "seriously mentally ill" are dying fifteen to twenty-five years earlier than normal; these statistics have risen so high recently due to the practice in the last two decades of placing an increasing number of patients on "antipsychotics" and on drug cocktails. Patients are dying from cardiovascular ailments, respiratory disease, diabetes, metabolic illnesses, and kidney failure to name just a few. Whitaker notes, "The physical ailments tend to pile up as people stay on antipsychotics (or drug cocktails) for years on end."[12]

In the comments above I focused on bipolar adults—the tip of the iceberg. The epidemic is far more disturbing when we take into account the children and infants now put on psychiatric drugs: the hazardous effects of Ritalin and Prozac and the neurological impairments caused by neuroleptics ("antipsychotics," as they are euphemistically termed). Neuroleptics are the most destructive drugs on the market, and many patients are forced to take them, sometimes by court order. The rationale for involuntary treatment is that anyone who is reluctant to take psychiatric drugs is too sick to know what is good for them.*[13] Nor did I describe electroshock—often forcibly administered to insufficiently submissive patients in state hospitals.[14]

Unfortunately there are "patients" who do not want to know about the effects of psychiatric drugs. It's painful to face the fact that the doctors in whom you placed all your trust are themselves misguided and—even with the best of intentions—may be prescribing "medications" that are harmful. But the sooner you face this fact, the sooner you can protect yourself.†

As of 2009 DuBrul had still had not read—or at least he never refers to it in any of his writings—*Toxic Psychiatry* by Peter Breggin, and yet Dr. Breggin has probably encouraged and empowered through *Toxic Psychiatry* (and other books) more people to get off psychiatric drugs than any other single person in the country. Dr. Breggin has been a major influence on Mind Freedom, as mentioned in chapter 3 on David Oaks. DuBrul had not read Kate Millett's *The Loony-Bin Trip*. Kay Jamison's book, *An Unquiet Mind,* is read by thousands of so-called bipolars; Millett's is not. Psychiatrists recommend that their educated patients read Jamison. They do not mention Millett, and why should they? Their goal is to make a living, not to affirm the sanctity of the soul.

In *The Loony-Bin Trip,* Millett wrote:

> The psychiatric diagnosis imposed upon me is that I am constitutionally psychotic, a manic-depressive bound to suffer recurrent attacks of "affective illness" unless I am maintained on prophylactic medication, specifically lithium. For a total of seventeen years I deadened my mind and obscured my consciousness with a drug whose prescription was based on a fallacy. Even discounting the possible harm of the drug's "side effects" it may seem little consolation to discover that one was sane all along. But to me it is everything.

---

*The idea that "mental patients" are more violent or dangerous than the normal population is a canard, as demonstrated by the well-known MacArthur Violence Risk Assessment Study.

†As Dr. Stastny pointed out in chapter 1, it should be common practice to not put patients on the more toxic drugs in the first place and, when prescribing drugs, to keep the dosages as low as possible.

Perhaps even survival for this diagnosis sets in motion a train of self-doubt and futility, a sentence of alienation whose predestined end is suicide. . . .

It is the integrity of the mind I wish to affirm, its sanctity and inviolability. Of course, there is no denying the misery and stress of life itself: the sufferings of the mind at the mercy of emotions . . . the divorces and antagonisms in human relationships, the swarm of fears . . . the crises of decision and choice. . . . They are the things we weather or fail to . . . they are the grit and matter of the human condition. . . . But when such circumstances are converted into symptoms and diagnosed as illnesses, I believe we enter upon very uncertain ground.[15]

With her successful weaning from psychiatric drugs after fourteen years, Millett indeed affirmed the integrity and sanctity of the mind, undermined the psychiatric narrative, and set an inspiring example for thousands of people who followed her.

11

The Icarus Project and the Future of Mad Pride

*I*n October 2011 DuBrul had developed a broader perspective than when I interviewed him in 2009. He wrote an eloquent statement just before I was going to submit my book for printing, and he asked me to include it. *To my surprise he did not mention reducing his intake of lithium as the cause of his problems, and in one of his recent e-mails DuBrul wrote,* "[H]opefully I'll figure out a way to get off the drugs all together some day."

Mad Pride and The Icarus Project
Revisited 2011—Some Final Thoughts
By Sascha DuBrul

Reading over the transcripts of our conversation I'm struck by a couple things. First of all, it's amazing to catch a glimpse of my own thought process as my anarchist sensibilities struggled to make sense of life in the ashram. It's been a really interesting two years of synthesis as my internal pendulum has swung closer to the middle and I've gotten creative about integrating spiritual practice and politics into my life. I've found a lot of inspiration and lessons in the history of the Human Potential Movement of the 1960s and '70s—the incredibly fruitful intersection of Eastern spiritual practices and Western psychology that merged with the political counterculture of the times. So many of the insights and tools from this period—from gestalt therapy to encounter—were lost and discredited amidst the neoliberal biopsychiatric backlash of the 1980s. More and more I find myself drawn to engaged Buddhist philosophy and the Generative Somatics community we have here in the Bay Area that mixes social justice analysis and grounded group practices. I see a lot of potential in the slow and deliberate foundation that is being laid by our work.

But Seth, the most important missing piece for me in this conversation of ours about Mad Pride has to do with the role that *trauma* plays for so many of us who struggle with madness. After just about a decade of working on The Icarus Project and crossing paths with, at this point, thousands of people who identify as "mad," one thing we all seem to have in common is that we have a lot of trauma and hardship woven through the stories we carry around about our lives. On a very personal level, it's clear to me that my "manic" and "depressive" episodes clearly have their roots in trauma from my past—they are reactions to early experiences. My inability to grieve my father's death as a child left me with so much confusion, anger, and despair that as I got older I channeled that intensity into what gets called mania. It's blocked energy and over the years I've learned how to work with it more effectively.

It's not a universal experience and that's an important piece of the story. There's a whole tribe of us that are wired in a way to have these particular kinds of breakdown/breakthroughs. But if you really believe that there is "a distinctive mad sensibility different from the normal person," I think we need to talk about how that narrative can leave room for the roles played by societal and familial trauma. And I think we need to distinguish between the "madness" of ecstatic vision and the "madness" of psychic anguish.

Us *madfolks*, we can throw *crazy* and *wingnut* and *mad* around as terms of endearment or insults as we please and I find it refreshing to hang out with the people who speak my language re-appropriated from oppression. It's a relief to find this oasis when we're surrounded by a society that's steeped in the stifling bio-psych DSM lingo of disorders and dysfunctions. In that way, I appreciate your efforts to reclaim and redefine madness in this arena of language and politics.

The LGBTQ (Lesbian, Gay, Bisexual, Transgender, Questioning) movement has made great strides in recent decades by raising awareness around queer issues ("Gay Pride!") opening all kinds of exciting doors of societal change. We have a lot in common in our struggles against what is considered straight and normal. But it's one thing to be proud of difference in sexuality (homosexuality/ queerness) and another to be proud of something that's been earned through strife and suffering and/or a mix of (please excuse the clumsy mechanistic meta- phor again) different wiring (madness.) This is not a cut and dry issue in my mind at all. It may be that everyone who's diagnosed with schizophrenia is having a spiritual emergence, but I don't think that's an obvious conclusion to draw. I think a trauma analysis can often be more useful than a spiritual one.

Leaving alone these tangled and complex questions of spirit and material, I want to bring up another aspect of strategy: what do we want our "Mad Pride" movement to look like on the ground and in real life?

Before my last hospitalization (and around the time I wrote those last blog posts you're quoting about the "*mad ones*") I was sleeping really badly. I was having visions and dreams of the end of the world. I was isolating from the people closest to me. I was spending hours every day walking in the woods and having conversations with dead people. I often thought I was a spirit in the material world. Was I "mad" by society's definitions? Clearly.

But more important for our conversation, was I "well" by my own standards and the standards of my community? Did our culture of "Mad Pride" help me in this case to stay healthy? In retrospect, I think the answer is no.

In the culture of The Icarus Project some years ago we developed a rough prototype of a document we call a Wellness Map (or affectionately a "Mad Map"). It's a very practical document to be written in good health and shared with friends and loved ones and it starts with the simple (yet not always easy to answer) question: *How are you when you're well? What does wellness look like to you?*

This question is followed by: *What are the signs that you're not so well?* and eventually: *What are the steps that you and your community need to take to get you back to wellness?*

In my case, I used my "Mad Pride" to totally ignore all the warning signs that I was going off the deep end. I wasn't being clear with myself or the people in my life about my wellness. I strongly believe that if we want to build an effective movement we have to prioritize our individual and collective *health and wellness*. And it needs to be way more nuanced and complex than the DSM. We need to weave this healthiness into our emerging culture. The psychiatric survivors movement [DuBrul is referring to the movement discussed in chapter 3 with which David Oaks is associated] doesn't have such a great track record in this regard. Hopefully we can do better in the future.

I write these words as the Occupy movement has taken the country by storm and set up encampments in public squares all over the United States. Mental health is one of the major issues the new movement is grappling with as people attempt to participate in group processes, sleeping outside and surrounded by police. It occurs to me that in this instance more *health and wellness* and less *madness* might be what is needed. Working in groups takes skill and my experience of creating a "mad" community is that it is hard to make decisions if there isn't a way for people to ground.

I'm not saying that "Mad Pride" can't be a really useful rallying cry for the tons of people who've been affected by the psych system and want a new empowering narrative and a way to connect with other like-minded folks. I'm saying that I've personally rubbed up against it's [*sic*] limitations in our movement work and I think that we need to be very clear about our intentions in using this powerful language as a way to bring people together.

So I hope this book ends up opening up some useful space for discussion in our greater community and that all the writings and thoughts you've put together help evolve the conversation in creative directions.

Let our Mad Pride movement be grounded in humility and kindness for each other in our diversity of life experiences, a recognition that social movements need good communicators and organizers more than charismatic leaders and messianic visions, and that the beautiful language we use to describe ourselves is only as powerful as the grounded actions we take to back up our words.

Mad love, Sascha

Sascha DuBrul raises a number of interesting questions here. I think everyone in this book—and those in the Mad Pride movement— realize that people experience trauma and that the standard psychiatric way of dealing with it, which is ignoring it and drugging the patient, does more harm than good (see the Dr. Stastny interview in chapter 1 and the discussion in chapter 10). DuBrul writes, "So many of the insights and tools from this period—from gestalt therapy to encounter—were lost and discredited amidst the neoliberal biopsychiatric backlash of the 1980s." The socially sanctioned way of dealing with all problems in living in this society is psychiatric drugs; for those who cannot afford to go to a private humanistic therapist or live where such creatures do not exist, the only option (in the mental health system) is modern psychiatric treatment, in other words, psychiatric drugs.

DuBrul uses the term *neoliberal backlash*. I presume he means the backlash associated with the "neoliberal" policies that became popular beginning in the 1980s: these policies include the unrestrained pursuit of profit and the collapse of the kind of ethical self-regulation that had prevented the APA until 1978 from accepting drug company money (see discussion in chapter 2). After the marriage of Psychiatry with the drug companies there was what DuBrul called a "neo-liberal backlash" against all the therapies that had become popular in the 1960s and 1970s. As the hunger strikers wrote, "The mental health system rarely offers options other than psychiatric drugs, and still more rarely offers people full, accurate information about the hazards of psychiatric drugs" (see chapter 2).

The impact of this was particularly devastating to clients due to Psychiatry's control of funding for mental health services by the government; as noted, after 1980 the NIMH would no longer provide any funding for places like Soteria, which did not use psychiatric drugs. Loren Mosher was fired from the NIMH. As Robert Whitaker showed, psychiatric drug treatment not only caused a variety of serious health problems but disabled the very organ it ostensibly was designed to fix: the brain.

DuBrul makes it clear that he was himself a victim of psychiatric single-vision. (This kind of approach to "psychotics" predated neoliberalism.) He saw numerous psychiatrists and therapists when he was a teenager and young adult, as he describes in his article in *The San Francisco Bay Guardian,* and every single one told him he had a chemical imbalance; not a single one related his mania to the trauma of his father's death. DuBrul eloquently writes, "My inability to grieve my father's death as a child left me with so much confusion, anger, and despair that as I got older I channeled that intensity into what gets called mania." (DuBrul had never mentioned this in our previous meetings, as can be seen in the previous chapters in part 3.)

After six years in the psychiatric system, DuBrul had been convinced in 2002 that his emotional pain was the result of a chemical imbalance, of a permanent incurable "bipolar disorder." Despite the fact that he grew up in Manhattan, the Mecca of psychotherapy, there was no therapist to say to him, "You are suffering because you went through hell watching your father die a slow and painful death when you were just twelve. You are not sick; you experienced a natural response. We need to talk about that and help you to mourn it." It did not occur to DuBrul in 2002 that his father's death might have contributed to his anguish: he did not even mention it in the article in *The San Francisco Bay Guardian;* I only found out about this when reading his blog entry for 2008, "And my Dad was slowly and painfully dying in front of me" (see chapter 8).

DuBrul had been misled for years and told he had a bipolar illness and that lithium was the solution to his problems. It took DuBrul over fifteen years, and several hospitalizations, to make the connection on his own—or perhaps with the help of a humanistic therapist in California—between his father's death and his breakdowns. There had been no need for DuBrul to be put on psychiatric drugs and told he had a chronic mental disorder. I saw these sorts of things happen every day when I worked as a therapist in clinics. In this way "chronic mental patients" are created and natural responses to the crises of life are converted into symptoms of "biochemical imbalances."

DuBrul raises another important issue: Are mad people simply mad because they have *more* trauma in their life? There has been a dispute about this, which has not been settled. On the one hand the trauma theory advocates argue that hospitalized schizophrenics have more trauma than "normal" persons and that "schizophrenia" can be completely accounted for by excessive trauma.

I am skeptical of this theory. Furthermore, while its proponents think this theory is the alternative to medical model, I think it tends toward reductionism. Over the past few decades investigators have discovered that the incidence of sexual abuse of female children was higher than previously imagined. For example at least 20 percent of female children have been sexually abused.[1] One would expect that a higher percentage of these children would exist among hospitalized mental patients. However, I don't believe trauma is the only variable that accounts for madness. Trauma theory advocates tend to overlook the large percentage of *nonhospitalized* persons who have undergone sexual abuse, which had been masked in the past.

There are studies of identical twins that found that if one was schizophrenic, there was a 45 percent chance that the other would be. The psychiatric dissidents who supported the hunger strikers believe these studies were flawed, that for example the similarity of the way in which identical twins are treated as compared to the treatment of fraternal twins can account for the higher concordance rate among identical twins (see chapter 2). There is no need to invoke genetic differences.

As I have explained in the introduction my own belief, based on reading and experience, is that those who get labeled psychotic, those who have breakdowns/breakthroughs, frequently have a distinctive type of personality. I am inclined to borrow Michael Thalbourne's felicitous term and assert that "psychotics" tend to be more "transliminal" than normal populations and are thus more emotionally vulnerable. (It is possible that this personality type is created by environmental factors.)

Thalbourne defines *transliminality* as "a largely involuntary susceptibility to, and awareness of, large volumes of inwardly generated psychological phenomena." The latter can more easily cross (trans-) the threshold into conscious awareness. Michael Thalbourne finds that transliminal personalities have a high rate of psychic, mystical, and manic experiences.[2] They tend to be more creative. (Thalbourne states he is himself "bipolar.") One could conclude that transliminality predisposes one to have "psychotic" experiences. I would draw the reader's attention to David Oaks's disclosure (chapter 2) that he now has so-called psychotic experiences while remaining calm, thus illustrating that the line between "schizophrenic" and "mystical" experiences is very fine. In fact, one cannot draw a line, as Dubrul suggests, between the traumatic and the spiritual-ecstatic, because they often go together.[3]

Thus the so-called psychotic disorders are frequently based on a transliminal personality that is constitutionally more sensitive and more aware. As we have seen, rather than an illness, a "breakdown" in a supportive environment—such as Diabasis or Soteria—could be a regenerative process. Thus madness can be personally adaptive. In part 4, I discuss the evidence for my contention that the schizophrenic or bipolar is frequently a prophet at an early stage of development—a process that is aborted by the psychiatric system.

I was surprised to discover Anthony Stevens had propounded the same thesis as I had from a different perspective. Stevens and Price write "[C]ertain life events could switch the individual carrying the genetic predisposition into a career either as a schizophrenic patient or a charismatic prophet."[4] A plethora of anecdotal and experimental evidence supports the thesis that as The Icarus Project collective had originally asserted, madness consists of "dangerous gifts" that can be of value to *humanity*.

Nevertheless, despite my agreement with DuBrul about many of these issues, I still sense that our perspectives are very different. DuBrul seems to have abandoned the ideas I found so exciting and inspiring in The Icarus Project's mission statement: the ideas that the mad have dangerous gifts and that because of these gifts they can make a major contribution to saving the planet. Ironically, DuBrul's views sound more like that of Mind Freedom (of which he originally was critical), with its focus on a revolution in the mental health field.

There is some inconsistency between DuBrul's theory and practice, just as there is with David Oaks. Both strongly believe in the ideal of a new order, nonviolent, anticorporate, based on equality, freedom, and fraternity. Both are (as of October 2011) very enthusiastic about the Occupy Wall Street movement, yet both seem to think the mad movement should focus primarily or exclusively on "mental health" issues: on the issues of creating more humanistic kinds of healing and opposing coercive treatments.

I agree with the need for a "healing narrative" (as I've made clear throughout this book), but I think it is a weaker and less expansive narrative than the messianic or utopian metanarrative. I think it is and should be encompassed by the greater messianic or utopian metanarrative. This metanarrative is not based on a fairy tale, however. Humanity is literally on the verge of annihilating itself and all life on the Earth. Mad people have seen the nightmare, and they have seen the promised land in their visions. DuBrul writes that "social movements need good communicators and organizers more than charismatic leaders and messianic visions." They need *both*, as I've tried to show. Right now more than anything we need many charismatic spokespersons whose actions and words are informed by a messianic vision of a collective spiritual life on Earth. ("Let the dead bury the dead and follow me," Jesus said.)

DuBrul is right, of course, that we need new ways of healing the wounded self. However, this is not a sufficient basis on which to build a movement of the mad. However important, it is too niggardly a goal in the light of the overwhelming magnitude of the problems that threaten our existence as a species. The political and economic elites that run the world are committing ecocide, and if we will not be around to experience it, our children will. Scientists leave no doubt that if we do not reverse the trajectory, the ravages of global warming will create millions if not billions of tragedies this century. We are staring into the abyss of doom—a doom our fellow human beings, the corporate elites, have imposed on us all.

It remains a fact that the problem of the world impinges on the psyches of our most psychologically vulnerable population in the United States—the mad. One of the most therapeutic things they can do for themselves is to bring their gifts to the new commons of those who are fighting to save the world. We need their visions, their contribution to *a narrative of redemption,* their sense—as Serine put it—that God has called them to help save the world. We need prophets who will call humanity to remembrance, we need messiahs who will remind the normal ones that they too have dreamed of paradise, of the homecoming. Perhaps the mad can evoke chords long forgotten because they know how to talk naturally in our native tongue—in the language of dreams, of madness.

What is the future for The Icarus Project? It has chapters all over the country, but can it contribute not just to helping the mad but healing the planet? In 2007 The Icarus Project published Harm Reduction Guide to Coming Off of Psychiatric Drugs.[5] It is available free online at the TIP website, and it's a valuable resource. Ashley McNamara—now known as "Jacks"—has not published anything on this topic since then. DuBrul and McNamara are both in the Bay Area now; DuBrul moved there in 2009. They have traveled together to promote the documentary about McNamara's life and artwork, *Crooked Beauty,* an extraordinarily moving documentary. The film is about her artistry (she is a painter and sculptor as well as a writer) and her emotional pain. It undermines the stereotype of mad people as helpless and pitiful. Unfortunately, it evades the topic of psychiatric drugs, but that was the decision of the filmmaker.

In 2007 McNamara had some sort of conflict with some of the people in TIP. She has not written anything on the TIP website since then. But she is active in the Bay Area Radical Mental Health Collective. I don't know if she, like DuBrul, has revised her views on Mad Pride. But both McNamara and DuBrul were the cocreators of the new Mad Pride narrative. She had big dreams for Mad Pride. McNamara attributed her proclivity to imagine grand possibilities to her own madness. In a brilliant essay "Drawing New Lines on the Map"—included in the first book The Icarus Project published—she wrote (the emphasis is mine), "We are people with a *dangerous gift* that sometimes grants us the vision to see new possibilities and to draw new lines on the map. Drawing new lines on the map requires free access to our imaginations. Drawing new lines requires the courage to resist authority—and ultimately the solidarity to do it well."

After discussing the parallel between shamans and mad people, she concluded,

> Is it possible that the very pieces of ourselves that get labeled pathological could also be like keys in the dark, their edges barely glowing, like silver question marks too easy to overlook? After all, would I [a so-called psychotic] be making the imaginative leaps necessary to write this piece you're reading if my mind wasn't prone to unifying visions, dendritic and unusual connections across vast swaths of thought, and *the "delusions of grandeur" that get labeled symptomatic of disease but also allow me to have a wide open vision that reconsiders the role madness can play in our culture and imagines big possibilities?*[6]

This is what I call the messianic-redemptive vision. To have a wide-open vision and to imagine big possibilities—for each individual, for Mad Pride, and for the Earth.

Part Four

Prophets of Madness
or Messiahs
among Us?

12

The Messianic or Postmodern Paradigm?

*A*s we have seen, Mad Pride began in America with the foundation of The Icarus Project in 2002 by DuBrul and McNamara. The Icarus Project (TIP) was created "for people living with dangerous gifts that are commonly diagnosed and labeled as 'mental illnesses.'" The bold mission statement of The Icarus Project declared, "We are a network of people living with and/or affected by experiences that are often diagnosed and labeled as psychiatric conditions. We believe these experiences are mad gifts needing cultivation and care, rather than diseases or disorders. By joining together as individuals and as a community, the intertwined threads of madness, creativity, and collaboration can inspire hope and transformation in an oppressive and damaged world. Participation in The Icarus Project helps us overcome alienation and tap into the true potential that lies between brilliance and madness."[1]

This statement is subversive of received wisdom in several ways. It emphasizes the idea of the distinctiveness of mad people, which, it is stated, enables them to make an unusual and indispensable contribution to the healing of the world. This is an extraordinary claim and one that had never been made by the patients' rights movement in the past. In the past, as we have seen, the patient's movement emphasized the commonality that the former "mental patients" shared with other (normal) citizens. Only R. D. Laing had praised the mad for being different, and Laing had been ignored by the patients' movement. After the Icarus statement proclaimed madness as a gift, other members of The Icarus Project who posted on its website made similar statements. Ashley McNamara highlighted this theme in several powerful essays. Note the mission statement also defines madness as a "gift"—a gift to the mad person and to the human community. Mad gifts entail responsibility: to care for and cultivate these gifts. Although the sentence with the word *transformation* is vaguely formulated, the implication is that mad persons as a community, as Mad Pride, can contribute to the profound transformation—ultimately, the salvation—of the world. It is based on the radical idea that the mad were not just equal but in some respects superior to normal people and thus could contribute to the redemption of the world. This is what I have termed a messianic-redemptive vision.

The Postmodern Vision

The secular pluralist zeitgeist seems to be dominant today within the Mad Pride movement, although The Icarus Project forum still teems with discussions about spirituality. In early 2008 DuBrul was experimenting with explorations in "the spirit world"—one can find a similar distinction between two worlds both in shamanism and in the literature on out-of-body experiences[2]—and he believed that as a mad person he had a natural penchant for exploring the spirit world. As discussed in chapters 9 and 10, in 2008 DuBrul went to a Hindu ashram in upstate New York to study, meditate, and worship and to develop a greater capacity for mental and spiritual discipline. After this DuBrul shifted from a future-oriented utopian model (what I call messianic) to a more moderate conception of social change, a conception consistent with the more distant and ironic stance encouraged by postmodernism. This is a perspective that I think sacrificed what was most interesting about the original perspective of The Icarus Project.

DuBrul's theoretical perspective has radically changed several times since he became an activist in the Mad Pride movement. In his 2002 article DuBrul had defined his belief that psychiatric drugs were indispensable (for some people) as the sensible "middle ground." As he states, "I think it's really about time we start carving some more of the middle ground with stories from outside the mainstream and creating a new language for ourselves that reflects all the complexity and brilliance that we hold inside."[3] To my mind, this last phrase—"creating a new language"—suggests that DuBrul had something else in mind besides a middle ground, if the middle ground means taking a politically moderate stance toward Psychiatry. Thus, it is not surprising to me in hindsight that by the time he coauthored the Icarus mission statement he was far away from the middle ground (although he continued to feel he needed psychiatric drugs) and was moving increasingly toward a commitment to a messianic-redemptive vision. As discussed, this trajectory came to a halt after his hospitalization in 2008.

The postmodern pluralist perspective (as defined by Tarnas in the introduction, under the subhead Mad Pride in Transition) is antithetical to the "totalizing" perspective of the redemptive vision. Mad Pride activists are increasingly attracted to postmodernism for a number of reasons. In the first place it accepts difference per se and promotes acceptance of madness in its myriad forms. Second, it is in accord with the ironically detached and skeptical temper of the times, unlike an explicitly spiritual messianic-redemptive vision, which sounds passionate, "fanatical," intolerant—too mad, a product of the feverish 1960s. As Mad Pride grows and becomes more socially visible, the temptation increases to accommodate to larger cultural forces and to sound "reasonable." Third, a relativistic even-tempered pluralism is friendly and inclusive of everyone; it avoids the risk of alienating those mad people who have not yet broken free of the influence of Psychiatry. Repeatedly, I was told by the more radical psychiatric survivors that different paradigms worked for different people—even the psychiatric paradigm.

It is not my intention here to attempt to address complex epistemological questions: I do not deny that postmodernists have incisively critiqued naively doctrinaire modernist and scientific approaches. In this case, I object specifically to postmodernism's stubborn tendency to disparage synthesizing visions while promoting relativism or nihilism. Postmodernism discourages the kind of unconscious archetypes—

visions of wholeness—that have a catalyzing effect. But it is precisely these kinds of messianic archetypes and narratives that have driven the movements beyond the narrow parameters of the status quo, as demonstrated in great revitalization movements, or Great Awakenings (see chapters 15 and 17). It is precisely the kind of unconscious archetypes that postmodernism discourages—visions of wholeness—that have a catalyzing effect. Paul Levy's quote from Jung clarifies the process of revolutionary change: "The new ideas spread rapidly because parallel changes have been taking place in the unconscious of other people. . . . If the translation of the unconscious into a communicable language proves successful, it has a redeeming [redemptive] effect" (see discussion in chapter 13).

Any great revolution inevitably evokes archetypes of new birth. Even the political moderate Abraham Lincoln evoked in the Gettysburg Address the natal archetype of a new birth of freedom that had been a motif for decades in the literature of the abolitionists. When Mad Pride first burst out it unleashed utopian or messianic aspirations. The danger is that postmodernism will suppress these archetypes in the name of its radical skepticism.

In its most extreme manifestation postmodernism engenders ethical relativism. I have even been told on a few occasions by different Mad Pride activists that it is cruel and dogmatic of me to tell people for whom psychiatry "works" that they are *not* "mentally ill." Their argument often goes like this: "For some people the psychiatric model works. Some of us need psychiatric drugs. Some of us bipolars cannot function without taking the drugs prescribed by the psychiatrists. The biochemical model has its place. For others, your mystical model may be more appropriate." One does not have to repudiate the doctrine of "mental illness," as I do, to see on an objective level that the medical model has been extraordinarily destructive, even to those who embrace it. The formerly mainstream psychologist Gail Hornstein wrote in 2009, "It is now absolutely clear that diagnosing people with 'schizophrenia' or 'bipolar illness,' giving them high doses of medications over long periods, and not talking to them about their experiences produces a chronically disabled population."[4] The psychiatric model produces the data that seems to validate it—a chronically disabled population, as Paul Levy has pointed out repeatedly. The psychiatric model has no value—even for those who claim it works for them. The only honest—indeed the only compassionate—way to talk to patients who think they are "mentally ill" is to tell them that they have been misinformed and deceived: they are not mentally ill, they do not have a chemical imbalance (see chapter 2), but they had undergone a crisis, they have dealt with a difficult problem in living, and they do possess the inner resources to overcome their personal problems and to contribute to saving the planet—and they do not need toxic psychiatric drugs. The psychiatric model deserves moral and epistemological condemnation, not "tolerance," much like previous institutions that were considered right at one time but that are now almost universally condemned (slavery, for example).

If one believes that the mad do not have to remain chronically disabled patients, then one has to tell them that the psychiatric model does *not* work—for anyone. If one believes that persons grow and evolve, it is only logical to assume that there will be leaders who are more evolved in some ways and will assist the process of growth and learning in others so that they can become leaders themselves. This requires taking a definitive point of view. A wishy-washy movement might succeed in helping the mad cope with life, but it has no chance of inspiring them, let alone spurring them to bring "hope and transformation" to "an oppressive and damaged *world*."

The reluctance of many of the leaders of Mad Pride to even admit they are in leadership positions is at least partially a reaction to the bullying they experienced as patients under the dominion of the mental health system. The "anything goes" position is appealing because it is antithetical to the kinds of spiritual and physical impositions to which patients are subjected in the mental health system. However, taking this position is an abdication of responsibility that is not conducive to the growth of a liberation movement. Whether certain leaders acknowledge that they are leaders or not, the fact is that there are still hundreds or thousands of persons deferring to their authority and looking to them for guidance.

Another shortcoming of the Mad Pride movement is the refusal of some of its leaders to read the work of theorists of previous generations. I get the impression from discussions with mad activists and readings that many Mad Pride leaders—who are mostly in their late twenties and thirties and who are mostly college-educated intellectuals—like to think of their movement as *sui generis*, as the product of bold innovation unfettered by any transgenerational intellectual bonds. This attitude severs the organic connection between the past and the present, and thus hinders Mad Pride activists from developing an alternative paradigm that draws on all the intellectual and spiritual resources of the past.

13

The Relationship of Mad Pride to Messianic Transformation

*H*ow can the Mad Pride movement create lasting change in a world on the brink of self-annihilation? How can we make the transition when humanity clings to the old ways? Laing did not attempt to grapple with the question of how to effect social change: after he wrote *The Politics of Experience* he stopped writing—or speaking—about his controversial idea that the mad were the avant-garde of a new order. In fact, he seemed to retreat from the 1960s idea of collective social change just as the collective spiritual ferment of the 1960s itself died out. In public lectures he often said he had no "answers" to the major problems of humanity, he was just "raising questions."

Unlike Laing, John Weir Perry had developed a theory of social change. Although he shared Laing's view that the normal world was self-destructive, he was optimistic that human beings would pull together in time to avert annihilation. The guiding thread throughout Perry's career was his death-rebirth theory of madness. However, Perry also was a student of cultural transformation, and he was convinced that society itself was undergoing an organic process of spiritual evolution.

He concluded that prophets are the catalysts of revolutionary change. He tells us that the prophet—like the mad person—undergoes a visionary experience: he or she plunges or is plunged into the myth world, the collective unconscious, into the deeper levels of the psyche.[1] The prophet, unlike the mad person, Perry believed, takes it upon himself or herself to solve not just their own growth crisis but the growth crisis of society. He or she emerges from madness with a new myth. "If his myth-making capacity is working well, he may deliver the new myth that is going to be accepted for the next phase of that culture's evolution. That then leads to a whole cultural renewal. Wallace [see chapter 15] calls it a 'revitalization movement.'"[2]

In other words, *the prophet is creatively maladjusted.* Someone *adjusted to society would not have the motivation or the capacity to solve the growth crisis of society and foster its spiritual evolution.* The maladjustment of the prophet, the mad person, is not a pathological aberration or a medical problem: it is a mutation in service of the spiritual evolution of humanity.

All of his adult life, Perry, who lived until 1998, believed that humanity was confronting a major crisis—as a result of our materialism, our rationalism, and "our aggressive self assertion that disregards the needs of the whole." We are destroying our fellow human beings and polluting beyond repair the resources of the Earth.[3] We need to accept that we are all interconnected. We need to make a transition—a revolutionary change—to a new way of life characterized by harmony and equality and cooperation with, not domination of, nature.[4] Revealingly, the Mad Pride activists interviewed in this book say the same thing.

"Dire straits are now upon us . . . awaiting us just ahead,"[5] Perry wrote prophetically in 1987. Perry believed that "history shows us that when a culture is in dire straits the collective psyche is activated"; it responds creatively somehow to crisis, to challenge, to necessity, to the specter of catastrophe.[6] Perry believes that prophets will arise, who I have argued will come largely from the ranks of the mad, who will become the "mouthpieces" of the new society, the catalysts of change (see The Sociobiological Function of Madness: The Spiritual Evolution Narrative in chapter 1 and part 5).

Let me interpolate here that Paul Levy's theory of change is identical to Perry's. (Both Perry and Levy are Jungians, so their similarity in this regard is not surprising.) Levy's theory of change posits that certain visionary individuals—those whom Perry calls prophets—are most likely to formulate the symbols and myths that can help society make the transition to a new mode of being. Levy writes:

> Jung said, "Social, political, and religious conditions affect the collective unconscious in the sense that all those factors which are suppressed by the prevailing views or attitudes in the life of a society gradually accumulate in the collective unconscious. . . . Certain individuals gifted with particularly strong intuition then become aware of the changes going on in it and translate these changes into communicable ideas. The new ideas spread rapidly because parallel changes have been taking place in the unconscious of other people. . . . *If the translation of the unconscious into a communicable language proves successful, it has a redeeming effect* [my emphasis]. The liberating vision of the artist [or prophets] attracts us into itself so as to make itself real in time, changing the world in the process."[7]

Unlike Levy, Perry consistently made a spurious distinction that weakens his theory of change—between the mad person and the prophet. Perry asserts that the mad person and the prophet both undergo the same kinds of transformative visionary experiences but invariably *choose different routes*—the mad person opting for self-change and the prophet opting to transform society.[8] (This sometimes happens, of course.) In recent history the mad person has little or no choice at all. However, we can see today if we look that *the Mad Pride movement is composed of mad persons who have opted not merely to change themselves, but to change society; contrary to Perry, many of them have a prophetic orientation.*

It is ironic that a radical thinker like Perry was so bound by cultural convention that he failed to notice or acknowledge that the great prophets in the past usually had been mad—that is to say, by the standards of psychiatry these prophets *were* psychotic. They had undergone the mad experience as Perry had described it. Perry's dichotomy of the mad person and the prophet is at odds with his many of his own observations. Perry had often noticed that the mad in general have a keen interest in social problems. For example, in an interview in the mid-90s Perry said that as soon as he finished medical school he began to discover that schizophrenics manifested an unusually strong interest in social problems and in the problems of the world.[9] This interest belies Perry's contention that "psychotics" choose to transform themselves, as opposed to prophets who opt to change society. Furthermore, Perry repeatedly noted that the "vision of oneness" that he believes is integral to social transformation was found in "the messianic ideation" of his psychotic clients; he found in their hallucinations a prefiguration of the new society that was "waiting to come about in the collective society of our time," in the next phase of our spiritual evolution.[10] This was very close to saying that the mad were prophets manqué or prophets in the making. In fact, this belief was sometime inaccurately imputed to Perry.

The fact is that there is a dearth of prophets today, in large part because so many potential prophets are "caught" and "squelched" (as Perry put it) early in their lives; they are inducted into "careers" as mental patients[11] before they have a chance to complete a process of spiritual rebirth. *The pool of visionaries from which modern prophets might emerge is depleted by the "mental health" system.* How many potential prophets, spiritual leaders, are there *among the mad*—among the so-called mentally ill—who are nipped in the bud, in the bloom of their spiritual development, by the treatment they are given by the psychiatric system?

It is my argument that our society has been unable to transcend its spiritual stasis despite the severity of its dysfunctionality—despite the fact that we face now the prospect of ecological doom—largely because it has been *so successful* for centuries in psychiatrically suppressing its nonconformists and prophets, its mad persons, those who are the natural catalysts for social transformation. This is why Mad Pride is such an auspicious development. The Mad Pride movement is changing this situation, opening up new possibilities by providing the mad with social support and alternative "maps" of madness. It seeks to free the mad from the chronicity of patienthood (caused by psychiatric drugs and indoctrination) so they can become creatively maladjusted. Perhaps some of them will thus realize their individual potential by becoming the prophets, social activists, and spiritual leaders who will help humanity to make the transition to a higher stage of consciousness and a new social order.

This development does not vitiate my criticism of the Mad Pride movement for abandoning a messianic vision. The question is not whether Mad Pride is having an impact but whether it is effective enough. The abdication of its original messianic-redemptive perspective is discouraging in light of the urgency of the crisis that confronts humanity, which has taken on even more ominous dimensions (e.g., the dire scientific expectations about global warming and other ecological crises that are developing) since Perry's death. It is unfortunate—I repeat—that the writings of visionaries like Perry and Laing have been ignored by the leaders of Mad Pride.

Perry wrote that most schizophrenics believe they have been in communication with God and that *they have been given a divine or messianic mission to fulfill*—to change society. (We saw in the introduction, under What Is to Be Done? Adopting a High Messianic Perspective, that many of the persons who wrote on the Icarus forum expressed this same belief.) This is the same belief that possessed Jesus, Moses, and the prophets from biblical times to the present. It is remarkable that Anton Boisen, born at the turn of the twentieth century—a religious pioneer, chaplain, and original thinker who had recovered (an especially rare, or undiscussed, feat in those days) from a mental breakdown in his youth— antedated Perry by decades, yet his observations are almost identical. On the basis of years as a chaplain in mental hospitals Boisen observed that the idea that one is going to play an important role in resolving a "world catastrophe" arises spontaneously in different persons—living *in completely different historical eras*—who are going through profound inner struggles.[12] *This sense of a social mission*, Boisen emphasized—this was in the mid-1930s—*is characteristic both of psychotics in "hospitals" and of men of "outstanding religious genius."*[13] Boisen's and Perry's observations (and those of others today, including my own) lead to the same conclusion, which they both stop just short of drawing: *Many mad persons are prophets in the making.* There are not many potential prophets in our society—not many persons who believe they have a messianic mission to fulfill. In a time of looming world catastrophe, our society desperately needs such people; we cannot afford to let psychiatry squelch them.

Messianic Mission or Grandiose Delusions?

Psychiatrists are certain that the mad person's claim to have a mission is a symptom of their illness. Anton Boisen pointed out that the founder of the Quakers, George Fox, would have been locked up immediately had he ever been examined by a psychiatrist[14]—a fact also noted by William James. After his religious conversion Fox repeatedly proclaimed to all who would listen that "the day of the Lord [the messianic era] was coming upon all flesh."[15] By modern psychiatric standards Fox was a schizophrenic, yet Fox had a brilliant mind, and the Quaker movement he founded became an important and valuable force for spiritual and social progress.

How many potential George Foxes are there among the mad today—how many prophets? It must be noted that by the standards of modern psychiatry the great Biblical prophets were all schizophrenics or bipolars. In fact, in the early twentieth century it became popular for psychiatrists to write books on Jesus's psychological condition: the majority opinion among these writers was that he was a paranoid schizophrenic. Psychiatrist Charles Binet-Sangle wrote in 1911 in his book *The Madness of Jesus,* "The nature of the hallucinations of Jesus, as they are described in the orthodox Gospels, permits us to conclude that the founder of the Christian religion was afflicted with religious paranoia."[16]

St. Paul and George Fox might not have become great spiritual leaders had there been psychiatrists around in their day: they would have been locked up, drugged into a stupor, and told it was scientifically determined that they were chronically mentally ill. Had Jesus "returned" in the 1950s in America he might have been lobotomized instead of crucified. If he returned today in the twenty-first century he would be put on a cocktail of psychotropic drugs and if he resisted it would be inferred that he had no "insight" into his "illness" and he would be forcibly injected with Haldol.

The greatest Christian prophet of the twentieth century, the Reverend Martin Luther King Jr., was also a martyr (his son and others believe he was assassinated by the FBI under orders of J. Edgar Hoover).

As stated, King was optimistic that "through . . . creative maladjustment, we may be able to emerge from the bleak and desolate midnight of man's inhumanity to man, into the bright and glittering daybreak of freedom and justice." As he said in 1961, "So let us be maladjusted, as maladjusted as the prophet Amos, who in the midst of the injustices of his day could cry out in words that echo across the centuries, 'Let justice run down like water and righteousness like a mighty stream. . . .' Let us be maladjusted as Jesus of Nazareth, who could look into the eyes of the men and women of his generation and cry out, 'Love your enemies.'"[17]

The question I will raise here again is, *Is it not possible that in the light of all the facts discussed above that mad persons—if liberated from the thralldom of the psychiatric "mind police" (Laing)—could play a decisive role in solving the Earth-threatening crisis, the world catastrophe, of the modern age?* Could some of them among us not be the prophets, the myth makers, and the "poetic mouthpieces" of the collective psyche whom Perry believed we are awaiting? If this is true, it means that the many mad people who think they have a messianic mission are correct. They *do* have a *mission;* this is not a "grandiose" delusion.

14

Interview with
Dr. Ed Whitney

Finding Oneself at the Age of Forty-five; Messianic Visions

One night in May 1994 I was stopped by the police as I wandered on the beach in my underwear and T-shirt, merging with the electrons in distant galaxies and looking for God. I was not sure whether Hitler, Elijah the prophet, or King Lear had gone mad. All I knew for certain was that I had surrendered my customary frames of reference and had chosen to trust a process over which I no longer had control.[1]

ED WHITNEY, M.D.

Ed Whitney is by degree a doctor of medicine; he is a former physician and works now as a medical researcher in Seattle. At the time of Dr. Whitney's first breakdown he was forty-four and working as a doctor. He had recently been thinking a lot about his father, who had died in a tragic mountain climbing accident when Dr. Whitney was fifteen. His father had been a successful internist, and Dr. Whitney felt himself to be "never as good as he was at being a doctor." The year Dr. Whitney had a breakdown he was the same age his father was when he was born. It was also the same age, Dr. Whitney remarked, as when Nietzsche—his favorite philosopher—went mad.

Dr. Whitney was raised in a liberal Christian family. He had an interest in spiritual questions, an interest that began when he was seven or eight, when he would lie awake at night wondering how anyone knew that God existed. Before his breakdown he had been a "normal," well-adjusted person, with no history of "psychiatric problems." He had moved to Santa Cruz from Colorado in 1990, ten years after he finished medical school. He was a financially successful doctor practicing in California, but as he said, "My heart wasn't in my practice." It was not the right livelihood for him. Furthermore, he had not married and "settled down," nor had he had kids.

Around this time Dr. Whitney began having an intense series of dreams. He remembers one in which he was on some kind of expedition hunting lions, which he had thought of as "forbidden," so he interpreted this dream as a message that he could go beyond his boundaries. Most of Ed's friends in Santa Cruz were Jewish, and in his new movement to transcend his boundaries he had become very interested in Judaism and in Jewish mysticism.

In 1992 he went to a concert by the guitarist-singer and New Age Jewish icon Rabbi Shlomo Carlebach. Carlebach said that if only we could be a "little better, a little kinder, a little more moral" then Elijah would return. (Elijah is the prophet whose return heralds the coming of the Messiah; every Passover a cup is filled with wine for Elijah.) In the Bible, Elijah has a confrontation with worshipers of Baal, a Canaanite deity. He challenges them to prove the power of their god. They keep summoning him, but nothing happens. As Dr. Whitney described it, "And Elijah pours a lot of water over his altar, calls out the name of the Lord, and whoosh!—out comes this fire and consumes the ox plus the altar, and all the people fall down on their faces and say, 'God! The Lord! He is God!' And that's where the reading ends the service in the synagogue, but in the Bible it goes on to say that Elijah then slaughtered the prophets of Baal." The slaughtering of the prophets of Baal seemed unrighteous to Dr. Whitney. It bothered him that Elijah, the herald of the Messiah who was to inaugurate the reign of peace on Earth, had committed this act of mass slaughter. In March and April of 1994, Dr. Whitney read numerous commentaries on this passage in the Bible. He began to talk constantly about the coming of the messianic age, which he felt was imminent.

In addition to studying Judaism, Dr. Whitney attended the Four Square Gospel Church, where they had "soul-lifting" gospel singing every Saturday night. He wandered around the beach a lot, marveling at every grain of sand. He also became obsessed with Rabbi Schneerson, the leader of the Lubavitcher Hasidim, an orthodox group of Jews centered in Brooklyn. Schneerson was ninety-two and had had a stroke. His followers were expecting a miracle as they had come to believe Rabbi Schneerson was the Messiah, which was a heretical position for an Orthodox Jew.

Dr. Whitney saw a program about this on CNN at the time, and his mind was divided. He thought maybe Schneerson was the Messiah, but on the other hand, he entertained the notion that perhaps what will happen at the beginning of the messianic age is that *everyone* will be the Messiah. Dr. Whitney had a sense of humor about this. He talked about this to his roommates: "I said, what's going to happen is, when the day comes, everyone's going to think everyone else is the Messiah. I was going on, and it was kind of like a version of *Life of Brian*. One person would say, 'I thought you were the Messiah.' Then the other person would say, 'No, I thought you were the Messiah.' And it would kind of go around and everyone would think everyone else was the Messiah."*

Dr. Whitney knew he was becoming "weird." His strange behavior worried his roommates and friends, who said, "Ed is getting kinda weird," but this was Santa Cruz, where mystics and seekers and gurus and holistic healers abounded, so Dr. Whitney's behavior was tolerated.

This was the background to his adventure that began that night in May when he went out onto the beach in his underwear looking for God. As Dr. Whitney writes:

I was intercepted by the police, and they shined this light in my eyes and asked me what I'm doing there at the beach. I tried to come up

---

*I mentioned to Dr. Whitney that the idea that humanity as a whole was the Messiah was common in esoteric circles. He had not known that at the time.

with a story that they might accept. I told them that I was a doctor who was deeply concerned about the Clinton health plan, that I lived four blocks away, and that I needed to go home. I was certain that they were angels sent by the Lord to prevent me from disrupting the flow of energy in the galaxies with which I was merging. Since God had sent them, then all was well; I could trust them.[2]

In 2009 I interviewed Dr. Ed Whitney over the telephone. He was at his home in Seattle.

Farber: This is what you were thinking then?"

Dr. Ed Whitney: Yes. I figured I was stirring up the electrons in the universe; they're going to be there to make the process safe for the rest of the universe. You see, I heard their police radio say something that included the words *seven four*. Thus they were checking the seventy-fourth decimal place of their calculations; this was the precision they needed to be sure that all the electrons in the universe were still in place. They were connected to the mind of God—even if they did not know it.

Farber: You did not tell them this?

Dr. Ed Whitney: Oh no, I knew that would sound too weird. I just talked to them about the Clinton health plan. And they let me go home.

Farber: Okay, you wrote, "I felt a deep transformation of the meaning of everything that had ever happened in my life. I was receiving assurances from Heaven itself that I needed to feel ashamed no longer, that I was loved for all eternity."[3] You felt this that night?

Dr. Ed Whitney: Yes.

Farber: Then what?

Dr. Ed Whitney: The next day I went for a walk. There was a bed-and-breakfast about three miles away from the house, called the Apple Lane Inn. Ahh! I thought. Apple Lane! The apple—Adam and Eve—and Eden! This was where everything began. I walked in—in that state—to get a room for the night, but the manager said they were all booked up.

So I walked away from the desk, went into a room, and picked up an apple from the bed.

Farber: From the bed?

Dr. Ed Whitney: They put apples on their beds! I'd just picked one up and chomped into it. This was *the* apple. I was Adam. This was the beginning all over again, except now God had given me permission to eat the apple. So this was a second chance—for all of us. Anyway, the proprietor was getting uptight. I told him I was leaving, but he became belligerent. I ended up bellowing at this guy, "I'm God Almighty!" I bellowed that with absolute full congruence, full commitment, with my whole being, and then I walked away, and I left my billfold behind; I wouldn't need it anymore. That was from the old world that had passed away.

Farber: You were God? Did you see yourself as running the universe? Or was everyone God?

Dr. Ed Whitney: Yes. I guess it was democratic. I thought everyone was God—although it was not clearly thought out in my mind.

Farber: Then what?

Dr. Ed Whitney: I was walking home, and I thought maybe I could fly through the air, and so I tried that a couple of times; I kept coming back down to the ground. Then I went to the ocean. I stood on the very limits of the water, and I stretched forth my hand, and I commanded the waves of the ocean to stop. The thing is, if they stopped I'd know that I was indeed the Omnipotent One.

Farber: Did they stop?

Dr. Ed Whitney: No, I was ankle deep in brine, not getting anyplace.

Farber: This is funny looking back, and you describe it with wry humor. But at the time it was serious stuff.

Dr. Ed Whitney: Yes, absolutely. Anyway, so I thought, I've got to find out my facts. I went back to the house. My housemates and I had a cat named Bandit. Years ago I was very attracted to a woman named Robin, and I reasoned that a bandit is a robber and robbers engage in robbin', therefore Bandit could be transformed into Robin for my carnal delight. I visualized the metamorphosis, lifted Bandit to my face, and rubbed noses with him. He blinked at me and meowed. "Fantastic!" Cats were cats, and women were women; reality had limits, and therefore my thoughts could not destroy the universe. Therefore, I was not God. I was relieved beyond measure.

Farber: It's like the logic of a dream. So you were not so keen on being God.

Dr. Ed Whitney: Not in the sense of absolute control. It was reassuring to learn that there is a structure to the universe.

The next day Dr. Whitney had some friends who had come down to visit from Berkeley. The police, who had been alerted by the manager of Apple Lane Inn, stopped over to ask his roommates questions. His roommates acknowledged that Dr. Whitney had indeed been acting a "little odd" lately.

Dr. Ed Whitney: My friends were trying to see if they could talk to me and keep me out of the hospital, because once the police get involved, people get a little more worried—and especially since I had created a disturbance that afternoon at the bed-and-breakfast. Of course, I kept having an answer to practically everything—everything they said—meaning that I was thinking about all of it, but I couldn't give a coherent account of where I'd been for the last twenty-four hours. I didn't know that, but I knew what must be done to bring the Messiah.

Farber: Which was?

Dr. Ed Whitney: It was mostly babbling. I still felt Elijah had screwed up, and that's why the Messiah had been delayed. . . . I was getting more and more emotional about things, crying a lot, my friends were watching the TV—there was an advertisement trying to get people to use condoms for prevention of AIDS, and in the middle of this commercial I just broke down sobbing, saying that fears were putting barriers in between people, which were signified by the condom, a kind of barrier.

Farber: Were you sobbing for the people with AIDS?

Dr. Ed Whitney: People who had AIDS, and I was sobbing for all of humanity. There was a spirit of fear put in there—like paradise lost. I had an awareness of the devastating effects of fear.

Farber: That was an astute insight for a mad man.

Dr. Ed Whitney: My friends were worried because I could not stop sobbing—although it was a release for me—and then they said, "Okay, we better take you to the hospital." At the same time, they were trying to find a more spiritual counselor. It was funny. They called the Spiritual Emergency Network, and the woman there said, "We have a great doctor in Santa Cruz who can help you, Ed Whitney." One of my housemates kept saying, "Ed's getting awfully strange. He seems to be falling apart."

So Ed went along cooperatively to the hospital. He figured that going to the hospital was also part of God's plan.

Farber: You had no fears about the hospital, about being abused, electroshocked?

Dr. Ed Whitney: I was taken to Dominican—where I went every week for medical grand rounds—so it was a general hospital. They did not do ECT. I think the thing that convinced me to go along to the hospital was this friend of my housemate who was visiting; I knew that he had lost his adolescent son to cancer, about twenty years ago. So I felt this perfect symmetry, because I had lost my father when I was fifteen, and he said to go to the hospital. So I thought that was what the universe had prearranged.

I got to the emergency room, and I was admitted for a three-day hold. I thought "Wow! Of course! Jonah, three nights in the belly of the whale"—and I was on a three-day hold. And the place was Dominican Hospital so that was associated with Thomas Aquinas, and he's the doctor of the church. And then, the other thing that happened was they said, "We're going to have the doctor see you. His name is Dr. Luther." So I thought, "This is where the Reformation is going to begin." Then they gave me an antipsychotic, Risperdol. Within thirty minutes I began seeing beautiful luminescent rivers of light, glowing right in front of me. I assumed that was the intended therapeutic effect of the drug. It meant I had been too uptight all my life and too closed-minded about psychedelic experiences, and I needed to be more open to them—because I thought they had given me a psychedelic drug.

Farber: You have previous negative associations with psychiatric hospitals.

Dr. Ed Whitney: I did! Hell, when I was in college in 1970 I worked weekends at the state hospital, which was horrible. But now the world was transforming; you no longer needed to be fearful. If I wasn't suspicious of them, then they weren't going to harm me, and all would be well. The drug they gave me that caused the psychedelic experience was proof, and then they started me on lithium. I thought "Aha!" Lithium was the lightest of the metallic elements, number three in the periodic table. It was the ideal conduit by which cosmic energies could be grounded. The stars were mostly hydrogen and helium; lithium was the vehicle through which their messages could come to Earth. How wise the psychiatrists were! They really knew what I needed.

Farber: Yes, of course. The irony, as you noted later, is that they had no idea what you were going through; they are not capable of construing such experiences as anything other than mental illness. Thus from their perspective your euphoria was a symptom of your illness. You had a "manic episode," the defining feature of which is "an abnormally and persistently elevated mood"*—elevated meaning euphoric, good, cheerful, or high. Furthermore, part of the problem according to them, is that persons experiencing "mania" often "do not know that they are 'ill'"—as the DSM puts it. That is, any attempt to interpret your experience as other than illness would be seen as a sign of illness! They had no idea what you needed, and the drug that triggered your vision of flowing light was intended to suppress your entire experience—even your happiness, your joy.

Farber: You wrote aptly in your essay:

---

*This is according to the Diagnostic and Statistical Manual of Mental Disorders (known as "the DSM") published by the American Psychiatric Association, used by all mental health professionals in clinics or privately—required for imbursement by insurance companies, including Medicaid.

[T]he mental health care system and I were at cross purposes; what I was experiencing as a wonderful healing process was construed by my doctors as a serious disease process. Neither of us had a clue about the other's perspective. They knew nothing about my issues with my father, the spiritual and religious interests I had had since childhood, and my recent fascination with the Lubavitcher Hasidim, who were saying publicly that their elderly and ailing leader was the promised Messiah. If the Lubavitchers were right, then the healing of the whole world was at hand, and we would have no more war. Fear and hatred would rule no longer. God would no longer be a tool of oppression. With my entire being, I wanted this to be true. For their part, the doctors knew messianic obsession as a symptom of illness, a medical disorder of the brain.[4]

Farber: What did you mean by your statement, "God would no longer be a tool of oppression"?

Dr. Ed Whitney: Just the two-thousand-year war persecution of Jews by the church.

Ed was released after three days and went back to work. He stopped taking the psychiatric drugs. He had intended to stay on the lithium but he found it was causing nausea and vomiting, and decided it had served its purpose. He was doing a lot of osteopathic manipulations in his practice and getting better results than ever before; he thinks his hands were more sensitive. Patients were saying, "Wow. I really feel better." He still felt that the messianic age was going to begin, but he was calmer and able to appear normal to his patients.

Farber: You were practicing, and you were doing better than ever before. Did this overcome your sense that you were inferior to your father?

Dr. Ed Whitney: Oh yes. The very last afternoon in my office, before my second hospitalization, I had a patient, a woman I saw for the very first time. She'd been referred by someone else, who was satisfied with what they got from me and said, "You should see this guy." She had some chronic pelvic and back pains, which had been around for a number of years, and she had a lot of stuff going on. And I said to her,

"Think of all the fear that we've been through in our lives, and how much that's affected our bodies." And meantime, I'm working with her. . . . I began to feel her unwind, the stuff with her legs . . . I just let her carry that process along the way a really good osteopath can do, till she settled down and sat quietly for a few minutes. Then she stirred, and she got off the table, and she said, "Wow!" And she touched her toes, and she said, "This is amazing!"

Farber: Was there an element of the miraculous there?

Dr. Ed Whitney: There was an element, certainly, of healing.

Farber: Do you think you were more intuitive than you had been?

Dr. Ed Whitney: Oh, yes.

Farber: Because of your state of consciousness, you were more intuitive?

Dr. Ed Whitney: Yes. An altered state of consciousness and just trusting my unconscious mind.

Farber: This actually resolved your complex about not being as good as your father?

Dr. Ed Whitney: Yes, it certainly did. I felt that I was there to be a healer.

Farber: And you didn't feel this inadequacy, as compared to your father anymore?

Dr. Ed Whitney: Right. That was gone.

Farber: Did you have a sense that it was finally resolved?

Dr. Ed Whitney: All the way, I was doing something new here.

Farber: So the altered state of consciousness—that began around the time you were the same age as your father's age at the time of your birth—was part of a healing process, as Laing or Perry would have seen it.

Dr. Ed Whitney: Yes. I felt it was a healing process.

Farber: But you now are a medical researcher, not a practicing doctor.

Dr. Ed Whitney: I decided I had to make a living. I found that the healing encounters worked well when there was no money changing hands. Most of the sessions I had done that worked so well that summer were gratis. I did not work so well as a doctor when I had to charge money and think about competing and making a living. So I went back and studied epidemiology, which had always fascinated me.

On June 12 the Lubavitcher Rebbe Rabbi Schneerson died. Dr. Whitney became very excited. As he said, "And I thought, 'Well, on the third day after the crucifixion of Christ, He rises from the dead.'"

Dr. Ed Whitney: And the thing is solid, the night after the Rebbe died, two of his leading followers were on *Larry King Live,* and Larry King said, "Was he the Messiah?" And one of them said, "Yes, he met every single criterion the Messiah must meet." And so I said, "I'm going to stay tuned. I'm going to watch." And it was on the third day that the newspaper had the story of the Vatican and Israel establishing full diplomatic relations. And that meant to me that the oldest wounds were healed and . . . soul . . . was made whole. And Maimonides had said eight-hundred years earlier that this was the kind of thing that would happen with the Messiah, not to look for miracles or supernatural events. So there, in *The New York Times,* was the confirmation.

Farber: So, did they claim it as the work of the Rebbe?

Dr. Ed Whitney: No, they had no idea. They weren't looking and hadn't noticed. I thought the whole world—I thought tens of thousands of people around the world would have done what I was doing and looked at the damn newspaper and listened to CNN—but there you go!

Farber: How could they claim that he was the Messiah, if he didn't usher in the messianic age?

Dr. Ed Whitney: Oh, because the messianic age was right there, three days later. And I thought, "Well, on the third day after the crucifixion of Christ, He rises from the dead."

Farber: That's what you thought. But what did they [the Rebbe's followers] say?

Dr. Ed Whitney: Oh, yes. I wondered what they must have thought, because I called them up a few weeks after. It was early on a Friday afternoon, before Shabbat. I'll always wonder what they thought when they heard this guy talking excitedly on their answering machine saying, "He did it! He's the Messiah! Hallelujah!" Some crazy guy that was obviously from another tradition.

Farber: So how were you able to function for so long with a view of the world that was so discrepant with the ugliness and things that were really happening in the world?

Dr. Ed Whitney: I was getting higher and higher, because there were these other signs I noticed. There was Castro showing up for the first time ever in a civilian shirt, and so that meant the swords will be beaten into plowshares, the instruments of war were turning to peace. And finding this again in *The New York Times* again; I still have the picture to prove it.

Farber: In your mind was this the messianic age as described by Isaiah and the biblical prophets? The lion and the lamb lying down and the Earth as house of prayer for all peoples?

Dr. Ed Whitney: Of course, that was absolutely central. This whole thing.

Farber: You were functioning, you were doing well, and the world wasn't doing so well, but you thought it was getting better.

Dr. Ed Whitney: I thought it was, yes.

Farber: You thought it was the messianic age?

Dr. Ed Whitney: Yes, once I went through all the evidence. I said, "No, I checked this out. No, I'll look once again at the videotape of Larry King." I began going around proclaiming, "Look! What more do you want?"

Farber: Oh, you still thought Rabbi Schneerson was behind it . . .

Dr. Ed Whitney: Simultaneously, when Jimmy Carter went to North Korea—when they were having that crisis, the nuclear inspections crisis, North and South Korea were on the verge of war—and Jimmy Carter goes there and sits down, takes his wife with him, introduces her to

Kim Il Sung, and pays him the goddamn common courtesy of listening to him for a few hours, which he had never experienced. Then he goes to the Torah.

Farber: The exact opposite of what George W. Bush is doing today.

Dr. Ed Whitney: Yes. That final piece fell into place. What more could you ask for? Because the question here becomes do we expect Elijah the prophet at Mt. Carmel?

Do you insist on fire and miracles; do you want a high amplitude signal or a low amplitude signal?

Farber: Were you aware there was still suffering in the world?

Dr. Ed Whitney: Yes, I was, because Rwanda was still happening. And the other thing was, O. J. Simpson was dominating the headlines. I couldn't forget about that; he just killed his wife the day the Messiah died. I was trying to incorporate all this stuff. You take some liberties with logic in order to get the process going, but what happened was, I began to . . .

Farber: But you thought all this bad stuff was going to stop?

Dr. Ed Whitney: Yes, and I was babbling to everyone I knew about *Larry King Live,* and my office manager said, "Let's go back to the hospital." So I went with her.

Farber: She felt this was necessary because of the things you were saying?

Dr. Ed Whitney: Yes, and I was talking excitedly and rapidly.

Farber: Not because you were doing anything dangerous?

Dr. Ed Whitney: No, nothing to endanger anyone, including myself. So it was eight days after the rebbe had died. I had another interview with some social workers at the hospital, and they said, "Well, okay, we'll let you leave the hospital, we're not going to bring you back in, but you'll have to have an appointment tomorrow morning with one of our doctors."

Farber: Oh, they let you go! This was a liberal hospital, then.

Dr. Ed Whitney: A friend was going to pick me up—a friend from church. I went to visit him that night, and we were sitting around talking about how maybe this is what the Second Coming looks like, and suddenly then: bang! Here's a moment I'm never going to forget. Suddenly I realized that everything I had thought was wrong, and I was actually Satan, and I was going to be punished: I would implode into the size of a proton, crushed down.

Farber: This is what you thought, just suddenly?

Dr. Ed Whitney: Yes. I was going to be crushed down to the size of a proton, and this being an implosion, like the big bang, into a nightmare universe, like it would go on forever and ever and ever, and I would be stomped on, I would be tortured, each one worse than the previous. That was the most intense experience that ever happened. And so, "Let's call the ambulance." And they whisked me . . .

Farber: Wait a minute. Even though you were going to go back to the hospital the next day, he called an ambulance?

Dr. Ed Whitney: Yes, this was way the hell out of what we'd planned for.

Farber: So you went from the so-called manic state to the so-called depressive state?

Dr. Ed Whitney: Yes. I thought, "Oh, nothing touches this!" I don't know what kind of—how the clinical terminology would work—but this was way beyond anything you would call depression. It was a full immersion in the dysphoric state.

Farber: A dark night of the soul, I would call it. Custance[5] describes the same kind of things—and many of the mystics—you know, being abominable to God. Of course the shrinks would call it a major depressive episode.

Dr. Ed Whitney: Yes, it was absolutely real, that the resurrection of the dead was going to take place. And each person, as they rose from the dead, all the pain that they'd had in their life was my fault, and they were going to stomp on me and inject their pain into me; I was the archfiend who had ruined a universe.

Farber: Very medieval.

Dr. Ed Whitney: It was going to get worse and worse and worse, forever and ever and ever, infinity upon infinity. And I was just screaming, eyes wide open, in absolute terror. So of course, they had . . .

Farber: Well, you know, James Joyce describes—these kind of things were said to people by the churches throughout the ages . . .

Dr. Ed Whitney: Yes, it was the whole thing from *Portrait of the Artist*, multiplied a hundred times.

Farber: This is part of what I call Augustinian Christianity.

Dr. Ed Whitney: Yes, it was kind of that, only more so.

Farber: It's part of Luther, and particularly, Calvin.

Dr. Ed Whitney: Yes. Except that I was Satan himself. I had always been Satan, from the foundation of the world till now.

Farber: And other people were bad, or they weren't as bad?

Dr. Ed Whitney: Well, the people were not as bad. They were going to stomp over me, and I would deserve it. And all their pain would be injected into me, and then—because I had felt so bad about the way that gays were persecuted—well, it meant they really were abominable in God's sight, and I was going to have a red-hot watermelon inserted into my rectum, and it would explode and tear my pelvis apart, and that would teach me to sympathize with the abominable. In other words, from God to death, and all this was going to happen. So the next thing that happened when I began to get oriented was that I was in the emergency room . . .

Farber: How many hours was this?

Dr. Ed Whitney: It was—not a clock time—maybe someday I can get the medical records.

Farber: Then it wasn't more than a few hours?

Dr. Ed Whitney: It was less than that. Once I was back in the hospital, it was very intensive, total immersion and was, clock time, half an hour to an hour, max.

Farber: You weren't going to kill yourself, though?

Dr. Ed Whitney: No, no.

Farber: But were you in a state of terror?

Dr. Ed Whitney: I was flat on my back, utterly unable to move. They strapped me onto a gurney and whisked me off to the emergency room, and then I realized that there was a bored-looking emergency room nurse, and she was taking my blood pressure, vital signs, and writing something down on a piece of paper. She was the most welcome sight I'd ever seen.

Farber: She was sympathetic?

Dr. Ed Whitney: No. She was kind of bored . . . but it wasn't the pit of hell. I was back! And all that wasn't going to happen. And then, about another seven-day hospitalization, with another yarn attached to it. Soon I went back into a highly euphoric state, I was . . .

Farber: The same kind of state again?

Dr. Ed Whitney: Yes. Except it was much more stable and sustained.

Farber: How did you get from that dark night of the soul back to a euphoric state?

Dr. Ed Whitney: Well, I said, "All this has cosmic significance, evidently."

Farber: When did you say this, right after you saw the nurse?

Dr. Ed Whitney: That same night I was taken off to the ward for the more seriously disturbed people. The first time I had been on the not-too-crazy side, but this time I was with the baddies. I sat very quietly on this couch on the ward, and I was really appreciative.

Farber: Was it seeing that woman that brought you out of that state?

Dr. Ed Whitney: Well, the nurse was the first person I saw who—I realized, "Wait, there's a clock on the wall, I'm still on planet Earth. This is the hospital, and I'm not going to be tormented. This is where I am, and I'm not being tortured."

Farber: In retrospect, that dark night of the soul had a meaning, as you saw it?

Dr. Ed Whitney: Oh, intense, yes.

Farber: And the meaning was obviously not that you were the devil. It was what?

Dr. Ed Whitney: The meaning was now I was Christ, after all, and I'd been through this to save humanity, like the crucifixion and resurrection.

Farber: So it was all part of God's plan for salvation. You thought that you were Christ? Or you were wondering?

Dr. Ed Whitney: Yes, my first thought was that I was Elijah the prophet after all, or one of those other bigwigs. But the hospital was undergoing accreditation at the time, so I thought, maybe I'd better be Jesus Christ, because if inspectors come through here, they might say, "How many Jesus Christs do you have?" And they didn't have any. So I feared the inspectors would say, "What kind of booby hatch is this? You don't have anyone here who says they're Jesus. We cannot accredit you." So I decided I'd be Jesus after all! So they'd check off on their list, "Okay, we've got at least one Jesus Christ."

Farber: Were you really were thinking that?

Dr. Ed Whitney: Oh, yes. I was talking to God and stuff. Stuff that amused me, also financial worries and my practice not going well—money; suddenly I realized, we're the only country in the world blasphemous enough to put "In God We Trust" on its currency. God knows we really worship the almighty dollar, and what God wants us to do is take "In God We Trust" off our currency and put it on our toilet paper. The toilet paper cleanses us, gives us comfort, and every time we use it we could be reminded that what toilet paper does for our bodies, God will do for our souls. It's going to remind us that it's a more appropriate place to say "In God We Trust," not on pieces of paper that only make excreting endlessly worrisome. That kind of stuff—hilariously funny to me, and self-evident that not everybody is similarly amused.

Farber: So you were now basically in a positive frame of mind?

Dr. Ed Whitney: Yes. They had a terrace, and I remember going out there and looking up at the sun. I could feel all the galaxies in the universe were singing, and all of the electrons in the universe were jumping in and out of their orbits just for the fun of it.

Farber: Singing praise to God?

Dr. Ed Whitney: Yes.

Ed was released on June 28, after seven days in the hospital. He began to see patients again in a spare room in his home; he had the place to himself because his housemates had "fled." The hospital had released him on a "mood stabilizer" (Depakote) and a neuroleptic, an "antipsychotic"; he was not sure which one. He stopped taking the neuroleptic as soon as he was released. Several days later he decided the Depakote had "served its purpose" and was no longer necessary, so he went to the beach and cast it into the sea.

Farber: Were you stable for the rest of the summer?

Dr. Ed Whitney: Yes, more or less stable, but the development of certain ideas was going on at the same time. It was that month, July I think, that Israel signed a formal peace treaty with Jordan—after forty years of warfare, they formalized a peace treaty—and also with the other Arab states. They had been in a state of war since the founding of the state. So I said, "Well, what more evidence does anybody want?"' And I continued to be accumulating evidence that the messianic age was here, and it was. In September I decided to go back to the hospital and talk to the doctor, to clear up some things. So I went to the administrator, and he directed me to the head psychiatrist, Dr. Weiss.

Farber: Why did you go?

Dr. Ed Whitney: I guess I was still looking for them to realize what had happened with me. Maybe it could help them with other patients. At that point I was more "sane," and I realized they might look at things differently than me. So I went in to talk with Dr. Weiss. I said that I had this kind of religious conversion experience. He sat there in his chair, and in a very condescending way was saying, "No, no, what you have is a biochemical disorder, a bipolar disorder, manic-depression. . . . You need to accept that, and you'll have to live with it the rest of your life and take your medication. Ted Turner has it, and Patty Duke has it," blah blah and, "It's biochemical, it's genetic," la de da de da.

Farber: In your essay you wrote:

> The head of psychiatry at the hospital told me that I was in denial if I insisted that I had been having a spiritual crisis. No, he said, this is a medical disorder like asthma or diabetes. When I finally understood that he meant what he said, I was devastated—and I was feeling suicidal within hours. I could not argue with his self-assured, expert manner. Where, I wanted to ask, were the mast cells, the inflammatory mediators, the glycosylated proteins of this allegedly medical condition? But I was too demoralized to speak. I felt only like dying. The whole episode meant nothing; it was just a case of bad DNA making defective protoplasm. If I had accepted the medical model of my experience, I would not have survived to tell this tale. Despair would have consumed me.[6]

Farber: Did he know you were a doctor?

Dr. Ed Whitney: Sure, but that didn't matter to him. I was just another mental defective in denial. He just wasn't listening to me. He was snide and condescending. I came away from there, and within half an hour I wanted to die.

Farber: You also wrote, "It is a very serious matter when a physician mistakes a healing process for a pathological one. The intention of the doctors was positive, but their expression was most destructive."[7] That's well put. This, by the way, was the basis of John Weir Perry's work—that these psychotic experiences are the psyche's way of healing itself and, of course, the mental health professionals who almost always interpret them as pathological are oblivious to the impact of this on the patient.

Dr. Ed Whitney: NAMI had this campaign to destigmatize mental illness, so I said to him, "Instead of stigmatizing these experiences by attributing them to a mental disorder and then trying to destigmatize the disorder . . . why don't we just not stigmatize the experiences in the first place by labeling them mental illness?" But it was like talking to a wall.

Farber: So this was the only time other than the dark night of the soul experience in which you felt—actually, even in the dark night of the soul, you didn't describe wanting to die.

Dr. Ed Whitney: I didn't feel suicidal then, I was just completely immersed in being Satan. This was a different kind of thing, a different feeling.

Farber: More mundane?

Dr. Ed Whitney: Yes, it was more mundane, but it was also very powerful; maybe everything *was* meaningless. But I was telling you, *this was the most meaningful thing I had ever experienced!* I couldn't even get some of my friends to go along with—to acknowledge—the synchronicities around the death of the Lubavitcher Rebbe. They said, "Drop it. You're reading too much into it."

Farber: You're talking about in September? After the fact?

Dr. Ed Whitney: Yes.

Farber: You mean, after you had the meeting with him, you went back to your friends and tried . . .

Dr. Ed Whitney: Yes, I was with a lot of the same—Jewish—friends. It was kind of the same, but they were saying, "Well, I think you're reading too much into the death . . ." It seemed most of them now believed I was sick, and so they were saying, "Well, you're probably reading too much into the whole . . ." And that, unintentionally, kind of kicked me down into the pits a bit more. I wanted to die. And that was when I called another doctor.

Farber: This was yet another dark night of the soul[8]—excuse the phrase again.

Dr. Ed Whitney: It was. Probably a more modern version.

Farber: There are people who think about everything like that—philosophers, scientists—that all life is meaningless, for example, Richard Dawkins. Were you contemplating suicide?

Dr. Ed Whitney: Well, not so much in terms of planning instruments, but feeling overwhelmed with misery and wanting to die, and feeling like . . .

Farber: Because you felt the whole world was meaningless and you were just a collection of biochemical elements?

Dr. Ed Whitney: A couple of bad nucleotides in my DNA was the whole explanation for—the entire explanation was an empty universe, la de da de da. But I found a psychiatrist who was part of the Spiritual Emergency Network; he was a board-certified psychiatrist.

Farber: You wouldn't have found that in most parts of the country!

Dr. Ed Whitney: No, I was lucky I was in Santa Cruz. He knew me and I knew him because we'd done some things together as doctors. He was interested in another model for taking care of people: what they call a sanctuary, having a place where people could have these experiences and be safe and not in a hospital setting.

Farber: Yes, this was what John Perry and Loren Mosher and R. D. Laing in England had done, and their asylums worked! (Laing's was another story.) But their funding was slashed under Reagan, and now there's no government funding for alternatives. How soon did you meet him?

Dr. Ed Whitney: I called him up and said, "Hey Bob, I think I need some help; I don't know what's going on." So he saw me, and we had about eight sessions. He was saying there's a mix of things going on, your personal issues, but you could also be having some spiritual emergence, this stuff, and I think the thing that really helped was about the nightmare experience.

Farber: The devil experience, yes.

Dr. Ed Whitney: He asked, "Did you feel whole and euphoric afterward?" I said, "Yes, absolutely. I felt wonderful afterward."

Farber: Like a purification?

Dr. Ed Whitney: Yes. And he said, "That is your archetypal night journey."

Farber: That is the archetypal night journey?

Dr. Ed Whitney: Yes, the hero's journey. They go through this ordeal, and this is part of the hero's journey—this night of the soul . . .

Farber: Descent?

Dr. Ed Whitney: Yes, descent. The ordeal. And that was fine. So I knew I'd be okay.

Farber: Because of what he said?

Dr. Ed Whitney: Yes. What he said was critical. He legitimized me. It was exactly what I needed—from one other human being, someone I respected. And I was getting there slowly, because I had some support from other people, including a guy—a friend of mine who never went to college—and he said, "This happened for a reason." And he said I seemed much improved by the whole experience, because he saw me before and after, and he said I was acting much less like a doctor now; of course, he meant that as compliment. It was a salutary thing as far as I was concerned.

Farber: Looking back on it, the whole thing became a healing—or rebirth—experience?

Dr. Ed Whitney: Yes, I wouldn't trade that entire experience for the world.

Farber: Obviously, your experiences were different from most people, who would not have met the doctor who helped them. There aren't many like him in the country.

Dr. Ed Whitney: Yes, because resources are scarce and because there aren't enough copies of John Custance in print. I was talking to my friend from Berkeley in the beginning of November, which happened to be my birthday. I was saying, "You know, what I've been through is going to mean something, because if I ever meet anybody who's been through a similar thing, I can affirm them and I can say, 'Yep, you're going to be okay, because I went through something a lot more psychotic than that.'"

Farber: Of course, most people—you were not on the psychiatric drugs in September either?

Dr. Ed Whitney: Now, I did take them for a little while. I kept the bottle; I actually wrote my own scrip for a bottle of Depakote.

Farber: But not neuroleptics?

Dr. Ed Whitney: No.

Farber: And not lithium.

Dr. Ed Whitney: No. But I said, "I'm going to keep the Depakote with me. I maybe should just have it around," because I took it for a while under this doctor's direction. I'd had it for a few weeks. I said, "I'm going to keep it around for a year," and I did that, just for security, but I had no need to take it after a couple weeks because I was reorienting. I said, "I'm going to go back to school, to study public health, epidemiology"— I'd always had an interest in that anyway—and recalibrate. I'm just an ordinary guy; it's okay to be ordinary. You don't have to be Nietzsche, you don't have to be God, you don't have to be any of that stuff. You can be Joe Shmoe, and that's good enough.

Farber: Did these experiences, as a whole, strengthen your belief in God?

Dr. Ed Whitney: It's kind of a wordless thing. I can't really—but he's real.

Farber: Was there an increased feeling that life was meaningful, in some sense?

Dr. Ed Whitney: Yes, it was meaningful, and other people's lives were meaningful, too. That was what seemed to me to be the unanswerable argument: I said that human life is meaningful, therefore, people's lives are meaningful, therefore, the episodes that make up people's lives are meaningful. Therefore, whoever has had a nutty experience—a mad experience—there's meaning in there too, and purpose.

Farber: This was the opposite of the psychiatric idea that we consist just of DNA and that if you have an experience like that, it's bad DNA—the medical model?

Dr. Ed Whitney: The medical model is, there's a bad stretch of DNA that sets your brain chemistry in the wrong direction.

Farber: According to psychiatrists, clearly you're supposed to be manic-depressive, bipolar today, and you're so . . .

Dr. Ed Whitney: Yes, and it gets worse if it's untreated and if you don't take the meds. That's the party line. And they were absolutely certain. They expressed no doubts whatsoever. I think of all the millions of people who believe them and become chronic cases *because* they believe them, because their experiences are all declared meaningless by the authorities.

Farber: And you didn't take the meds, and you haven't had a "psychotic" episode since; you proved them wrong.

Dr. Ed Whitney: Yes. A few weeks after I started with the new psychiatrist—in November—I went down to Esalen. I was a whole month down there, to try to decompress from this thing. I could talk to people there about angels and stuff. They said, "Oh yeah. Amazing." I could talk to somebody about how I was seeing auras at one point.

Farber: (Laughs.) Back in the late '80s, it was still possible to get a job in the mental health system and not believe in the medical model, because they weren't insisting everyone go on drugs. After I lost my job in 1989 for getting people off of the psych drugs, I couldn't get hired—as soon I said anything critical about the drugs, as mild as not believing in long-term use—at least not in the New York area where I tried.

Dr. Ed Whitney: They were saying on *60 Minutes* last night how kids are being diagnosed now as bipolar at the age of three and four . . .

Farber: Oh, yes. It's a big thing now. Even younger: they have infants they call bipolar. I guess they cry too much. It's really insane. Babies laugh and cry, but now a baby is not supposed to have "mood swings."

Dr. Ed Whitney: They want to use neuroleptics on everybody.

Farber: I had a patient, John, in 1988, before I was fired from this clinic. He was a young man of about twenty who was diagnosed as quote-unquote, schizophrenic. He was hearing a voice. I had just been in California three years before, and I knew how many people there were channeling spirits. So I told him he could call himself a channeler and make lots of money. I told him he did not need the "antipsychotic" drugs. . . . I told him there was nothing wrong with him, that mental illness was a myth, et cetera. Other than hearing the voice, he was like anyone else. He was coherent and very intelligent. Also I gave him a book on mysticism, on Sri Aurobindo, and he said it cleared everything up in his mind. . . . I told his mother he wasn't schizophrenic. . . . His mother tried to get me fired from the clinic. She was in NAMI, she threatened to sue me, and she threatened to sue the clinic. Eventually, the head of the clinic, even though he liked me, had to fire me, because I was encouraging too many people to get off the drugs and I got on the psychiatrist's nerves.

Ten years later, John called me, and he was perfectly normal. He was making a lot of money as a carpenter. The voice had disappeared. (I contacted him in 2011, and he was still doing fine.) He said that what I had told him—that he was not psychotic—had encouraged him to get off the drugs. He said once he did this he felt like a new person, and he hasn't taken a drug or been to a psychiatrist in ten years. (As of now, it's been twenty years.) His parents would not talk to him for many years; they told him unless he took his meds they would not talk to him. I had not told him to try to get rid of the voice; I just advised him not to take all his orders from the voice. That was just one intervention, because he really wasn't with me that long before I got fired from that clinic. Then I heard from him a few years ago, and he was still doing okay.

Dr. Ed Whitney: I knew a schizophrenic. He heard voices. He kind of knew some of them were actual people talking to him and some of them weren't, but he didn't know which was which. So he said, "I'm going to get a dog." He got a dog, and he knew that if the dog reacted to the voice, it was probably another person, but if the dog did nothing, it was a voice in his head. That was how he could tell them apart, noticing the dog's reaction.

Farber: This was for him a functional way . . .

Dr. Ed Whitney: That was how he learned to distinguish real voices of people.

Farber: And it works . . .

Dr. Ed Whitney: The dog reacted to one and not the other.

Farber: Did you know how he was doing a few years later?

Dr. Ed Whitney: No idea.

Farber: Oh, so this worked for a few months—that you know?

Dr. Ed Whitney: Yes, but he seemed to be okay; at least he wasn't in the hospital.

Farber: Well, let me go to what you say here, because you worded it eloquently, I think:

> Mania, in my experience of it, is a process of giving birth to hope in the soul. It is opposed from within by an equally intense nihilism and fear that the entire creation is nothing more than a cesspool of doom. . . . Inner conflict can make a person labile.* The cosmic grandiosity comes from trying to answer the question, "Is the universe a friendly place or a hostile place?" This is ultimately a religious question; hence the preoccupation with religious and spiritual issues.[9]

Farber: That's good.

Dr. Ed Whitney: These issues are as old as mankind. This stuff you're grappling with, these issues have come up in the last few years with the advent of modern psychiatry, which in its hubris thinks it

---

Labile is a psychiatric term that means "inclined to mood swings."

can reduce all these big questions to aberrant biochemistry. It's all the kind of stuff that is for these bigger traditions, the great religious and spiritual traditions of humanity—they were the bigger issues. They grappled seriously with these issues. Psychiatry wants to silence the great existential questions, as if the question itself was a symptom of aberrant biochemistry.

Farber: Actually, if you read some of the stuff on Christian mysticism, the mystical experience of the universe as a manifestation of divine love is frequently, at least in the Western tradition, followed by the dark night of the soul, along with nihilism and fear that the entire creation is nothing more than "a cesspool of doom," as you say. The two frequently go together at this stage in our spiritual evolution. How could they not? Look at the Earth today; look at how human beings are destroying everything. I blame this on man, not God. It makes sense that the vision of paradise would be followed by a fear of doom, because this is the choice we face, but modern psychiatry considers it a bipolar disorder.

Dr. Ed Whitney: Yes. The thing is, we're trying to approach the religious and spiritual. We used to repress sexuality, now with psychiatrists it's spirituality. They do not consider homosexuality a mental illness anymore, but the kinds of spiritual experiences I had are not permitted; they are considered psychopathology. Spiritual histories are just not part of their paradigm, but this is a big part of human experience, and it's a damn shame that they're not—because they should be. And they should be able to respond, to ask questions such as, "Do you feel something meaningful is happening?"

Farber: That's the antithesis of what they do and what they're supposed to do, which is to adjust people to quote-unquote reality.

Dr. Ed Whitney: Well, it is the pharmaceutical industry—a great many symptoms, that is their bread and butter. Psychiatrists have sold out to the pharmaceutical industry. They have to decide what they want to be. It seems like they just want to be drug pushers. If they want to be physicians, that's another thing. They need to want to be that, and that means you'd have another way of being with people.

Farber: Do you think your experience would have resolved itself had you not gone to the sympathetic psychiatrist?

Dr. Ed Whitney: That is an interesting thing; I don't know. He was a very important part of it, and these friends of mine also. I think it would have taken a lot longer, but because I had access to other resources, including several sympathetic friends, and my family was supportive, I would have made it.

Farber: Your family didn't want you locked up? They didn't have a typical psychiatric NAMI attitude?

Dr. Ed Whitney: No, no. It is very different with them.

Farber: Do you think your state of elation, given the fact that the world wasn't changing, would have died down eventually anyway?

Dr. Ed Whitney: Yes, I think it would have. I'd have been facing a rock, eventually.

Farber: What are your philosophical or spiritual beliefs today?

Dr. Ed Whitney: In practice, I don't go to church much. But still I think basically there's some Christian framework.

Farber: You have a Christian framework?

Dr. Ed Whitney: Yes. I'm not much of a fundamentalist, clearly.

Farber: If you're a Christian, you must still believe in God in some . . .

Dr. Ed Whitney: Oh, yes. Absolutely, yes. This universe came from somewhere.

Farber: Some personal . . .

Dr. Ed Whitney: Yes. Some higher intelligence.

Farber: And do you believe that the Earth—the climate —will get better?

Dr. Ed Whitney: Yes, oh sure. No doubt. The kingdom of God will come, eventually. Eventually we'll wake up.

Part Five

Awakenings in History and Social Activism

15

Cultural Revitalization Movements

*J*ohn Weir Perry's theory of cultural change was adapted from Anthony Wallace, who refers to these collective renewal efforts as cultural revitalization movements. Wallace says they arise in times of stress—defined as a condition in which a part or the whole of the social organism is threatened with more or less serious damage.[1] Many revitalization movements successfully changed the dysfunctional paradigm or worldview that dominated during their era and thus resolved the cultural crisis. Both Perry and Wallace provide numerous historical examples of revitalization movements—Christianity and Islam, and perhaps Buddhism, originated in revitalization movements.

The prominent historian of American religion William McLoughlin finds Wallace's model is generally applicable to the "Great Awakenings" in America, with several modifications that will be discussed later. McLoughlin has argued that there have been four major cultural revitalization movements in American history.

The first two Great Awakenings are accepted as historic events by all American historians. The first took place between 1730 and 1760. McLoughlin notes, as do most historians, that the First Great Awakening created the revolution in consciousness that gave rise to the American

Revolution: "The Revolution, implementing the new republican ideology was in fact the secular fulfillment of the religious ideals of the First Great Awakening." Or, as the eminent American historian Gordon Wood put it, "After 1765, the concept of political independence became not only political but moral. Revolution, republicanism, all blended in American thinking."[2] The Second Great Awakening took place in the early nineteenth century. McLoughlin, unlike most historians, believes there was a third awakening in the early twentieth century—the Social Gospel movement. McLoughlin was the first to propose that the 1960s constituted a Great Awakening

The first two awakenings were instigated by waves of Christian revivalist meetings. All revitalization movements, McLoughlin notes, were "periods of fundamental ideological transformations" that made possible "the growth of the nation in adapting to social, ecological, psychological and economic changes." Cultural revitalizations constitute "the awakening of a people caught in an outmoded, dysfunctional world view to the necessity of converting their mindset, their behavior, and their institutions to more relevant or more functionally useful ways of understanding and coping with the changes in the world they live in."[3]

What is relevant to note here is that in America's Great Awakenings, rather than one or several central prophets (as Perry's model implied), there have been a wide variety of prophets. Yet despite the diversity of the religious affiliations (e.g., Methodist, Quaker, Presbyterian, Unitarian) of the spiritual leaders in the first two Great Awakenings, their vision and theological beliefs had common salient features as compared to those of the religious establishments against which they were spontaneously rebelling. McLoughlin's revised model of revitalization is of particular relevance for the situation we are facing today in the context of the multicultural society America has become. It highlights the importance of developing a unifying messianic-redemptive vision based on universal symbols.

McLoughlin's account of America's revitalization movements provides historical mooring for Perry's theory concerning the decisive role of spiritual leaders as catalysts of change. Prophetic leaders emerge in times of cultural revitalization, and they also foster a revitalization process. The changes effected in the past by visionaries undergirds the hopeful perspective I am conveying in this book: the Mad Pride movement that is just now emerging propitiously in the midst of the greatest crisis humanity has ever faced—our survival is at stake—could develop into a revitalization movement. It could spark a new awakening or rekindle the embers that remain from the fires lit during the days that McLoughlin calls America's Fourth Great Awakening—the social movement and counterculture of the 1960s. (The Occupy Wall Street movement began just before this book was ready to go to press. Although the future is unpredictable, OWS belied the contention of some commentators that the 1960s was the last period of progressive popular revolt.)

The Second Great Awakening and the Messianic-Redemptive Vision

These revitalization movements provide a model for an alternative to secular (e.g., Marxist) paradigms of transformation that are not fully adequate to the exigencies of our current crisis. The messianic-redemptive vision was prevalent in America's past, though it has been buried in the course of history. For example, although many left-wing activists are committed to a redemptive (secular) vision (e.g., a socialist revolution), virtually none of them are aware that evangelical post-millennial Christianity provided the foundation and inspiration for the most powerful reform movement in American history prior to the 1960s—the Second Awakening. Many of them would deny their narrative is "messianic" or "redemptive," since they have adopted the scientific positivism of modernity. Unlike the left-wing reform movements in the 1930s, the Second Awakening of the early nineteenth century (which included the abolitionist movement) was based on an explicitly messianic narrative and vision—one that has since been eclipsed and suppressed in the course of history. This was partly because Evangelical Christianity began to become transformed after the Civil War, in large part into a reactionary premillennial right-wing cult, today composed of millions of Americans. (There are socially progressive tendencies within Evangelical Christianity, but as of yet they are relatively small and weak.) The messianic *postmillennial* Christian vision was the source of the Second Awakening's endurance and power.

According to historians, the first third of the nineteenth century was the period of the Second Great Awakening (Smith argues it extended until the Civil War.)[4] Robert Abzug and others showed that the most ardent religious reformers in those days—Christians of sundry denominations—believed the millennium was near and that its realization depended on human righteousness and progressive (to use the modern term) activism, including abolitionism, to bring society into conformity with the Christian prescriptions of justice and love. The majority of American Christians believed that Christ would return to Earth to launch a thousand years of peace and prosperity, but *as postmillennialists* they believed that Christ would return only after humanity was acting in accord with God's will. (The nineteenth-century evangelical Christians were reformers of all sorts; they did not subscribe to the fatalistic, premillennialist, and militaristic beliefs of most "Evangelical Christians" today.) Christianity in the early nineteenth century espoused messianic beliefs that were in accord with Buber's definition of messianism (see the introduction under the subheading Mad Pride in Transition), inspired as it was by the prophetic strain in Judaism (e.g., from Isaiah to Jesus): *the coming of the messianic age, the recovery of heaven on Earth, depended on the righteousness of humanity, it required the creation of a society based on Christian norms of justice.*

Since the responsibility for change in postmillennial Christianity lies with humanity and with God acting through humanity, the literal return of Jesus seems to be a superfluous part of this narrative, but no one at that time seemed to notice. It was only in the twentieth century that some Christians began to develop a profound and esoteric interpretation of the Second Coming; they claimed it would not involve the literal return of Jesus, but the coming of the "cosmic Christ." Paul Levy has explained Jung's esoteric interpretation of Christianity.

God is incarnating not just through one man, as it did through Christ over 2000 years ago, but is incarnating through all of humanity. Jung talked about, ". . . a broadening process of incarnation. Christ the son begotten by God, is the first-born who is succeeded by an increasing number of younger brothers and sisters." Christ was the first attempt by God to incarnate and transform itself. Now humanity as a whole will be the subject of the divine incarnation process. What is happening in our world right now is the second Coming of Christ, what Jung calls the "Christification of many."[5]

Thus according to Jung there *is* a divine initiative—this is the supernatural dimension to transformation—but it seeks expression through as many human beings as possible.

The foundation for the Second Great Awakening in the nineteenth century and the social activism that marked it was the spontaneous theological revolution that developed in the decades after the American Revolution. This was a new Christian Reformation, a theological revolution marked by a widespread attack on the reigning Calvinist doctrines of original sin and determinism—predestination. John L. Thomas describes this as an upsurge of the Romantic faith in human perfectibility, which found expression in prophets as diverse as Charles Finney, William Ellery Channing, Ralph Waldo Emerson, and a motley assortment of radical utopians and abolitionists.[6]

The historian of theology Dan McKanan argues that *the Awakening was the spiritual theological fruit of the growth of the Jeffersonian ideal of equality planted fifty years before, during the American Revolution.*[7] This is a cogent explanation, as one would expect that the ideal of equality would naturally find its theological expression in a rejection of the fatalistic Calvinist doctrine (derived from St. Augustine) that only an elect would be saved—that the majority were consigned by God to eternal torment. Clearly this idea was not conducive to social reform.

In religious terms perfectionism was the antithesis of the Protestant idea of original sin—that each person as a result of "original sin" was "totally depraved," as Calvin had expressed it. As opposed to total depravity, perfectionism affirmed—although this was made explicit only by a few intellectuals and reformers—the "infinite worthiness," as Emerson called it, of each human soul and her ability to actualize her potential here and now, with God's help.[8]

Thomas captures the sweep of the movement, "Salvation . . . lay open to everyone. Sin was voluntary: Men were not helpless and depraved by nature [as Calvinism asserted] but free agents and potential powers for good. Perfectionism spread rapidly across the whole spectrum of

Protestantism. The progress of the country suddenly seemed to depend upon the regeneration of the individual and the contagion of example. . . . As it spread, perfectionism swept across denominational barriers and penetrated even secular thought."[9] Perfectionism meant that the perfectibility of each individual would be accomplished as soon as oppressive social conditions were transformed.[10] As Evangelicals saw it, this was the precondition for the advent of the millennium.

As the legitimacy of Calvinism was undermined in the early nineteenth century, Americans were consequently instilled with a new sense of power and ethical responsibility. Many believed it was within their power to create the conditions for the realization of the kingdom of God on Earth. A new humanistic Christianity was emerging in a wide variety of different denominations that set loose a wave of reform activities—from abolitionism to women's rights, to Christian anarchism, to the first ecumenical Christian pacifist organizations, to the creation of utopian communes. "What a fertility of projects for the salvation of the world," exclaimed Emerson.[11] Christian historian Timothy Smith argued, "The [nineteenth-century] evangelicals played a key role in the widespread attack on slavery, poverty and greed. They thus prepared the way . . . for what later became known as the Social Gospel [a Christian socialist movement that flourished in the early twentieth century]."[12]

The belief that the kingdom of God was at hand had swept up many Americans in the first half of the nineteenth century. The messianic-redemptive vision had sunk its roots in the collective psyche. Such messianic expectations would be considered psychotic—madness—if they were expressed by a patient being examined by a psychiatrist today, but the zeitgeist at that time was radically different from the secular worldview of the modern world. Christianity in the first half of the nineteenth century was imbued with the "utopian" expectation of the dawning of the millennium, the breaking into this world of a new supernatural miraculous order.*[13] It must be emphasized how normative that ideal was at that time. It was only in the late twentieth century that mainstream

---

*Abzug argues that the "essence" of the antebellum reform movement was "the radical joining of heaven and earth. . . ."

American religion and culture—after the traumas of the horrors of the world's bloodiest century—became robustly antimetaphysical, anti-utopian and, under the guise of scientistic secularism, banished messianic hope in its all its various guises (secular or religious) to the hinterlands of superstition or madness.[14]

The Second Awakening did not bear any resemblance to modern Christian evangelicalism or fundamentalism, which with its premillennialist doctrines and emphasis on human innate sinfulness is similar to the fatalistic perspective that had been repudiated in the revolt against Calvinism in the late eighteenth and early nineteenth centuries. The antebellum Evangelicals (at least in the North) were dedicated to changing the world, whereas modern premillenialist Evangelicals believe that human beings have no power to avert the apocalyptic destruction of the Earth—Armageddon—which God has already commanded to punish unbelievers. How this strange doctrine melded in the 1980s with the militaristic xenophobic politics of the Christian right is a long story. The point here is that it involved the inversion of *antebellum* Evangelical Christianity from a worldview that inspired utopian hope and movements for progressive reforms into a worldview empowering forces of reaction.[15]

Charles Finney, the most prominent Christian evangelist of the nineteenth century and a strong opponent of slavery, rejected the legacy of his own Calvinist background—which affirmed the impotence of the human will and that salvation would be effected for the predestined by grace alone—and based his sermons on his conviction that human beings are "active participants with God in both their own salvation and the affairs of the world."[16] Finney preached that human activism in partnership with the Holy Spirit was the means for "the creation of a new heaven and a new earth."[17] In 1835 he exulted that "the millennium can come in three years" if Americans and their churches would "do their duty."[18]

Cushing Strout describes revivalist meetings on the frontiers: "Gathered in homemade tents for several days thousands of families would eat, drink, sing, shout, pray and cry together. . . . It was a jamboree and an awesome rite, a family picnic and a religious crisis, one community under God . . . with free will and heavenly justice for all."[19]

Finney's revivals took place in the East in churches and were generally more sedate than frontier revivals, but his fiery sermons produced many converts. "He aimed his sermons toward one goal—to make the stakes of salvation burn in the mind of his listeners. Religious experiences, once private dialogues between God and man, now took places in public settings; men and women, realizing and confessing their sinfulness before all who would listen."[20]

Finney's conviction that the millennium was in reach was not anomalous for the era. One historian aptly wrote that "America in the early nineteenth century was drunk on the millennium." The great theologian and historian H. Richard Niebuhr (brother of Reinhold) captures the popular mood well in *The Kingdom of God in America,* written in 1937, "[A] great wave of expectancy came over men. . . . A Christian revolution was evidently taking place; a new day was dawning." This gospel of the coming kingdom that had begun with individual conversions of heart had become social. "It insisted that the fruits of the personal revolution needed to appear and, insofar as the revolution was genuine would appear in the whole common life, in science, art, agriculture, industry, church and state."[21] The leaders of revivalism disagreed on many particulars, but they agreed on two major points. There was no way into "the kingdom of God on Earth" that did not entail crisis on Earth and "the loss and death to the self." Today we would call it the death of the ego. Second, they agreed on the necessity of meeting the future crisis by *pressing into the kingdom,"* which was coming with both judgment and promise.[22]

The expectation of the coming kingdom on Earth was "nurtured by the continuing revival until it became the dominant idea in American Christianity."[23] Let me emphasize this: Christianity at the time was based on a messianic-redemptive vision of social change. This gave rise to the burgeoning of a sense of collective hopefulness. By psychiatric standards this mood would be considered "manic." (Note the similarity to the experiences of Dr. Ed Whitney, interviewed in chapter 14.) William Ellery Channing[*24]—the great mentor of Emerson—saw in

---

*Niebuhr writes that due to his emphasis on social reform as integral to Christianity, Channing can be "legitimately counted . . . as one of the great heirs of the *Evangelical* movement and the Awakening"—even though Channing was a non-Evangelical Unitarian.

"the victory of Christ's spirit the coming of his kingdom to earth." Channing wrote, "Christ comes in the conversion, the regeneration, the emancipation of the world." Channing believed Christ's spirit demands the abolition of war and slavery, the practice of philanthropy, and the "government of all life by reference to the dignity and worth of men."[25] To those who participated in the awakening, the humanitarian reform and evangelical movements were simultaneously *evidence* of the kingdom's coming and "instruments whereby [the advent of] the kingdom was being hastened."[26]

The antislavery movement was also a product of Christian evangelicalism, of the spiritual revitalization. This kind of utopian revitalization is strikingly similar, as will be shown, to the spirit of the 1960s, in spite of the fact that in the 1960s the idiom of the rebels was not Christian. It is striking, however, that in both the Second and Fourth Awakenings it was believed that a combination of individual regeneration with a commitment to social reform would have eschatological consequences. Despite the secularism of the 1960s' counterculture and New Left resistance, they seem to have been possessed by a vision similar to that of their nineteenth-century forebears—the recovery of paradise on Earth, of the return to the Garden of Eden.

Theodore Weld was a stellar example of the fusion of the personal and political dimensions represented by the awakening. He was a Finney disciple who became one of the leading abolitionists. He went from town to town preaching against slavery and braving the wrath of proslavery mobs in the Midwest. Abzug, Weld's biographer, raises an important issue: What was it that gave Weld and his comrades the courage to persevere in the face of staunch opposition and such meager material remuneration for their work? There were several factors. First, like the Biblical prophets, they saw themselves as rebels against the injustices of society, and they cared little for earthly rewards. But this negative factor would not have been enough to inspire such sacrifice.

The second factor was probably more important: Weld and men like him "ordered their lives around one idea . . . that admitted of no compromise . . . they believed in the Millennium, to be made by men and made quickly." That is, it was a messianic-redemptive vision—based upon human endeavor—that was the source of their power of endurance. "When all else was going badly they could place their faith in eventual triumph as prophesied in the Bible, and as heralded by signs of the times. One only needed to keep working at it."[27]

Abzug notes that Weld often used a metaphor in describing society. He "saw society as sick."[28] This is a striking parallel with the radicals of the 1960s. If he had access to the language of the twentieth century, Weld, like Erich Fromm and R. D. Laing, may have said that society was "insane." He did not view conformity to a "sick" society as normative; the new world that the Christian reformers were seeking to give birth to was normative. Society needed to be restored to health. To those who warned Weld of the dangers of upsetting the social order, he scoffed and responded that the task of the Christian was not to preserve order but to determine "what would quicken the church, turn the nations from their idols, pioneer into being the glories of the millennium, and cause earth to bloom with the hues of heaven."[29] The radical abolitionists (men like Weld and Garrison) were creatively maladjusted, and they knew it! Their compass was not set to the sights of "normal society"—which they believed was itself existentially "off course"—but to the millennium, the new order, the kingdom of heaven on Earth (see chapter 4).

Niebuhr noted that even a slight success in the movement was enough to prompt Weld to exalt, "If these are the first fruits what will be the Harvest? If the gatherings of handfuls wakes up such loud acclaim, what will be the song when the morning stars break out together . . . as the whole mighty growth that now stands as a forest . . . comes before the Lord of the harvest, and is gathered into his garner?"[30] It was the same spirit that led Edward Beecher to cry out in 1865, "Now that God has smitten slavery unto death, he has opened the way for the redemption and sanctification of our whole social system." Weld was passionately convinced that the abolitionists would triumph because ending slavery was the "cause of God."[31]

As Niebuhr put it, for Weld and the abolitionists the coming kingdom was "*judgment as well as promise.*"[32] The abolitionists believed that only repentance could save sinful men from the wrath of God. Weld said confession and restitution were necessary—abolishing slavery, feeding the poor, and giving jobs to the unemployed. "This may save us.

God grant it may not be too late."[33] But God's mercy in this era was as deep as his wrath at human sinfulness; Weld saw sin in social as well as individual terms, much like liberation theologists over a century later. When Lane Seminary asked Weld and his students to dissolve their organization and to desist from their abolitionist agitation, Weld wrote, "Is this the time to destroy our society [i.e., organization] when truth is fallen in the street and judgment turned away backward? When the pulpit is overawed, the press panders to power, conscience surrenders to expediency. . . ? When the heart of the slave is breaking with the anguish of hope deferred, and our free colored brethren are persecuted even into strange cities?" Weld answered his own question: "No! God forbid that we should abandon a cause that strikes its roots so deep into the soil of human interests, and human rights, and throws its branches upward and abroad, so high and wide into the sunlight of human hopes and human well-being."[34] Yet despite all obstacles, Weld persisted in the confidence that the days of slavery are numbered in "this land of liberty and light, and revivals of millennial glory."[35]

Timothy L. Smith's controversial but extensively documented classic *Revivalism and Social Reform* (1957) corroborated two of the main ideas expounded above: that the messianic expectation was present in the nineteenth century and that it led to what we would call today "progressive" social action. He attempted to demonstrate that the Second Awakening did not end until the eve of the Civil War, when it had unleashed a crescendo of antislavery and social reform sentiment. The revivalists, the evangelists, played a key role in the "attack on slavery, poverty and greed" and thus prepared the way "both in theory and practice for what later became known as the social gospel."[36] (The Social Gospel adherents were liberals or socialists.) Smith's book, as he puts it, "indicates that revivalism and perfectionism become socially volatile only when combined with the doctrine of Christ's imminent conquest of the earth."[37] In other words, Smith's study of this period indicates the social power of the messianic-redemptive vision and thus strengthens the argument for what I call the messianic-redemptive paradigm.

According to Smith, by the time of the Civil War, the conviction had become "commonplace" (in the North) that "society must be reconstructed through the power of a sanctifying gospel and all the evils of cruelty, poverty and greed done away with." From this perspective a rag-tag band of radical reformers, as, for example, the abolitionists were at the start, effected a major change in several decades. (Of course, there were also historical and economic factors creating antagonism to the "slave-ocracy.") It was the "enlargement of millennial [messianic] hopes" that engendered this new sense of "social responsibility."[38]

To take one eloquent and more philosophical example of a common sentiment, William Hosner, a Methodist abolitionist, author, and newspaper editor, wrote in an editorial in 1852, "Wicked laws not only may be broken, but absolutely must be broken: there is no other way to escape the wrath of God." Slaveholders must be banned from the church. The mission of the Church "is to establish the Kingdom of God on earth by the banishment of unrighteousness and the introduction of universal holiness."[39] Both Smith and Niebuhr (unlike his brother Reinhold) present messianic-redemptive paradigms of social transformation or revitalization. It should be noted, of course, that as usual the shadow side of messianic possibility was also present: the terrible wrath of God at the injustice of women and men. Thus, if human beings do not rise to the occasion, the wrath of God will consume saint and sinner alike.

In Wallace's and McLoughlin's terms the economic and moral tensions of the nineteenth century—most prominently the moral disturbance provoked by the scandal of slavery in a republic dedicated at its founding to the principle of equality—constituted the conflict that inevitably engendered the religious revitalization of the Second Great Awakening. According to McLoughlin there have been many revitalizations in the course of history, and they inevitably spill over into social reform movements.

To put it in more theological terms befitting this particular revitalization, the Second Awakening had all the markings of a kairos—a moment of human decision in history marked by "the entry of the Kingdom of God into human affairs"—a period in which an "eschatological leap" becomes possible if not imperative, one that "overcomes demonic powers and then transcends the limits of previous political, racial and economic history."[40] We see how during the Second Awakening the Kingdom of God initially comes to life in the inner life of men and women; it starts first in the visions of those who become the leaders of the movement—mostly revivalists—who express it in words that, to use Jung's term, reverberate in the psyches of the ordinary men and women. (See the discussion of the power of leadership in Aurobindo's work, chapter 17.) The power of the messianic vision is combined with new theological concepts and a new mythos and communicated through books, sermons, and revivals.

What Paul Levy says about music of the '60s could be said about the revivals of the Second Awakening. "The music of the '60s was both an expression of an expanded consciousness, while simultaneously being the vibration, which precipitated and catalyzed the very expansion of consciousness of which it was an expression." To put it in Jung's terms, "If the translation of the unconscious into a communicable language that reverberates proves successful, it has a redeeming [redemptive] effect. The liberating vision of the artist [or prophets] attracts us into itself so as to make itself real in time, changing the world in the process."* Thus, the kingdom of God enters into history and constitutes a kairos.

The kingdom of God, or the messianic expectation, enters the psyche in moments of acute social crisis, as it did during the Second Awakening, when the future of slavery, of democracy, became a matter of collective decision. It is human beings who then place it—the kingdom of God—on the historical agenda as the task of human beings aided by God. (The deterministic worldview as we saw was repudiated during the Second Awakening.) Thus, the kingdom of God as a utopian or messianic vision enters history, galvanizes human beings, and gradually but suddenly seems imminent or at least within the realm of possibility.

Of course, it must be said: judged by eschatological standards, the Evangelical reformers' own standards, the Second Great Awakening was a failure; the eschatological leap was not made, the defeat of the demonic powers turned out despite all the blood shed to be but temporary, the millennium was not ushered in. Moral suasion—contrary

---

*Redemptive is the correct word. The term redeeming may have been an inaccurate translation, as it trivializes the point and is not the adjective for redemption.

to the expectations of abolitionists like William Garrison, Theodore Weld, and others—had not led Southerners to voluntarily abolish slavery, although it greatly increased antislavery sentiment in the North and increased the rancor between North and South, thus becoming a catalyst for the Civil War, which led to the legal abolition of slavery. Contrary to the expectations of the abolitionists, the abolition of slavery was not followed by programs to implement racial equality. Racial caste oppression took on a new and ugly face in the Jim Crow system. Despite the limits of its accomplishments, the awakening of the first half of the nineteenth century "created the most powerful reform era in American history."[41] It eventually changed the norms of society: it anchored into the moral firmament of American culture the ideal of equal rights—first articulated by Jefferson—for women and men, as well as black and whites. But this is a far cry from the redemption of humanity that the great reformers had expected. The march of progress turned out to be a cycle of eternal return, as today we face, as a species, the greatest crisis in the history of humanity, one that could lead to the very annihilation of the species.

But according to H. Richard Niebuhr, in one sense the Second Awakening was a breakthrough: its most distinctive feature, one that endowed it with its vitality, was its recovery of the sense of immediacy and universality of the messianic vision (this had been first recovered in the First Awakening a century earlier)—what John L. Thomas described above as the era's Romantic "perfectionism." H. Richard Niebuhr stated that the idea of the imminence of God's kingdom—with all that it promised for humanity—was "the dominant idea" of the nineteenth century (as discussed in this section above).

We have seen something of its power: how the messianic vision steeled abolitionists like Theodore Weld and informed Weld's thought. It led the masses to reject established or ancient Christian church doctrines (some that Protestant Reformers borrowed from Augustine or the Catholic Church) and affirm a radically new interpretation of Christianity. It forged Christianity into an instrument of social reform as well of spiritual regeneration. It led the abolitionists to the revolutionary conclusion—asserted with prophetic fervor—that justice requires the abolition of slavery and the equality of all men. The messianic ideal has not been realized, but the memory of its power reminds us of the power of its memory as a potentially transformative force.

In the terms frequently used by Christian theologians, it is the promise of God.

The 1960s and the New Spiritual Awakening

William McLoughlin argues that there was a more recent revitalization movement in America. According to McLoughlin's unique theory, the 1960s' revolt and counterculture was the Fourth Great Awakening in American history.* Unlike the previous awakenings, it did not take a Christian form. This revitalization movement was a response to the crisis of liberalism and technocracy,[42] as McLoughlin and others have documented. The events of the 1960s' revolt and counterculture, as described by many participants and historians, bear a striking similarity to the Second Great Awakening, although McLoughlin was the only one who explicitly drew the analogy. Both upheavals combined a collective passion for social justice and equality with profound messianic hopes, and both were fueled by the belief in the perfectibility of human beings and society.

As I recall, by 1969 the 1960s' political activists were possessed by a strong sense, a virtual certainty (I know I was, at seventeen years old), that the struggle to right the wrongs of the world would soon lead to "the revolution"—just as Weld, Finney, and the participants of the Second Awakening expected that their endeavors would bring about the millennium. The ideal of perfectionism (as exemplified in the nineteenth century) was reborn. The revolution would be an era of justice and peace and happiness. The intellectual leadership of the New Left of the 1960s had no sympathy for the state-socialism (or "state-capitalism," as some Marxists saw it) of the Soviet Union, which they saw as a betrayal of the true socialist revolution. For the previous generation of former leftists who had become political conservatives, the totalitarian nature of the Soviet Union was not a product—so they argued—of betrayal but of the

---

*McLoughlin considered the Social Gospel movement to be a third Great Awakening. Most historians refer to only two "Great Awakenings."

messianic utopian ideology itself, Marxism, which by failing to accept the tragic limits of the human situation unleashed destructive passions that inevitably undermined the social order and paved the way for the advent of totalitarianism.

Although Christianity was out of favor in the 1960s, many activists and cultural rebels were inspired by the mysticism of the East as well as the pagan nature-religions of native Americans.[43] The use of LSD and other consciousness-altering drugs led many of the young to turn to the more disciplined pursuit of mystical illuminations through transcendental meditation and other Eastern mystical disciplines. The fledgling ecology movement cultured a new reverence for the Earth. As in the nineteenth-century awakening, spiritual revitalization was fused with political activism, except that in the 1960s this movement was primarily restricted to the young, unlike previous eras.

The popular imagery of the counterculture as expressed in the poetry, popular literature, and folk and rock songs (such as the Beatles, Dylan, Joni Mitchell) was profoundly messianic and often drew on Judeo-Christian imagery and prophetic themes while rejecting or ignoring Christianity itself. Additionally, there were striking resemblances between rock concerts and hippie events (from Woodstock to "be-ins") on the one hand and the revivalist meetings of the Second Awakening on the other.[44] One might note also that the 1960s had its own equivalent of nineteenth-century preachers: savvy and eloquent spokespersons with a message of change and revolution were transformed into celebrities overnight and gained access to the media, where they preached their perfectionist gospel.

I include here a list of a few cultural icons who were messianic preachers of the 1960s. All presented their messianic ideal in different terms and images. None that were well-known used the terms *messianic,* or *the kingdom of God*—except for Martin Luther King Jr. and the Jewish rabbi, theologian, and civil rights and antiwar activist Rabbi Abraham Joshua Heschel, who marched with King. Heschel did not become an iconic figure until he was rediscovered after his death in the early 1970s. The Berrigan brothers emphasized the prophetic more than the messianic, but the prophetic derived its strength from the messianic vision in Isaiah of "beating the swords into ploughshares." These figures convey a sense of the variety of messianic archetypes evoked in the 1960s and early 1970s. The similarity to the revivalists of the Second Awakening is striking. They were not similar to modern revivalists, whose conservative or right-wing premillennialist beliefs are dissimilar from the early nineteenth-century preachers.

The visions of these cultural icons overlapped in many ways. Timothy Leary was the LSD guru who preached, "Turn on, tune in, drop out." Leary himself was a Harvard psychologist who first used LSD in psychology experiments and ended up soon thereafter resigning from—dropping out of—Harvard. In the late '60s he was imprisoned for possession of marijuana and was busted out of prison by a underground revolutionary group composed of former student leaders, the "Weathermen." The Weatherman preached combining violent revolution with doing psychedelic drugs and listening to rock music. They hoped to recruit young hippies to their organization.

In music, there were the Beatles and Bob Dylan. In the early 1960s there was Abbie Hoffman, a New Left Jewish student who went south to participate in the civil rights movement; in the midsixties he became an antiwar activist, a political prankster (a "Groucho Marxist"), and a political hippie who took psychedelics and went on to politicize and radicalize many hippies in the mid- to late 1960s. In 1968, Hoffman, Jerry Rubin, Paul Krassner, Stew Albert, and a few others formed the Youth International Party (YIP). They had launched a new movement of "Yippies"—politically radical hippies devoted to the antiwar movement and social revolution. Allen Ginsberg was a peace activist, world famous beat poet, Hindu/Buddhist, preacher of "flower power," who would sing Hindu hymns and chant "Ommm" at antiwar demonstrations. There was the elderly Herbert Marcuse, utopian Marxist philosopher, who was deemed "the ideological godfather of the New Left" by *The New York Times*. There was John Lennon, the Beatle who combined transcendental meditation with peace activism and who famously embarked on a "bed-in" in which he and Yoko Ono stayed in bed naked for several days in 1969 to protest the war in Vietnam (they invited the press in to look and received enormous publicity). Lennon also wrote a brief antiwar anthem that was repeatedly sung by millions at antiwar rallies, "All we are saying is, 'Give peace a chance.'" That was sung as a refrain over and over, sometimes for a half an hour at a time. There was Bobby Kennedy and Martin Luther King Jr. and Malcolm X. There was Baba Ram Dass, a.k.a. Richard Alpert, former Harvard professor turned LSD guru (a colleague of Leary's) who spent several years in India and became a Hindu swami, denounced the use of LSD, preached meditation, and wrote the famous bestseller *Be Here Now.*

There was Eldridge Cleaver, former criminal and prisoner who wrote an autobiography that was compared by critics to the work of James Baldwin. Cleaver became a Marxist and joined with street hoodlum turned revolutionary Huey Newton (unfortunately Newton remained secretly a hoodlum with a drug habit and a penchant for raping women) to form the Black Panther Party, which advocated cooperating with white people to agitate for a socialist revolution. There was psychiatrist R. D. Laing, discussed throughout this book. There were the two pacifist antiwar Catholic priests, the Berrigan brothers, who made headlines everywhere when they broke into Selective Service offices and destroyed the draft files. There was Tom Hayden, cofounder of the Students for a Democratic Society (SDS), a New Left student activist who married movie star turned peace activist Jane Fonda. Hayden became a left Democrat politician in the 1970s. These are just a few of the many well known spokespersons and revolutionary icons of the 1960s.

McLoughlin observed that "the pietistic element in the counterculture found its symbol in the Woodstock Nation after a particularly idyllic concert festival in 1969." McLoughlin thinks Joni Mitchell's song *Woodstock* captured the revivalist mood of the three hundred thousand persons who participated in the event, the most famous symbol of the sixties era. The last verse follows.

> *By the time we got to Woodstock*
> *We were half a million strong*
> *And everywhere there was song and celebration*
> *And I dreamed I saw the bombers*
> *Riding shotgun in the sky*
> *And they were turning into butterflies*
> *Above our nation*

> *We are stardust*
> *Billion year old carbon*
> *We are golden*
> *Caught in the devils bargain*
> *And we've got to get ourselves*
> *Back to the garden.*[45]

"We've got to get ourselves back to the garden" is as explicit and poignant a Judeo-Christian messianic archetype as one could imagine.

McLoughlin writes, "In many respects the rock concerts and festivals deserve comparison to the old camp meetings, where people entered into a special arena of religious enthusiasm with like-minded souls seeking release from confusion and ready to 'let loose' in orgies of emotional enthusiasm. . . . In between these mass celebrations they carried the aura back into daily life" by listening to the songs on their radios or stereos. "They sang the new songs of liberation like gospel hymns."[46] It was as if the kingdom of God was stirring within the collective imagination of the youth of the 1960s. Once again a messianic-redemptive vision had captivated the hearts of young men and women.

It is a remarkable fact: the same kind of archetypes of renewal, redemption, death-rebirth, and messianic transformation that were activated in the Great Awakening of the nineteenth century—that were so clearly connected to the Jewish-Christian mythos—were reactivated among the youth of the 1960s who had repudiated Christianity and Judaism in favor of secular ideologies (e.g., neo-Marxism) or Eastern mysticism, which usually lacked a messianic element. Insofar as there was a messianic influence it was derived from secular philosophers who were neo-Marxists, like Herbert Marcuse. Or it was derived from the lyrics to the music. One ought also to mention the radicalizing effects of LSD and marijuana, which, when used—as was typical—in a sacramental way, almost always relativized the reality of modern Western culture and gave users the sense that it was one among many cultural constructs—and not a very good one at that.

Paul Levy describes how art and music helped the new consciousness to spread and change the world. In the following quote Levy explains the power of sixties "music"; these observations could also be accurate if one substitutes for "the music of the '60s" the many dem-onstrations, slogans, and the happenings led by the secular preachers mentioned above, all of which received extensive publicity. The effect was cumulative.

> Contagious in its effects, art can "virally" spread via the unconscious of our species in a way which liberates and unleashes a latent, creative energy lying dormant in the unconscious of humanity, which has the power to effect real change in the world. An example is the gal-vanizing influence that music began having in the 1960s—socially, politically, and on consciousness itself. The music of the '60s was both an expression of an expanded consciousness, while simultane-ously being the vibration, which precipitated and catalyzed the very expansion of consciousness of which it was an expression. In cre-atively translating what is being touched inside of themselves into a communicable language, the artist taps into forms, vibrations, and realizations that exist in the formless, atemporal realm—a dimen-sion existing "outside of time"—that are waiting to be discovered, formulated, and brought forth at the right moment "in time."[47]

The "revolution" the 1960s rebels dreamed about and expected did not occur—just as the millennium the reformers and abolitionists believed in did not occur. The masses were not converted. However, the 1960s had a powerful impact on social norms. Author, cofounder of Students for a Democratic Society, and 1960s radical activist Tom Hayden lists the accomplishments of the 1960s in his book *The Long Sixties*. These include the abolition of the military draft, voting rights for black people and for those aged eighteen to twenty-one, the Freedom of Information Act, and "tougher environmental and consumer and health and safety laws than any passed since." In addition, there was "the decline of censorship" and the passage of the Equal Rights Amendment in the early 1970s by both houses of Congress, though it failed to gain ratification before its 1982 deadline.[48] Oddly, Hayden does not spe-cifically mention the establishment of a new cultural norm of equal-ity between men and women. Some of these reforms have been vitiated by policies passed by George W. Bush and continued by Obama. The effects of the environmental laws have been vitiated by the far more toxic kinds of environmental practices that are now permitted and by the captivation of the regulatory agencies by representatives of the industries they are regulating. This is referred to as "the revolving door" between industry and government.

The Fourth Awakening did not succeed in effecting the kind of institutional changes that McLoughlin, the liberal historian of religion, still thought (in 1978) would soon be forthcoming in the form of political implementation of more cooperative, socialist (but not Marxist), and ecological policies. In fact, two years after McLoughlin made his predictions, Ronald Reagan was elected president. As Hayden put it, the gains of the 1960s were "not enough to stop the movement of repression still contained in a system that seeks pervasive control over lives and resources."[49]

To the extent to which the 1960s counterculture was not aborted, in the ensuing decades it lost its subversive thrust as it became assimilated into modern society—reduced to a trend of fashion and identity politics and relegated to cultural niches such as the "the New Age" and academia.

It is possible that Mad Pride will be able to help to re-evoke messianic archetypes or even to develop a messianic paradigm like I have started to do in this book. The messianic imagery of the counterculture still ferments on the margins of the collective imagination, and it blazes today in the psyches of the mad alongside their apocalyptic terror: for, in the moments of their "mania," the mad have always been convinced that the millennium is near.

16

Interview with Paul Levy

"They May Say I'm a Dreamer"

From Paul Levy's biography, posted on his website:

In 1981 Paul Levy had a life-changing spiritual awakening, in which he began to wake up to the dream-like nature of reality. During the first year of his spiritual emergence, Paul was hospitalized a number of times, and was diagnosed with having had a severe psychotic break. Much to his surprise, he was told that he had a chemical imbalance and had manic-depressive (bipolar) illness, and would have to live with his illness for the rest of his life. Fortunately, he was able to quickly extricate himself from the medical and psychiatric establishment. Little did the doctors realize that he was taking part in some sort of spiritual awakening/shamanic initiation process. . . . In 1993, after many years of struggling to contain and integrate his experiences, he started to teach about what he was realizing. He has been in private practice for fifteen years, assisting others who are spiritually emerging and beginning to wake up to the dreamlike nature of reality. In a dream come true, psychiatrists now consult with him and send him patients. A pioneer in the field of spiritual emergence, Paul is in the book *Saints and Madmen: Psychiatry Opens its Doors to Religion.*

325

Paul has developed and teaches a unique and creative vehicle to introduce people to the dreamlike nature of reality that he calls "the Dreaming Up Process," which is based on the realization that the same dreaming mind that dreams our dreams at night is dreaming our life. He teaches this dreaming up process, where people who are awakening to the dreamlike nature of reality come together and collaboratively help each other to wake up in the dream together.

Deeply steeped in and inspired by the work of C. G. Jung, Paul is an innovator in the field of dreaming (both night dreams as well as waking dreams). He has had innumerable articles published on consciousness, dreaming, and spirituality, and has lectured about his work at various universities. Paul is the founder of the Awakening in the Dream Community, and his work is the inspiration for the Awakening in the Dream Center, a psychospiritual healing center in Mexico. A visionary artist, Paul is helping to create the Art-Happening Called Global Awakening, a work of living art in which we, as a species, collaboratively help each other to become lucid in the dream of life.

A long-time practitioner of Tibetan Buddhism, Paul has intimately studied with some of the greatest masters from Tibet and Burma and serves as the coordinator of a local Buddhist center. Paul is the author of *The Madness of George W. Bush: A Reflection of Our Collective Psychosis* and is currently writing a book about his work in dreaming.[1]

During the summer of 2009 I was grateful to be able to speak with Paul Levy by phone. Levy has never been in the patients' rights movement. However, as he describes in the interview, he was hospitalized numerous times and diagnosed as a bipolar psychotic. He knows about and is a supporter of the Mad Pride movement.

Farber: Albert Schweitzer rediscovered the historical Jesus back in the later nineteenth century; this is confirmed by most of the scholars involved today in the "quest for the historical Jesus." Schweitzer was right; the historical Jesus wasn't the domesticated figure that liberal Protestantism made him out to be in the early twentieth century. Forget about fundamentalism, that's off the map, it's not even worth discussing. Jesus, in fact, thought he was going to usher in the kingdom of God. Now Anton Boisen, the theologian who had had a breakdown and miraculously recovered—I say miraculously because this was in the 1920s, and the mental hospitals then were worse than they are now—he went on to become a chaplain and worked in mental hospitals. He pointed out that many of the hospitalized mental patients had similar ideas to the great spiritual geniuses. That was the most radical conclusion he drew. Jesus thought he was the Messiah and he was going to usher in the kingdom of heaven, and he didn't. Many people in mental hospitals think they are going to usher in the kingdom of God. This is considered a sign of schizophrenia, thus the question that could be raised is, Was Jesus mad? Was Jesus schizophrenic?

Paul Levy: Okay, is that the question? It makes me think of my experience. When I was having my spiritual awakening and when it first started, and I was having the realization of being the Messiah too, but I was realizing we all are—we all are the Messiah. I actually made out these business cards that just said "the Messiah," and I was giving them out to people, and I was saying "Look, here's my card, and if you want some you can have some too, you can give them out to people." The point is for us to remember who we are, and that's exactly, I think, my understanding of what Christ was saying. He would say, "We are God, his scripture can not be broken." He was pointing out that outside of time, in the atemporal dimension, we already are these enlightened beings; that's our true nature. Jesus was having the realization of his own self; if it's a genuine realization it's not inflation, it's not you thinking you're the Messiah and no one else is, it's the realization that that's who we all are. I think that's what Jesus was experiencing, and that definitely, to some degree, that's what happened for me.

Farber: I think Boisen also said, Well, these patients are not completely wrong; maybe they're on to something. The modern secular idea is that a human being is just a mix of chemicals and epiphenomena of a biochemical process. The people in the mental hospital who say they're Jesus actually have a higher conception of themselves and their calling. They typically have this kind of inflation that you talk about; that's inevitable I think because most of them don't have any spiritual cultural context in which to put this sense that they are more than the little ego. So without this context they just conclude, "I am Christ."

Paul Levy: Sure, the thing is to just point out we are card-carrying members of the consensus reality under a collective spell, and part of awakening almost always involves some sort of ego inflation. It's necessary to break out of that inertia. Almost like when you have like a rocket, it needs a certain amount of energy to break out of the Earth's atmosphere, out of its gravitational field. If it's an organic spiritual awakening, the ego inflation—which was necessary to break out of the consensus reality trance—very organically and effortlessly falls away and becomes integrated into a broader perspective. That's very much in contrast to people who then stay in the inflation and they inflate the ego with the self; that's a form of insanity. It's just important to understand that when we have the recognition of our divine true nature, there is always a phase of ego inflation, and that actually helps us to break out of the collective trance.

Farber: That would also be in accord with the Laingian theory that I'm trying to advance: this process of awakening to one's true Christlike nature is happening among many people in the mental hospitals, and it is suppressed by the psychiatric establishment. This cultural stasis is a deeper crisis of modern civilization; we can't get out of this spiritual stagnation we are in where the pursuit of more and more money by the elite is leading to the destruction of the planet. So, in fact, the people who are really the most likely to be attuned to the cosmic rhythms and universal things that are happening on the planet have particular vulnerabilities because they're so personally disturbed by the destructiveness of the world. If these people's higher attunement is leading them at that time to be singled out as bipolars or schizophrenics and taken away and removed from the social body, then the process of social transformation that might ordinarily take place in terms of an awakening and of taking collective responsibility would be prevented by the psychiatric priesthood itself. Do you agree with that?

Paul Levy: Absolutely. I mean the thing is that the people who are really sensitive, the ones who really have like a permeable boundary between their ego and unconscious both individually and collectively, they're very attuned to the collective unconscious in the field to what's going on, just like any artist, poet, or seer or anything like that. They're also being altered and receptive; they might not have a solid ego structure that protects them, they might not have developed that strong of a persona, or they have fallen under the hypnotic spell to such a degree that they're just more vulnerable. Then when they try to share their gift they're maybe even in more of a fragile state; they're not as grounded as someone who just has the nine-to-five mentality. You know if they get in the clutches of the psychiatric system—which is trained to interpret any sort abnormal behavior as being pathological—they just act to suppress it. That's a tragic thing because so many of these people are potential shamans. The archetype of the shaman gets activated precisely by being emotionally disturbed: there's something in the psyche that hasn't been able to fully adjust to a crazy culture. So inwardly we become a little bit out of balance and disturbed, and that constellates the shamanic archetype. The indigenous cultures would understand this is somebody who might be called by the spirits and might actually have a real gift for the community—and they'd be honored as such—but in our culture we don't have any understanding of that, so anybody who might actually be a potential shaman, a being in whom the shamanic archetype can incarnate, is typically labeled psychotic and medicated and suppressed. It's tragic: they can spend their whole lives just having bought into this label of being mentally ill, there are lots of people who that's happened to; it's unbelievably tragic, because it's taken away this incredible gift for society that we potentially have. In sacred cultures when somebody accomplishes the whole shamanic ordeal, as he or she comes back from the underworld, they have the wisdom to share with the rest of the tribe, which in this society is the human species, which can potentially be of incredible benefit for all of us. And we're actually aborting that process by pathologizing them and medicating them. The following is from "We Are All Shamans in Training":

> The shaman's descent into the darkness can be agonizing, a veritable crucifixion. Part of the (arche)typical shamanic experience is to become dis-membered, which is a cooking and smelting of psychic

contents that have become rigidified, ossified, and have outlived their usefulness. To quote Jung, "The shaman's experience of sickness, torture, death and regeneration implies, at a higher level, the idea of being made whole through sacrifice, of being changed by transubstantiation and exalted to the pneumatic man—in a word, apotheosis," or elevated from an ordinary person to a "god." The goal of the shaman's death and dismemberment experience is to "re-member" himself, which like true soul retrieval, brings all of his dissociated parts back together into a more integrated synthesis. By embracing, assimilating, and metabolizing what has gotten triggered in them, however, shamans are able to heal themselves and in so doing non-locally send healing to the whole "community." In our current moment in time, as interdependent members of an ever-more interconnected global village, our "community" is the entire planet.[2]

Farber: I was going to say Perry said at one point, "My God! What is society doing to its visionaries?"

Paul Levy: Exactly, it's these people who are the visionaries, totally. It's exactly what happened to me. I had this incredibly abusive father in the family system—I was the only child—I was the recipient of the emotional energetic abuse, and I was the one who actually got propelled out of my egoic perspective very much into a way more expansive point of view.

Farber: Expansive in a more cosmic sense?

Paul Levy: Yeah, yeah. Expansive in a cosmic sense in that on the one hand I was the one who was seeing the deeper field—the deeper nouemal* field—and the abuse that was playing out in the interpersonal

---

*In Western metaphysics, a noumenon refers to an object in itself, which is supposedly beyond the ability of the senses to perceive. A phenomenon, on the other hand, is the object as filtered through our senses. The mystic often claims that her intuition gives her direct non-sensual knowledge of the object itself. Levy is using this distinction metaphorically, as it often is used, to distinguish between the spoken text and the unspoken subtext of interpersonal interactions.

psychological area; the family system. Concurrent with that I was stepping out of my identification with myself as a discrete skin-encapsulated ego, I'm realizing that I'm actually interconnected and interdependent with everyone and so is everyone else. I was stepping out of the limited point of view of the ego and stepping into the more expansive view of the self where I saw that we could actually—you know as being the Messiah—help each other to activate our collective genius, that we could conspire to co-inspire each other. I have a zillion different ways of saying it, but we can basically configure ourselves in a way that we could actually help each other to awaken. That's the cosmic visionary aspect you know, and there was also the interpersonal stuff that I was seeing going on between my family. Then the mental health system got involved, and instead of helping, they actually made the matters worse . . .

Farber: You said the more you attempted to communicate authentically the crazier the mental health system became. As you put it:

> In essence, the more I authentically expressed my experience, the more I was convincing the doctors that I was crazy. It was like I had stepped through the looking glass and found myself in a dimension of existence that was truly bewitched, as if I had entered a domain which felt, qualitatively speaking, under a curse of black magicians. It felt like I had shamanically journeyed into the underworld and wound up in some sort of weird, perverse hell realm where reality was inverted in a way, which was get-me-out-of-here crazy. Little did I realize at the time, however, that this was all part of the deeper awakening process that I was going through.
>
> By myopically seeing people's behavior as being pathological, the psychiatrists literally drew out the pathology in the person, which only further confirmed to them [the psychiatrists] the correctness of their diagnosis in a self-fulfilling prophecy, as if they were both under a spell and casting one at the same time.[3]

Paul Levy: The crazier they became . . . The more I expressed myself authentically and gave voice and articulated my experience, the more they saw me as crazy. There was like this diabolical feedback loop: it was like falling into this other psychiatric universe that was ruled by black magic. It was completely like—fuck, really—it was so abusive. I don't have a family; psychiatry destroyed my family. I'm still trying to wrap my mind around the unbelievable toxicity and abuse that the psychiatric community played out.

Farber: One woman who suffered from incest said she was "reincested" when she went into the psychiatric system.

Paul Levy: Totally—that's in a sense true. For me it was like you are trying to heal the trauma and you get retraumatized sort of a thousand-fold: it was like the reiteration of the same fractal process that occurred in my family, and it got played out totally unwittingly in the psychiatric system under the guise "it's all for your own good." What they're doing is just enacting their own unconscious will-to-power of the shadow.

They have no idea they're doing that, and the more you point out to them that you're experiencing that, the more that proves to them how crazy you are in that diabolical negative feedback loop. I can just tell you I have a lot of stories between 1981 and '82 or something, it was a number of times I was thrown in mental hospitals, and I always got diagnosed. I was called bipolar, but then it was called manic depression.

Farber: Because you were literate enough to escape the schizophrenic diagnosis would you say?

Paul Levy: Yeah, I think that's what it was. Also I did not hear voices, but I had certain so-called manic behaviors, like maybe I was spending a lot of money or talking a lot or not sleeping.

Farber: Did you know *manike* means "prophet" in Greek?

Paul Levy: Right and also the word *entheos,* enthusiasm, means "to be filled with spirit."

When I got out of the last hospital I had found this supposedly real good psychiatrist. At that point when I got out of the hospital in 1982, I was really fucked up. I was really traumatized—not only with the abuse from my father but also from the trauma of the psych system. So, I found what I thought was a good psychiatrist, who I saw for seven years twice a week.

Farber: Was he a Freudian?

Paul Levy: Yes, she was, but the thing was here I was commuting from the suburbs twice a week for seven years, and then at a certain point I really began to have an experience of her unconscious and her shadow. It was fine, because we all have that, but as soon as I began pointing that out . . .

Farber: Which in Freudian terms is good; she's supposed to become aware of her "countertransference."* She should have welcomed your pointing.

Paul Levy: Instead of welcoming it, she was immediately like, "I'm the doctor and you're the sick one." She actually said that, and then she said, "How come none of my other patients are saying this?" I said very clearly, "Well they probably aren't as aware as I am to see this". . . but the point was we were like actually reenacting the very process that I was trying to heal with my father: he was an authority figure, and I was trying to step into my power and speak my voice. Instead of her having that realization and being able to follow that process and unfold it and self-reflect, she immediately got caught in the role of being the one with the power and the authority figure and that I'm crazy if I'm saying things that she can't see. So then it was actually a reenactment or the retraumatization of the process I was trying to heal from. That's when I left her, that's when I stopped the therapy.

It has come out in my family since then that my father was a genuine psychopath, he was a criminal and he should have been behind bars, literally. His sister, his only sibling, said to me probably a few years before she died—she asked me if I knew who Hannibal Lector was, and she's an eighty-year-old Jewish woman. I replied, "Of course Aunt Helen, I know who Hannibal Lector is." She says, "Paul, that's the sort of person your father is; before you were born he did something so

---

*In the Freudian model, transference is the redirection of a patient's feelings for a significant person (usually a parent) to the therapist. Countertransference is the redirection of these feelings by the therapist onto the patient. The therapist is supposed to be aware and mature enough to be aware of countertransference when it occurs. The ideal for an adult is to overcome transference through therapy, but since no one achieves that ideal the more realistic goal is to be aware of transference and countertransference.

horrible and so terrible, our parents died brokenhearted because of this. I'll never tell you what it was because it was so horrible." She never did; she died and took the secret to her grave.

Farber: Was it something like murder?

Paul Levy: I think it was something sexual. I think he definitely acted out—I think he raped—I think he raped her, I'm almost sure of it. I would bet bottom dollar that it was something sexual or something with rape, because when I described issues with my father, he was into domination: objectifying me, getting off on his narcissistic pleasure— like a rape, but without the sex—and then from many dreams I've had about it. I'm not sure what happened, but that's what I hypothesized. The whole point is I've tried now, a number of years later, to connect with the psychiatrist I was seeing—who was a very loving, good, intelligent person. Once a month she would see my parents, and I was seeing her twice a week. Of course, I was the identified patient. Here I am a number of years later, and I called her up to say, "By the way it came out my father was a world-class psychopath and you didn't know that. I would like to complete the process with you because I have feelings about this," and she has made it a point in no way to be in contact with me. She won't return my phone calls. I have had other therapists of mine call her, and she won't even return *their* phone calls. That's just another more subtle form of psychiatric abuse; I'm not wanting to sue her or get any money or anything. I'm just wanting to say, "Hey look, I appreciate all your help, yet session after session, I was telling you what was going on with my father, and instead of you having the recognition of something going on here, you just saw me as crazy." Anyway, it still pisses me off to this day.

Farber: This psychoanalytic thing is a continuous battle within the field to compete for higher status, to stay on top of the client, to stay on top of each other. Did you ever read Jeffrey Masson, who wrote these books against Freud? He was a psychoanalyst who rose very high in the Freudian establishment and was given access to the Freud archives when he was doing research. He was very disillusioned when he found out Freud had been suppressing evidence that women were sexually abused by their fathers. He thought the psychoanalytic field would welcome his discovery, but Anna Freud tried to shut him up and they tried to destroy him once he started writing about these things. Jeffrey Masson's last book on that topic was a memoir called *Final Analysis*. When he first became a Freudian he was socializing with others and going to all their meetings: he shows that not only are they trying to maintain their one-up status with the patient, but they're always talking about each other behind their backs. One would say, "You know Kernberg is a narcissistic personality disorder, blah blah blah," and of course Kernberg (for example) was the expert on personality disorders—borderline [personality disorder]—but they seem to prefer to use the term *narcissistic* for each other. It's continual preoccupation with their own intellectual-spiritual status. They're describing other analysts all the time in psychoanalytic terms.

Paul Levy: Wow.

Farber: Of course, these are very stigmatizing labels when they call someone narcissistic personality disorder. It's not like the colloquial use. A narcissistic personality disorder is supposedly not capable of intimacy. They use these "diagnoses" as insults—behind the back of their peers.

Paul Levy: It's really just here we're all fluid open-ended holograms. When you stigmatize someone like that and you're concretizing their infinitely fluid hologram, it's a form of abuse—particularly when you're doing that with a patient, somebody who is in a role you have authority and power over; when you're concretizing them it's like you're casting a spell.

Farber: I don't recall you mentioning being on psychiatric drugs. They must have put you on psychiatric drugs. Am I wrong, you don't refer to that much?

Paul Levy: On some of my articles I have mentioned drugs, I don't know offhand which ones, it was a very short time They had me with lithium, and they had me on Haldol, an antipsychotic, which I experienced as an anticreative; it just completely shut down my creative impulses.

Farber: That's a pretty typical response.

Paul Levy: It's horrendous. They also put me on antidepressants, because I was like, "Wow, I'm on all these drugs, I don't feel my creative impulse; I feel really shut down." Then they say, "Oh you're really depressed, let's put you on an antidepressant, too." The thing is I was really on these drugs probably a whole number of months; it wasn't a long time. The Haldol was for a week, and they had me on lithium probably for six months or so, but then I just stopped taking it. I stopped taking the antidepressant really quick. It wasn't that long that I was actually on some sort of psychiatric drugs; during that year between 1981 and '82, there were like six or ten or twelve times—I even lost count—I was put in mental hospitals, diagnosed, and forced to take drugs. The thing which was weird, I was telling them I'm not manic-depressive, I'm emotionally disturbed because my father was an abuser, which to them proved even more how crazy I was. There was that first year I was on like SSI or social security; it was fucked up, I couldn't work.

Farber: You said you had to go back to live with your family for a year, and you knew how abusive they were at that time. You knew how traumatizing your parents were when you went back.

Paul Levy: Here's the thing: my parents from the surface seemed like really good people. My mother was a beautiful person, my father appeared normal, everybody thought he was a normal guy, but he was a complete narcissist, a sociopath, and a criminal. The thing to keep in mind, even though I knew it was the last place I wanted to be living, back with my parents, I didn't have the insight I have now. I was in my early to mid-twenties when that was happening. I was a normal, healthy, happy kid growing up, very bright with lots of friends, but my father was a failure; he owned a cigar store in Queens that wasn't doing well. He was happy his only child was like a superstar academically. I went to Binghamton University. I was hired by Princeton University; they were paying me money to do research in economics. I was a straight-A student; the whole point is he was, in a vicarious way, identified with me, living his life out through me like a lot of parents do. It was positive until I decided I did not want to be a doctor, lawyer, or economist: I wanted to become an artist. They say the mythic Chronos,* the negative father, gets constellated when the son begins to separate individually from the parent. As soon as when I was in college, when I was like nineteen or twenty, I was beginning to get into art, philosophy, and spirituality. That's when just in essence—to describe the abuse, when I would express any sort of separation or differentiation, my father, who was so unconsciously identified with me, would become completely possessed and go into demonic rages. The mantra was, "You're killing me," and he would literally be having heart attacks. The worst time it ever happened, I woke with a fever that lasted for a year. At the end of that year, that entity that had taken over my father—it was like that entity was inside of my psyche and it was getting constellated. Every impulse I had toward expressing myself in any way, in any of my own natural healthy impulses, whenever I would express them would constellate this raging demonic father that was now living inside of my psyche telling me I was killing it and having heart attacks. . . . Let me explain the archetypal process here. My father fell totally into his unconscious and acted out his darker impulses; we could say he was fully possessed by an unconscious complex. Because of this, his person became an instrument for a nonpersonal, archetypal energy to come through him. Much to my horror, I found the entity that had possessed and taken over my father was now living within and introjected within my psyche; it was raging, saying I was killing him whenever I would express my true self. Seen symbolically, this translates as me stepping into and expressing my authentic self, who "kills" the negative father Chronos; in essence, I found myself enacting an archetypal, mythic process in, as, and through my personal life. Once I understood this later, once I got beyond seeing it in purely personal terms and saw it as a universal archetypal process, then I could begin to heal, but that was later.

---

*In Greek mythology Chronos was the god of time, serpentine in form, with three heads—that of a man, a bull, and a lion. Chronos is usually portrayed through an old, wise man with a long, gray beard, such as Father Time.

The Way of the Shaman

Paul Levy has written extensively regarding the interaction or mirroring of the inner and the outer, of the individual and the cosmos. I include three quotes from his work here because they help to understand his theory that what manifests itself as a personal problem is a reflection on the inner plane of a more extensive problem in the macrocosmic world.

> It is very seductive to personalize, and pathologize, our inner experiences, believing they are just our own problems, without realizing that we might be unwittingly being dreamed up by the underlying field to pick-up, like a would-be shaman, the split-off, unconscious energies that are playing out all around us.[4]

> Interestingly, linear time is symbolized by the mythic Saturn/Chronos, Father Time, whose shadow aspect is the negative patriarchy, which happens to be one of the deeper, underlying archetypal patterns wreaking unspeakable havoc in our world through its obsessive addiction to power, control, and domination. Saturn/Chronos' peculiar form of "blessing"—restraining us as it seemingly takes away our freedom—is always "cursed" by its recipient, and yet it is the very thing that inspires us to discover our own power and authority.[5]

> Like an iteration of an inter-nested fractal, the (macro)cosmic, collective process that is happening on the world stage reflects and reveals itself on the inner, personal plane [of the individual] at the same time, as well as vice versa. Different dimensional reflections of each other, the outer collective process and the inner personal process, are beyond interconnected—they are the same process simply explicating itself in different dimensions of our being simultaneously. The microcosm (our inner, personal process) and macrocosm (the world process) directly, instantaneously, and reciprocally affect each other, as the two are one and the same. This means that the way to effect real change in the world is to transform ourselves by becoming more conscious, as, holographically speaking, the world is enfolded within us while at the same time "We are the World."[6]

Farber: Okay, you had introjected this entity. Did you hear a voice?

Paul Levy: I wasn't hearing voices. It was like feeling that energy that my father was literally possessed by embodying, it was literally like I was reenacting that moment of trauma again and again. At the end of that year, after the fever, I moved to the West Coast to get away from my parents. You know, I was in my early twenties, I graduated college, I wanted to move away from home like any normal healthy kid does, after that year of having the fever. At the end of 1979 finally the fever went away. By late '79 through '82 I was living in Berkeley.

Farber: You were also conscious of your father raging?

Paul Levy: Once the fever went away—when I'd moved to Berkeley—it was then I was realizing, "Oh my God, I'm like reenacting that trauma, it's now inside of my psyche"—that every impulse I have, like if I had a thought to go for a walk on a beautiful day or to play basketball or to draw or paint or anything, any healthy activity that is in the service of myself, that would reactivate it.

Farber: Had you been somaticizing your experiences, meaning were they repressed and assuming a physical form?

Paul Levy: It was like my mind-body's way of dealing with what basically happened. I was afraid I was going to get murdered, my father was taken over by rage, by a demon, to the point I thought he was going to literally kill me. At the same time he was having a heart attack, he was jumping up and down, he disowned me, he threw me out of the house. It was over the house. Think of me as a glass vase, like a container; it was like I was a glass vase that got shattered, my boundaries of myself shattered, something entered me, something penetrated that was not me. That's when I had the fever for a year. The way I see it was it was my mind and body's way of trying to metabolize what happened.

Farber: When you say something penetrated you, what was this something?

Paul Levy: For me it wasn't a physical rape; it was an energetic psychic rape. We all have these natural boundaries of a self, and that's why I was using the image of a glass vase to convey a sense of the integrity and fragility of my personality at that time, which got shattered and transgressed by my father—who on the one hand completely unconsciously identified with me. Here I was separating from him and becoming my own person, and he was going into his raging and dying and laying a guilt trip on me and unconsciously saying, "You're killing me," while he was having heart attacks: it was unbelievable. The thing is, once I got out to Berkeley after that year of the fever a lot of these kind of paranormal things began happening to me. One example of it was there was a black shadowy substance that began coming out of my head.

Farber: Literally?

Paul Levy: Totally literally. It was like a vapor. I would see it. Other people saw it. Sometimes it would happen a hundred times a day, sometimes it wouldn't happen for months, sometimes it would come out of my eyes, and when it came out of my eyes it was like coming out of a camera, when the shutter opens and all of a sudden your field of vision expands. The whole point of why I'm telling you this part was the suffering I was going through made me go inward, and that's why I began meditating and watching what was happening. I very quickly figured out that I couldn't figure my way out with my intellect, and I was very fortunate that I began to meet the greatest enlightened teachers in the world. I met these teachers who I'm still really close with. One of them is a Buddhist nun from Burma, a very great healer.

Farber: Rina?

Paul Levy: Have you met her? You know Rina?

Farber: Yes. She led meditations at the California Institute for Integral Studies in San Francisco when I was there in the early 1980s.

Paul Levy: We are very close; we're like family members. One night I was with her and she said, "I want you to meet this great clairvoyant who just arrived from Burma, he has this special power, whatever he predicts automatically comes true." This person wasn't a monk, he was a clairvoyant, and basically when I went to meet him in the next room he said, "I'll answer any question. You ask me, I will answer." It stopped my mind; I didn't know what to say; I described to him in much detail the black vapor that was coming out of my head. He said to me, "There is an incredibly negative evil force that's trying to stop you; the only thing you can do is to take refuge in your self, in the truth."

Farber: The self, not the Buddha and the sangha?

Paul Levy: That is the Buddha; he might have said Buddha too, I don't have the exact words. I had already done the formal vow, he was saying to just depend on the truth of yourself and just put it in simple language, you'll soon see the light, there's nothing else I can do for you. And that sort of contextualizes the stuff with my father. When someone becomes taken over by deeper archetypal energy they're just an instrument for some sort of darker force to come through, and more and more I'm understanding it was initiatory. The key was to not to allow myself to get stuck in the personal dimension, in which case I would've stayed stuck in despair and resignation. By expanding my awareness and realizing I had gotten drafted into a deeper, archetypal process, I had recontextualized my experience, expanded my consciousness, and concurrently enlarged my sense of identity and the process I was involved in, which allowed for healing to occur. I saw that by going through this I could become a healer for others, and that was why I had to go through it. It really fucked me up and created enormous suffering, and it made me very sick. But it was a healing crisis, over the course of my life; as I'm healing and integrating I'm more and more discovering the work I do, which is hopefully helping people.

The following is from Paul Levy's work "We Are All Shamans in Training."

> Fortunately, soon after getting out of the last hospital I began meeting my spiritual teachers, some of the greatest living Buddhist masters from Tibet and Burma, who, unlike the psychiatrists, helped to evoke the healthy part of me. When I described to them what I was subjectively experiencing, instead of being pathologized, they reflected back to me that I was beginning to remember what in Buddhism is called our "true nature." In finding my teachers, I had dreamed up the part of me that was seeing and relating to the part of me that *was* awakening. Having someone else bear witness and reflect back the healthy part of me created a bridge that helped me to see it, too. It was as if my teachers became engaged with me in an intimate relationship that

helped me to not get stuck in the trauma of it all, to not get caught in being "sick." By simply relating to the healthy part of me, which was an expression of their own level of health and wholeness, they helped me to step into and incarnate the part of me that was well. My teachers and I had instinctively created a supportive, nourishing container between us, which cultivated healing. As if figures in a fairy tale, they had gotten dreamed up to help me learn how to "dis-spell" and transmute the darker forces with which I had been wrestling. . . .[7]

Farber: This healing took place in spite of the whole so-called mental health system. Did you feel that your psychiatrist was helpful or mostly harmful?

Paul Levy: The psychiatrist was a good person: well intentioned, very bright. On the one hand, she helped me a lot, because I had a real transference with her, a positive transference. As I said, I saw her for seven years twice a week, and she was a very good person. Keep in mind, I see now that she didn't even have a clue that she was so completely and totally incompetent. I was coming to her every session, and I was having dreams about my father being a bad guy, and I was telling her the abuse he was enacting. Her point of view was Paul seems to be obsessed with his father, when is he going to get over his father? Not realizing that his father should be in jail and his father is a complete criminal. She was helpful in one sense. When I found her after I got out of the hospital I was totally shattered. . . . She was a good person with good intentions. Keep in mind she was seeing me twice a week, and she was seeing my parents once a month; she never saw us together. She never got that the real sick one in the family was my father.

Farber: So the major transformation took place soon as you moved; just the act of getting into a new environment initiated this?

Paul Levy: You're talking after that year of the fever? What happened Thanksgiving night 1978 was the worst of the abuse, and the next day I got the fever. That next year I was sick with the fever, then at the end of that year I moved to the West Coast. That's when all of a sudden the abuse really came out. It was when I felt like my father was living inside of me, but he had gotten possessed by this demonic entity. That entity was getting constellated inside of me every moment. So for that next year or two I was completely trying to deal with that.

Farber: Were you healing or were you still under the thralldom of this force?

Levy: Oh, I was totally under the thralldom. That was the beginning when I realized, "Oh fuck, I have a problem." Until then I was a healthy normal kid. I was seeing a normal therapist, and all of a sudden, I went inward and was doing intense meditation because that was the only thing that made me feel better. That's when all of a sudden I got hit by a bolt of lightning inside of my brain; I went into this total altered state, got brought to a hospital, where I met this blind woman and was able to help her heal her sight. That was the start of that next year. Probably ten different times I was thrown into mental hospitals and told, "Oh, you are manic-depressive."

Farber: Ten different times! This was in Berkeley?

Levy: This was between 1981 and 1982 in Berkeley, and at certain points I got flown back to New York.

The Healing of the Blind Lady and the Crucifixion by Psychiatry—By Paul Levy

I had begun acting so unlike my ordinary, conditioned, and repressed self that a close friend thought I was going crazy and had me brought, by ambulance, to Highland Hospital in Oakland, California. In the very first room I was brought to in that hospital, some sort of lounge for psychiatric patients, was a blind woman. Immediately upon seeing her, without any thought on my part at all, I went right up to her and found myself looking at her eyes and saying over and over the following words: "All you have to do to see is open your eyes and look." These words were literally coming through me. It was as if the words I said to her had fallen into my head, as if I myself hadn't consciously thought them, as if I was channeling them.

I kept on getting closer and closer to her as I repeated these words, staring at her eyes all the while. Her eyes were a blind person's eyes, opaque with no color or radiance at all.

What happened next I will never forget. In front of my very eyes her eyes began regaining their color and luminosity, going from the dead, diseased eyes of a blind person to normal, healthy, seeing eyes. She had regained her sight.

At that moment, as if it was divinely choreographed, a doctor brought me into another room and strapped me on a table. And there I spent the night.

I remember lying there knowing I was going through some sort of spiritual experience and feeling that whoever I would think of I was in some way "bringing along." So I began trying to think of everybody I had ever known.

The next morning I was brought to a room and the only other person in the room, sitting across a table from me, was, coincidentally, that ex-blind woman. She was looking at me and smiling from ear to ear, not having said one word to me as of yet.

All of a sudden it was like a closed fist that was in my heart just completely opened. It was perfectly clear to me that this was my heart chakra blossoming. It is described as the opening of a thousand-petaled lotus, and though I had never had this happen to me before, it was an experience that I immediately recognized.

At a certain point I had the spontaneous realization of what had happened with this woman the day before. I intuitively understood that her eyes were physically fine, it was just that she was not letting herself open her (inner) eyes to look. It was like she herself was keeping them closed. I somehow had "seen" this the day before and I had known what to do. It was like I had become a conduit for some deeper, healing force. It was also clear to me that it was no accident that she and I had come together. It was clearly a synchronistic meeting, one in which we were both playing roles in a deeper drama.

At a certain point she said to me "Aren't you going to answer the phone call from Roy (my father's name)?" These were, literally, the first and only words she ever spoke to me. Moments later the nurse came into the room and said my father was on the phone.

Even though the situation with that blind woman actually happened in waking life, it is quite profound to contemplate what happened symbolically, as if it were a dream. To see our life in this way is to view the events in our life as if they are a dream that a deeper part of us, what I call the "deeper, dreaming Self" dreamed into materialized form in and as our life itself. Just like doing dreamwork about a night dream, we can then ask ourselves, what is the meaning of this dream? How would I interpret it? What parts of myself are embodied in the different dream characters?

This was clearly a dream that the two of us were collaboratively dreaming up together. We can look at what got dreamed up between us from either of our point's [sic] of view (what dream character am I in her dream, and what part of myself was she?), as it was a mutually shared dream. Who was I in her dream, but an awakening part of herself that she was split-off from, and hence projected out and dreamed up into and as a (dream) figure in her (waking) dream? It was as if I was open and sensitive enough to simply pick up a role that was being dreamed up in the dreamfield, waiting for someone to give it fully embodied, incarnate form.

I began to realize that what happened between the two of us, when contemplated symbolically as if it were a dream, was revealing what is happening all of the time, with everyone, only it's happening unconsciously. We are all mutually, interdependently dreaming each other up, in a nonlinear, acausal process that happens outside of time, in no time, faster than the twinkling of an eye. In this waking dream of ours, we are all picking up roles in each other's dreaming processes. We are all dreaming up the deeper dreamfield as well as, concurrently, being dreamed up by it, a process that Buddhism calls interdependent co-origination, in which every part of the universe is evoking, while simultaneously being evoked by, every other part. Having experiences with this (ex-) blind woman, and contemplating them symbolically, was a key that helped me to extract the blessing of what these situations were revealing, becoming the seeds that later helped me to articulate and develop "The Dreaming Up Process."

In the waking dream that I was having, who was this blind woman but the part of myself that wasn't really blind, but was literally refusing to look at something. To see this as a dream would be to realize that she is an embodied reflection of a part of myself that is actively refusing to look at something. Doing dreamwork, I immediately have two associations. First, I think of the part of me that has been definitely unwilling to directly look at and come to terms with the depth of the darkness, the shadow, the pain inside of myself. But I also think of the saying of Christ, when he says, "The kingdom is spread all over and people just don't see it." There is definitely something about opening one's eyes and simply seeing what is there. I notice that at times when I am teaching, this is exactly what I am trying to get across, for us to simply open our eyes, so to speak, and recognize our situation. And of course, you teach what you need to learn.

I also found it interesting to contemplate how the very moment that her eyes got healed, I got taken into another room and strapped, Christ-like, on a table. To view this actual event as if it were a dream and read it symbolically is to realize that somehow it is expressing and reflecting a process happening not only deep inside my psyche, but deep inside the collective psyche of humankind. For a dream is our inner process, going on deep inside our being, being projected out, and both literally, as well as symbolically, "dreamed up" into materialized form in, as and through the dream. So a dream is not separate from the psyche, it is the deeper psyche externalized. The seemingly outer events in the dream are themselves, in symbolic form, the very inner process of the psyche.

To view my getting strapped up as if it were a scene in a dream makes me immediately associate to being crucified right at the moment I had stepped into my light; the symbolism is very clear. It was as if a deeper archetypal mythic dimension was enacting itself through me, through events in my life. Upon reflection, this makes sense, as if the archetype of the Self, to use Jung's language, was birthing itself through me, and these events were all symbolically expressing the deeper process that I had fallen into.[8]

Farber: Did the healing begin after you met this Rina and this clairvoyant?

Paul Levy: I met Rina in '81, and I met the clairvoyant in the early '90s—much later. Here's the chronology: Thanksgiving 1978 was the worst of the abuse there, I had the fever for a year, late in '79 I moved to the West Coast; that was when the abuse came out, when I was completely feeling my father inside of me for the first time in my life. That was also when I had the realization, Well, I really have a problem. I have to deal with this. That's when I went inward and mediated to try to understand, to try to watch what was happening. In May of 1981 was when the thing with the blind woman happened, that was the first mental hospitalization. During the next year, May 1981 to September 1982, I was put in mental hospitals a lot because I was having this huge awakening and I was out in the world. I wasn't in a monastery; I wasn't in an ashram; I was totally uncontained. When I got out of the last hospital, I think that was in September '82, that's when I was really depressed and traumatized by all the hospitalizations, conditions, and the abuse. That's when I found that psychiatrist, and I worked with her up until I moved to Portland in 1990. It was in the early '90s in Portland when I had the realization, "Oh well, I've actually discovered something: I can be of help to other people." I integrated my own process, and that's when I opened up my private practice and began giving lectures and writing articles. That was in the early '90s.

Farber: When did you feel you were over the worst parts of the breakdown?

Paul Levy: The thing was when I had gotten out of that last hospital, which I believe was '82, that next year I was living with my parents was the real dark night of the soul. At the end of the year I found a place to live, I found a girlfriend, and I found my lamas, the Tibetan lamas that are living in New York. That's when I found a psychiatrist who was actually helpful at first. That's when I began having, you know, really sort of a normal life.

Farber: You moved back to New York in 1982?

Paul Levy: I was flown back for final hospitalization for three weeks to be stabilized with meds.

Farber: Why did they fly you back to New York?

Paul Levy: I got in trouble with the law, and part of the court agreement was that they would make sure I got flown back to New York and stabilized on meds. I was acting out in such an uncontained, unrestrained way that the authorities got alerted; I was breaking the rules of society.

Farber: You're one of those people who are supposed to be a chronic mental patient today.

Paul Levy: And so it is. I haven't been on any sort of psychiatric medication for over twenty-five years; I haven't been in mental hospitals for over twenty-five years. Here I am; I have psychiatrists who consult with me, study with me, and send me patients. I'm a little bit off the radar.

I was one of the lucky ones, however, as I was able to extricate myself from the Stone Age horrors of the mental health community as soon as I was able. Tragically, many others are not as fortunate, and their potential spiritual awakening/shamanic initiation process becomes aborted as they become bound and captive to the psychiatric establishment. The psychiatric system and the pharmaceutical companies (Big Pharma) are codependently intertwined with each other in a genuinely pathological, mutually profitable, and crazy-making relationship. . . . In essence, the sick part of the psychiatric system/Big Pharma is that it/they are in the business of "making crazies" so as to support its/their pathology, which is to be guilty of genuine "mal-practice." To people who have fallen into the black hole and become caught in the double bind of the psychiatric/ Big Pharma "field-of-force," it is a very dangerous situation, as if an insect had gotten too entangled in a spider's web to extricate itself. I was lucky to escape with my sanity intact.[9]

Farber: Pretty much you're now a spiritual teacher?

Paul Levy: I'm not putting myself as an enlightened person like I think of with my teacher; they're really integrated, and they're enlightened, like Rina and the Tibetan lamas. I'm in a role where I'm a teacher, but the way I do it is I openly share my wounds, my trauma, my unhealed suffering. I'm not saying I'm this enlightened person. Yeah, I've been through a incredible ordeal I'm still healing from, and still integrating and assimilating. I genuinely and authentically share my struggles. People are really inspired by the honesty of that.

The following is from "We Are All Shamans in Training"

> It's been very helpful for me as I continually deepen my own healing to remember that my experience of trauma in myself is simultaneously a microcosmic, personalized fractal reflecting the greater trauma resonating throughout the collective field. This realization allows me to not personalize the moment of feeling the trauma, or concretize myself as being traumatized, but allows me to give myself over to and embrace my experience. . . .
>
> We then can envision ourselves from this more expansive point of view to have, like a shaman, the intention to take into ourselves the madness in the field [the universe] which ultimately is our own madness, so as to creatively assimilate it into our wholeness in our own unique manner as a way to help serve the field.[10]

Farber: Through the 1980s would you say that you reached a satisfied creative life?

Paul Levy: That happened as soon as I moved out of my parents' house, which was probably in '83. That's when I'd gotten my teaching certification, and I'd gotten teaching appointments.

Farber: Teaching kids?

Paul Levy: I have a degree both in economics and art. I'm an artist, and I was teaching art, having a girlfriend, and having a normal life. I still am healing from the torment of having had the father I did. Keep in mind I was a very happy normal person as a teenager. I used to play sports all the time, and I was introspective, too. There are a lot of people I know whose teenage years were like nightmarish; mine were very happy. That is why my father was so kind of living his life through me and so identified his success with me because I was so accomplished.

Farber: He didn't lose it until you started diverging from what he wanted you to become.

Paul Levy: Exactly, that's the whole myth of the negative father, that Chronos the negative father gets constellated as soon as the son begins to separate and individuate from the father. As soon as I began to step into my own self separate from my father, that's when he began to go insane. The thing which is sad is I would have loved—my parents are both dead now—I would have loved to deal with the sort of unconscious abuse that was in the family system. I was hoping that's what the mental health system was going to do, but unfortunately and ultimately it wound up being complicit in the abuse I was wanting to help liberate.

Farber: I studied family therapy with Jay Haley and Salvador Minuchin, and for a couple years I was doing that kind of thing in clinics. Unfortunately, I kept getting fired for getting people off drugs, and by 1990 I could not get hired in the public sector as a psychologist because I opposed keeping people on psychiatric drugs—and that is not tolerated. After being involved with psychiatry you became a Jungian right? It sounds like you've read more Jung than most Jungians.

Paul Levy: I'm not a Jungian. I studied Jung every day for twenty-five years; I'm a self-taught Jungian. There's sort of a way I have of being able to translate Jung—which hasn't been done in the modern idea of Jung—that a lot of people feel is very helpful. I don't have any degree in Jung. I studied him on my own.

Farber: But was that a part of your spiritual growth? When did you start becoming optimistic about solving the crisis of humanity?

Paul Levy: Right when I was having my awakening in '81. I had this clear vision. It's not a theory but a total vision of clear being who we are. That we all are the Messiah, that all this is a mass shared dream, that when a certain sufficient number of us recognize that fact and become lucid we can connect with each other and we can literally change the dream, and that's evolutionary. I had that idea from the beginning, and that's a vision I had imprinted in my psyche so fully. My work is about these incredibly imaginative ways of trying to get that across to people.

Farber: That's similar to the kind of archetype that possesses me, the idea of the messianic consciousness, separating it from the tradition of one individual coming back.

Paul Levy: That's totally in line with what Jung talks about when he talks about the Christification of the many. He said they are incarnating within ever-increasing numbers of brothers and sisters in humanity. It's only if we're able to withstand that tension of opposites, to not just split off and project out one of those opposites but to hold that creative tension that the transcendent function can manifest through. That was exactly his vision. I feel like I'm almost one of the translators of Jung.

Farber: Jesus put it that the kingdom of heaven is at hand, the kingdom of God is at hand.

To say that nowadays would immediately arouse suspicions among most people that you are psychotic—or quixotic at best—even among many people who call themselves Christian. This is why I say either Jesus was insane or modern society is insane.

Paul Levy: I talk about it in my book, that we are enlightened, and this is the kingdom of heaven spread all over, and we don't recognize it. That's the deepest teaching in Buddhism too, that our true nature is right here right now, and even our impurities' obscurations are the form our true nature is taking.

Farber: That's one of the reasons that my hopes are resting on being able to interest people who were called mentally ill and schizophrenic not in just trying to heal themselves but in trying to heal the world. You talk about various different roles, you talk about the creative artist, and when you talk about the artist it sounds more like a prophet than the artist because your creative artist is not the one who is writing books for the entertainment of individuals but trying to change the zeitgeist.

Paul Levy: Totally; what I'm pointing at is that the figure, whether you call him the artist, the shaman, or the wounded healer, is in all aspects of the deeper archetype because we are interconnected in the field. Somebody's able to get in touch with what's constellated inside of them, keeping in mind we're not just these discrete egos separate from the universe, we are actually all oracles of the collective. The microcosm and the macrocosm are reflections of each other. When any of us, whether you call them the hero, shaman, artist, boddhisattva, prophet, or whatever, are able to somehow creatively express and give shape and form to what is going on inside of us—which is not separate from what's going on inside the collective unconscious of our species—by us expressing that it actually affects, in a powerful way, the whole collective unconscious, the whole field. It can actually be transfused and activate in others the same realization that we're giving shape and form to. That's why I say that the figure of the wounded healer, shaman, artist, whatever is the figure that's going to heal our planet.

Farber: So if the people who are today mental patients locked inside a hospital can make the same transition you did to being a creative artist or the shaman in training, I'm hoping that reading this book will help them to do that. Who else has the motivation to do it? Most people want to belong to the rat race, that's what Laing said. He said our society has become biologically dysfunctional and some forms of schizophrenic alienation from the alienation of our society may have a sociobiological function we have yet not recognized.

Paul Levy: You know Seth, you are so right on that there are probably so many people in mental hospitals or even outpatients who just bought into the diagnosis, which is then to fall under the psychiatric spell; it's like we talked about before in the self-fulfilling prophecy or the infinitely self-perpetuating feedback loop. The mental patients are having the space, having the container, to creatively express what they're envisioning, what they're seeing, what they're experiencing, and what they're saying could be incredible—not to just heal themselves but it could be helpful to help the world.

Farber: Jesus thought he could bring about the kingdom of heaven on Earth. As I said, it turned out that, from a conventional viewpoint, Jesus was mistaken. Inversing the usual thing that Jesus was pathological, I say that the mental patients who, like Jesus, want to bring about the kingdom of God, if there were enough people who had that consciousness, who went through what you and Jung refer to as inflation, we'd have a number of people committed to the messianic transformation.

Paul Levy: Right. What I'm saying is that that's the way, what you just described, that's the way I see it happening. It's one thing if you or I wake up right now and stabilize and have the lucidity and the realization that this is a mass shared dream. So what? The point is that the way you understand this if you have the lucidity in the night dream—that's one thing—but when you connect with other dream characters in that night dream, other aspects of yourself who are also turned on and lucid and realizing the nature of the situation they find themselves in (i.e., that they're dreaming), which means that the environment they're in is nothing other than their own thoughtforms, their own energy, their own consciousness—what they discover is, "Wow, we can configure ourselves together." It's what I call our sacred power of dreaming: we can reconfigure ourselves together and change the dream we're having. We can dream whatever we want into materialization. That's what this is all about, and that's evolutionary, that's what's available to us.

Farber: For one thing it entails coming to the realization—which the schizophrenics and the bipolars, as they're called now, can accept, but can the normal people accept it?—that the laws of nature are not laws of nature. They're not the eternal laws of nature. As Rupert Sheldrake said, these are habits of nature: everything from death to disease to all the things we regard as inevitable parts of the human situation.

Paul Levy: Like this friend of mine, who also was thrown in mental hospitals when he was younger, he's a genius now. He's an incredible physicist, and when he has the realization he's dreaming he does physics experiments in the lucid dream state. What he's discovering endlessly in his life is that it's all a function of consciousness: if we are fed a particular axiomatic viewpoint that we become entrenched in, then, being like a dream, this world will supply all the evidence we need to confirm the seemingly objective truth of that viewpoint. We're just entrancing ourselves by our own ability to create reality.

Farber: One of these spiritual kind of books at . . . I think you might have been alluding to it—was the idea of individual realization and just becoming oblivious to the world. It seems to work for some people, but it's not doing anything to save the Earth. You find that in Buddhism; you find it in many spiritual traditions.

Paul Levy: That's not the real Buddhism, because the real Buddhism is talking about when you wake up. It's the Mahayana, it's the boddhisattva; it's like the boddhisattva's about to enter nirvana, and they look back and they see all their brothers and sisters, and the boddhisattva says "I'm not going to enter nirvana until I bring everybody else there first." And who is everybody else except aspects of me?

Farber: But Theravada Buddhists are pretty much into individual realization, are they not?

Paul Levy: Yeah, they are, and yet I also have to say, because I'm connected with some Theravada teachers, they're also some of the most incredible and loving, some of the most wisdom-filled and compassionate people I know.

Farber: That's in spite of the theory?

Paul Levy: It's somehow in spite of it. I almost think it's a question of semantics; when somebody has some degree of realization, they understand that we're not separate from each other and that we're interconnected and interdependent; me and separate self don't exist.

Farber: I guess all religious mystics have had that kind of . . .

Paul Levy: I don't get caught up in the semantic thing about the Hinayana being just about personal salvation and forgetting about everybody else.

Farber: If you want to change the communal mind you have to recruit people who are not advocating individual liberation.

Paul Levy: That's what I talk about in my book, about being a spiritually informed political activist. You can't be a spiritual practitioner without being a political activist, and you can't be a political activist without being a spiritual practitioner; we're at the point where they really have to cross-pollinate each other.

Farber: In the entire Indian tradition, the ultimate goal is seen as disincarnation. Isn't that true in Buddhism, too?

Paul Levy: The point is that when you become enlightened, then when you pass away you don't get blown by the winds of karma and incarnate back into a body. You want to break the incarnation cycle, but then that needs to be complemented by the idea of the boddhisattva who attains the realization and breaks from the incarnation cycle and consciously chooses to come back.

Farber: Sri Aurobindo says that—I don't mean to cite him as the authority—but the ultimate goal is the highest realization will take place on Earth, even the motive coming back at this point may be not to help other people attain freedom but ultimately to transform the whole Earth consciousness. There would then be incarnation but, as Aurobindo puts it, continuous evolution in the Knowledge rather than evolution in the Ignorance. It would be the realization of the ancient dream of the kingdom of God on Earth.

Paul Levy: I fully agree with that, and that's why, in the last chapter of my book *Creating an Art Happening Called Global Awakening*, I present the idea of these dreamers and artists whose canvas is this universe, and if we could actually have the recognition of the nature of our situation, then just like an artist, we can create an art happening where we actually help each other to wake up. That's like a radical thing, and that, I think, is what Aurobindo was pointing at.

Farber: Are you aware of the split in society between spirituality, which is seen as a kind of get-yourself-together thing, and politics, which is seen as a change society type of thing?

Paul Levy: To answer that I go back to Jung, who talks about how the real change in the world is going to happen through the individual: it doesn't happen through making new legislation. Any one of us doing our own work and actually waking up to a degree has a real effect, and that's where we can be really active and an activated agent. Particularly when people like that connect with each other, and of course, then there's the whole idea of whether its in the revelations, they talk about a 144,000 or the hundred-monkey phenomenon. There's a certain critical mass; the thing is that any one of us, you know if you in this moment and me in this moment, we integrate our shadow and wake up or whatever and individuate to whatever degree—that might be the sort of putting this grain of sugar in the saturated solution that forms this crystal. It might be any one of us in this moment waking up who might be that very . . .

Farber: How would it then manifest in society? We couldn't continue to go to war, and even the slaughter of animals—the things we take for granted as we eat our food—the enormous amount of suffering that's being inflicted upon other beings . . .

Paul Levy: The point is that when there are a sufficient number of people getting together and not only just actually getting together but even just the way we affect the field, if I wake up in this moment even more that has an . . . effect on the whole thought field of consciousness that actually exists. I can't say how that's going to get incorporated or institutionalized into the existing paradigm; what we're stepping into is more and more the realization that we have to have for the survival of our species, that we're actually on the same side, that we're actually interdependent and interconnected, and it's really like a stepping out of the illusion of the separate self. I mean that's really what it's about.

Farber: What would be an example of a global—can you give a historical example; you make passing reference to the sixties—of an art happening called global awakening?

Paul Levy: I don't even know if there is such an example because it's such . . . like an epochal radical evolutionary event arising that we're approaching, you know? What I think in terms of when you think about our species, however many 6.5 billion of us there are . . . think about in a family system, or even a relationship, where all of a sudden there will be polarity, there will be conflict. And then all of a sudden something will happen where that will shift and the whole configuration will change, where all of a sudden it will go from kind of war and adversarial diabolical creating separation to all of a sudden . . . connection, instead of separation. That's what I call a microcosmic freckle; that's like showing up the minutest microcosmic level, whether it be personal relationships or family dynamics, it's what's available to us as a human species. The thing I'm saying is that whether it be the women's movement, the gay rights movement, the blacks movement, all of these movements maybe would be examples on a smaller scale, but instead of it having to do with just a specific thing, what about it being just a fully human movement, where we're *all* having a realization? So yeah, I'm saying these things have happened, whether it be on the smaller scale of relationship or group dynamics or even within a particular group.

Farber: Do you remember the Harmonic Convergence?

Paul Levy: Oh, I know—I know who started that; he's a friend of mine.

Farber: Do you expect any transformation in 2012? You've been in contact with Arguelles? He's still very much a believer.

Paul Levy: He's married now to my ex-girlfriend; we are really good friends. The point is for me I don't know what's going to happen in 2012. My imagination is that it's some form of potential conscious expansion, but I can't say. The thing that really gets my attention as someone who tracks the dreaming is just the fact that there are tons and tons of people who are even contemplating or asking the question, What's going to happen in 2012? It just seems like something's going to shift. Just that itself is a psychic phenomenon that merits our attention.

Farber: Do you see the sixties as some sort of global—you make reference to the music of the sixties and the contagious effect of that?

Paul Levy: Yeah. I see the sixties as totally an example of some form of global awakening, and the thing that is sad is that so many people who in the sixties were the proponents of these more progressive liberal expanded points of view have now become card-carrying members of the machine, so to speak. It's kind of tragic in a way. There are lots of people who grew up in the sixties who still carry that frequency and that vibration in their own way. So yeah, that might be a good example of that.

Farber: I guess you're not pessimistic when you see all these efforts to change the world. I don't know how much hope you had in the Obama movement. One would have thought with the campaign or whatever, you saw a reaction to the horrific things that Bush did.

Paul Levy: I didn't have much hope with him because I was aware that he was just, whatever, in the pockets of big business. I do study a lot of what's happening in the world, because I have to be tracking what the dreaming is doing—cause I see it all as a dreaming process. The big danger is to get really absorbed in despair and pessimism because it's very convincing how terrible things are. I also feel there are so many people who are awakening and who are these visionaries, whether or not they're mental patients, and that gives me incredible hope, so I definitely am an optimist.

Farber: What about the fact that people that are not awakening are the ones who have the guns and bombs and police and all that?

Paul Levy: Right, that's true, and I'm not going to debate that; it's really unfortunate, you know.

Farber: You may have read about internment camps; I don't think we're putting them in now, but they definitely have them and have been building them.

Paul Levy: I have no doubt about that, and that really concerns me. I don't know what to say; I'm not this naive person who is like, "Oh no, everything is going to turn out great; let's hope for the best." No. I mean things on one hand look very bleak and are very . . . I sort of see it as like the powers-that-be are really wanting to centralize power and control and have dominance over the planet, over everyone. I want to say that's a dreaming process, that's an archetypal process that has enacted itself all throughout history on a smaller scale.

Farber: What makes you feel that now is the time—within the next century or our lifetime—that we can transcend this?

Paul Levy: One way of understanding what's happening collectively is to just take a look at an individual and when she, when the unconscious creates a situation that puts her in a corner or a potentially fatal situation, this also can precipitate her to wake up individually. It's a similar thing on the collective scale: if you look at this thing of dream and the unconscious of our species, that we're dreaming ourselves into this incredible corner and potentially creating a fatal situation for ourselves, but the other half of that is that it could potentially snap us out of our spell.

Farber: Even on mainstream TV there's commentary that no one's going to take global warming seriously until there's a catastrophe. It's an inconvenient truth, to use Gore's phrase.

Paul Levy: Right, and so the thing is that stuff on so many fronts— whether it be economic, environmental, or militarily or political or social—they're all converging, and we're given a choice: Are we going to wake up to a degree or are we just going to be like sheep and be led along and go over a cliff?

Farber: Going back to the Mad Pride movement, do you see a positive shift as I say in the kind of transition from the psychiatric survivors' movement, which seemed to be focused just on the mental health system and its crimes, to the Mad Pride movement, that seems to be expanding its focus?

Paul Levy: I don't know, I'm not really plugged into that community. I'm just sort of an independent agent doing my own thing. I might be open to kind of connecting with more groups like that; I've just felt so strongly pulled to do my own thing. I guess the one thing I want to say is that, if we're talking about Mad Pride and having these visionary gifts and awakenings, you can't take out of that equation that you are a member of the human community and that part of what gifts you are bringing forth have to do with helping our species and the greater collective field to heal and to wake up. I don't see any way to separate that from your own personal healing. It's sort of like the way I saw it, because I was so committed to my own healing, but at a certain point I had the realization, "Wow, I'm not gonna be fully healed until the whole universe is healed."

Farber: I've come to the point where I see the mental health system as just completely incapable of change, and if we change society what need would there be for a so-called mental health system, anyway?

Paul Levy: That's true. I think the mental health system is a sort of self-sustaining system, particularly when you factor in the Big Pharma companies involved there. Change isn't going to come within that system, particularly with Big Pharma involved. The thing is I feel like any of us stepping into our light, which involves, of course, integrating the shadow, but really stepping into our genius and particularly connecting with other people who are doing the same, it activates the collective genius, which is greater than the sum of its parts. When I talk about this in my work—that's the way we're going to change things, whether it be the mental health community or the world.

Farber: Just to sum up, it seems to me you pretty much accepted what I saw as many if not all of the basic assertions implied by the Mad Pride movement. You did seem to agree that people who get labeled schizophrenic or bipolar seem to have a distinctive kind of personality characteristic in terms of being more sensitive or more aware?

Paul Levy: Yes, but the thing is maybe it's not fully integrated. Thus they can get overwhelmed by being more sensitive and aware that they can feel the unconscious, the shadow in the field, but they don't necessarily know what to do with it. A healer feels that unconscious shadow stuff, but they're able to metabolize what gets activated in them, so that they integrate it and then they can be of help, whereas the mental patient is sensitive and aware and feels that stuff, but he or she hasn't developed the container to be able to metabolize it.

Farber: No, they haven't gotten much help. The point I was making is that this group, who are more constitutionally sensitive and aware, has been marginalized for a long time, and they continue to be marginalized.

Paul Levy: I want to point out that marginalization is a reflection of how we people in the consensus reality tend to marginalize our own sensitive parts or our own parts that are a little bit idiosyncratic or abnormal. That then plays out as a reflection collectively in the world.

Farber: You have noticed that many people who are psychiatrically labeled are more mystically inclined than the average Joe?

Paul Levy: Totally; they're more mystically inclined. Is it grounded; is it integrated? No. Where people tend to think they're Christ, or the Messiah, and that's seen as part of the pathology, but yet what we're pointing out is that it can be ego inflation, ungrounded, and out of balance, but they can still actually be onto something. We only need to keep the realization they're not getting metabolized or integrated in a certain way.

Farber: I'd like to think of St. Paul, who was blind for all that time, and these people who developed a messiah consciousness that was not egocentric: St. Paul, George Fox.

Paul Levy: I agree.

Farber: When you say that human beings are dreaming the dream and we could dream it together, do you also see that as a manifestation of a kind of evolutionary tendency, a telos?

Paul Levy: Definitely. I totally see that. The way I see it is that when you step into the atemporal dimension, from that point of view we already are enlightened and woken up. All exists in that atemporal dimension, and its almost like it's an attractor, that everything going out as linear time is the medium through which we as a species are actualizing and having that realization in time.

Farber: How do you see these attractors?

Paul Levy: I'm not sure, because *attractors* is also a term in physics, and so I don't quite know. I just think of it in the realm of the mind, where there are archetypes, and they get activated and act as attractors. They attract both the inner and outer environment as to give form to themselves. That could be potentially negative or positive.

Farber: So then what you believe is realized in the atemporal world manifests itself as purpose and striving in our created universe?

Paul Levy: I definitely see this as some form of telos, like a teleology thing . . . the whole purpose or a goal. That's like a deep sense I have, whether in the individual life and also in the collective life of our species. I immediately associate with Christ when he says that you're gods and scripture cannot be broken; he was actually speaking from that place where he actualized that realization.

17

Revitalization and the Messianic-Redemptive Vision of Sri Aurobindo

hy have I discussed in detail two cultural revitalizations in America? What does this have to do with Mad Pride? The worlds that sprung up during these revitalizations were infused with a far greater sense of human possibility; I think they bring us into a different universe of the imagination and allow us to recover a sense of how different these worlds were from the one we inhabit today. Thus they help to convey to readers and activists who have accommodated themselves to the postmodernist zeitgeist, a sense of the transformative power of the messianic-redemptive vision. I think these accounts also illustrate the cogency of the Perry-Wallace-McLoughlin-Levy theory as well as the Christian perspective of H. Richard Niebuhr.

As Levy might put it, during cultural revitalizations new leaders emerge who put forward myths and symbols and enact dramatic rituals that mobilize the masses and resonate with the messianic-redemptive archetypes in the collective unconscious. It is my contention—based on evidence presented in the interviews in this book and in the works of those such as Laing and Perry—that it is from the ranks of the mad (those who are today seen as "psychotic") that such new leaders are most likely to emerge.

The life and writings of Sri Aurobindo also provide some confirmation for the revitalization theory. His ideas on social change (even less well read than his writings on yoga) are in some ways similar to that of Perry and the others I have mentioned. Sri Aurobindo was the only Eastern thinker who formulated a philosophy that fused mysticism—defined in most general terms as the cultivation of "higher" states of consciousness through meditation—and messianism.[1] Aurobindo believed that just as life superseded matter and mind superseded life in the process of evolution, humanity would evolve—not biologically, but under the teleological press of the Spirit—to a higher state of existence. This state would be governed not by mind but by an intuitive faculty of knowing that is conscious of its oneness with all beings and with the divine Spirit immanent in nature.

Sri Aurobindo, it is clear, was himself—after his transformation—a forerunner of this type of human being. This next phase of evolutionary transformation requires a conscious cooperation on the part of humanity—a conversion of consciousness. "What is necessary," Aurobindo wrote, "is that there should be a turn in humanity felt by some or many toward the vision of this change, a feeling of its imperative need, the sense of its possibility, the will to make it possible in themselves and to find the way."[2] Aurobindo rarely discussed the social preconditions of this conversion, but in his essay "The Human Cycle" he posits that those advanced souls he views as the pioneers of humanity can help to prepare the species to make the eschatological leap into a higher phase of our spiritual and historical evolution: the realization of the divine life on Earth.[3]

Sri Aurobindo is best known not for his political writings but for his books on integral yoga (meditation)* and metaphysical philosophy. Although he was strongly influenced by the Indian religious tradition

---

*Most Americans confuse yoga with hatha yoga (stretching exercises), but in India the term refers more generally to set of practices (usually involving some sort of meditation), including hatha yoga, whose goal is to enable one to attain unity with the Divine.

and its Vedic scriptures, his perspective was singular in one essential respect. Until Sri Aurobindo, all of the Hindu spiritual traditions and their philosophers agreed on one point—that the culmination of the spiritual quest is reached when one has completely overcome and exhausted one's attachments to the world (one's karma) and is thus freed from the necessity to reincarnate. In all my research, I have not found any exceptions to this ideal. One then attains the permanent state of absorption of one's soul into God, or as typically formulated in Hinduism, into "Brahman," the impersonal absolute (or into Krishna, in the theistic schools of Hinduism). Even the leaders of the great twentieth-century renaissance of Hinduism—from the popularizers like Swami Vivekananda (who brought Hindu Vedanta in its most universal form to the West) to the renowned philosopher Sarvepalli Radhakrishnan (also the president of India in the 1960s)—for all their worldly activism and advocacy of social reform, accepted this traditional ideal of liberation as escape from the world.

While Eastern Christianity has posited a vision closer to Aurobindo's based on this worldly transformation,* Western Christianity—from the time of its alliance with the Roman empire in the fourth century up until recently—has presented a postmortem "heaven" as the realm of salvation, despite the messianic vision of earthly paradise preached in Isaiah, Jeremiah, and the New Testament, including the sermons of Jesus. Thus, Aurobindo states that Christian and Hindu cultures have "joined the great consensus," crying that "not in this world can there be our kingdom of heaven but beyond."[4] Sri Aurobindo's messianic-redemptive vision was made all the more forceful by his elaborate, polemical, and luminous deconstructions of the many of the great metaphysical philosophies—particularly the dominant Vedic philosophy of Sankara—that denied the value and potentialities of earthly existence. Aurobindo termed Sankara's interpretation of Vedanta "illusionism." As opposed to these world-denying perspectives, Aurobindo testified that the highest attainment of the spiritual life entailed a col-

---

*Although similar ideals exist today in pockets of Western Christianity, the Christianity Aurobindo was exposed to in England, where he studied in the late nineteenth century, was the otherworldly version based on reward or punishment in an afterlife.

lective endeavor that would result in the realization of the divine life on Earth.

Sri Aurobindo's messianic-redemptive vision—articulated in volume after volume of philosophical prose as well as in his epic poem *Savitri*—was endowed with a depth and specificity it lacked in its Judeo-Christian formulations: Aurobindo sketched out in detail (based on his own spiritual revelations, the result of a lifetime devoted to the practice of meditation) how the realization of this vision would alter the psychology of human beings and the ontology and phenomenology of embodied existence. The attainment of the divine life would even alter the "laws" of nature, making it possible for human beings to attain immortal bodies as well as immortal souls. As one of Aurobindo's disciples put it, the transformation would not be limited to the creation of a new humanity but would "extend to the entire earth-life—to animals, plants and eventually to matter itself. This change would take place not only within the laws governing their present nature—but more and more by a change of these laws themselves."[5] He notes that these observations are bound to appear "preposterous" to the "circumspect mind of rational man." Sri Aurobindo's lifelong spiritual partner and fellow yogi Mira Richard, known to ashram residents as "the Mother," said, "This looks like madness but all new things have always seemed madness before they became realities."[6]

Aurobindo typically spoke not just of changing humanity but of changing the Earth consciousness. Aurobindo stated poignantly, in response to a question by a disciple, that he was seeking through his yogic work to "make life something better than a struggle with ignorance and falsehood and pain and strife. . . . I am seeking to bring some principle of Truth, Light, Harmony and Peace into the earth-consciousness. . . . I feel it ever gleaming down on my consciousness from above. . . . I believe the descent of this Truth opening the way to the development of a divine consciousness here to be the final sense of the earth evolution. . . . Let all men jeer upon me if they will . . . for my presumption. I go on until I conquer or perish."[7]

Aurobindo was born in 1872. His father was an Indian doctor, an intellectual and Anglophile who sent Aurobindo to England as a child of seven to make sure he received a superior education. Aurobindo decided to return to India in 1893, shortly before completing college at the University of Cambridge. Aurobindo worked in civil service and then in teaching. He spent all his free time reading and writing poetry in English, the language in which he was most proficient. After a few years he became involved in the movement against British domination—at first from behind the scenes. By 1906 Aurobindo had become a leader in the Nationalist Party and was the first Indian leader to become a vocal advocate for national independence; most of the activists favored greater autonomy for Indians in government. This goal was eventually adopted by the Indian movement due largely to Aurobindo's influence, which had crescendoed after his second arrest by the British in 1908.

Aurobindo expressed his views through the paper of which he became the editor, *Bande Mantaram*. Aurobindo's astute editorials and impassioned calls for "national independence" won the paper "unprecedented popularity and influence." Even in South Africa, Gandhi read the paper and was impressed.[8] In addition to his writings, Aurobindo's powerful speeches on behalf on his exalted vision of Indian nationalism struck a chord within the community of Indian activists and made him one of the heroes and prophets of the movement. His two arrests and famous trial in 1909 had made Aurobindo a "legendary figure" by the time he retired from political activism in 1910.[9]

Aurobindo's first arrest by the British was in 1907, for "seditious" writings. A month later he was acquitted, but the trial had made him a celebrity. Aurobindo resumed the struggle with redoubled energy. India was not an abstraction to Aurobindo. As he wrote in a personal letter in August 1905, "[W]hile others look upon their country as an inert piece of matter . . . I look upon my country as the Mother. I love her. I adore Her. I worship Her as the Mother."*[10] He compared the British to a demon sitting on his mother's breast and sucking her blood. He could not just continue his normal activities but felt compelled to "rush out" and rescue his mother. He was confident: "I know I have the strength to deliver this fallen race. God sent me to earth to accomplish this great mission."[11]

---

*Aurobindo had little contact with his own mother, who was reportedly too self-absorbed by emotional problems to assume a maternal role.

But from the beginning Aurobindo saw the liberation of the nation as a means to an even greater goal. As he stated in June 1909, "Our aim will be to help in building up India for the sake of humanity."[12] The West had achieved technological and scientific superiority, but India had developed its spiritual resources based on the ancient scriptures of India. India could help solve the problems of mankind by teaching it to rise to a higher level of spiritual existence. In his historic Uttaparic speech in May 1909 Aurobindo stressed the universal significance of India's liberation. In the "seclusion of the [Indian] peninsula from of old," Hinduism "was cherished" by its sages "for the salvation of humanity." "It is to give this religion that India is rising. . . . She is rising to shed the eternal light entrusted to her over the world. India has always existed for humanity and not for herself and it is for humanity, and not for herself, that she must be great."[13]

Aurobindo had started the practice of yoga in 1904; his primary motive, he wrote later, was to gain through meditation the psychic power to help him liberate India. Over the next few years, as he immersed himself in the study of India's spiritual traditions, his spiritual experiences became increasingly intense.[14] In January 1908 he sought guidance from an accomplished yogi and had his first experience of the silent formless Brahman.[15] This is believed by followers of the Sankarite school to be the "highest" spiritual experience possible, prefiguring the ultimate merger with Brahman when one is freed from the cycle of incarnations. For Sri Aurobindo, whose goal was *not* escape, the experience of Brahman *in the world* (which he had in prison later) was equally high. In February 1908 he wrote in a personal letter, "From now on all that I do is done not at my will but at the command of God. . . . I hope that God will show you the light he has shown me in his infinite Grace."[16] At the time, Aurobindo had learned to follow a voice from within that gave him guidance—a tradition in India. The experience of the union of the silent Brahman and the active Brahman, a turning point in his yogic practice, took place in 1912 and seemed to follow naturally from his two previous experiences—and he believed it to be a "higher" revelation.[17]

Life was transformed when Aurobindo was arrested by the British in 1908 for conspiracy to "wage war against the government," a crime that could result in execution or deportation. Aurobindo's first response was despair. He thought he had a mission to work for the people of his country and that until that work was done he would have God's protection.[18] Had God abandoned him? Aurobindo was placed in solitary confinement for over a week. He suffered "intense mental agony," and for the first time his efforts to meditate were futile. His thoughts became so wild and uncontrollable he wondered "whether he was going insane." In desperation, he called on the Divine for help, and suddenly "his heart was flooded with happiness."[19] From then on, prison life became bearable. Shortly afterward a voice within told him that the Divine had placed him in prison in order to loosen the bonds he had to the independence movement because God had a different task for him to do. He was told his training would begin in prison.*[20] Ten days after his imprisonment he was allowed to read. He sent home for the Gita and the Upanishads.

During the year in prison Aurobindo devoted himself to meditating. Much of the time he was in a trancelike state. He had his second profound mystical experience in prison, that of Brahman in the world, "I walked under the branches under the tree in front of my cell but it was not the tree. . . . I knew it was Sri Krishna [God in manifest form] whom I saw standing there and holding over me his shade. . . . Everyone and everything seemed to be a manifestation of God." "I looked at the prisoners in the jail, the thieves, the murderers, the swindlers" in "these darkened souls and misused bodies," and "as I looked at them I saw Vasudeva (Krishna)."[21] Everything was alive with an "all pervading consciousness."[22]

A year after his imprisonment, the trial took place. Aurobindo was acquitted by the judge. As Heehs writes, the charges were nebulous enough that another judge might easily have convicted him. Aurobindo's brother had been engaged in terrorist activities and had stored the bombs in Aurobindo's house with Aurobindo's knowledge. Although Aurobindo did not support his brother's actions, he *was* guilty of conspiring to deprive the British of sovereignty of India.[23] As he stated later, his goal was even-

---

*Aurobindo heard many voices when in prison, but he had learned to distinguish the voice coming from God—issuing *adeshas,* meaning "direct commands from the Divine."

tually to help provoke "an armed revolution in the whole of India."[24] After his release he continued to give speeches until, under threat of being arrested again, an inner prompting from the Divine, an *adesh*, directed him to take refuge in Pondicherry (the capital of the French settlements in India) and to devote himself to spiritual work.

Thus in 1910 he settled in Pondicherry and began the *sadhana** that would last until his death. After 1926 he decided his spiritual work required complete isolation (in his bedroom/study meditating and writing) so he only saw the disciples who had gathered around him on special occasions to give them blessings three times a year. The only person he saw regularly was Mira Richard, "the Mother," whom he recognized as his spiritual partner shortly after she became his disciple in 1920; without the Mother, Sri Aurobindo said he could not have accomplished his spiritual work. (Aurobindo's relationship with the Mother was not physical, as they were both spiritual renunciates.) It was a profound partnership; "The Mother and I are one but in two bodies."[25]

Sri Aurobindo explained his retirement from politics later (writing in the third person).

> But this did not mean, as most people supposed that he had retired into some height of spiritual experience devoid of any further interest in the world or in the fate of India. It could not mean that, for the very principle of his Yoga was not only to realize the Divine and attain to a complete spiritual consciousness [for the individual] but also to take all life and all world activity into the scope of this spiritual consciousness and action and to base life on the Spirit and give it a spiritual meaning. In his retirement Sri Aurobindo kept a close watch on all that was happening in the world and in India and actively intervened whenever necessary with a spiritual force and silent spiritual action.[26]

Mysticism may be an individual endeavor (although in accord with Indian tradition, Aurobindo acquired disciples, and less conventionally—

---

*Sadhana is the spiritual practice that one is given by the Divine or the "guru" to realize one's spiritual potential, to fulfill one's life mission.

uniquely—he had formed a partnership with "the Mother"), but its ultimate goal in Aurobindo's view was the collective transformation of society—of the Earth.

Despite the fact that Sri Aurobindo wrote several volumes on social and political developments after his retirement from active politics, these books were less well known than his more voluminous writings on yoga and metaphysics. One question stands out, How does one get from the present society based on an absence of unity and murderous discord to the society envisioned by Aurobindo? Aurobindo cogently explains the spiritual conditions for a new social order, which in turn is necessary for the attainment of the divine life on Earth. As stated, Aurobindo regards the ideal of individual liberation as specious.*[27] The question thus remains: Considering the allegiance of the masses and the economic and political elites to the present order, how is the transition to be effected?

Sri Aurobindo stated that his goal of his sadhana was to bring the Divine (the "Supermind," he called it, which is the Divine in one of its poises) down to Earth, so that it would make the complete transformation of society possible to accomplish. Aurobindo did not succeed in this task at the time of his death in 1950. However, there is also another theory of change that is implied in Sri Aurobindo's writings; it parallels Wallace's theory of cultural revitalization. The theory gains credibility in the light of Aurobindo's own success as an activist in persuading the Indian movement to take up independence from Britain as a goal.

At the beginning of his activism Aurobindo had written of the necessity for "propaganda intended to convert the whole nation to the ideal of independence which was regarded by the vast majority of Indians as impractical and impossible, an almost insane chimera."[28] Several years after he retired from politics his goal had been accomplished. According to Aurobindo's biographer, "He succeeded in infusing this will [for freedom] into the mind of a whole generation."[29] Most authors agree that Aurobindo was virtually single-handedly responsible for effecting this change—primarily through the power of his writings and speeches (*propaganda* is too crude a term), which imbued indepen-

---

*"No salvation should be valued which takes us away from the love of God in his manifestation and the help we can give to the world."

dence with a spiritual significance and had an electrifying effect on the younger generation (his peers and younger). In Perry's terms, Aurobindo was the prophet who emerged in the time of India's cultural crisis with a myth to energize and channel the direction of the emerging movement for change.

Long after his retirement from activism, Sri Aurobindo continued to follow political developments and even, he said, to intervene on the occult plane to effect a favorable outcome on worldly happenings. He believed throughout his life that the independence of India had been an important accomplishment for humanity, although after his death it became clear that his highest hopes for India had not been realized. He believed that Hitler represented a danger to humanity. Unlike Gandhi, he proclaimed his support for the Allies in World War II (to the consternation of the majority of Indian nationalists) and believed that the victory over Hitler had been essential to prevent a terrible retrogression of humanity.

Yet the transformation of humanity that he believed to be the goal of the next phase of our development is a far greater task. Nevertheless, it relies on the same principles. It cannot be achieved by the yoga of a handful of disciples alone. Although Aurobindo knew that people were at different stages of spiritual development and the masses were less evolved and less ready for change than a small number of individuals who were more spiritually advanced, any radical change in life required the support of a majority. As he wrote in "The Human Cycle," "There may even be a glorious crop of saints and hermits in a forcing-soil of spirituality but unless the race, the society, the nation is moved toward the spiritualization of life or move forward led by the light of an ideal, the end must be weakness, littleness and stagnation."[30]

It would have been far easier to adopt the traditional goal of individual liberation from the world. Aurobindo lived through two world wars. He had no naïve belief in human "progress." All of Aurobindo's writings reveal that his faith was not based on a facile optimism. As he wrote in *Savitri:*

> *This mortal creature is his own worst foe*
> *His science is an artificer of doom*

He ransacks earth for means to harm his kind
He slays his happiness and others' good
Nothing has he learnt from Time and its history . . .
Battle and rapine, ruin and massacre
Are still the pastimes of man's warring tribes
An idiot hour destroys what centuries made . . .
All he has achieved he drags to the precipice
His grandeur he turns to an epic of doom and fall . . .
A part author of the cosmic tragedy
His will conspires with time and death and fate,
His brief appearance on the enigmaed earth
Ever recurs but brings no high result.
His soul's wide search and ever recurring hopes
Pursue the useless orbit of their course
In a vain repetition of lost toils
Across a track of soon forgotten lives . . .
Why is it all and wherefore are we here?[31]

Aurobindo writes that "the coming of a spiritual age must be preceded by the appearance of an increasing number of individuals who are no longer satisfied with the normal existence of man but perceive that a greater evolution is the real goal of humanity and attempt to effect it *in themselves,* to lead others to it and make it the recognized goal of the race."[32] Are there an increasing number of individuals in the United States who perceive the need for a greater evolution? It does not seem so at this time, but it certainly was the case in the 1960s.* Such a development would be auspicious, the precondition for the change of society. "All great changes find their first clear and effective power and their direct shaping force in the mind and spirit of the individual or a limited number of individuals."[33]

In "The Human Cycle," Aurobindo repeatedly states that there must be an interaction between the spiritual vanguard and the masses, between the individual and the masses, "the communal-mind," the

---

*As we go to press, I am encouraged by the emergence of the Occupy Wall Street movement.

"group-soul."[34] The pioneers must not only change themselves, they must somehow move the masses, presumably by articulating spiritual ideals that may exist in inchoate form in the chaos of the communal mind. "[I]f the common human mind has begun to admit ideas proper to the higher order . . . and the heart of man has begun to be stirred by aspirations born of these ideas, then there is a hope of some advance in the not distant future."[35]

Even in "The Human Cycle" much of what Aurobindo teaches about how the pioneers can transform the communal mind is suggestive rather than explicit; it was exemplified as much by his own practice, as a yogi, as a writer, and in his past as an activist. After Aurobindo had retired from activism, his own contribution to humanity now lay in writing, in meditating, in giving guidance to those who were practicing yoga in his ashram, and in his own occult efforts to bring the divine down to Earth; he tended not to give much thought to the strategy of the activist. Furthermore, as indicated above, he was well aware that all worldly efforts to produce great changes were never more than partial successes—that the Earth was still a vale of suffering and that the human being remains "his own worst foe" despite all our "progress." More inclined to ravage and destroy than to strive to realize the high ideal of equality, liberty, and fraternity, humanity dwells still in the shadow of Ignorance. Nevertheless, despite the cautionary notes throughout "The Human Cycle," the formulations hedged with caveats, Aurobindo repeatedly states that the future hinges on the *relationship* between the human pioneers and the masses.

It is revealing that Aurobindo's own work consisted not just in yoga but in writing thousands of pages (most of it, except his letters to his disciples, cerebral by the standards of the common man), to communicate to others his own vision of the future. His clearest statement in "The Human Cycle" on how the vanguard can prepare the masses is, "There must be the individual and individuals who are able to see, to develop, to re-create themselves in the image of the Spirit and *communicate* both *their idea and its power* to the *mass*" (my emphasis).[36]

How?

Sri Aurobindo addressed his books to an elite of intellectuals, yet, judging from the well-known writers of our time, they have remained undiscovered or ignored even by those intellectuals one would expect to be most receptive. (Ken Wilber is an exception, but his understanding of Sri Aurobindo was distorted by his own exaltation of Sankara's Advaita Vedanta and his attachment to Freudianism.[37]) As an activist, Aurobindo had written and spoken in simpler terms but with a similar message: he appealed to the masses by placing the goal of independence for India within the context of a messianic-redemptive vision for humanity. And he was successful, although his hopes for India were not realized with its liberation. So his books and his life present the same message for activists and for pioneers of a new order. They must work to remold themselves and find ways to communicate *the power* of their vision to the masses.

What is the idea that must be communicated? It is not new: it lies in the depths of humanity's collective imagination. "We have to return to the pursuit of an ancient secret which man, as a race, has seen only obscurely and followed after lamely, has indeed understood only with his surface mind and not in his heart of meaning—and yet in following it lies his social no less than his individual salvation—the ideal of the kingdom of God, the secret of the reign of Spirit over mind and life and body." "There [will be] a growing inner unity with others. Not only to see the Divine in oneself, but to see and find the Divine in all . . . is the complete law of the spiritual being. But he who sees God in all will serve freely God in all with the service of love. . . . Therefore too is a growing inner unity with others. . . . [Man] will seek not only his own freedom, but the freedom of all, not only his own perfection, but the perfection of all."[38]

The "perfectionism" of the nineteenth-century Evangelical Christian reformers (see chapter 15) is paralleled a century later by Aurobindo, who supports it with a philosophical foundation that the reformers lacked. Philosophically, the realization of the divine life, the messianic vision, is marked by a shift in consciousness that enables one to grasp the One behind the many. The law of the perfected being is "unity fulfilled in diversity. . . . The individual would not be cast according to a single type of individuality; each would be different from the other, a unique formation of the Being, although one with all the rest in foundation of self and sense of oneness . . ."[39]

Besides the perfectionism of nineteenth-century Christianity, Aurobindo's messianic vision finds another parallel as well. To quote

Laing again, "If the human race survives, future men will look back on our enlightened epoch as a veritable Age of Darkness. . . . The laugh's on us. They will see that what we call 'schizophrenia' was one of the forms in which, often through quite ordinary people, the light began to break in the cracks in our all-too-closed minds."[40] John Weir Perry writes, "The vision of oneness is expressed in the messianic ideation, along with the recognition that the world is going to be marked by a style of living emphasizing equality and tolerance, harmony and love. This hope is almost universally seen in persons in the acute [psychotic] episode."[41]

Many of the mad have had this vision. Few have taken it seriously. I can think now of half a dozen people who were persuaded by psychiatrists that their messianic visions were symptoms of illnesses, and thus they gave them up. I can think of others who believe that these visions are private matters. I know there are many who have had such visions in their times of mania and madness, who could communicate these visions, both the idea and its power, to others. As I stated above, I think that the secular pluralism of the patients' liberation movement is based on the mistaken idea that these visions do not have any relevance to the public. Aurobindo's hope was that there would be a vanguard, pioneers who had experienced the new order of life and would seek to find a way to communicate "their idea and its power" to the masses. Among the mad are these pioneers. This is the basis for Mad Pride and for the Mad Pride movement.

Furthermore, Aurobindo says that the aim of a spiritual age would be one with the essential aim of subjective religions: "a new birth, a new consciousness, an upward evolution of the human being, a descent of the Spirit into our members, a spiritual reorganization of our lives."[42] Aurobindo acknowledged in another book that when Christianity first originated there was such an "awakening."[43] With Christianity in mind, no doubt, he warns of the danger of a new sectarian religion that begins with inspiration and devolves into "a set of crystallized dogmas" and "sanctified superstitions." Finally "the spirit is dominated by the outward machinery, the sheltering structure becomes a tomb." The root of this problem is the tendency of a particular religious belief and form "to universalize and impose itself," which runs "contrary to the variety of human nature and the need of the Spirit . . . for a spacious inner freedom and a large unity into which each man must be allowed to grow according to his own nature."[44] The idea of salvation in an after-life is also a diversion. What is essential is not man's ascent into heaven "but rather his ascent here into the Spirit and the descent of the Spirit into his normal humanity." "For that and not some post mortem salvation is the real new birth for which humanity waits as the crowning movement of its long obscure and painful course."[45]

And yet although religion poses these dangers I think Aurobindo realized that the new birth would find its expression and motivation in forms and symbols and archetypes derived from one religion or another, just as Aurobindo's own books were laced with phrases and ideas from the Hindu scriptures. Thus Aurobindo's terminology even here is religious— "rebirth," "conversion." "Even as the animal man has been largely converted into a mentalized humanity . . . so too now or in the future an evolution or conversion . . . of the present type of humanity into a spiritualized humanity is the need of the race and surely the intention of Nature."[46]

At the same time as Aurobindo warns the pioneers against imposing religious uniformity, he also acknowledges that a (tolerant) religious diversity is not just the alternative to uniformity but is also a positive feature, an asset. The "evolution or conversion" of humanity will be "the ideal or endeavor" of the pioneers. These pioneers will be "indifferent to particular belief and form and leave men to resort to the beliefs and forms to which they are naturally drawn." The pioneers will hold as "essential" "the faith in this spiritual conversion, the attempt to live it out and [they will hold essential] *whatever knowledge*—the form of opinion into which it is thrown does not so much matter—*can be converted into this living*" (my emphasis).[47] Obviously, by "belief" and "form of opinion," Aurobindo is referring to what is commonly called religion, and he recognizes human beings are "naturally drawn" to one kind or another of religious mythos and that these religious forms (that is, *some kind or another of religious form, regardless of which*) are themselves essential. But the religion must serve the ideal of spiritual and collective transformation, not divert persons into a quest for nirvanic escape or a postmortem salvation. Any kind of individualist soteriology is only a diversion from the deepest aspiration of the species.

My impression from my readings is that this kind of spiritual transformation took place among many Christians during the Second Awakening. Clearly by the end of the century, after the trauma of the Civil War, it was also followed by the sordid denouement Sri Aurobindo describes—and worse. The atavistic nature of Evangelical Christianity today is a major obstacle to change in America. Nevertheless, "The Human Cycle" is a sort of manual for those pioneers of the kingdom of God on Earth who need to go out and make converts—converts not to an exclusivist creed but to the way of life Aurobindo describes. No secular utopia can possibly have this kind of ontological reach; for secularists and those who do not accept reincarnation (or resurrection), salvation is only for other future generations, each doomed to extinction in its turn. The messianic element conveys the force of the ideal, its promise to liberate humanity from those very "laws" of nature—in reality, habits of nature—that keep us subject to disease and death.

I think Sri Aurobindo conveyed his vision most powerfully in *Savitri*—his epic 700-page poem that he considered his most important work. More powerfully than anywhere else, Aurobindo affirms the as yet unfulfilled promise of life on Earth, the potentiality also of romantic love, and reveals the relative effeteness of the ideal of liberation into unembodied existence. Adapted from a Hindu myth, in *Savitri* the heroine is not only a princess but also, as we discover, an avatar who has incarnated in order to do battle with death ("the last enemy," to quote St. Paul) and win the final victory for humanity. (Aurobindo manifests his feminism in his presentation of a woman as an avatar—unprecedented in the Hindu tradition.)

The heroine Savitri confronts the god of Death and scorns him when he advises her to accept the death of her husband, Satyavan—who, doomed to an early death, dies one year after Savitri's meeting with him. She pleads with Death to return her husband. Death tells her that she shares the fate of all human beings and that love on Earth is doomed, that no joy of the heart can last beyond death. Furthermore, by confronting Death, Savitri is quixotically pitting herself against the "laws" of nature, the decree of God. Savitri responds that human love has the sanction of the Divine. Death scoffs and advises her to realize that the world will always be a vale of sorrow and to seek instead the greater bliss (*ananda*) of extraworldly nirvana.

But Savitri rejects the postmortem nirvanic soteriology of Death. She scorns the boon of bodiless nirvana; she has another vision:

> *How sayst thou Truth can never light the human mind*
> *And Bliss can never invade the mortal's heart*
> *Or God descend into the world he made?*
> *If in the meaningless Void creation rose,*
> *If from a bodiless Force Matter was born,*
> *If Life could climb in the unconscious tree,*
> *Its green delight break into emerald leaves*
> *And its laughter of beauty blossom in the flower,*
> *If sense could wake in tissue, nerve and cell*
> *And Thought seize the grey matter of the brain,*
> *And soul peep from its secrecy through the flesh,*
> *How shall the nameless Light not leap on men,*
> *And unknown powers emerge from Nature's sleep? . . .*
> *Even now the deathless Lover's touch we feel:*
> *If the chamber's door is even a little ajar,*
> *What then can hinder God from stealing in*
> *Or who forbid his kiss on the sleeping soul?*
>
> *Already God is near, the Truth is close:*
> *Because the dark atheist body knows him not,*
> *Must the sage deny the Light, the seer his soul?*
> *I am not bound by thought or sense or shape;*
> *I live in the glory of the Infinite,*
> *I am near to the Nameless and Unknowable,*
> *The Ineffable is now my household mate.*
> *But standing on Eternity's luminous brink*
> *I have discovered that the world was He.*[48]

Savitri has discovered God in the world. She rejects the teaching that God can only be experienced apart from the world. She tells him that she too has experienced the blissful union with the Brahman beyond the world that is considered by Advaita Vedanta* to be the great-

---

*The philosophical system (of Sankara) most revered by scholars of Hinduism.

est mystical experience; she has met "Spirit with spirit," but she has also experienced human love, and that has changed everything.

Finally after hundreds of pages of a colloquy between Savitri and Death in which Savitri refutes all of Death's arguments that other-worldly union with the Divine is superior to the experience of God in the soul and body of her mate, Death finally concedes defeat. Death releases Satyavan, and Savitri and Satyavan are united again. They stand entwined "their kiss and passion-tranced embrace a meeting point, in their commingling spirits, one for ever, Two-souled, two-bodied for the joy of time."[49] They are now at the beginning of a new mission. God sends Savitri and Satyavan back to Earth, "a dual power of God in an ignorant world" to persuade humanity to forsake the ways of the past, to prepare humanity for the New Age, when man will "light up Truth's fire in Nature's night" and God will "annul the decree of death and pain." Thus will take place, as Mehta puts it, the indissoluble "marriage between Heaven and Earth."[50] (See the appendix for an excerpt describing the reunion and eternal bonding of Savitri and Satyavan.)

Despite all his caveats, Sri Aurobindo believed a cultural revitalization was the prerequisite for the inner change of the spirit among the masses, which would finally enable us to transcend what Hegel called "the slaughterbench of history." Such a revitalization requires a conversion of the masses—at least a significant portion of them. Aurobindo warns, "In this as in all great human aspirations . . . an a priori declaration of impossibility is a sign of ignorance and weakness. . . . A true beginning has to be made; the rest is a work for Time in its sudden achievements or its long patient labor."[51] Or in other words, "In proportion as they [the pioneers] succeed, and to the degree to which they carry this evolution, the yet unrealized potentiality which they represent will become an actual possibility of the future."[52]

It should be noted that besides perfectionism there is another similarity between Sri Aurobindo's messianic-redemptive vision and that of nineteenth-century postmillennial Christianity: the transformation will be a result of divine-human cooperation. (For reasons that require too much space to be explained here, Aurobindo believes the force that will assist the transformation will be the Divine Feminine—the Divine Mother.) This, as I noted in the introduction, was also the way Martin

Buber interpreted Jewish messianism—as a task involving both humanity and God. Aurobindo writes that "a fixed and unfailing aspiration that calls from below" will be met by "a Supreme grace from above that answers."[53] Mehta explains the fundamental dialectic of Sri Aurobindo's messianic vision of transformation: "Ascent without descent is a gospel of personal salvation, but Descent without Ascent is a gospel of passive existence. These two must constitute a rhythm of spiritual life—one without the other is incomplete."[54]

In summary, if one reads carefully "The Human Cycle" and other essays in *Social and Political Thought,* it is clear Sri Aurobindo believed, as did Perry and McLoughlin, that a process of cultural revitalization based on conveying a sense of the messianic vision—effecting a social conversion—could provide the conditions necessary for a profound spiritual transformation. He stated that the first step was for a sufficient number of people to become convinced that we could realize the kingdom of God on Earth. Unfortunately, the two revitalizations discussed in chapter 15 (the Great Awakenings) failed to achieve even the worldly changes to which they aspired. However, I would argue that both periods were actualizations of the messianic-redemptive vision and they were prefigurations, however imperfect, of the social-spiritual transformation that is yet to come. How long this will take we do not know, nor do we know how much destruction humanity will wreak first on the Earth. Scientists now tell us that if humanity does not mitigate global warming and reduce carbon emissions that humanity could be entirely destroyed.* Aurobindo tells us only that "a true beginning has to be made; the rest is a work for Time in its sudden achievements or its long patient labor."

---

*A problem that Aurobindo does not discuss, despite his egalitarianism and his sympathy to socialism, is the tremendous resistance to change presented by the ruling classes in the world with their control of the enormous military forces of the state. Aurobindo died in 1950, when it was still possible to be cautiously optimistic about the development of the United States—as he was—but America's trajectory has been steadily downward with the ascendancy of the American empire and, since 1980, with the subordination of all realms of life to corporate control and exploitation.

18

Whither Mad Pride?

The social activism of the nineteenth century and the 1960s was the product of and gave rise to a messianic-redemptive vision. The idea of the advent of the millennium engendered in the early nineteenth century several decades of a spiritualized political activism and of creative discontent with the status quo. Abolitionism itself was integrally connected to the messianic-redemptive vision—as illustrated so vividly in the life of that great America hero, Theodore Weld. As McLoughlin demonstrated, even the activism of the 1960s gained much of its strength from a messianic vision—albeit less explicit and more scattered than the unifying Christian ideal of the nineteenth-century Great Awakening.

My purview of the messianic periods in America and recapitulation of the arguments in favor of the efficacy of the messianic-redemptive vision by Perry, (H. Richard) Niebuhr, McLoughlin, Smith, and Sri Aurobindo constitutes an effort on my part to rehabilitate the messianic-redemptive vision and restore to it its credibility and luster in an age in which it has become an object of derision due to various factors. These factors include the corruption or evisceration of Christianity, the failure of secular messianic visions like Marxism, and the rise to hegemony of postmodern pluralism, which maintains a distrust or skepticism or cynicism about all "metanarratives," meaning all Romantic philosophies that envision an end of the conflict of man and nature, all unifying visions.

In nineteenth-century America, the messianic vision grew organically out of the Christian paradigm, although it was a Christian paradigm that had been revolutionized by the ideals of the American Revolution and the repudiation of Calvinism. By the 1960s American Christianity did not provide support for a vision of radical transformation—not among white students who regarded institutional Christianity as part of the past against which they were rebelling, and thus had no interest in reforming it. In the 1960s many in the counterculture, including some of its most well-known figures (e.g., the Beatles, Allen Ginsberg) turned East to Hinduism or Buddhism for spiritual wisdom and nurturance. Since Eastern religion did not have a messianic tradition, the radicals of the 1960s did not forge an enduring vision of messianic transformation. Although Sri Aurobindo had created a powerful messianic paradigm—he wrote thousands of pages on meditation, yoga, metaphysics, and social change and spent a lifetime in contemplation exploring the furthest reaches of human consciousness[1]—his work was too new to be assimilated by the masses (his books became available in America in the 1960s) and too philosophically recondite to have any popular appeal. One would have expected that the spiritually oriented countercultural intellectuals would have familiarized themselves with his books, but this never happened. Neither Allen Ginsberg nor Baba Ram Dass (Richard Alpert) nor R. D. Laing showed any awareness of Aurobindo's work. (Ultimately, the failure of Western intellectuals to read Aurobindo is one of the tragic enigmas of our time.)

Consequently, countercultural spokespersons tended to preach a spiritual existentialism, as expressed by Ram Dass's famous aphorism (and book title)—"Be Here Now"—and disparaged those who held messianic-redemptive visions as living in a fantasy, instead of the "now." In fact many countercultural gurus (Alan Watts, Krishnamurti) would have dismissed such a vision as the baggage of Western religion. Eckhart Tolle disparages utopianism as an escape from the present. These Eastern-oriented apostles of "the epiphany of the eternal present" (to borrow a phrase from left-wing Christian theologian Jurgen Moltmann) tend to forget that humanity currently lives under a regime of intolerable suffering and that historically a messianic vision of the future has resonated with our most profound—albeit suppressed or forgotten—aspirations and thus could motivate us to make the kind of sacrifices necessary to create a world in which all suffering is transcended. Like many "New Age" gurus, Tolle ignores the catastrophic threat of the environmental crisis. (Deepak Chopra is more socially aware than most "gurus.")

Many of today's New Age utopians have exchanged the 1960s' democratic and communalist vision (philosophically expounded by Sri Aurobindo) for an individualistic redemptionist vision imbued with the ethos of capitalism and the spirit of consumerism (e.g., "Abraham," channeled by Esther and Jerry Hicks), not to mention the various technocratic secular utopias spawned in the age of cybernetics.

The failure to ground messianic aspirations in a philosophical spiritual paradigm like Aurobindo's or a living spiritual tradition is one reason that Eastern mysticism and radical social transformation became sundered after a brief courtship in America in the 1960s and 1970s. (Liberation theology attempted to revitalize Christian theology in Latin America, but it had no impact in the privileged countries and was soon violently suppressed in Latin America.) The messianic-redemptive vision of the American Left had been based on secular theories like Marxism (often in new Romantic twentieth-century forms). The "New Age movement," which at first attempted to synthesize Eastern mysticism with a radical reformist political agenda, devolved in the 1980s for the most part into individual escapism and a potpourri of packaged shortcuts to "enlightenment"; thus it was susceptible (particularly a decade later) to the charges of "narcissism" leveled against it by leftist social critics.[2] The point should not, however, be overstated—this subculture still contains spiritual resources of resistance.

The messianic sensibility is rare today: one finds it in some New Age circles, and one can find it in European and British pockets of left-wing Christianity. It exists in a highly muted form in some schools of liberal or left-of-liberal American Christianity (e.g., process theology). However, it is unfortunate that although some of these theologians had famously entered into an extended and reportedly enriching dialogue with Buddhism, they have ignored Aurobindo's work, despite its similarities in some respects with their own philosophical forbear,

Alfred North Whitehead.*[3] In a secular form it is found among the radical left and the Greens. The messianic sensibility made a bold emergence (as shown in part 4) with the start of the Mad Pride movement in the United States—only to disappear soon thereafter. DuBrul and McNamara had been its strongest spokespersons in the Mad Pride movement, but DuBrul repudiated his Romantic vision (although not his activism) and McNamara stopped writing for The Icarus Project. The messianic-redemptive paradigm has not yet been clearly formulated by any of the current leaders in Mad Pride. (Although Mad Pride decries leadership it was obvious to me in 2007 that many Icaristas deferred to DuBrul and his ideas.) Paul Levy, an ally of Mad Pride, formulated a messianic vision explicitly in his writings (and in the interview in chapter 16), but Levy is not a spokesperson for Mad Pride and his ideas reach only a small readership. *The messianic consciousness typically appears spontaneously in the experience of madness itself* (as shown in the interviews with Whitney, DuBrul, and Levy), *but it has not been fully and consciously affirmed as a foundation of the Mad Pride movement.*

The various historical developments described above explain the eclipse of the messianic-redemptive perspective. It is my hope that the examples I have recalled and the argument I have made will help to restore interest in a messianic-redemptionist vision or at least to make it less easy for people to dismiss it with postmodernist condescension.

In the light of these considerations, I conclude this exploration of madness and Mad Pride by asking, What identity will Mad Pride assume in the future? Its hallmark today is the celebration of difference and diversity—in accord with the values of the postmodernist ethos.

---

*Despite some fundamental differences between Sri Aurobindo and Whitehead and Griffin, one would have expected, for example, that the ecumenical Christian theologian David Ray Griffin would have grappled with Sri Aurobindo's work, (as he does with many spiritual traditions) but it is evident from Griffin's writings that although he has heard of Aurobindo, he has not read him. Aurobindo's perspective, in fact, anticipated many of the very same points made in Griffin's scathing critique of what Griffin terms "deconstructive postmodernism"—as opposed to what Griffin terms "revisionary/constructive postmodernism," which, he contends, preserves such modern concepts as the self and historical meaning, while at the same time seeking to reveal or recover a positive meaning for such "pre-modern ideas" as divine reality or cosmic meaning. Clearly there are remarkable similarities with Sri Aurobindo's work.

(I will reiterate that I think there is much that is salutary about postmodernism. It has become the focus of my critique because of its effort to preempt unifying visions and because of its unsympathetic criticism of Romantic philosophies inspired by a redemptive vision.) Mad Pride is engendering a vital self-help movement. Will Mad Pride become a widespread self-help movement like the Twelve Step programs? This is not an unworthy goal in light of the destructiveness of the psychiatric system; as stated above it could rescue many persons who might become the prophets of a new order, as described by John Weir Perry.

More importantly, will Mad Pride also stake a claim to making a contribution to solving the problems of an "oppressive and damaged world," of a world that is insane and in need of redemption? The Icarus Project expressed this goal as part of the original agenda. Why *should* Mad Pride resign itself to representing only the mad? Could Mad Pride not become an instrument for the salvation of humanity? Is a "revolution in the mental health system"*—as Oaks calls for—sufficiently radical and inspiring as a goal to motivate the mad to great acts of sacrifice and devotion? I do not think so. It fails to strike the deeper chords in the collective imagination of the mad. The Mad Pride movement must set its heights much higher: it must learn to take its bearings from the mad themselves, who have said so often in private moments (in moments of authentic madness) that they were the prophets and messiahs of a new messianic age.

A truly authentic revolution will wipe away the entire professional "mental health" system. The "mental health system" is just another symptom of an insane and spiritually deranged society. Its purpose is to stabilize society. The "mental health system" cannot be "revolutionized." Attempting to humanize this system is not the solution. (Certainly Oaks's effort to limit its coercive power is valuable, but that cannot be an ultimate goal.) Now *for the first time in history* there exists a Mad Pride movement that collectively searches (sometimes) for light and guidance in the visions of the mad and resists the dismissal and denigration of these visions as symptoms of mental illness. I suggest that a messianic-redemptive vision would enable the mad to fulfill their

---

*Frankly, I personally find the very idea of a "mental health system" dispiriting.

role as natural catalysts of social/spiritual transformation—of a revolution in society.

The Mad Pride movement then faces a choice. It can embrace a messianic-redemptive vision or resign itself to becoming just a self-help movement or a pressure group inside the psychiatric system. What methods it might use to influence others in this age of multimedia—to bring about the cultural transformation—is another question, beyond our scope here. It would require thought and deliberation and imagination. Paul Levy gives an interesting example in his book of a practice that could be adopted by Mad Pride. He writes in his essay "Art-Happening Called Global Awakening":

> We can become what I call an "in-phase dreaming circle," which is actually an organism of a higher dimension. Instead of there being x-number of seemingly separate, fragmented selves, in an in-phase dreaming circle we recognize our interdependence and interconnectedness. We realize that we are all on the same side, that we are not separate, but all parts of a greater being. Once we realize this, we discover that it is literally within our God-given power to collaboratively hook up with each other and put our sacred power of dreaming together in such a way that we can change the dream we are having and literally dream ourselves awake. This is a radical, revolutionary, and epochal quantum leap in consciousness that is fully capable of being imagined into being in this very moment.[4]

There could be Mad Pride dreaming circles coordinated all over the country, all over the world—based on the images and visions experienced by the mad as prefigurations of the world to come. There are, of course, also Mad Pride events that have already taken place, as David Oaks discusses, and will continue to be sponsored. (Many of these focus on reforming the "mental health system.") My point is that if Mad Pride is to become more than a self-help movement, if it decides changing the mental health system is too meager a goal for a society on the verge of self-extinction, then the first and most important step is to commit itself as a movement to a vision of the salvation and messianic transformation of humanity, of nature, and of the Earth.

There can be no gainsaying the gravity of our situation. Furthermore, I repeat, it is now clear that humanity is facing the greatest and most decisive crisis in its 2.5 million-year-old history or, more aptly, in our ten-thousand-year history as a civilization: will we survive? "We have exhausted our natural resources to engage in an orgy of consumption and waste that poisoned the earth and degraded the ecosystem on which human life [and that of other species] depends," wrote Pulitzer Prize winning author Chris Hedges. Most Americans do not know about the dangers because there is a complete blackout on the news. Noam Chomksy wrote, "Practically every country in the world is taking at least halting steps to do something about [global warming]. The United States is taking steps backward. A propaganda system, openly acknowledged by the business community, declares that climate change is all a liberal hoax: Why pay attention to these scientists? . . . Something must be done in a disciplined, sustained way, and soon. It won't be easy to proceed. There will be hardships and failures, it's inevitable. But unless the process that's taking place here (at Occupy Boston) and elsewhere in the country and around the world continues to grow and becomes a major force in society and politics, the chances for a decent future are bleak. You can't achieve significant initiatives without a large, active, popular base."[5] Although it is too late to stop climate change, most of the experts writing about it think that if we act quickly (within five to ten years) we can avoid its most catastrophic effects: we can save humanity from extinction. But the United States, under President Obama, refuses to make a commitment to lowering carbon emissions before 2020.

Hedges states, "We face a terrible political truth. Those who hold power will not act with the urgency required to protect human life and the ecosystem. [Not just human life—two hundred species die every day.] Decisions about the fate of the planet . . . are in the hands of moral and intellectual trolls. . . ." "Our corporate and political masters are driven by a craven desire to accumulate wealth at the expense of human life. The leaders of these corporations now determine our fate. Their greed has turned workers into global serfs and our planet into a wasteland."[6] Our political leaders, like Barack Obama, depend on these corporations for millions of dollars in campaign contributions, and they repay them by opening up vast regions for deep water drilling—like the kind done by British Petroleum.

This is a time of kairos. It is up to us to decide: Do we want to continue life on Earth? Was this the meaning of our origins over two million years ago—that humanity, led by men and women who debase themselves worshipping the idol of greed, would be destroyed? These are gangsters and sociopaths who have taken hold of America and are content to put an end to humanity forever, insane men drunk with a sense of their own power. There must be a new awakening if there is to be a chance of saving life on Earth. What could be more alarming, what greater motivation to change our actions, than the apocalyptic warnings of ordinarily staid scientists—ecologists, geologists, systems analysts, physicists—transformed by indignation and concern for their children into thundering prophets.

The Eastern Christian theologian Father Georges Florovsky (1893–1979) explained the Eastern Christian diagnosis: "According to St Anthanasius the human fall consists precisely in the fact that man limits himself to himself, that man becomes as it were in love with himself. . . . And through his concentration on himself man separates himself from God, and broke the spiritual and free contact with God. It was a spiritual narcissism, a despiritualization of human existence. . . . Separated from God, personality vanishes, is stricken with a spiritual sterility."[7]

Will we allow the corporate CEOs and their political minions to burn out the universe in the rapacious hunger for more money, more profits, more more more more—trapped in loveless existences, in their virtual reality bubbles, in spiritual narcissism? There will be an awakening because there must be an awakening, because we have squandered the gifts of God. There must be a nonviolent revolution—not to change the mental health system, but to change this insane society, to determine whether there will be any future life on Earth.

Why have human beings and the mad had these messianic visions? It is as if the cosmos, or God, wills that our messianic dream be realized in history. Richard Tarnas writes that the human intelligence is the cosmos's intelligence, expressing the cosmos's creative brilliance, the human imagination is "grounded in the cosmic imagination," is in fact the cosmos's intelligence expressing its creative spirit, expressing its sense of infinite plenitude in time. Tarnas says that the larger spirit, intelligence, and imagination—God?—"all live within and act through the self reflective human being who serves as a unique vessel and embodiment of the cosmos. . . . unfolding the whole, integral to the whole, perhaps even essential to the whole."[8] One might add that all suffering, all wars, whether between humans or between "man" and "nature," result from our failure to recognize or remember our relationship to the whole, to humanity, to nature, to the cosmos, to God. We need only draw on the power of this imagination to bring unity to the splintered body of humanity, to heal the created order, thus realizing the messianic vision of our prophets and seers, from Isaiah to Jesus to Sri Aurobindo, the dream of harmony, of immortality, of eternal love, of paradise on Earth.

Every time there is a kairos, an opportunity to make an eschatological leap, demonic forces rally to oppose it and have sabotaged us each time. We have one weapon we rarely use: the power of the messianic vision. The alternative, the "wrath" of God as the prophets and revivalists called it, has become more destructive each time. This time it threatens to destroy all life. We must make the ontological leap.

To empower the vision, those in Mad Pride—those who have been labeled psychotic— need to reaffirm the mission statement of The Icarus Project. This also means going beyond the single-issue focus of Mind Freedom, which did not even discuss political developments on its website during the years of the radical changes implemented by the Bush administration. (It is clear to those who know him that politically David Oaks is, like his hero Martin Luther King Jr., far "left" of "center," although he wisely wants to avoid "left-right" terminology.) Mad Pride organizations can and should participate, for example, in Occupy Wall Street—as representatives *of* Mad Pride.

They should participate in popular movements against the kind of wars that the United States has initiated since the Vietnam War ended. I suspect that the reason that psychiatric survivors' organizations (like Mind Freedom) and Mad Pride groups (like The Icarus Project) did not participate in such protests *qua Mad Pride organizations* was for fear of "dividing" its membership, but this is a bugaboo. I do not know a single person who had been labeled a "psychotic"—a single mad person, and I know many—who was not opposed, for example, to the United States bombing of Iraq in 2003. The values that emerge from the crucible of madness are in accord with the yearning for world peace and ecological harmony—as Perry contended above. (I know that *every* person interviewed in this book was against the Iraq war from the start.) The same is true with the environmental crisis, the financial crisis, the torture of prisoners (this is a mad issue akin to torture of mental patients), animal rights, and other human rights and ecological issues.

Mad Pride activists should join in public protests as a Mad Pride group. Mad Pride needs to define itself in broader political terms than it does at present—even if it loses a few members. Mad people need to go beyond acting like, and being seen as, just another special interest group. Mad people are a group particularly concerned with the plight of humanity, as DuBrul and McNamara wrote in the mission statement and in essays or blog entries during the first few years after they founded The Icarus Project.

Mad Pride should allow its messianic vision(s) to inform and guide and impel its political activism, for the sake of humanity. For all earthly beings it is important for the Mad Pride movement to keep alive, through cultivation, its vision *of world transformation, not of the transformation of the mental health system.* It should insist on its power and right to "imagine big possibilities," of a vision so "vast" that it gets labeled "delusions of grandeur" by psychiatrists—as Ashley McNamara wrote in her essay on shamanism (see chapter 8). Mad Pride should affirm a vision as grand and profound as that of Sri Aurobindo and the Mother.

> *O Sun-Word, Thou shalt raise the earth-soul to Light*
> *And bring down God into the lives of men;*
> *Earth shall be my work-chamber and my house*
> *My garden of life to plant a seed divine.*
> *The mind of earth shall be a home of light,*
> *The life of earth a tree growing towards heaven,*
> *The body of earth a tabernacle of God.*[9]

This book has told the story of six "psychotics" who did the impossible, the miraculous—they lead healthy, full lives as creatively maladjusted persons. It gives a sense of how human beings can and do venture far beyond the limits of consensus reality, but at the cost of being labeled "psychotic." I have also attempted to illustrate the viability of the messianic-redemptive vision. It is my opinion that this is the only solution to the insanity of the world. If nothing else, this book is a call to all those who are mad, or just heretics, to commit ourselves to a utopian or messianic-redemptive vision, to a realization of the kingdom of heaven, of God/Goddess, the divine life on Earth, as the basis for a new, spiritually informed political activism.

Epilogue

Beating the System

*A*s I stated in the preface, I hoped to accomplish a number of goals with this book. One of the goals is to encourage "patients" by telling "true stories" of persons who were captured by the mental health system and diagnosed as chronically mentally ill, yet who broke away and far exceeded psychiatric expectations. I hope to break the evil spell cast by Psychiatry on the minds of its victims. Thus it is my hope that many of these persons reading this book will think "Aha! There is hope for me. If Caty Simon or David Oaks or Paul Levy could go through all that, if they could be so mad—so 'mentally ill'—and wean themselves off their 'meds' and stay out of psychiatric hospitals and become examples to others, then so can I. These stories prove that the psychiatrists who tell me I have an illness like diabetes and that my brain is flawed are wrong. I want to make contact with other people who are going through something like me and are breaking away from psychiatry. I want to join the Mad Pride movement." It is my hope that many of the persons who have this response will aspire not to be well-adjusted but to become creatively maladjusted. So to facilitate this process I will briefly note below a few of the characteristics the six heroes and heroines of this book have in common.

The Hero's Journey

Every person I interviewed was diagnosed as seriously mentally ill by the mental health system—either schizophrenic or bipolar and usually both at different times depending on the individual psychiatrist. Each of them in different ways proved the system wrong. All but one got off the psychiatric drugs that they supposedly needed to function. All are involved in creative work and/or working to change society.

One of the subjects takes psychiatric drugs (or one drug) and is convinced that he needs them. However, as I demonstrated, it is notable that unlike the other interviewees he has long held to the notion that he needs these drugs in order to stay sane. I have argued that his dependence on the drugs is created in large part by his belief that he needs these drugs. This conviction constitutes a self-fulfilling prophecy. Thus every person interviewed in this book—and thousands of others I have met over twenty years—proves the mad are not "mentally ill." Every person who has been given a psychiatric diagnosis can read this book and be assured that she is not mentally ill and that with support she can also wean herself off of psychiatric drugs. (If she has been on them for years and she has developed an addiction to them, then the addiction would be extremely hard to break.) *Mad people can take heart from the extraordinary accomplishments of the persons interviewed in this book.*

Sascha DuBrul is the cofounder of the organization that launched the Mad Pride movement in America. David Oaks is the leader of the largest patients' rights' organization that ever existed. In the late 1970s he had a breakdown/breakthrough and was diagnosed as schizophrenic by multiple psychiatrists. If psychiatry had been correct or if Oaks had followed their recommendations, he would be in "day treatment" today, performing menial tasks and taking antipsychotic drugs. Paul Levy, who is a brilliant spiritual teacher today—consulted for advice by many teachers and therapists, including psychiatrists—was overwhelmed by madness for many years. He regards this ordeal as an initiation. However, he also believes that had he found help from the mental health system—family therapy, for instance—his problems would have been resolved in a brief period of time. Caty Simon spent years in anguish until she found that the solution for her problems was getting off of psychiatric drugs, assuming responsibility for her actions, and becoming a creatively maladjusted member of a Mad Pride community. It was the Mad Pride community, not the mental health professionals, that helped this woman who putatively was afflicted by "bipolar" and "borderline personality disorder."

The stories presented in this book prove psychiatry is a failure—a failure for those who looked to it for help. It is hugely successful at making money—at the cost of its clients' well-being and lives. Most of the persons interviewed felt that their experiences on psychiatric wards were far more traumatizing than the original problems that led them to fall into the clutches of the psychiatric system. Each subject illustrates the destructive effects of psychiatric labeling. Dr. Ed Whitney's account is striking. He was "psychotic" for a year, and he had undergone an experience he called the "dark night of the soul." However, by far the worst experience, the one that almost destroyed him spiritually, took place when he went back a few months later to talk to the head of psychiatry at the hospital where he had been incarcerated.

He was told in no uncertain terms that all of the strange, marvelous, and terrifying experiences he had were purely the result of aberrant biochemistry. Dr. Whitney wrote, "The head of psychiatry at the hospital told me that I was in denial if I insisted that I had been having a spiritual crisis. No, he said, this is a medical disorder like asthma or diabetes. I was devastated, and I was feeling suicidal within hours. I could not argue with his self-assured, expert manner." Dr. Whitney told me, "The whole episode [his spiritual revelation] meant nothing as far as the psychiatrist was concerned; it was just a case of bad DNA making defective protoplasm. If I had accepted the medical model of my experience, I would not have survived to tell this tale. Despair would have consumed me."

Paul Levy also illustrates the negative effect of diagnosis. He says repeatedly that he could only begin healing once he understood that his experiences were not merely "personal," not merely the result of personal quirks, but were archetypal experiences. They were fractal reflections in his life of the universal obstacles with which all of humanity has to contend in its struggle to find itself.

In considering each person in this book, account must be taken not only of the considerable trauma inflicted on them by Psychiatry but also what the psychiatric system failed to do—to help resolve the problems of living that led them to go for help in the first place. There is not a person in this book who could not have been spared considerable suffering if Psychiatry was the healing force it claimed to be. Once in a while, the subject would find a therapist who was helpful, but for the most part the only "angels" my subjects encountered were fellow patients. The fact is that every person in this book is a hero or heroine who fought the dark angel, the demon of Psychiatry, and survived—and was stronger for the experience. Unlike Jacob or Israel they did not receive a blessing and a new name *from psychiatry* to compensate them for their injury. Psychiatry insisted to the end that they were mentally ill. *They were rechristened by their peers*—as mad persons, as shamans, as creatively maladjusted political activists, as wounded healers, as artists, as visionaries, as messiahs.

There are many similarities between the experiences of the different subjects that would be fruitful to explore, but that is largely outside the scope of this book. However, and just to take one example: note how both DuBrul and Levy felt they were possessed by the spirit of their fathers, or rather a spirit that had taken over their fathers. Since DuBrul's father was dead, his theory may sound far-fetched—"delusional," Psychiatry would say. But Levy's account of the archetypal nature of this kind of experience makes DuBrul's account more plausible. DuBrul's father was far more benevolent than Levy's, but like Levy's father, DuBrul's father identified strongly with his adolescent son and wanted to guide him. There is no reason, besides metaphysical prejudice, to exclude the theory that he may have been attempting to do so from the other side of the grave.

The stories also accomplish another goal; they convey a sense of what Mad Pride is doing. By creating alternatives to psychiatry, the Mad Pride movement is helping many of the mad to wean themselves off psychiatric drugs and is literally saving thousands (of course, this is only a small minority of those in the mental health system) from being inducted into lifetime careers as chronic mental patients, of being emotionally and intellectually disabled by psychiatric drugs, being infantilized and spiritually destroyed by Psychiatry, spending their lives as zombies in residential houses, and of participating daily in degradation rituals in day treatment. These day treatment centers are extremely demeaning. For example, one woman I know—who is perfectly trusting and rational—is in a program where the patients do menial labor for a few cents an hour and are forced by the program managers to wear badges pinned to their chest, with their diagnosis written on the badge: hers reads "Paranoid Schizophrenic." (I know her well enough to state she is not paranoid at all; on the contrary, she is very trusting.) Mad Pride is thus multiplying by a thousandfold the ranks of the *creatively* maladjusted, of the prophets and visionaries who may help to bring about a process of cultural revitalization, who may help to formulate the myths (see chapter 16) that will help society to make a transition to a new order.

Yet this may not be sufficient. It may require a Mad Pride community dedicated to changing the world. At present, Mad Pride is not oriented to the goal outlined in the mission statement of The Icarus Project. To reiterate, "We believe we have mad gifts to be cultivated and taken care of, rather than diseases or disorders to be suppressed or eliminated. By joining together as individuals and as a community, the intertwined threads of madness, creativity, and collaboration can inspire hope and transformation in an oppressive and damaged world."

Appendix

Extracts from Sri Aurobindo's *Savitri*

The poignancy of Sri Aurobindo's messianic vision can best be experienced through his own words. I have selected a few extracts from *Savitri*, which is described above in chapter 18 on Sri Aurobindo. Sri Aurobindo's work is the greatest example of a modern messianic vision.* By reconciling the ancient messianic vision with its modern context it demands to be taken seriously; it cannot be facilely dismissed as the product of archaic society unenlightened by the highest knowledge of science. As well as a gift to humanity, Sri Aurobindo wrote this poem for his own soulmate (to use a modern term that became popular years after Sri Aurobindo's death), a French woman, Mira Richard, known as "the Mother." They met when Richard, a longtime student of occult wisdom, came to India to be a disciple of Sri Aurobindo. Soon thereafter he recognized her as his equal and his partner. Their relationship was not physical as both believed sexual union would impede their spiritual work and their spiritual union. (As stated in chapter 17, Sri Aurobindo spent years in seclusion, which he believed necessary for his yoga. During that time he spoke to one person only—the Mother.) Sri Aurobindo was the only well-known Indian sage who had a spiritual partner. (Despite his reverence for her, Ramakrishna's wife was submissive, as tradition dictated.)

---

*This poem is over 700 pages. I can only convey a general sense of his vision in these short excerpts.

Most of the disciples found in *Savitri* a thinly veiled autobiographical account of Sri Aurobindo and the Mother's spiritual paths. Although Aurobindo's vision of the attainment of physical immortality is the focus of *Savitri*, Aurobindo also discussed it in many of his philosophical works. (For a superb discussion of the metaphysical and scientific aspects see *The Destiny of the Body*[1] by one of Aurobindo's disciples.) We also find the idea of attaining an eternal spiritualized body in Christianity. For example, St. Gregory of Nyssa in the fourth century depicted death as a result of our estrangement from God. Many Russian Christian theologians thought death was unnatural, a product of sin, as St. Paul said.

In the poem, Savitri confronts the god of Death and scorns him when he advises her to accept the death of her husband, Satyavan—who, doomed to an early death, dies one year after Savitri's meeting with him:

> *My spirit has glimpsed the glory for which it came*
> *Beating of one vast heart in the flame of things*
> *My eternity clasped by his eternity*
> *And tireless of the sweet abysms of Time*
> *Deep possibility always to love*
> *This, this is first, last joy and to its throb*
> *The riches of a thousand fortunate years*
> *Are a poverty.*

But Death tells her that she shares the fate of all human beings. And that love on the Earth is doomed, that no joy of the heart can last beyond death:

> *If God there is he cares not for the world;*
> *All things he sees with calm indifferent gaze,*
> *He has doomed all hearts to sorrow and desire,*
> *He has bound all life with his implacable laws; . . .*
> *He sees as minute details mid the stars*
> *The animal's agony and the fate of man:*
> *Immeasurably wise, he exceeds thy thought;*
> *His solitary joy needs not thy love . . .*

Furthermore, Death says Savitri is quixotically pitting herself against the "laws" of nature, the decree of God, and that even God is subject to the laws he made. This theology is common among those Christians who believe that theology must be subordinated to science. For many liberal Christians today, "reality" is revealed by scientific naturalism. Such a reification of science conflicts with the understanding of Christianity emphasized in St. Paul and preserved in Eastern Christian theology: death is a product of the fall, science describes the "laws" in the "fallen" universe only, the universe estranged from its divine source.

Aurobindo's perspective is similar to Eastern Christianity: laws only seem eternal. Laws are, in fact, habits of man/woman and nature; they are subject to inertia as all habits are. Although many modern scientists also believe laws are really habits of nature, most treat laws as if they are independently decreed by nature and eternal, an inference questioned by the great skeptic David Hume. So when Death responds to Savitri, his words carry the inflection of modern science:

> *The cosmic law is greater than thy will,*
> *Even God himself obeys the Laws he made*
> *The Law abides and never can it change*
> *The Person is a bubble on Time's sea . . .*
> *This truth I know that Satyavan is dead*
> *And even thy sweetness cannot lure him back.*
> *No magic Truth can bring the dead to life*
> *No power of earth cancel the thing once done*
> *No joy of the heart can last surviving death*
> *No bliss persuade the past to live again.*

But Savitri responds that human love has the sanction of the Divine:

> *My will is greater than thy law, O Death;*
> *My love is stronger than the bonds of Fate:*
> *Our love is the heavenly seal of the Supreme . . .*
> *Love must not cease to live upon the earth;*
> *For love is the bright link twixt earth and heaven,*
> *Love is the far Transcendent's angel here . . .*

Death scoffs and advises her to realize that the world will always be a vale of sorrow and to seek instead the greater bliss (ananda) of extra-worldly nirvana. This soteriology posits that the greatest and most authentic happiness* can be found only by those who are liberated from worldly existence and absorbed into Brahman, the godhead. This is different from the Western idea of heaven, but the similarities are salient. Death says:

> *Dream not to change the world that God has planned . . .*
> *If heavens there are whose doors are shut to grief*
> *There seek the joy thou couldst not find on earth.*
> *Turn then to God, for him leave all behind;*
> *Forgetting love, forgetting Satyavan,*
> *Annul thyself in his immobile peace.*
> *O soul, drown in his still beatitude.*
> *For thou must die to thyself to reach God's height.*

But Savitri rejects the postmortem nirvanic soteriology of Death. She scorns the boon of bodiless nirvana; she has another vision (see chapter 18 for Savitri's rebuttal to Death's claim above that lasting joy cannot and will not be found on Earth.) In the verse below, Savitri tells Death she has discovered God in the world. She tells him that she too has experienced the blissful union with the Brahman beyond the world; she has met "Spirit with spirit," but as she sees it, this experience no longer seems unsatisfying to her. To one who has also experienced human love at its height, the beloved appears as a manifestation of God. This experience has given her a sense of kinship with all mortals who love and who die:

> *I have met Spirit with spirit, Self with self,*
> *But I have loved too the body of my God.*
> *I have pursued him in his earthly form.*

---

*The Hindu term for bliss, *ananda,* has a different meaning in the Hindu context, closer to bliss-happiness. It has the intensity of bliss, but unlike the English term, *ananda* connotes a spiritual and existential bliss, as opposed to a mere pleasurable sensation.

A lonely freedom cannot satisfy
A heart that has grown one with every heart:
I am a deputy of the aspiring world,
My spirit's liberty I ask for all.

Finally, Savitri has answered all Death's arguments and stands waiting before him, a testimony to the power of will, the will to love that has conquered all the lower aspirations in humanity, even the aspiration to be merged into God. Death is silent, revealing that his power is not supreme. Savitri hears the voice of God:

I hail thee almighty and victorious Death
Thou art my shadow and my instrument
And the sharp sword of terror and grief and pain
To force the soul of man to struggle for light . . .
But now O timeless mightiness stand aside . . .
Release the soul of the world called Satyavan
That he may stand master of life and fate
The mate of Wisdom and the spouse of Light
The eternal bridegroom of the eternal bride.

In this last line Sri Aurobindo explicitly formulates what he believes is our destiny as humans, God's will for men and women: that each shall be paired and bonded eternally, in bodies not subject to death. Book Ten, "The Book of Eternal Night" ends:

The dire universal shadow disappeared
Vanishing into the Void from which it came.

God offers Savitri and Satyavan the freedom to live in a realm free from ignorant humanity. But Savitri replies:

In vain thou temptst with solitary bliss
Two spirits saved out of a suffering world;
My soul and his indissolubly linked
In the one task for which our lives were born,

To raise the world to God in deathless Light,
To bring God down to the world on earth we came,
To change the earthly life to life divine.

God acknowledges Savitri's choice, and tells Savitri and Satyavan of their mission:

Descend to life with him thy heart desires.
O Satyavan, O luminous Savitri,
I sent you forth of old beneath the stars,
A dual power of God in an ignorant world,
In a hedged creation shut from limitless self,
Bringing down God to the insentient globe,
Lifting earth-beings to immortality.
In the world of my knowledge and my ignorance
Where God is unseen and only is heard a Name
And knowledge is trapped in the boundaries of mind
And life is hauled in the drag-net of desire
And Matter hides the soul from its own sight,
You are my Force at work to uplift earth's fate,
My self that moves up the immense incline
Between the extremes of the spirit's night and day.
He is my soul that climbs from nescient Night
Through life and mind and supernature's Vast
To the supernal light of Timelessness
And my eternity hid in moving Time.

God tells Savitri and Satyavan that human beings live in ignorance, but there shall come a time soon when all this will change. Savitri has demonstrated that she is the "Mighty Mother"—the Divine Mother—who has taken birth in time. This is how Sri Aurobindo regarded his partner, Mira Richard, and this is also how the disciples viewed her. God tells Savitri and Satyavan of the future that will be. (This is the consummation of the messianic vision Sri Aurobindo shared with the Mother.)

The Traveller now treads in the Ignorance,
Unaware of his next step, not knowing his goal . . .
But when the hour of the Divine draws near,
The Mighty Mother shall take birth in Time
And God be born in human clay
In forms made ready by your human lives
All earth shall be the Spirit's manifest home,
Hidden no more by the body and the life,
Hidden no more by the mind's ignorance . . .

This world shall be God's visible garden house
The earth shall be a field and camp of God
Man shall forget consent to mortality
And his embodied frail impermanence . . .

Man too shall turn towards the Spirit's call . . .
Awake to his hidden possibility
Awake to all that slept within his heart
And all that Nature meant when earth was formed
And the Spirit made this ignorant world his home,
He shall aspire to Truth and God and Bliss . . .

The frontiers of the Ignorance shall recede
More and more souls shall enter into light . . .
These separate selves the Spirit's oneness feel
These senses of heavenly sense grow capable
The flesh and nerves of a strange ethereal joy
And mortal bodies of immortality

Thus shall the earth open to divinity
And common natures feel the wide uplift
Illumine common acts with the Spirit's ray
And meet the deity in common things.
Nature shall live to manifest secret God,
The Spirit shall take up the human play,
This earthly life become the life divine . . .

Notes

Introduction.
Discovering the Higher Sanity within Madness

1. Levy, "God the Imagination," www.awakeninthedream.com/wordpress/?p =170 (accessed October 24, 2011).
2. *Newsweek,* "Listening to Madness," www.newsweek.com/2009/05/01 /listening-to-madness.html (accessed October 24, 2011).
3. Kutchins and Kirk, *Making Us Crazy.*
4. Laing, *Politics of Experience.*
5. Morrison, *Talking Back to Psychiatry,* 103, 104–5.
6. Ibid., 103.
7. Breggin, *Toxic Psychiatry,* 354–62.
8. Laing, *Politics of Experience,* 76.
9. King, "Speech to American Psychiatric Association" and "Speech to Lincoln University," www.mindfreedom.org/kb/mental-health-global/iaacm (accessed November 8, 2011).
10. Laing, *Politics of Experience,* 120.
11. Reddy, *Footnotes to the Future,* 124.
12. Ibid., 125.
13. Aurobindo, *Social and Political Thought,* 350.
14. Heinberg, *Memories and Visions of Paradise.*
15. Reddy, *Footnotes to the Future,* 154.
16. O'Callaghan, "Interview with John Weir Perry," www.global-vision.org/papers /JWP.pdf, 14 (accessed October 24, 2011); and Perry, *The Heart of History,* 207.

17. Gosden, *Schismatic Mind,* 165, 170. Available at http://sites.google.com /site/richardgosden/phd (accessed October 24, 2011).

18. Levy, *Madness of George W. Bush,* 215–16.

19. Perry, *Trials of the Visionary Mind,* 48.

20. Ibid., 48–49.

21. Laing, *Politics of Experience,* 129.

22. Ibid., 120.

23. Kumar, *Religion and Utopia,* 65.

24. Luzkow, *What's Left,* 83.

25. Ibid., 82–85.

26. Lowy, *Redemption and Utopia,* 51.

27. Ibid., 51.

28. Ibid., 55.

29. Ibid.

30. Ibid., 13.

31. Idel, *Messianic Mystics,* 323.

32. Levy, "The Artist as Healer of the World," www.awakeninthedream.com /wordpress/?p=162 (accessed October 24, 2011).

33. The Icarus Project, *Friends Make the Best Medicine.*

34. The Icarus Project, "Mission Statement," http://theicarusproject.net/about -us/icarus-project-mission-statement (accessed October 25, 2011).

35. McNamara, "In This Society the Mystics Will Always Live on the Margins," 68.

36. Ibid., 68.

37. Ibid., 66.

38. Ibid., 70.

39. Morrison, *Talking Back to Psychiatry,* 78; Chamberlin, *On Our Own.*

40. Tarnas, *Passion of the Western Mind,* 401.

41. Ibid.

42. Jacoby, *End of Utopia.*

43. Millett, *Loony-Bin Trip,* 85.

44. Serine, "Anybody else think god gave them a mission to save the world?" online discussion in The Icarus Project Forum: Alternate Dimensions or Psychotic Delusions?, started February 7, 2007, http://theicarusproject.net /forums/viewtopic.php?f=21&t=8135 (accessed October 25, 2011).

45. Levy, "Are We Possessed?" www.awakeninthedream.com/wordpress/?p=211 (accessed October 25, 2011).

46. Levy, *Madness of George W. Bush,* 146–47.

47. Laing, *Politics of Experience,* 28.

48. Ibid., 157.

49. Abzug, *Cosmos Crumbling,* 5.

50. Ibid.

51. McLoughlin, *Revivals, Awakenings, and Reform,* 8.

52. Smecker and Jensen, "You Can't Kill a Planet and Live on It Too," www.truth-out.org/you-cant-kill-planet-and-live-it-too/1310403275 (accessed November 9, 2011).

53. Speth, *Bridge at the Edge of the World,* 26–27; Orr, *Down to the Wire.*

54. Smecker and Jensen, "You Can't Kill a Planet and Live on It Too," www.truth-out.org/you-cant-kill-planet-and-live-it-too/1310403275 (accessed October 24, 2011); O'Callaghan, "Interview with John Weir Perry," www.global-vision.org/papers/JWP.pdf, 14 (accessed October 24, 2011).

55. Perry, *Trials of the Visionary Mind,* 48.

Chapter 1. Interview with Peter Stastny, M. D.: The Psychiatric-Pharmaceutical Complex and Its Critics

1. Breggin, *Toxic Psychiatry,* 354–60.

2. Farber, *Madness, Heresy, and the Rumor of Angels.*

3. Stastny and Lehmann, eds., *Alternatives beyond Psychiatry.*

4. The International Network toward Alternatives and Recovery, intar.org (accessed October 25, 2011).

5. Breggin, *Toxic Psychiatry,* 362–64.

6. Hornstein, *Agnes's Jacket,* 30–43.

7. Harris, Carey, and Roberts, "Psychiatrists, Children, and the Drug Industry's Role," www.nytimes.com/2007/05/10/health/10psyche.html?pagewanted=all (accessed October 25, 2011).

8. Stastny and Lehmann, eds., *Alternatives beyond Psychiatry.*

9. Whitaker, *Mad in America.*

10. Seikkula, "Open Dialogues."

Chapter 2. The Mind Freedom Hunger Strike

1. Boysen, "An Evaluation of the DSM Concept of Mental Disorder," 164.

2. Boysen, ibid. For a discussion of the weaknesses of Freudianism, see Farber, "Institutional Mental Health and Social Control," www.academyanalyticarts.org/farber.htm (accessed October 26, 2011); and Farber, "Augustinianism and the Psychoanalytic Metanarrative."

3. Boysen, "An Evaluation of the DSM Concept of Mental Disorder," 164.

4. Breggin, *Toxic Psychiatry*, 354.

5. Ibid., 354.

6. Ibid.

7. Ibid., 355.

8. Ibid.

9. Ibid.

10. Szasz, *Coercion as Cure*, 12.

11. Ibid., 59–60.

12. Ibid., 58–59.

13. Ibid., 59.

14. Farber, *Eternal Day*.

15. Pagels, *Adam, Eve, and the Serpent*.

16. Farber, *Eternal Day*.

17. John Breeding's website, www.wildestcolts.com (accessed October 26, 2011).

18. Mosher, "Resignation from APA," www.moshersoteria.com/articles/resignation-from-apa (accessed October 26, 2011).

19. Morrison, *Talking Back to Psychiatry*, 99–130.

20. Edds, "California Hunger Strike Challenges Use of Antidepressants," www.whatcausesmentalillness.com/research/mindfreedom-hunger-strike/the-washington-post (accessed October 26, 2011).

21. "Original Statement by the Fast for Freedom in Mental Health," July 28, 2003, www.whatcausesmentalillness.com/research/mindfreedom-hunger-strike/original-statement-by-the-fast-for-freedom-in-mental-health (accessed October 26, 2011).

22. Ibid.

23. "Response from APA," August 12, 2003, www.whatcausesmentalillness.com/research/mindfreedom-hunger-strike/response-from-apa (accessed October 26, 2011).

24. "Fast for Freedom Scientific Panel Reply to the APA," August 22, 2003, www.whatcausesmentalillness.com/research/mindfreedom-hunger-strike/scientific-panel-addresses-apa-claims (accessed October 26, 2011).

25. Boysen, "An Evaluation of the DSM Concept of Mental Disorder," 164.

26. "American Psychological Association 'Statement on Diagnosis and Treatment of Mental Disorders,'" September 26, 2003, www.whatcausesmentalillness.com/research/mindfreedom-hunger-strike/apa-statement-on-quot-diagnosis-and-treatment-of-mental-disorders-quot (accessed October 26, 2011).

27. "Scientific Panel Replies to APA Statement," December 15, 2003, www.whatcausesmentalillness.com/research/mindfreedom-hunger-strike /scientific-panel-replies-to-apa-statement (accessed October 26, 2011).

Chapter 3. Interview with David Oaks: From Harvard to the Psychiatric Survivors' Movement

1. Oaks, "Mind Freedom International," 334.

2. Ibid.; www.mindfreedom.org; and personal communication.

3. Mind Freedom International, "Eco Madness!!! Or, Humans Are Killing the Planet and I Feel Fine," www.mindfreedom.org/campaign/madpride (accessed October 28, 2011).

4. Chamberlin, *On Our Own.*

5. Farber, "The Challenge of Cosmic Optimism: An Appeal to the Mad and Other Cultural Dissidents," 11–13, 31–37.

Chapter 4. Mental Patients' Liberation

1. Szasz, *Myth of Mental Illness;* and Szasz, *Ideology and Insanity.*

2. Leifer, "Medical Model as the Ideology of the Therapeutic State"; and Schaler, *Szasz under Fire.*

3. Sarbin and Mancuso, *Schizophrenia.*

4. Szasz, *My Madness Saved Me,* 10; and Szasz, *Coercion as Cure.*

5. Laing, *Politics of Experience,* 120.

6. Ibid., 28, 167.

7. Magnet, *Dream and the Nightmare.*

8. Laing, *Politics of Experience,* 125.

9. Ibid., 127.

10. Ibid.

11. Ibid., 140.

12. Ibid., 142.

13. Ibid., 140–42.

14. Ibid., 119.

15. Ibid., 129.

16. Ibid., 144–45.

17. Mullan, *Mad to Be Normal,* 378; Laing also used the word *disheartened* in a 1987 interview with Richard Hefner on the television show on NET, *Open Mind,* and in seminars he led, which I attended in New York City in 1986 and 1987.

Chapter 5. R. D. Laing, John Weir Perry, and the Sanctuary for Visionaries

1. Burston, *Wing of Madness*, 78–92.
2. Perry, *Trials of the Visionary Mind*, 147.
3. Ibid., 63.
4. Ibid., 39.
5. Ibid., vii.
6. Whitaker, *Mad in America*, 225.
7. McNamara, "In This Society the Mystics Will Always Live on the Margins," 70.
8. Stastny and Lehmann, eds., *Alternatives beyond Psychiatry*.
9. Goffman, *Asylums*.
10. Perry, *Trials of the Visionary Mind*, 7.
11. Ibid.
12. Laing, *Divided Self*.
13. Laing, *Politics of Experience*, 129.
14. Burston, *Wing of Madness*, 77–92.
15. Campbell, "Schizophrenia—The Inward Journey," 219–20.
16. Perry, *Trials of the Visionary Mind*, 123.

Chapter 6. Interview with Chaya Grossberg: Spiritually Informed Social Activism

1. Chaya Grossberg's Keynote Address to National Association for Rights Protection and Advocacy (NARPA), 2005.
2. Podvoll, *Seduction of Madness*.
3. See, for example, Breggin and Cohen, *Your Drug May Be Your Problem;* Farber, *Madness, Heresy, and the Rumor of Angels;* and interview with Dr. Stastny in chapter 1.
4. *Newsweek*, "Listening to Madness," www.newsweek.com/2009/05/01/listening-to-madness.html (accessed October 27, 2011).
5. Farber, *Madness, Heresy, and the Rumor of Angels*.
6. Haley, *Leaving Home*.
7. Farber, *Madness, Heresy, and the Rumor of Angels*.
8. Morrison, *Talking Back to Psychiatry*.
9. Minuchin, *Families and Family Therapy;* and Haley, *Leaving Home*.
10. Laing, *Sanity, Madness, and the Family;* and Haley, *Leaving Home*.

Chapter 7. Interview with Caty Simon: The Communitarian Vision

1. Simon, "Caty's Story," www.theicarusproject.net/articles/catys-story (accessed October 24, 2011).
2. Breggin, *Toxic Psychiatry;* and Jackson, *Rethinking Psychiatric Drugs.*
3. Breggin, *Toxic Psychiatry,* 67.
4. Jackson, *Rethinking Psychiatric Drugs,* 52.
5. Laing, *Politics of Experience,* 71.
6. Ibid., 57–64.
7. Jackson, *Rethinking Psychiatric Drugs,* 63.
8. Minuchin, *Families and Family Therapy.*
9. Millett, *Loony-Bin Trip.*

Chapter 8. The Roots of The Icarus Project

1. Swami Prabhupada, ed., *Bhagavad Gita,* ch. 1, text 26, 55; ch. 1, text 46, 71.
2. Gandhi, "Gita According to Gandhi," www.wikilivres.info/wiki/The_Gita_According_to_Gandhi/Introduction (accessed October 28, 2011).
3. Laing, *Politics of Experience,* 144–45.
4. Ginsberg, *Howl,* 9.
5. DuBrul, "Bipolar World," 10–14.
6. The Icarus Project, "The Icarus Project Mission Statement," www.theicarusproject.net/about-us/icarus-project-mission-statement (accessed October 28, 2011).
7. The Icarus Project, *Navigating the Space between Brilliance and Madness,* inside cover; and Mitchell-Brody, "The Icarus Project," 144.
8. The Icarus Project, Mission Statement.
9. DuBrul, "Bipolar World."
10. DuBrul, Scatter's blog, theicarusproject.net/blog/scatter (accessed October 28, 2011).
11. Breggin, "Suicidality, Violence, and Mania Caused by Selective Serotonin Reuptake Inhibitors (SSRIs)," 31–49.
12. Whitaker, *Anatomy of an Epidemic,* 179, 188.
13. Farber, *Madness, Heresy, and the Rumors of Angels.*
14. Millett, *Loony-Bin Trip.*
15. DuBrul, Scatter's blog, theicarusproject.net/blog/scatter (accessed October 28, 2011).
16. Buhlman, *Adventures beyond the Body.*
17. The Icarus Project, *Friends Make the Best Medicine.*

Chapter 9. Interview with Sascha DuBrul: The Reluctant Warrior, May 2009

1. Bey, *Temporary Autonomous Zone, Ontological Anarchy, Poetic Terrorism.*
2. Ram Dass, *Be Here Now.*
3. Campbell, "Schizophrenia—The Inward Journey."
4. Boisen, *Exploration of the Inner World.*

Chapter 10. The Warrior in Retreat

1. Breggin, *Toxic Psychiatry,* 174; and Whitaker, *Anatomy of an Epidemic,* 185.
2. Breggin and Cohen, *Your Drug May Be Your Problem,* 130.
3. "Project on the Decade of the Brain," Presidential Proclamation 6158, www.loc.gov/loc/brain/proclaim.html (accessed October 28, 2011).
4. Laing, *Sanity, Madness, and the Family;* and Haley, *Leaving Home.*
5. Millett, *Loony-Bin Trip,* 310–12.
6. Whitaker, *Anatomy of an Epidemic,* 195–96, 35.
7. Ibid., 186–87.
8. Ibid., 187.
9. Ibid., 192.
10. Ibid., 191.
11. Ibid., 193.
12. Whitaker, *Anatomy of an Epidemic,* 211; also Breggin, *Brain-Disabling Treatments.*
13. McNally, "Misconceptions about Mental Illness," Harvard University Press Blog, February 7, 2011, http://harvardpress.typepad.com/hup_publicity/2011 /02/misconceptions-madness-mayhem-what-is-mental-illness.html (accessed October 28, 2011).
14. Breggin, *Brain-Disabling Treatments;* and Andre, *Doctors of Deception.*
15. Millett, *Loony-Bin Trip,* 310–11.

Chapter 11. The Icarus Project and the Future of Mad Pride

1. Finkelhor, "Current Information on the Scope of Child Sexual Abuse," www.unh.edu/ccrc/pdf/VS75.pdf (accessed October 28, 2011).
2. Thalbourne et al., "Transliminality: Its Nature and Correlates," 305–32.
3. Grof, *Realms of the Human Unconscious.*
4. Stevens and Price, *Prophets, Cults, and Madness,* 32.

5. The Icarus Project and the Freedom Center, *Harm Reduction Guide to Coming off of Psychiatric Drugs.*
6. McNamara, "Drawing New Lines on the Map," 63, 66.

Chapter 12. The Messianic or Postmodern Paradigm?

1. The Icarus Project, "The Icarus Project Mission Statement," www.theicarusproject.net/about-us/icarus-project-mission-statement (accessed October 28, 2011).
2. Buhlman, *Adventures beyond the Body.*
3. DuBrul, "Bipolar World."
4. Hornstein, *Agnes's Jacket,* 274.

Chapter 13. The Relationship of Mad Pride to Messianic Transformation

1. Perry, *Far Side of Madness,* 8.
2. O'Callaghan, "Interview with John Weir Perry," www.jungianschizophrenia.blogspot.com/2009/01/inner-apocalypse-in-mythology-madness.html (accessed November 6, 2011).
3. Perry, *Heart of History,* 206.
4. Ibid., 204–5.
5. Ibid., 205.
6. Ibid., 205–6.
7. Levy, "The Artist as Healer of the World," www.awakeninthedream.com/wordpress/?p=162 (accessed November 6, 2011).
8. Perry, *Heart of History,* 40.
9. Gosden, *Schismatic Mind,* 165–66. Available at http://sites.google.com/site/richardgosden/phd (accessed October 24, 2011).
10. Perry, *Trials of the Visionary Mind,* 48–49.
11. Goffman, *Asylums.*
12. Boisen, *Exploration of the Inner World,* 131.
13. Ibid., 134.
14. Ibid., 63.
15. Ibid., 62.
16. *Dementia of Jesus,* 393, as cited in Havis, *Not Resigned,* 146.
17. King, "Speech to American Psychiatric Association," 1967; King, "Speech to Lincoln University," June 6, 1961. Available at www.mindfreedom.org/kb/mental-health-global/iaacm/MLK-on-IAACM (accessed November 6, 2011).

Chapter 14. Interview with Dr. Ed Whitney: Finding Oneself at the Age of Forty-five, Messianic Visions

1. Whitney, "Mania as Spiritual Emergency," www.spiritualrecoveries.blogspot.com/2006/07/personal-account-mania-as-spiritual.html (accessed November 6, 2011).
2. Ibid.
3. Ibid.
4. Ibid.
5. Custance, *Wisdom, Madness, and Folly.*
6. Whitney, "Mania as Spiritual Emergency."
7. Ibid.
8. Underhill, *Mysticism,* 380–412.
9. Whitney, "Mania as Spiritual Emergency."

Chapter 15. Cultural Revitalization Movements

1. Wallace, *Revitalizations and Mazeways,* 11.
2. McLoughlin, *Revivals, Awakenings, and Reform,* 97; ibid., 96.
3. Ibid., 8.
4. Smith, *Revivalism and Social Reform.*
5. Levy, *Madness of George W. Bush,* 146–47.
6. Thomas, "Romantic Reform in America," 155; and Hatch, *Democratization of American Christianity,* 162–89.
7. McKanan, *Identifying the Image of God,* 48.
8. Thomas, "Romantic Reform in America," 153.
9. Ibid., 156.
10. Ibid., 153–54.
11. Sweet, *Evangelical Tradition in America,* 143.
12. Smith, *Revivalism and Social Reform,* 8.
13. Abzug, *Cosmos Crumbling,* 8.
14. Jacoby, *Utopian Thought in an Anti-Utopian Age.*
15. Robbins and Magee, *Sleeping Giant Has Awoken.*
16. Rosell, "Charles G. Finney," 142.
17. McLoughlin, *Revivals, Awakenings, and Reform,* 130.
18. Ibid.
19. Strout, *New Heavens and the New Earth,* 106.
20. Abzug, *Passionate Liberator,* 46.

21. Niebuhr, *Kingdom of God in America,* 148.

22. Ibid., 149.

23. Ibid., 150.

24. Ibid., 152.

25. Ibid., 153.

26. Ibid., 152.

27. Abzug, *Passionate Liberator,* 108.

28. Ibid.

29. Ibid., 109.

30. Niebuhr, *Kingdom of God in America.*

31. Ibid., 157; and Abzug, *Passionate Liberator,* 109.

32. Niebuhr, *Kingdom of God in America,* 158.

33. Ibid., 159.

34. Abzug, *Passionate Liberator,* 28–51, 121–22.

35. Niebuhr, 157.

36. Smith, *Revivalism and Social Reform,* 8.

37. Ibid., 225.

38. Ibid., 161.

39. Ibid., 206.

40. Abzug, *Cosmos Crumbling,* 5.

41. McLoughlin, *Revivals, Awakenings, and Reform,* 130.

42. Ibid., 179–85.

43. Roszak, *Making of a Counter Culture.*

44. McLoughlin, *Revivals, Awakenings, and Reform,* 208.

45. Ibid., 210.

46. Ibid., 208.

47. Levy, "The Artist as Healer of the World," www.awakeninthedream.com /wordpress/?p=162 (accessed October 24, 2011).

48. Hayden, *Long Sixties,* 19–20.

49. Ibid., 19.

Chapter 16. Interview with Paul Levy: "They May Say I'm a Dreamer"

1. Levy, "Bio," www.awakeninthedream.com/wordpress/?page_id=2 (accessed November 6, 2011).

2. Levy, "We Are All Shamans in Training," www.awakeninthedream.com /wordpress/?p=160 (accessed November 6, 2011).

3. Ibid.

4. Levy, "The Artist as Healer of the World," www.awakeninthedream.com /wordpress/?p=162 (accessed November 6, 2011).

5. Levy, "The Wounded Healer, Part 2," www.awakeninthedream.com/wordpress /?p=157 (accessed November 6, 2011).

6. Levy, "God the Imagination," www.awakeninthedream.com/wordpress /?p=170 (accessed November 6, 2011).

7. Levy, "We Are All Shamans in Training."

8. Levy, "The Healing of the Blind Lady and the Crucifixion by Psychiatry," unpublished.

9. Levy, "We Are All Shamans in Training."

10. Ibid.

Chapter 17. Revitalization and the Messianic-Redemptive Vision of Sri Aurobindo

1. Heehs, *Lives of Sri Aurobindo.*

2. Aurobindo, *Life Divine,* 1060.

3. Aurobindo, "Human Cycle."

4. Bruteau, "Sri Aurobindo and Teilhard De Chardin," 203.

5. Gandhi, *Social Philosophy of Sri Aurobindo and the New Age,* 329.

6. Van Vrekhem, *Patterns of the Present,* 135.

7. Purani, *Life of Sri Aurobindo,* 223–24.

8. Heehs, *Lives of Sri Aurobindo,* 123.

9. Varma, *Political Philosophy of Sri Aurobindo,* 168.

10. Heehs, *The Lives of Sri Aurobindo,* 33.

11. Purani, *Life of Sri Aurobindo,* 82.

12. Gandhi, *Social Philosophy of Sri Aurobindo,* 5–6.

13. Purani, *The Life,* 118.

14. Ibid., 57–58.

15. Ibid., 97–99.

16. Heehs, *Lives of Sri Aurobindo,* 178, 232.

17. Purani, *Life of Sri Aurobindo,* 106.

18. Heehs, *Lives of Sri Aurobindo,* 160.

19. Ibid., 164.

20. Ibid., 178.

21. Purani, *Life of Sri Aurobindo,* 118.

22. Heehs, *Lives of Sri Aurobindo,* 165.

23. Ibid., 183.

24. Purani, *Life of Sri Aurobindo,* 61.

25. Aurobindo, *On Himself,* 457.

26. Gandhi, *Social Philosophy of Sri Aurobindo,* 7.

27. Aurobindo, *Upanishads,* 189.

28. Heehs, *Lives of Sri Aurobindo,* 61–62.

29. Ibid., 213.

30. Aurobindo, "Human Cycle," 212.

31. Aurobindo, *Savitri,* 441.

32. Aurobindo, "Human Cycle," 248.

33. Ibid., 231.

34. Ibid., 232.

35. Ibid., 233.

36. Ibid., 232.

37. Hemsell, *Ken Wilber and Sri Aurobindo,* www.integralworld.net/hemsell .html.

38. Aurobindo, "Human Cycle," 225.

39. Ibid., 244; Aurobindo, *Life Divine,* 1008.

40. Laing, *Politics of Experience,* 129.

41. Perry, *Trials of the Visionary Mind,* 48.

42. Aurobindo, "Human Cycle," 248.

43. Heehs, *Lives of Sri Aurobindo,* 342.

44. Aurobindo, "Human Cycle," 249.

45. Ibid., 250.

46. Ibid.

47. Ibid.

48. Aurobindo, *Savitri,* 648–49.

49. Ibid., 721.

50. Mehta, *Dialogue with Death,* 351–53; and Aurobindo, *Savitri,* 706.

51. Aurobindo, "Human Cycle," 251.

52. Ibid., 248.

53. Mehta, *Miracle of Descent,* 67.

54. Ibid., 67.

Chapter 18. Whither Mad Pride?

1. Heehs, *Lives of Sri Aurobindo.*

2. Lasch, *Culture of Narcissism.*

3. Griffin, *Varieties of Postmodern Theology,* xiii.

4. Levy, *Madness of George W. Bush,* 209–10.

5. Hedges, *Death of the Liberal Class,* 202; and Chomsky, "Occupy the Future," www.truth-out.org/occupy-future/1320154096 (accessed November 15, 2011).

6. Hedges, *Death of the Liberal Class,* 204.

7. Florovsky, *Creation and Redemption,* 85–87.

8. Tarnas, *Cosmos and Psyche,* 492.

9. Aurobindo, *Savitri,* 699.

Appendix. Extracts from Sri Aurobindo's *Savitri*

1. Mukherjee, *Destiny of the Body.*

Bibliography

Abzug, Robert. *Cosmos Crumbling: American Reform and the Religious Tradition*. Oxford, UK: Oxford University Press, 1994.

———. *Passionate Liberator: Theodore Dwight Weld and the Dilemma of Reform*. New York: Oxford University Press, 1980.

Andre, Linda. *Doctors of Deception: What They Don't Want You to Know about Shock Treatment*. New Brunswick, N.J.: Rutgers University Press, 2009.

Aurobindo, Sri. "The Human Cycle." In *Social and Political Thought*. Pandicherry, India: Sri Aurobindo Ashram, 1970.

———. *The Life Divine*. Pondicherry, India: Sri Aurobindo Ashram, 1977.

———. *On Himself*. Pondicherry, India: Sri Aurobindo Ashram, 1985.

———. *Savitri: A Legend and a Symbol*. Pondicherry, India: Sri Aurobindo Ashram, 1981.

———. *Social and Political Thought*. Pondicherry, India: Sri Aurobindo Ashram, 1970.

———. *The Upanishads*. Pondicherry, India: Sri Aurobindo Ashram, 1981.

Bey, Hakim. *The Temporary Autonomous Zone, Ontological Anarchy, Poetic Terrorism*. New York: Autonomedia, 1985.

Boisen, Anton. *The Exploration of the Inner World: A Study of Mental Disorder and Religious Experience*. Philadelphia, Pa.: University of Pennsylvania Press, 1971.

Boysen, Guy. "An Evaluation of the DSM Concept of Mental Disorder." *The Journal of Mind and Behavior* 28, no. 2 (2007).

Breggin, Peter. *Brain-Disabling Treatments in Psychiatry: Drugs, Electroshock, and the Role of the FDA*. New York: Springer Publishing Company, 1997.

———. "Suicidality, Violence, and Mania Caused by Selective Serotonin Reuptake Inhibitors (SSRIs): A Review and Analysis." *International Journal of Risk and Safety in Medicine* 16 (2003/2004): 31–49.

———. *Toxic Psychiatry.* New York: St. Martin's Press, 1991.

Breggin, Peter, and David Cohen. *Your Drug May Be Your Problem: How and Why to Stop Taking Psychiatric Drugs.* New York: Perseus Books, 2007.

Bruteau, Beatrice. "Sri Aurobindo and Teilhard De Chardin on the Problem of Action." *International Philosophical Quarterly* 12 (June 1972): 193–204.

Buhlman, William. *Adventures beyond the Body.* San Francisco: Harper, 1996.

Burston, Daniel. *The Wing of Madness: The Life and Work of R. D. Laing.* Cambridge, Mass.: Harvard University Press, 1996.

Campbell, Joseph. "Schizophrenia—The Inward Journey." In *Myths to Live By.* New York: Viking Press, 1972.

Chamberlin, Judi. "The Ex-Patients Movement." In "Challenging the Therapeutic State," edited by David Cohen, *The Journal of Mind and Behavior* 11 (1990).

———. *On Our Own.* New York: McGraw Hill, 1979.

Chomsky, Noam. "Occupy the Future." *Truthout,* November 1, 2012. Available at www.truth-out.org/occupy-future/1320154096 (accessed November 15, 2011).

Cohen, David, ed. "Challenging the Therapeutic State: Critical Perspectives on Psychiatry and the Mental Health System." *The Journal of Mind and Behavior* 11 (1990).

Curtis, Ted, et al. *Mad Pride: A Celebration of Mad Culture.* London: Spare Change Books, 2000.

Custance, John. *Wisdom, Madness, and Folly: The Philosophy of a Lunatic.* New York: Pellegrini and Cudahy, 1952.

Davis, David Brion, ed. *Ante-Bellum Reform.* New York: Harper and Row, 1967.

DuBrul, Sascha. "The Bipolar World." In *Navigating the Space between Brilliance and Madness,* edited by The Icarus Project, 10–14. This work was first published in the *San Francisco Bay Guardian* in September 2002.

Edds, Kimberly. "California Hunger Strike Challenges Use of Antidepressants." *Washington Post,* August 30, 2003, www.whatcausesmentalillness.com /research/mindfreedom-hunger-strike/the-washington-post (accessed October 26, 2011).

Farber, Seth. "Augustinianism and the Psychoanalytic Metanarrative." *Review of Existential Psychology and Psychiatry* 25, no. 1 (2001): 105–32.

———. "The Challenge of Cosmic Optimism: An Appeal to the Mad and

Other Cultural Dissidents." *Inside Out Magazine,* November–December 1988, 11–13, 31–37.

———. *Eternal Day: The Christian Alternative to Secularism and Modern Psychology.* Salisbury, Mass.: Regina Orthodox Press, 1998.

———. "Institutional Mental Health and Social Control: The Ravages of Epistemological Hubris." *The Journal of Mind and Behavior* 11, nos. 3–4 (1990). Available at www.academyanalyticarts.org/farber.htm (accessed October 26, 2011).

———. *Madness, Heresy, and the Rumor of Angels: The Revolt against the Mental Health System.* Chicago: Open Court Press, 1993.

Finkelhor, David. "Current Information on the Scope of Child Sexual Abuse." *The Future of Children,* 4 no. 2 (1994): 31–51. Available at www.unh.edu/ccrc/pdf/VS75.pdf (accessed October 28, 2011).

Florovsky, Georges. *Creation and Redemption.* Belmont, Mass.: Nordland Publishing Company, 1976.

Foucault, Michel. *Madness and Civilization: A History of Insanity in the Age of Reason.* New York: Random House, 1965.

Fromm, Erich. *The Sane Society.* New York: Holt, Rinehart and Winston, 1955.

Gandhi, Kishor. *Social Philosophy of Sri Aurobindo and the New Age.* Pondicherry, India: Sri Aurobindo Ashram, 1991.

Gandhi, Mahatma. Foreword to *The Gita According to Gandhi.* www.wikilivres.info/wiki/The_Gita_According_to_Gandhi/Foreword (accessed November 16, 2011).

Ginsberg, Allen. *Howl.* San Francisco: City Light Books, 1959.

Goffman, Erving. *Asylums: Essays on the Social Situation of Mental Paients and Other Inmates.* New York: Anchor Books, 1961.

Gosden, Richard. *Schismatic Mind: Controversies over the Cause of the Symptoms of Schizophrenia.* Ph.D thesis, University of Wollongong, Australia, 2000. http://sites.google.com/site/richardgosden/phd (accessed November 6, 2011).

Greenberg, Gary. "Is it Prozac? Or Placebo?" *Mother Jones,* November-December 2003. http://motherjones.com/politics/2003/11/it-prozac-or-placebo (accessed November 6, 2011).

Griffin, David Ray. *Varieties of Postmodern Theology.* Albany, N.Y.: State University of New York Press, 1989.

Grossberg, Chaya. "Keynote Address to National Association of Rights, Protection and Advocacy (NARPA)." Keynote address, 2005.

Haley, Jay. *Leaving Home.* New York: McGraw Hill, 1980.

Harris, Gardiner, Benedict Carey, and Janet Roberts. "Psychiatrists, Children, and the Drug Industry's Role." *New York Times,* May 10, 2007. www.nytimes.com/2007/05/10/health/10psyche.html?pagewanted=all (accessed October 25, 2011).

Hatch, Nathan. *The Democratization of American Christianity.* New Haven, Conn.: Yale University Press, 1989.

Havis, Don. *Not Resigned.* Bloomington, Ind.: XLibris, 2010.

Hayden, Tom. *The Long Sixties.* Boulder: Paradigm Publishers, 2009.

Hedges, Chris. *The Death of the Liberal Class.* New York: Nation Books, 2010.

Heehs, Peter. *The Lives of Sri Aurobindo.* New York: Columbia University Press, 2008.

Heinberg, Richard. *Memories and Visions of Paradise.* Los Angeles, Calif.: Jeremy Tarcher Inc., 1987.

Hemsell, Rod. *Ken Wilber and Sri Aurobindo.* www.integralworld.net/hemsell .html (accessed November 6, 2011).

Hoffman, Lynn. *Foundations of Family Therapy.* New York: Basic Books, 1987.

Hornstein, Gail. *Agnes's Jacket: A Psychologist's Search for the Meaning of Madness.* New York: Rodale, 2009.

Icarus Project, The. *Friends Make the Best Medicine.* New York: The Icarus Project, 2006.

———. "Icarus Project Mission Statement." http://theicarusproject.net/about-us /icarus-project-mission-statement (accessed October 24, 2011).

———. *Navigating the Space between Brilliance and Madness.* New York: The Icarus Project, 2006.

Icarus Project, The, and the Freedom Center. *Harm Reduction Guide to Coming off of Psychiatric Drugs.* New York: The Icarus Project, 2007.

Idel, Moshe. *Messianic Mystics.* New Haven, Conn.: Yale University Press, 1998.

Jackson, Grace. *Rethinking Psychiatric Drugs.* Bloomington, Ind.: AuthorHouse, 2005.

Jacoby, Russell. *The End of Utopia: Politics and Culture in an Age of Apathy.* New York: Basic Books, 2000.

———. *Utopian Thought in an Anti-Utopian Age.* New York: Columbia University Press, 2007.

Karon, Betram. "Psychotherapy versus Medication for Schizophrenia." In *The Limits of Biological Treatments for Psychological Distress,* edited by Seymour Fisher and Roger Greenberg. Hillsdale, N.J.: Lawrence Erlbaum Associates, 1989.

King, Martin Luther Jr. "Speech to American Psychiatric Association." September 1, 1967. www.mindfreedom.org/kb/mental-health-global/iaacm/MLK-on-IAACM (accessed November 6, 2011).

———. "Speech to Lincoln University." June 6, 1961. www.mindfreedom.org/kb/mental-health-global/iaacm/MLK-on-IAACM (accessed November 6, 2011).

Kumar, Krishan. *Religion and Utopia*. Canterbury, U.K.: Center for the Study of Religion and Society, 1985.

Kutchins, Herb, and Stuart A. Kirk. *Making Us Crazy*. New York: Free Press, 1997.

Laing, R. D. *The Divided Self.* London: Tavistock, 1960.

———. *The Politics of Experience*. New York: Pantheon Books, 1967.

———. *Sanity, Madness, and the Family*. Great Britain: Penguin Books, 1964.

Lasch, Christopher. *The Culture of Narcissism*. New York: Norton, 1978.

Leifer, Ron. "The Medical Model as Ideology of the Therapeutic State." In "Challenging the Therapeutic State: Critical Perspectives on Psychiatry and the Mental Health System," edited by David Cohen. *The Journal of Mind and Behavior* 11 (1990).

Levy, Paul. "Are We Possessed?" www.awakeninthedream.com/wordpress/?p=211 (accessed November 6, 2011).

———. "The Artist as Healer of the World." www.awakeninthedream.com/wordpress/?p=162 (accessed November 6, 2011).

———. "God the Imagination." www.awakeninthedream.com/wordpress/?p=170 (accessed November 6, 2011).

———. "The Healing of the Blind Lady and the Crucifixion by Psychiatry." Unpublished.

———. *The Madness of George W. Bush*. Bloomington, Ind.: Author House, 2006.

———. "We Are All Shamans in Training." www.awakeninthedream.com/wordpress/?p=160 (accessed November 6, 2011).

———. "The Wounded Healer, Part 2." www.awakeninthedream.com/wordpress/?p=157 (accessed November 6, 2011).

Lewis, Bradley. *Moving beyond Prozac, DSM, and the New Psychiatry: The Birth of Post-Psychiatry*. Ann Arbor, Mich.: The University of Michigan Press. 2006.

Lowy, Michael. *Redemption and Utopia: Jewish Libertarian Thought in Central Europe*. Stanford, Calif.: Stanford University Press, 1988.

Luzkow, Jack. *What's Left: Marxism, Utopianism, and the Revolt against History*. Washington, D.C.: University Press of America, 2006.

Magnet, Myron. *The Dream and the Nightmare: The Sixties Legacy to the Underclass.* New York: William Morrow, 1993.

McKanan, Dan. *Identifying the Image of God.* Oxford, U.K.: Oxford University Press, 2002.

McLoughlin, William. *Revivals, Awakenings, and Reform.* Chicago: University of Chicago Press, 1978.

McNally, Richard. "Misconceptions about Mental Illness." *Harvard University Press Blog,* February 7, 2011. http://harvardpress.typepad.com/hup_publicity/2011/02/misconceptions-madness-mayhem-what-is-mental-illness.html (accessed November 15, 2011).

McNamara, Ashley Y. "Drawing New Lines on the Map." In *Navigating the Space between Brilliance and Madness,* edited by The Icarus Project, 63–66.

———. "In This Society the Mystics Will Always Live on the Margins." In *Navigating the Space between Brilliance and Madness*, edited by The Icarus Project, 68–70.

Mehta, Rohit. *The Dialogue with Death.* Delhi, India: Motilal Banarsidass, 1983.

———. *The Miracle of Descent.* Baroda, India: Sri Aurobindo Society, 1973.

Millett, Kate. *The Loony-Bin Trip.* New York: Simon and Shuster, 1991.

Minuchin, Salvador. *Families and Family Therapy.* Cambridge, Mass.: Harvard University Press, 1970.

Mitchell-Brody, Maryse. "The Icarus Project." In *Alternatives beyond Psychiatry,* edited by Peter Stastny and Peter Lehmann, 137–45.

Morrison, Linda J. *Talking Back to Psychiatry.* New York: Routledge, 2005.

Mukherjee, Jugal Kishore. *The Destiny of the Body.* Pondicherry, India: Sri Aurobindo Ashram, 1989.

Mullan, Robert. *Mad to Be Normal: Conversations with R. D. Laing.* London: Free Association Books, 1995.

Newsweek. "Listening to Madness." May 1, 2009. www.newsweek.com/2009/05/01/listening-to-madness.html (accessed October 24, 2011).

Niebuhr, H. Richard. *The Kingdom of God in America.* New York: Harper, 1937.

O'Callaghan, Michael. Interview with John Weir Perry. 1982. www.global-vision.org/papers/JWP.pdf (accessed November 6, 2011).

Oaks, David. "Mind Freedom International." In *Alternatives beyond Psychiatry,* edited by Peter Stastny and Peter Lehmann, 328–35.

Orr, David. *Down to the Wire: Confronting Climate Collapse.* New York: Oxford University Press, 2009.

Pagels, Elaine. *Adam, Eve, and the Serpent.* New York: Random House, 1988.

Perry, John Weir. *The Far Side of Madness*. New York: Prentice-Hall, 1974.

———. *The Heart of History*. Albany, N.Y.: State University of New York Press, 1987.

———. *Roots of Renewal in Myth and Madness*. San Francisco: Jossey Bass, 1976.

———. *Trials of the Visionary Mind*. Albany, N.Y.: State University of New York Press, 1999.

Podvoll, Ed. *The Seduction of Madness*. New York, HarperCollins, 1990.

Prabhupada, Swami, ed. *The Bhagavad Gita*. Australia: Bhaktivedanta Book Trust, no date given.

Purani, A. B. *The Life of Sri Aurobindo*. Pondicherry, India: Sri Aurobindo Ashram, 1991.

Ram Dass, Baba. *Be Here Now*. Taos, N.Mex.: Lama Foundation, 1971.

Reddy, V. Madhusudan. *Footnotes to the Future*. Hyderabad, India: Institute of Human Study, 1993.

Robbins, Jeffrey, and Neal Magee. *The Sleeping Giant Has Awoken*. New York: Continuum, 2008.

Rosell, Garth M. "Charles G. Finney." In Leonard I. Sweet, *The Evangelical Tradition in America*. Macon, Ga.: Mercer University Press, 1997.

Rosenhan, David. "On Being Sane in Insane Places." *Science* 179 (1973).

Roszak, Theodore. *The Making of a Counter Culture*. New York: Doubleday, 1969.

Sarbin, Theodore. "Toward the Obsolescence of the Schizophrenia Hypothesis." In "Challenging the Therapeutic State," edited by David Cohen, *The Journal of Mind and Behavior* 11 (1990).

Sarbin, Theodore, and James Mancuso. *Schizophrenia: Medical Diagnosis or Moral Verdict?* New York: Pergamon, 1980.

Schaler, Jeffrey. *Szasz under Fire*. Chicago: Open Court Press, 2004.

Seikkula, Jaakko. "Open Dialogues." In *Alternatives beyond Psychiatry*, edited by Peter Stastny and Peter Lehmann.

Silverman, Julian. "Shamans and Acute Schizophrenia." *American Anthropologist* 69 (1967).

Smecker, Frank Joseph, and Derrick Jensen, "You Can't Kill a Planet and Live on It Too." *Truthout*, July 16, 2011. Available at www.truth-out.org/you-cant-kill-planet-and-live-it-too/1310403275 (accessed on November 1, 2011).

Smith, Timothy L. *Revivalism and Social Reform*. New York: Harper, 1957.

Speth, James Gustave. *The Bridge at the Edge of the World: Capitalism, the Environment, and Crossing from Crisis to Sustainability*. New Haven, Conn.: Yale University Press, 2008.

Stastny, Peter, and Peter Lehmann, eds. *Alternatives beyond Psychiatry*. Berlin, Germany: Peter Lehmann Publishing, 2007.

Stevens, Anthony, and John Price. *Prophets, Cults, and Madness*. London, England: Gerald Duckworth and Co., 2000.

Strout, Cushing. *The New Heavens and the New Earth: Political Religion in America*. New York: Harper and Row, 1974.

Sweet, Leonard I. *The Evangelical Tradition in America*. Macon, Ga.: Mercer University Press, 1997.

Szasz, Thomas. *Coercion as Cure: A Critical History of Psychiatry*. New Brunswick, N.J.: Transaction Publishers, 2007.

———. *Fatal Freedom*. Westport, Conn.: Praeger, 1999.

———. *Ideology and Insanity*. New York: Anchor, 1970.

———. *The Manufacture of Madness: A Comparative Study of the Inquisition and the Mental Health Movement*. New York: Harper and Row, 1970.

———. *My Madness Saved Me*. New Brunswick, N.J.: Transaction Publishers, 2006.

———. *The Myth of Mental Illness*. New York: Hoeber-Harper, 1961.

Tarnas, Richard. *Cosmos and Psyche*. New York: Viking, 2006.

———. *The Passion of the Western Mind*. New York: Ballantine Books, 1991.

Thalbourne, Michael, et al. "Transliminality: Its Nature and Correlates." *Journal of the American Society for Psychical Research* 91 (October 1997): 305–32.

Thomas, John L. "Romantic Reform in America: 1815–1865." In *Ante-Bellum Reform*, edited by David Brion Davis. New York: Harper and Row, 1967.

Underhill, Evelyn. *Mysticism*. New York: Dutton, 1961

Van Vrekhem, Georges. *Patterns of the Present*. New Delhi, India: Rupa and Co., 2002.

Varma, Vishwanath Prasad. *The Political Philosophy of Sri Aurobindo*. Delhi, India: Motilal Banarsidass, 1976.

Wallace, Anthony. *Revitalizations and Mazeways*. Lincoln, Neb.: University of Nebraska Press, 2003.

Whitaker, Robert. *Anatomy of an Epidemic*. New York: Crown Publisher, 2010.

———. *Mad in America: Bad Science, Bad Medicine, and the Enduring Mistreatment of the Mentally Ill*. Cambridge, Mass.: Perseus Press, 2002.

Whitney, Ed. "Mania as Spiritual Emergency." *Spiritual Recovery Blog*, July 3, 2006. http://spiritualrecoveries.blogspot.com/2006/07/personal-account-mania-as-spiritual.html (accessed November 6, 2011).

Index